THE NUMBER ONE NAZI JEW-BAITER

THE NUMBER ONE NAZI JEW- BAITER

(A Political Biography of Julius Streicher,
Hitler's Chief Anti-Semitic Propagandist)

by William P. Varga

A Hearthstone Book

Carlton Press, Inc.   New York, N.Y.

CONTENTS

TABLE OF ILLUSTRATIONS

TABLE OF ABBREVIATIONS

Parties and Organizations

DAP:	Deutsche Arbeiterpartei	German Workers Party
DNVP:	Deutsche Nationalistische Volkspartei	German Nationalist Peoples Party
DSP:	Deutsch-Sozialistische Partei	German Socialist Party
DW:	Deutsche Werkgemeinschaft	German Working Community
GVG:	Grossdeutsche Volksgemeinschaft	Greater German Peoples Union
HJ:	Hitler-Jugend	Hitler Youth Organization
KPD:	Kommunistische Partei Deutschlands	German Communist Party
NSAG:	Nationalsozialistische Arbeitsgemeinschaft	National Socialist Working Association
NSDAP:	Nationalsozialistische Deutsche Arbeiterpartei	National Socialist German Workers Party
NSFP:	Nationalsozialistische Freiheitspartei	National Socialist Freedom Party
SA:	Sturm-Abteilung	Party Militia of the NSDAP
SS:	Schutzstaffel	Protective (Elite) Guard of the NSDAP

PREFACE

Although more than three decades have elapsed since the end of World War II, widespread interest in Hitler's Germany and the holocaust suffered by European Jews has still not abated. This is evidenced partially by the continued marketing success of books and documentary films about the Nazis and 20th-century anti-Semitic persecution. Recent best sellers among these books have dealt almost solely with Hitler. The television documentary film, "Holocaust," has attracted record numbers of viewers wherever and whenever presented. Considerable attention has also been focused on publications about some of the Nazi sub-leaders involved in the barbaric treatment of the Jews. Among the better known of these are biographies of Heinrich Himmler, Adolph Eichmann and Reinhard Heydrich.

Publications and presentations such as those mentioned above portray vividly the brutality involved in the implementation of Hitler's "solutions to the Jewish problem." While most readers and viewers have remained transfixed by the horror of the historical facts presented to them in these books and films, they have usually been left with a feeling of disbelief that such massive criminality could have sprung from an "advanced" nation such as Germany. The question of *what* happened to European Jews at the hands of the Nazis has been thoroughly examined and presented. Yet, the more important question persists: *How* could these atrocities have happened in the 20th century at the hands of a culturally developed nation?

A key to understanding this question lies in gaining knowledge of Nazi propaganda methods and deeds which created fear (of both Jews and Nazi reprisals) among older Germans and which poisoned the minds of young people as well as some immature or naive adults. In northern Bavaria an anti-Semitic program was initiated by Julius Streicher even before the Nazi party was organized. Streicher, who was to become Hitler's chief anti-Semitic propagandist, was perhaps the most hated individual in the world at the time of the Nuremberg Trials in 1945 and 1946. He was rightfully blamed for generating widespread racial hatred and for poisoning the minds of thousands of young Germans by means of his written and verbal demagoguery. He rivaled Hitler as a forceful and effective speaker and was a prolific author and publisher of anti-Semitic polemics.

Streicher was probably best known for his fanatic and sensational anti-Semitic newspaper, *Der Stuermer*, which he published without interruption from 1923 to 1945. During most of this period Streicher was the chief editor and a feature writer for the *Stuermer*. He was also a contributing author or publisher of other Nazi newspapers and a number of books and magazines dealing with racial topics. Among these were grammar-school textbooks and children's picture books describing the "evils of the Jews."

This biography involves the factual story of Streicher's rise from an obscure schoolteacher to the most powerful Nazi political figure in Franconia, a sizable district around Nuremberg in northern Bavaria. Shortly after the end of World War I, Streicher emerged as a popular political figure. Largely on the strength of his style and forcefulness as an anti-Semitic speaker and political organizer he attracted a large following which he later developed into a strong, active local Nazi party. His political successes were also due to the fact that anti-Semitism was enthusiastically accepted in Franconia, where prejudice against Jews was by tradition deeply rooted. Additionally, millions of Germans during the Weimar period accepted the Jews as scapegoats to blame for their wartime losses.

In 1922 Streicher joined forces with Hitler and remained totally loyal to him for the rest of his life. Because of this personal loyalty and Streicher's valuable contributions as a party organizer, Hitler supported him in the Nazi party oftentimes over the severe complaints of other Nazi leaders who disliked or despised him because of his extreme racial fanaticism, his belligerent mannerisms, and his suspected personal immorality. In addition to countless intra-party squabbles, Streicher was continuously involved in quarrels and legal entanglements with other political opponents.

Much of Streicher's behavior can be traced to one or more of his dominant personality characteristics—which are all traceable to abnormalities attributable to clinically observed mental patients of known anti-Semitic tendencies. Partially because of these particular traits, Streicher's anti-Semitism developed into an obsessive crusade which dominated all his other activities. After the Nazi seizure of power, Streicher was rewarded for his zealous anti-Semitic activities by Hitler in being named national chairman of the first boycott of Jewish businesses held in early April, 1933. Determined to make Nuremberg the leader of German anti-Semitism, Streicher arranged for the most severe boycott measures to take place in his *Gau*. Throughout the balance of the 1930's, the Nuremberg area became known as the focal point of Nazi anti-Semitic persecution. Evidence indicates that the Nazi government in Berlin issued anti-Semitic laws which followed the pioneering of increasingly harsh persecution methods devised by Streicher and his cronies in Franconia. Eventually, Streicher and his henchmen also led the way in lining their pockets with profits exacted from forced sales of Jewish properties. Details of the anti-Semitic "aryanization" program carried out in Franconia provide the reader with an in-depth view of the process by which the Jews were systematically stripped of their property and forced into economic and political helplessness in a single district in Germany.

As in the case of Hitler, Streicher married his mistress after realizing that World War II was lost. He fled with his bride southward as American troops approached the Nuremberg area. In a bizarre and fatefully coincidental occurrence he was captured shortly after his flight by a Jewish-American officer of the 101 Airborne Division.

During approximately seventeen months of imprisonment, interrogation and trial, Streicher talked incessantly about his anti-Semitic beliefs and also wrote a lengthy political testament detailing his "lifelong religious crusade." Description and interpretation of these racial absurdities provide an informative insight into the workings of a neurotically obsessive anti-Semitic mind. In the end, however, Streicher received the justice due him for the human suffering and tragedy he caused. Even though there was no proof that he committed murder or directly caused the death of a single individual, he was convicted of crimes against humanity at the Nuremberg Trials and executed in October, 1946.

Unfortunately, some information concerning Streicher's personal and political activities and thoughts are missing in this study because of the lack of necessary resource material. An explanation for the scarcity of correspondence was offered by Streicher himself in a statement that he was too impatient to spend time writing letters. In addition, much more vital documentation may have been available to aid in this research if Streicher had not destroyed great quantities of papers as American troops were approaching the Nuremberg area in April, 1945. Streicher's second wife, Adele, testified to American military officers that she had helped her husband burn bundles of documents for some fourteen nights just prior to their flight near the end of the war.

In conducting research for this study, I have received help and cooperation from a number of sources. I am especially indebted to Mr. Robert Wolfe, Specialist in German Records at the National Archives, Washington, D.C., with whom I conversed for long hours during the early stages of my research, and who provided me with valuable information about the location of certain vital research material. I am also grateful for the cordiality and assistance of Dr. G. Hirschmann, Director of the Nuremberg Stadtarchiv; Dr. P. Lehnert, Assistant Director of the Nuremberg Stadtbibliothek; Dr. J. Zittel, Director of the Munich Bayrische Staatsarchiv; the head archivist at the Munich Institut fuer Zeitgeschichte; and Fraeulein J. Kinder, Assistant Director of the Koblenz Bundesarchiv.

I have also received valuable help from the staff at the Library of Congress, Washington D.C., and the librarians at the Ohio State University as well as the Columbus Public Library.

I was fortunate in gaining the cooperation of Dr. Benno Martin, former Police President of Nuremberg, and Mr. Fritz Nadler, of Nuremberg, an author and former newspaper journalist, who both granted me long hours of their time in personal interviews. I also spent additional enjoyable hours conversing with many individuals in Munich, Koblenz and Nuremberg about questions dealing with this study.

I am also indebted to the faculty committee of the Ohio State University History Department for granting me assistantships to allow the origination of my research work. The administrative officers of Urbana College have also shown me cooperation by granting a sabbatical leave from my teaching duties to complete this writing. In addition, I owe a large debt of gratitude to Dr. Andreas Dorpalen, who directed me towards this study and who counseled me during the writing of the early chapters of this book.

My wife, Susan, offered me countless hours of encouragement and help in reading and editing the final drafts. Without her assistance and patient understanding, it is doubtful that this work could have been completed.

W.P.V.

PROLOGUE

During the peak years of his political dictatorship in Franconia, Julius Streicher usually appeared in public strutting arrogantly on the sidewalks of Nuremberg, exuding authority with his ever-present riding whip, dressed impeccably in a tailored Nazi SA uniform and black, shiny boots. A few weeks after the collapse of Germany, his bearing and appearance had changed remarkably. Perhaps symbolic of the ruination and shame that was Nazi Germany by that time, Streicher acted hesitant and confused and looked like a broken, disreputable old man when he was arrested by American soldiers on May 23, 1945. He spoke haltingly and contradicted himself when first approached by Major Henry Blitt, of the American Army's 101st Airborne Division. In an effort at disguise he had grown a shaggy, white beard, which made him look older than his sixty years. His face and bald head were streaked with dirt or paint and he was dressed in a collarless, dirty blue-striped shirt and ragged trousers.[1]

In early April, Streicher and his bride, Adele, had fled their residence near Nuremberg in order to avoid the advancing forces of the American Army. They had driven south to the Bavarian Tyrol region. Posing as an artist by the name of Sailor, Streicher had secured lodging and board near the town of Weidring from an unsuspecting farmer. He had planned to remain in hiding at this farmhouse until he could return to his home. But he must have realized the futility of these plans after he had heard his name mentioned during a radio broadcast listing the Nazi officials who had been classified as criminals and were being sought to stand trial for the crimes and atrocities committed during the war.

Interestingly, Streicher might have escaped the man-hunt being conducted by American Military Police for an indefinite period except for his innate arrogance and confused state of mind. However, he blundered into captivity in a manner reminiscent of a third-rate Hollywood film scenario. The farm-house was in full view of anyone traveling the main road between Innsbruck and Munich. During recent weeks traffic on the road was brisk with American military vehicles of all description. Adele was frightened at the thought of her husband's arrest and cautioned him repeatedly to stay out of the sight of enemy soldiers. Dismissing her warnings, Streicher brashly set up his easel each morning on the front porch and sat openly painting watercolor landscapes throughout most of the daylight hours.

It was almost inevitable that he would attract the attention of at least one of the thousands of American soldiers passing along the road each day. As if acting out a key role of a prophetic script, the person motivated into action at the sight of the unrecognizable figure on the porch was an American officer who was of German-Jewish ancestry. Major Blitt was returning in a jeep in an eastward direction to his company headquarters that afternoon. He was thirsty and when he saw a man on the porch of the farm-house he impulsively ordered his driver to turn into the narrow lane because he wanted to ask for a drink of fresh milk.[2]

Blitt had no idea of the true identity of the shabby-looking old man on the porch. Yet, he was thoroughly familiar with the reputation and facial features of the infamous anti-Semitic propagandist, known widely as the "Number One Nazi Jew-Baiter." Mounting the steps to the porch, Blitt addressed Streicher courteously in Yiddish-accented German. After a brief and polite chat, the officer mentioned his desire for a drink of milk. Somewhat arrogantly Streicher retorted that he was a visiting artist, not the man of the house, who was a "dirt-farmer." At this, Blitt scrutinized the bearded face and said: "You look like Julius Streicher!" Responding as if he were flattered, Streicher blurted: "How did you recognize me?" Then, realizing too late what he had said, he tried to act calm and friendly and mumbled that he was very sorry but he had made a mistake—his name was not Streicher, but Sailor. By this time Blitt had drawn his revolver. Leveling it at Streicher he concluded the scene on the porch with a quiet but stern command: "Put your hands up, you're under arrest!"

Within a few hours, Streicher and his wife were taken in Blitt's jeep to a U. S. Army headquarters compound, where they were interrogated briefly, then placed in separate jail cells in a small-town police station between Munich and

Salzburg. By the next day, news of Streicher's capture brought war correspondents and reporters to the site of his confinement. The journalists were shown the seedy-looking figure, sitting dejectedly on the floor of his cell, which was totally devoid of furniture. He was grumbling to himself about his undignified circumstances, being "treated like an animal in a zoo." The guards told reporters that he had been constantly asking them why he was being handled as a killer; that he had never harmed anyone in his life. They said that he had been repeatedly claiming that he was innocent of any crime and that a great injustice was being committed against him.[3]

The journalists who heard this knew otherwise. Most of them were aware of Streicher's reputation as Hitler's political ruler of Franconia. In this district of over one million persons, anti-Semitic persecution had begun earlier and had been carried out more severely than in any other region in Nazi Germany. He was widely known and hated because of his radically anti-Semitic weekly newspaper, *Der Stuermer*, which he had published almost without interruption from 1923 to 1945. Streicher was considered by many observers to have contributed as much as any Nazi to the torment and tragedy of European Jews. In his role as Hitler's most consistent anti-Semitic propagandist, he was considered by many Franconians as responsible for creating the climate of hatred which contributed largely to the enactment and enforcement of anti-Semitic measures which culminated in the mass-execution of millions of Jewish people.

During the first full day of his captivity, Streicher revealed to attending soldiers and reporters a glimpse of his contradictory and volatile behavior. In the early part of an interview he responded to questions in quiet and sincere tones, claiming that he had never intended physical harm to a single Jew, and that he had always tried to protect the Jews and had hoped to get them out of Germany and into Palestine. Then he fell silent for a short time and fixed his gaze on some of the soldiers standing outside his cell. Suddenly he screamed: "Jews, Jews, Jews! Since I was taken in all I've seen is Jews!" This outburst was followed by a rush of words describing his utter contempt and hatred of "all things Jewish."[4]

The sudden emotional change from calm sincerity to

violent diatribe as exhibited by Streicher on this occasion was to be a behavioral pattern repeated by him on countless occasions throughout the ensuing seventeen months of incarceration and trial. His mercurial disposition in prison typified his bizarre and fanatic behavior as a Nazi political boss and racial propagandist. Perhaps more than any other National Socialist official, he displayed the characteristics of an unstable, split personality. On most occasions he behaved in a manner deserving of his evil and unsavory reputation—as a brutal anti-Semite and as an unintelligent *Grobian*.* At times, however, Streicher showed the capability of acting like an intelligent and sensitive human being.

He had risen from humble origins to become a popular political leader. At times crowds had adored him and women had strewn flowers in his path. He had sometimes performed unusual acts of kindness, such as raising huge sums for the poor, seeking out jobs for unemployed war veterans and arranging Christmas dinners and visits home for prisoners of opposing political views. He painted landscapes in soft, pleasant colors. These works of art have been described as aesthetically pleasing to the eye and delicate in composition. He was kind to animals and fed a small herd of deer on his estate from his hand. He rarely drank alcohol and would tolerate no drunkenness around him. Long after his conviction and death as a criminal, some of his former employees and acquaintances still spoke of him in kindly terms.[5]

Because of the paradoxical nature of Streicher's behavior, even a partial understanding of the motivation or causes of his actions and words will be difficult to achieve. Some questions about his deeds will remain unanswered because of the lack of reliable evidence. Some gaps in his life story will never be filled because he was habitually disinclined to write letters or keep a personal journal, and because Streicher and his wife destroyed a large amount of documentary evidence in nightly bonfires during the two weeks prior to their flight to the Bavarian Tyrol region.[6] Despite these problems and drawbacks, enough material has survived to enable the piecing together of a near-complete political biography of

---

* A *Grobian* is a German colloquial term for a person with an overabundance of coarseness and grossness in personal habits and thoughts.

this complex and stormy character. Throughout the narrative some attempts at psychological interpretation will be made in an effort to analyze Streicher's behavioral patterns and personality characteristics and to add substance to the bare facts of his adult life-story.

CHAPTER I

BEFORE THE VERSAILLES TREATY

Friedrich Streicher never rose in rank above the position of village elementary school teacher, which was his first Bavarian civil service appointment. Born and raised in the household of a small-town hand-craftsman, Friedrich was evidently a person of limited intelligence. He grew to adulthood schooled with the minimum educational requirements necessary for a beginning teacher. Even though he made no attempt at improving his professional status by further education, he bored anyone who listened with his pedantic monologues. He seemed to delight in bragging ostentatiously about his knowledge of the Church's rules, especially those considered unimportant and trivial to most villagers.[1]

As most Bavarians, Friedrich was an ardent Catholic. He was dubbed by his neighbors as the local priest's lackey. He usually volunteered to perform the village church's necessary janitorial duties and faithfully lit the candles at all masses celebrated by the priest. In addition, he consistently followed all dictates of the priest in matters pertaining to the curriculum taught to his young students. Friedrich married a young Bavarian peasant girl, Anna Weiss, in the mid-1870's and the couple settled down in Fleinhausen, a small village in Swabian Bavaria. By the end of approximately ten years of marriage, Anna had given birth to nine children. The last of these was a son, whom they named Julius.[2]

The youngest of the Streicher brood was born on February 12, 1885. He was reared in a dull environment bordering on poverty and with little knowledge of the world outside of Fleinhausen. Among his few reminiscences about his childhood days, Julius described his father as one who seemed more concerned with spiritual matters and with church business than with the ever-present needs of his family. In a statement made during his later adult life, Streicher said that his father seemed oblivious to the struggle in the household against the pervasive cold and hunger that darkened "most of the days of my childhood." Streicher also remembered that his father dominated his mother and all the children with his insistence on rigid adherence to arbitrary rules dealing mostly with household religious practices.

It is interesting to note, however, that while the elder Streicher ruled his family quite objectively with strict discipline, and at the same time seemed unconcerned about their personal and material needs, the children, including Julius, held no resentment against him as they approached maturity. Evidently striving to emulate their father, three of the four Streicher sons who survived to adulthood became school teachers, as did one of the daughters. The remaining two daughters married school teachers.[3]

Anna Weiss Streicher must have led a drab life, dominated by a husband who was obsessed with spiritual matters and struggling with inadequate means to provide meals and clothing for her large family. In view of her peasant background and burdensome adult existence, there is little possibility that Anna was able to endow any of her children with such characteristics as high ideals of social refinement or ambitious goals of intellectual achievement. Streicher made only one reference to his mother during his adult years. This was a statement that when he was five years old he remembered that she spoke in anger about the dishonesty of a Jewish mail order agent from whom she had ordered some material for clothing.[4]

During his formative years, Julius received his early education at the village Catholic school. He then successfully completed a two-year program at the Royal Bavarian Teacher's School at Lauingen an der Donau in July, 1903.

In November, 1903, he was assigned his first teaching position at Irsee, in the district of Truthaven, as a substitute school teacher. He remained in that position approximately six months. He then fulfilled substitute assignments at two nearby village schools until he was transferred to a "Correction Boys' School" in Lauingen in December, 1906.[5]

In January, 1907, the district and local school inspectors visited the Lauingen School to evaluate Streicher's teaching practices. The report on this visitation was somewhat critical of the young teacher because the class did not meet the normal standards in reading, writing, and arithmetic skills.

Because Streicher had taken charge of this class less than one month earlier, the report was doubtless intended to be as instructive as it was evaluative. Numerous suggestions on improved teaching techniques were listed before the notation that the previous teacher had performed inadequately. Because of this the report mentioned that Streicher would have to make a special effort to bring the class up to academic standards. The report ended with the minor complaint that the young teacher should keep a more detailed daily record book.[6]

Streicher remained at Lauingen until October, 1907, when he took his state teaching examinations. That same month he began serving his one-year military obligation in the 6th Company of the 2nd Bavarian Infantry Regiment.[7] During this training period, Streicher was punished because he was not able to control his verbal outbursts which usually accompanied his refusal to obey commands he felt to be nonsensical. In later years he braggingly told of this experience in a public speech:

> Sergeant Weiss will confirm the truth of what I say. I served my one-year training period (1907 and 1908). I was locked up because I could not keep my mouth shut. On my discharge papers the following words were noted and underlined in red: "Streicher is not a good candidate for non-commissioned officer status."[8]

Steicher's conduct here was the first open manifestation of the abnormal behavior which was to become commonplace throughout his adult life. Streicher's volatile reactions to orders by his superior officers most likely resulted from an undisciplined mind which refused to accept the tedious regimentation of a peacetime military training camp. This interpretation has been forwarded by the American historian, Arthur Peterson. In discussing Streicher's adult behavior, it was noted that Streicher would rarely accept orders from superiors, and, despite serious threats, he would not comply with the rules of a social system or political organization which he did not agree with or which in any way limited his impulses of the moment.[9]

Upon completion of his one-year military training period in October, 1908, Streicher was released to reserve status and returned to civilian life. He immediately assumed the duties of his new civil service assignment as School Administrator in Mindelheim at a sizable increase in pay.[10] In view of his questionable teaching and military-training performance during the previous two years, this promotion appears somewhat surprising. One possible explanation of this apparent contradiction might be that the young teacher enjoyed the favor of influential government administrators because of his family connections in the school system. It is also possible that military performance did not concern school authorities, or, more likely that Streicher's military records were not available to the school administrators at the time of the assignment.[11]

Streicher remained at the Mindelheim post from October, 1908, until September, 1909 when he was transferred to the Nuremberg school system. Here he worked as teacher and administrator in the *Volksschule* at Lenaustrasse and Kupferstrasse, in the first and second classes of girls. He remained in this position until August, 1914.[12]

Streicher later described these years in Nuremberg as his "years of political development." He said that living in the city put him in close contact with working-class families and the social inequities he observed prompted him to become interested in politics.[13] Streicher's accounts of his first venture into politics are as vague as they are contradictory. In one interview he stated that in 1911 he joined the "Democratic Party." He had earlier referred to this group as the "Young Social Democratic Party" and the "Young Democratic Party."[14] On the one hand he claimed that he was drawn into politics because of local social issues but later asserted that he often spoke on behalf of the party's unsuccessful Reichstag candidates and that on these occasions he usually discussed "nationalistic matters." The incongruity between his alleged interests and his actual speeches is puzzling. One can only learn from this evidence that Streicher may have been stressing the fact that he never spoke against the Jews in these meetings because he stated in later testimony that he was not familiar with the racial question at the time.[15]

For unknown reasons, Streicher disassociated himself from this obscure party in early 1914, when he and two other men, Otto Wintermantel and Julius Nuremberger, organized a small political club called Young Progress *(Jung-Fortschritt).*[16]

This club existed only for a few months, and its accomplishments were negligible. Of interest, however, is the fact that anti-Semitism had not yet emerged as an issue in Streicher's political circle. Concerns of the club members at this time were reflected in the titles of the speeches delivered at meetings in February and April 1914: "The Development of the German Economy and the Tasks of the Industrial Classes"; "The Question of General Voting Rights of the Three Classes"; and "Voting Rights and Voting Duties."[17] There is no other record of Streicher's political views or activities prior to August, 1914.

At the outbreak of World War I, Streicher joined the 6th Company of the 6th Bavarian Infantry Regiment. He was sent to the front lines in the Flanders campaign as a cyclist in a machine-gun platoon.[18] His performance as a combat soldier differed markedly from his earlier peacetime record as a military trainee. By September 6, 1914, he was awarded the Prussian Iron Cross, 2nd class, and four days later he was promoted to the rank of a non-commissioned officer. During the same month he was advanced to vice-sergeant of the reserves. On August 1, 1916, he was promoted to temporary officer rank and the following April was awarded the Austrian Silver Medal with Crown. In July, 1917, he was officially promoted to Lieutenant of a machine-gun company. In January, 1918, the young officer was transferred to the Italian front where he received two more decorations— the Bavarian Military Service Medal, 4th class, and the Iron Cross, 1st class.[19]

Streicher's early decorations and promotions indicate that he entered the war with enthusiasm and thrived under battle conditions. To his superiors, Streicher seemed to possess a passion for dangerous or deadly combat. It was under the heaviest engagements with the enemy that he distinguished himself by his unflagging energy and fearless acts. Streicher's combat performance was discussed at a staff meeting of his battalion officers just before he was promoted to temporary officer rank. One officer speculated that perhaps Streicher acted so bravely because he wanted to erase his poor record as a military trainee. Another commented that if many soldiers followed Streicher's example in front of enemy fire the casualty losses would be staggering. It was decided, however, that the promotion could not be denied. In rendering this decision, the senior officer added that he hoped that more combat experience would shape Streicher into an inspiring, though more cautious leader.

There is no evidence to indicate that Streicher's enthusiasm for fighting waned after his promotion to officer rank. He received three more decorations with citations praising his outstanding bravery in front of enemy fire.

Streicher's battlefield heroics illustrated a second unusual personality characteristic which remained with him almost to the end of his life. This was a willingness to fight recklessly, regardless of the possible serious consequences of his actions. This characteristic by itself does not explain why Streicher constantly exposed himself to death on the battlefield. Such behavior was not normal for front-line soldiers. In Streicher's case it was a type of irrational fearlessness which indicated an imperviousness to reason regarding danger and which probably developed into an attitude that his destiny was guided by fate. This belief was undoubtedly reinforced with each successive narrow escape from death. After the war he spoke openly and frequently about the fact that fate—or an "inner voice"—was the principal motivating factor of his life and destiny, which, he claimed, was coupled irrevocably with the destiny of his country.[20]

CHAPTER II

HIS EXCELLENCY HAKENKREUZ

After the armistice, Streicher returned to his home in Nuremberg. By this time he was the head of a growing family. His wife, Kunigunde, whom he had married in late 1913, had borne him two sons during the war years. Lothar, the elder son, was born on January 2, 1915, while the younger son, Elmar, was born on March 16, 1918. Streicher immediately resumed the teaching position he had left four years earlier. Although he had stated publicly that when he left the army he intended to devote all of his time to his teaching profession, he soon became actively involved in local politics a few weeks after his military release.[1]

In December, 1918, Streicher joined a growing movement opposed to the Socialist regime of the new Bavarian Republic by entering a local branch of the Society for Protective and Defense Action *(Schutz und Trutzbund).*[2] Formed "to counter the growing power of the Bolshevik Jews," the society was bitterly opposed to what was called the "Jewish government" of the Independent Socialist, Kurt Eisner, who was actually the only Jew in the government. Eisner had also led the uprising against the Wittelsbach dynasty in Bavaria in early November, 1918.[3] Streicher became an occasional speaker at meetings of the *Schutz und Trutzbund.* His topics generally reiterated most of Germany's present problems which, he claimed, were "all caused by the Jews and their friends."[4] Almost overnight he became known as one of the most virulent anti-Semitic speakers in the Nuremberg area.

His early racist speeches attracted large audiences and thrust him quickly into political prominence. By early 1919 he had already outgrown the role of a secondary speaker at small meetings of the local society. He began to schedule political rallies where he was always the principal speaker. He later described one of his experiences in this role:

My first meeting in the Hercules Velodrome was crowded. Ten thousand people were standing in front of the assembly hall, and the crowd had to be kept in order by the police. I spoke at this assembly for three hours. . . .Until the year 1921, I had a big mass meeting in Nuremberg every week. Besides that, I participated several evenings during the week in discussions. . . .[5]

Streicher's success at drawing large audiences to his early meetings was due partially to widespread acceptance of *voelkisch* political doctrines in post-war Germany, especially in Bavaria. To many of Streicher's listeners, *voelkisch* ideology seemed to provide the best answers to the political, social and economic problems that existed in the months and years immediately following the war. A vernacular word in German political language, the term *voelkisch* refers essentially to right-wing elements seeking to build a united German political system on the basis of racial affinities among the people. Even before the final peace terms were signed at Versailles, the *voelkisch* views of pseudo-scientific writers such as Paul de Lagarde, Theodor Fritsch and Houston Stewart Chamberlain were being read avidly in Bavaria. Political and social dissidence was especially rampant in that section of Germany because it was torn, in late 1918, by the left-wing takeover led by Eisner. In general, these writers presented the history of mankind narrowly, as a bitter struggle between spirituality, embodied in the German "race," and materialism, embodied in the Jewish "race." These works stressed, in varying degrees, the need for a new national consciousness of the Germanic *Volk:* "a *voelkisch* society, living once more as it had lived in the remote past, bonded together in unity by pure Aryan blood."[6] All of these writers focused on the problem of the Jews, whom they portrayed as the embodiment of fear and hate. The Jews were shown not simply as evil, but as the source of depravity, existing not solely in their religion, but in their very blood.

In many of his speeches, Streicher quoted directly from the works of these *voelkisch*-racist writers. It is uncertain whether he did this because of a sincere belief in the philosophies of these authors or because he learned quickly that references to de Lagarde and the others were always met with enthusiastic responses from his audiences.

To persons who knew of Streicher's benign political opinions and moderate activism before the war, his sudden emergence as a leading *voelkisch*-anti-Semitic spokesman was viewed with considerable surprise. When questioned later about this dramatic shift in his political attitude, Streicher explained that his interest in anti-Semitism was kindled when he read Theodor Fritsch's *Handbook on the Jewish Question* during the closing months of the war. Then he added that after he had returned home, "something told him" that his life task was to fight the Jews.[7]

Streicher would offer no other reason for his sudden dedication to anti-Semitism besides this vague allusion to an inner voice which he described later on several occasions as the unseen hand of fate, which guided his destiny.[8] The timing of this change, however, suggests that other factors reinforced this mystic "conversion" to a career dedicated to anti-Semitic propaganda. Streicher may have learned quickly that he could capitalize on the growing popularity of *voelkisch*-racism in post-war Germany. Many of his countrymen willingly accepted the argument that the Jews were the foremost villains causing the humiliating loss of the war. Strengthening this belief was the fact that it was a Jewish Socialist, Kurt Eisner, who had led the recent and chaotic revolution in Munich.

Another factor which undoubtedly reinforced Streicher's plunge into anti-Semitism was the love of struggle and conflict which he had developed during the war. This personality characteristic was so intense at times that Streicher was once described as possessing an "almost demonic passion for fierce fighting."[9] After November, 1918, the Jews appeared to be the ideal group on whom all discontent, hardship and humility could be blamed. In his own words, Streicher said that when he returned home in late 1916, he saw that the Socialists and Jews were threatening to take over Germany, and already a "Polish Jew named Eisner Kosmanowsky" (Kurt Eisner) had seized the Bavarian government in the November revolts.[10]

The most unique aspect of Streicher's anti-Semitism was his fanaticism which became so extreme that he was often viewed with awe by National Socialists. In fact, Hitler once called Streicher the pioneer of the anti-Semitic movement.[11] His unceasing diatribes often reached the point of blind, almost religious fervor and ultimately it was this that later earned him the unsavory epithet of "Number One Nazi Jew-Baiter."

In an attempt to explain Streicher's extremism in the Jewish question, the American author, Edward Peterson, hypothesized that Streicher might have had a Jewish grandparent and thus was part Jewish himself. With the resurgence of the anti-Semitic movement after World War I, he may have struggled to conceal his background in all conceivable ways. Despite later efforts to verify the questionable aspects of Streicher's heritage, it was impossible to prove that he was not "pure" German as defined by Nazi legal terminology. However, a large shadow of doubt about his ancestry remains because when this question arose in the mid-1930's, examiners found that the birth records of Streicher's maternal grandmother had been removed from the Bavarian Government Office of Vital Statistics upon Streicher's orders after the Nazis took over political power.[12] Streicher's concern with his questionable heritage may have had something to do with his rapidly developed interest in anti-Semitism and with his extremism about the racial subject, but other motivational factors appear more relevant when the attempt is made to understand his racial fanaticism as well as his antagonistic and volatile personality.

It has been suggested that Streicher may have adopted anti-Semitism when he did simply because it was politically expedient. Undoubtedly, many disgruntled Germans joined *voelkisch* groups or became outspoken anti-Semites for selfish political reasons. But Streicher was not merely a typical *voeklisch*, anti-Semitic enthusiast. After his interest in racial issues was initially captivated by the views of Fritsch, he apparently plunged into active anti-Semitism with far more intensity than most other politically minded Germans who had accepted, or had agreed with the *voelkisch* ideologies of the racist writers. Even though Streicher found willing listeners at his early anti-Semitic speeches, his immediate fanaticism about racial issues indicates that he had become abnormally imbued with the totality of the subject almost overnight.

By his extremist behavior regarding racial issues, it was evident that Streicher had to be classed among the "crackpots" described by the American historian, Hannah Arendt, as having accepted anti-Semitism as an ideology. Arendt notes the differentiation between the large class of educated Europeans who had simply decided to dislike the Jews and support anti-Semitic doctrines and those who were confirmed anti-Semites, believing it to be the foundation upon which a political, social and economic system should be built.[13]

The French author, Jean-Paul Sartre, points out that the confirmed, or total anti-Semite is not motivated by outside influences (such as political expediency) but rather by his own free choice. In the following quotation from his book, *Anti-Semite and Jew*, Sartre seems to be directing his remarks toward Streicher as he states:

Anti-Semitism is a free and total choice of oneself, a comprehensive attitude that one adopts not only to Jews but toward men in general, toward history and society; it is at one and the same time a passion and a conception of the world.[14]

Sartre provides further insights into the question of Streicher's initial attraction to the anti-Semitic cause. He explains that most of the 20th century racists belonged to the lower middle class that possessed nothing. "They have chosen anti-Semitism as a means of establishing their status as possessors." Sartre then continues that by treating the Jew as an inferior, the racist affirms at the same time that he belongs to the elite.[15] Streicher's occupation as a lower-grade schoolteacher was viewed by many Germans as the lowliest of all civil service positions. As an anti-Semite he could represent the Jew as a crooked businessman or a robber to be guarded against. In this way, he could cast himself in the enviable position of a proprietor, a possessor of assets and property. In direct reference to the petty bourgeoisie of Germany in the 1920's, Sartre states that it was among this class that anti-Semitism flourished because the principal concern of the "white-collar proletariat" was to distinguish itself from the real proletariat.

From the above discussion it seems apparent that Streicher's initial interest in anti-Semitism was motivated by more than a single cause or force. His rapid indoctrination into the racial struggle was undoubtedly fostered to some extent by the above-mentioned, definable historical and environmental factors that existed in Germany after the loss of the war. However, the key elements attributable to Streicher's overly-enthusiastic reaction to the doctrines of the anti-Semitic writers are almost impossible to define or understand clearly because they deal with the complex and subtle realm of human motivation.

The question of behavioral tendencies in confirmed or historical anti-Semites has been the subject of clinical studies by psychiatrists and psychologists as well as the topic of certain books dealing with the phenomena of racial radicalism. These sources generally agree that a variety of recognizable clinical syndromes have been displayed by large numbers of anti-Semitic patients.[16] Further understanding of Streicher's radical racism as well as other personality characteristics can be gained best by discussing his outstanding behavioral patterns as they emerge in the narrative and parallel the principal traits recognized in professionally-observed anti-Semitic personalities.

In the early 1920's, political events in Bavaria seemed to play into the hands of Streicher and other *voelkisch* leaders. Eisner was assassinated in early 1919. Then a moderate Socialist government took over, but was unable to establish authority. It was temporarily superseded by a Communist regime, which was also short-lived and removed by military force after a bloody struggle. In the end, the pendulum of political authority swung to the extreme right.[17]

A deputation of the regular German army, the police and the volunteer army "Free Corps" installed a conservative judge, Gustav von Kahr, as virtual dictator over Bavaria. Kahr had little political experience or imagination. He had been a privy councilor in the wartime government and, for unknown reasons, was considered in some circles to be the "strong man" of Bavaria.[18]

More important than Kahr himself were some of the key civil servants such as Ernst Poehner, the chief of police, who was a rightist revolutionary at heart. When questioned by a politician about the growing number of political terrorist organizations in Bavaria, Poehner answered: "Herr Representative, there are not nearly enough of them for me."[19] Under Poehner, Munich became a haven for radical rightists, such as disgruntled militarists, monarchists, conservatives, and a large mob of uprooted, unemployed war veterans. These groups formed political clubs and parties according to their interests which were generally aligned in their negative political opinions. They all shared a common hatred for the Weimar government, the Versailles Treaty and the "worst enemy of all—the Jew."[20]

As noted previously, a strong anti-Semitic movement began to spread rapidly throughout Bavaria. In late 1919 a police report noted that there might be serious pogroms against Jews in the near future, and that many Jews had already left Munich because of this. Some political leaders, such as Kahr, began advocating secession from the Weimar Republic. Kahr publicly wrote and spoke against the "Jew-dominated Berlin government."[2 1] And a political newcomer, Adolf Hitler, was beginning to attract large audiences as he spoke against the national government and the "evil Jews."[2 2]

The Nuremberg *Schutz und Trutzbund* held a large demonstration on January 20, 1920, and issued an official memorandum *(Denkschrift)* condemning "many Jewish practices."[2 3] This, however, seems to have been an exceptional undertaking, for by that time Streicher was at odds with many members of the Nuremberg *"Bund."* He resented the fact that "they wanted to work only in small circles." These narrow goals were obviously not suited to his activism and fighting spirit. He resigned from the *"Bund"* in early 1920 and sounded out larger *voelkisch* parties with more ambitious programs.[2 4]

In April he joined a newly founded organization, the German Socialist Party *(Deutsch-Sozialistische Partei)* (DSP). This group was founded by an engineer, Hans Vey, and its political tone was anti-Catholic and anti-Semitic. In view of Streicher's Catholic parentage and upbringing it seems surprising that he would join an anti-Catholic party. The German publicist, Manfred Ruehl, explains that constant censure by rigid Catholic school inspectors during his early teaching years must have turned Streicher against the Catholic faith.[2 6] It is also possible that Streicher was subconsciously hostile to the Catholic Church because of the unpleasant experiences during his childhood days, when his father had insisted on rigid obedience to Catholic dogma in the household. In addition, he may have resented the Catholic faith because the elder Streicher usually considered his children's welfare secondary to affairs of the village church.

At the founding of the DSP at Hanover in April, 1920, it was decided that a party newspaper should be published. The need for urgency was noted especially because Reichstag elections were scheduled for June 6. A professor named Bohneberg was the choice of the party's central committee as the official editor. But when he did not act immediately, Streicher seized the initiative, and on June 4 published the first official newspaper of the DSP, entitled the *German Socialist (Deutscher Sozialist).*[2 7] In the first issue, devoted mostly to the elections, Streicher's name appeared as the first DSP candidate for a Reichstag seat. In his brief, last-minute campaign efforts in this hastily compiled and published newspaper, Streicher authored articles reflective of his own opinions at that time. These issues included denunciations of certain Catholic churches and Jewish leaders. Other themes included the need for unification of all German people and the allegation that all German families deserved a "piece of land and a little garden of their own."[28] In subsequent issues of the *Deutscher Sozialist*, Streicher referred to himself as public spokesman of the party, but his articles mentioned party policies only rarely. His interests appeared to concentrate increasingly on racial issues. His articles on anti-Semitism became more numerous and rabid.

On the day after the elections, little space was devoted to the results of the voting. Most likely this was because Streicher did not win on this try. He continued publishing the *Deutscher Sozialist* and in subsequent issues his articles on anti-Semitism became even more numerous. For example, the first two issues of the newspaper published after the elections were devoted almost entirely to the "evils of world Jewry." He claimed that it was Jewish money that had corrupted the voters and that an organization of international Jews planned to dominate the world. He further alleged that the Jewish plan included the de-flowering of all Aryan virgins.[29]

Streicher's attacks against the Jews in the *Deutscher Sozialist* became so base and bizarre that many of the members of the DSP began complaining openly that such radical journalism was ruining the respectability of their party.[30] Streicher was urged to tone down his anti-Semitic articles but he adamantly refused and a series of violent arguments over this matter ensued. He openly defied this segment of the party in May, 1921, when he shouted to these men that the *Deutscher Sozialist* was his private paper and therefore he could write anything he desired. The newspaper had a circulation of almost 10,000 at this time, but lacking the support of many DSP members it began experiencing financial problems. This was noted in the following appeal to his readers which also illustrated Streicher's clever tactic of associating clean physical and moral habits with his anti-Semitic propaganda:

....There are many ways to help (the *Deutscher Sozialist*). A saved drink, an unsmoked cigarette, a filthy cinema not visited. Get rid of these habits! You will make yourselves conquerors and feel filled with satisfaction. Recruit readers! Order blanks are available free of charge at the business office.... Everyone should give as he can. Even a little becomes a lot by its number....[31]

Despite such pleas the *Deutscher Sozialist* continued to flounder financially until Streicher stopped its publication in September, 1921. At that time he also resigned from the DSP.[32]

He soon joined another political group, the German Working Community *(Deutsche Werkgemeinschaft)* (DW). This party was headed by a Nuremberg doctor, named Beck. Among the stated goals of the group were the creation of a "pure Germanic State"; a more equitable tax system; and the development of a strong rightist movement.[33] Streicher became a very active DW member, and in October, 1921, published the first issue of its party newspaper, the *German People's Will (Deutscher Volkswille)*, (DV). The financing of the new paper, like that of its predecessor, was accomplished in devious ways—by pocketing money collected at party meetings, by begging and borrowing from friends, and by repeatedly changing printing houses instead of paying printing costs incurred.[34]

The first few issues of the *Deutscher Volkswille* were somewhat subdued on racial matters, but Streicher's articles soon became as virulent as those of the *Deutscher Sozialist*. For example, one leading front page article was entitled: "Why the German People Must Break the Chains of Slavery to the Jews." In another issue he argued at length that Jews and other foreigners should "leave Germany or die."[35]

These vicious anti-Semitic attacks were severely criticized by some members of the DW for the same basic reasons about which certain members of the DSP had complained in the earlier vitriolic racial articles. Despite these reprimands, Streicher soon became a leading voice of the party, whose membership had increased markedly.[36] An important reason for the sudden growth of the DW was the fact that many of the more radical members of the DSP left that organization and followed Streicher. Prominent among this group was Walther Kellerbauer, well-known anti-Semitic journalist, who, with Streicher, led the powerful new radical wing of the DW.[37]

After Streicher joined the DW he became increasingly active in politics and newspaper work. In December, 1921, he participated in the founding of the German House in Nuremberg. This establishment developed into a central library of German books and other printed material specializing in nationalism and anti-Semitism.[38] Lengthy articles written by Streicher appeared regularly in the *Deutscher Volkswille*. He usually wrote in a radical and sensational manner. Although his targets were mostly Jews, occasionally he also attacked non-Jewish public figures. In November, 1921, he wrote an article ridiculing General Erich Ludendorff for taking so long to understand "what others saw long ago, that the greatest people in the world, the German people, were being destroyed by the poison of the Jews."[39] He also criticized great industrialists, such as the Krupp family, for their social and economic privileges and their greed. Former Emperor William II was blamed for beginning and losing World War I because he had listened to the poor advice of "strangers."[40]

DW meetings were always well attended when Streicher was the featured speaker. Contrary to Hitler's roaring voice and rapid delivery, Streicher spoke in low tones at a moderate pace.[41] His speeches, however, were never well organized. He usually appeared to be reiterating the spontaneous thoughts of an undisciplined mind. Although his topic was almost always some form of anti-Semitic attack, his particular point was difficult to discern because he habitually confused his theme by inserting irrelevant or erratic statements. For example, he interrupted a long racial tirade in February, 1922, to make comments about Hitler and Walter Rathenau, the Jewish foreign minister. He referred to Hitler as "a former house painter who should be complimented because he spoke well on the Jewish question." This statement was followed by the remark that he (Streicher) was being accused by Jewish newspapers of planning the murder of Rathenau.[42]

In March, 1922, Streicher suddenly and inexplicably began displaying the swastika, or *Hakenkreuz*, wherever he spoke. This created an additional measure of agitation among segments of his audiences. At the first public display of this symbol at a DW meeting in Neustadt, his speech was interrupted frequently by hoots and catcalls. Streicher described this chaotic meeting himself in the *Deutscher Volkswille*. He claimed that the disturbances were caused by Jews and "Jew-sympathizers" who resented his "truth" about Semitic evils. He further alleged that the swastika added to the excitement and dissension of his "enemies" because this symbol was already well known in southern Bavaria as a banner of a growing anti-Semitic movement. He concluded his article with the warning that in the future he would "give these Jews something to think about."[43] Later that month the mayor of Ipsheim, a small town in Middle Franconia, complained to the government police office that Streicher had caused "great agitation" when he placed a large, red swastika over the door of the electric plant and made a fiery speech condemning all things Jewish.[44]

A few days after his introduction of the swastika at Ipsheim, Streicher spoke at another Franconian town, Schonungen, where the DW meeting ended in a bloody riot. In a long harangue he accused Jews of practicing ritual murder. He claimed that sixteen newspapers had told about the disappearance of some one-hundred German children before the Jewish Passover season of 1919, and that in Nuremberg three young boys disappeared mysteriously at this time in 1920. Since none of them were ever found, Streicher concluded that they must all have been victims of the Jewish blood ritual. He explained that his reasoning was based on the teachings of the *Talmud*, which instructed Jews to kill Christians, especially children, and to drink their blood in a certain ritual during the Jewish Easter season. Streicher escaped unharmed from the ensuing riot but was subsequently sued by a group of Jewish men for openly insulting the Jewish religion.[45]

Streicher was brought to trial September 5, 1922, and the jury found him guilty of the charge. He was sentenced to fourteen days in prison.[46] The case went to an appellate court, and the sentence was reduced to a fine of 2000 marks and costs of the legal proceedings. The lighter sentence was imposed by an appeals judge who seemed to be sympathetic to Streicher and his strong racial feelings. He stated in his verdict that Streicher was a very impulsive man and was an enthusiastic anti-Semite because of his strong loyalty to the motherland. In a final display of his partiality and bias, this judge concluded his verdict by noting that Streicher "fights the Jews as a race because he feels their existence is a threat to the German people."[47]

In both trials the judges assumed that Streicher was sincere in his belief that the murder ritual was still practiced by some Jews. As evidence, Streicher had presented two books, written in the twentieth century. Yet both authors referred only to suspicions that the Jewish ritual might still be practiced. They also offered interpretations of the *Talmud* which, they claimed, made it "quite certain" that the ritual had been customary in certain Jewish sects during past centuries.[48] Following up on this vague evidence, Streicher advanced his main argument—a story about an alleged conversation with the mayor of a small town in Italy during World War I. He claimed the mayor had told him that he was sure that some Jews in Italy still practiced the murder ritual because each year, just before the Jewish Passover season, several children disappeared mysteriously from his village.[49]

After Streicher's Schonungen speech, he received much publicity which served to boost his reputation as a controversial, if not interesting, political figure. On March 28, the civil director of the town of Neustadt refused to issue a permit for a DW meeting, saying he "did not want Streicher and his swastika and speech."[50] In early April, Streicher was the featured speaker before large audiences during two successive weeks in Nuremberg. The first meeting was considered a success by attending police because there were no disturbances. At the second one, however, Streicher had spoken only a few minutes when hecklers, presumably Socialists or Communists, created so much turmoil that police dismissed the audience.[51] The police report stated that this meeting was disorderly because of Streicher's ominous words at the previous meeting. He had reminded his listeners that the season for Jewish murder rituals was coming soon and that he (Streicher) would inform his audience the following week how the Jews could be stopped from "gaining full power."[52]

By mid-summer, 1922, Streicher had fallen from favor with large segments of DW moderates too, who argued that he "always put too much emphasis on the Jewish question." Anti-Semitic radicalism was repulsive to these moderates who saw the goal of the DW as a "more spiritual and cultural development."[53] Because of this conflict, the *Deutscher*

Volkswille was boycotted in the large district of Augsburg, which was the stronghold of the moderate faction.[54] Streicher was also at odds with many DW members because he had adopted the swastika as a political symbol without party consent. His insistence on its further use caused such irritation within party ranks that he was contemptuously dubbed "His Excellency Hakenkreuz" by some of his critics.[55] Streicher and his fellow radical, Kellerbauer, became embittered over this increasing opposition, and after a violent argument in early October, both resigned from the party.[56]

CHAPTER III

JOINING FORCES WITH HITLER

On October 20, 1922, Streicher announced during a Nuremberg speech that he had joined Hitler's National Socialist movement. He also stressed that he had pledged his personal loyalty to Hitler and urged those in the audience who were his own followers to join local NSDAP (Nazi) groups which, he said, would soon be forming throughout Franconia.[1]

The speech was the first public notice that Streicher had subordinated himself to Hitler's leadership. The abruptness of this move must have raised questions among the ranks of his local *voelkisch* constituents. For those who were familiar with Streicher, it would have been a normal reaction to ask why he had suddenly accepted the leadership of any other person in the *voelkisch* movement. Streicher was already known as a person who rarely took orders from anyone else in a political organization. Mainly through the force of his domineering personality he had gained a sizable following of enthusiastic supporters and his political rallies and speeches were consistently attended by capacity crowds.

The timing of his move, coming within a week after he resigned from the DW, suggested to some observers that the merging of Streicher and his political followers into Hitler's party may have been the result of careful and crafty planning. When he was questioned by his local followers about the merger, Streicher refused to provide information other than the weak explanation that he had met with Hitler several times and was convinced that he (Hitler) should be the one and only *voelkisch* leader in the whole of Germany. He patently refused to offer substantive reasons for his abrupt decision. Instead, he usually launched into a lengthy monologue praising the super-natural qualities of Hitler.

When asked the same question in 1946, he stated under oath that he became convinced that Hitler possessed super-human qualities the first time that he heard him speak and that he (Streicher) submitted to Hitler's leadership then and there. His 1946 description of his first meeting with Hitler appears more like the fantasy of a neurotic mind than a factual recollection. Streicher described his earlier meeting with the Nazi leader:

42

I went to the Munich Buergerbraeukeller. Adolf Hitler was speaking there. I had never seen the man before...I saw this man...after he had spoken three hours, drenched in perspiration, radiant. My neighbor said he thought he saw a halo around his (Hitler's) head; and I, gentlemen, experienced something which transcended the commonplace. When he finished his speech an inner voice bade me to get up...I approached him and told him my name.[2]

It is apparent that Streicher was either deliberately untruthful or else fantasizing when he repeated, during his later years, that he was so captivated by Hitler's magnetic personality at their first meeting that he placed himself under Hitler's leadership immediately. The fact that Streicher did not succumb to Hitler's magnetic personality until late 1922 is somewhat surprising in view of his recognized emotional instability. Other men, reputedly more stable emotionally than Streicher, were unable to resist dedicating themselves to Hitler after their first encounter with him. A typical example of such immediate transformation is the case of Kurt Ludecke, an ardent Nazi organizer in the "early days" of the party. After his first meeting with Hitler, Ludecke wrote: "I had found myself, my leader, and my cause...I had given him my soul."[3]

The exact date of Streicher's first meeting with Hitler is uncertain, but there is reliable evidence indicating that it must have occurred in the later months of 1921, after Hitler had consolidated his control over the recently reorganized Nazi party in July of that year.[4] Yet, approximately one year elapsed before Streicher agreed to join Hitler's forces. A brief examination of some of the factors which may have caused Streicher to resist Hitler's charisma during that year serve to clarify an important, but somewhat confusing, segment of Streicher's early political career. At the probable time of his first encounter with Hitler, in late summer, 1921, Streicher was the leading voice of the political party, DW, and the owner of that party's newspaper the *Deutscher Volkswille*. He was already known as a person who insisted on being the leader, or leading voice, in his various political affiliations. Streicher's personality also included a penchant for egocentricity and for undisciplined behavior. From the standpoint of these psychological characteristics alone it is understandable that he would not be anxious to bind himself quickly to the rules of a larger party or endanger the popularity and prestige he enjoyed as a leading figure of smaller, local *voelkisch* parties.

In addition to likely psychological reasons for Streicher's hesitation in this case, there are several other possible factors to be considered in the overall question of the Streicher-Hitler merger.

It has been suggested by at least one widely-known American historian, William Shirer, that in mid-1921 Streicher was intensely disliked by Hitler and because of this Streicher may have been discouraged from joining the Nazi movement until a year later.[5] This theory emanated originally from the account of a plot by a number of dissident NSDAP members who sought to deprive Hitler of his growing dominance of the young party. While Hitler was in Berlin, in early July, 1921, these members allegedly negotiated an agreement which would lead to a merger of the NSDAP and the DW. It was felt that the influx of members from another *voelkisch* group would stratify the leadership of the enlarged Nazi party. Hitler heard of this plot and hurried back to Munich and immediately resigned from the party. This move came as a shocking surprise to the "rebels." Within a few days they realized the indispensibility of Hitler to the future of the party and implored him to withdraw his resignation.

At a party conference later in July, Hitler became sole leader of the NSDAP and he promulgated a new code of party regulations which provided among other things that no other groups outside Munich were to be recognized until they had accepted Munich's (Hitler's) leadership.[6]

There is no reliable evidence that Streicher was an active protagonist in this plot. However, Shirer states that Streicher was an active participant in the intrigue and that Streicher was then a "bitter enemy and rival of Hitler." Shirer's allegations are not documented and thus can be considered only a hypothesis. Yet, if this point is valid, one might assume that after the plot was exposed and failed, and after Hitler had taken complete control and promulgated the new Nazi party code, Streicher had reason to feel that he was in Hitler's bad graces and would be rejected then if he applied for membership in the Munich movement.

Shirer's allegation that a bitter rivalry existed between Streicher and Hitler in 1921 and early 1922 is supported by

Ludecke, who was a close party associate of Hitler at that time. However, Ludecke's recollections of these events are not substantiated and were written many years after the period in question. Since neither of these accounts is documented they cannot be considered factual. Whether or not differences existed between the two men in the earlier days poses an unanswerable question of minor significance. Of far greater importance is the fact that after the rapprochement a long-lasting and unusually close relationship developed between the two *voelkisch* leaders.

There seems to be little question that Streicher was forced by reasons of financial and political necessity to join Hitler when he did regardless of his personal political ambitions or possible psychological restraints. Both his financial and political positions in the months immediately prior to the merger were precarious. By mid-summer, 1922, his *Deutscher Volkswille* was in dire straits mainly because it had been banned in the district of Augsburg, where nearly one-half of the DW members lived.[7] After he resigned from that party a few months later, the financial future of his publishing business became hopeless.

The German author, Manfred Ruehl, offers some evidence that Streicher's financial dilemma in late 1922 was an important factor in his decision to join Hitler. Ruehl discusses a letter that Streicher allegedly wrote to Hitler on October 8, 1922. The contents describe the hopeless financial position of the Franconian *voelkisch* press organs. Ruehl's source of information was the *Neuer Kurier*, which featured an article in 1946 about the Hitler-Streicher relationship. According to this article, the letter had been discovered by the president of the Nuremberg police in 1935 or 1936, and subsequently turned over to the Franconian Nazi Archive.[8] Shortly afterwards, however, this letter disappeared and it was intimated that Streicher was responsible for its mysterious disappearance because the contents, if disclosed publicly, would have been an embarrassment to him as political ruler of Franconia. The newspaper article offered no specific details of the letter, nor did it substantiate the intimation that a firm agreement was made between the two men before the merger was officially announced. Nevertheless, the *Neuer Kurier* concluded that Streicher agreed to join forces with Hitler only after he was promised handsome rewards.

Streicher's record of political activism in the early post-war years indicated an inability to solidify his leadership position in any of the three *voelkisch* groups with which he had been associated. By early 1922 it must have appeared inevitable to him that his days with the third group, the DW, were numbered and he faced political oblivion. He may have been planning to seek affiliation with Hitler's party in Spring, 1922, when he suddenly and without explanation adopted the swastika as his political symbol in early 1922. This emblem, a red and white banner, emblazoned with a black, hooked cross, had been designed by Hitler almost two years earlier as the official insignia of the National Socialist movement.[9]

In all likelihood, Hitler must have learned of Streicher's adoption of the swastika flag. He also probably knew of his disenchantment with the Nuremberg DW group. In early October, Hitler directed one of his recruiting agents, Ludecke, to visit Streicher and urge him to join the Munich-based Nazi movement. Ludecke recalls in his memoirs that he approached Streicher with Hitler's invitation and that he accompanied him to Munich where a stormy luncheon debate between the two leaders ensued.[10] After this luncheon, Streicher indicated to Ludecke his willingness to secede with his followers from the DW and join the Nazi party. Ludecke further remarked that he considered this a valuable meeting because the Hitler movement had gained not only a powerful *voelkisch* activist but 1500 of his followers as well. No details of the discussion at the luncheon were provided in this account. Ludecke merely added that Hitler subsequently agreed to a private meeting with Streicher to iron out details of the pending merger. Although there exists no documentary evidence of agreements concluded between the two leaders at the time of the merger, it is presumable that Hitler granted Streicher broad party authorities on the local level because as soon as Streicher publicly accepted Hitler's leadership he took full charge of Nazi organizational activities in Franconia.

Almost from the moment of the merger, Streicher became fanatically loyal to Hitler, and remained so for the rest of his life. In his book, *Mein Kampf*, Hitler publicly acknowledged his warm feeling for Streicher. In reference to the merger, Hitler pointed out that he appreciated the unselfishness of "this individual who sacrificed his own party for a larger goal."[11] In a further accolade to Streicher, Hitler continued that this voluntary contribution greatly aided the early development of the NSDAP because it had provided a "bridge to the north" for his party. This phrase suggests that Hitler felt that the merging of Streicher and his followers to the Munich party provided an important link which connected the south Bavarian Nazi movement to scattered National Socialist groups which existed in the north of Bavaria at that time.

Hitler's friendly feelings toward Streicher were to be exhibited in several other forms. In addition to granting Streicher positions of privilege and honor, the Nazi leader also remained a loyal supporter even in later years after Streicher had become an embarrassment to the party and the Nazi government.[12] An indication of Streicher's high personal standing with Hitler is notable by the fact that he was one of only four men ever permitted to use the German familiar *du* salutation in addressing Hitler.[13]

An interesting feature of the personal relationship between Streicher and Hitler is the rapidity with which it developed. It may be possible that this occurred as it did because there existed a long-standing compatibility between the two individuals that did not surface until they began working together in a common cause. This possibility bears consideration in light of the unique parallelisms in the personalities and lives of the two men.

Both Streicher and Hitler were born of humble parentage within a few years of each other. Their mothers were from the lower classes and led dreary lives. Their fathers were minor civil servants who were overbearing in the home and unconcerned about their children's needs. Streicher and Hitler were both suspected of Jewish ancestry and in later years these charges, although unproven, were used by some historians as a possible explanation for their rabid anti-Semitic attitudes.[14] Both became interested in politics before World War I and when that disastrous conflict finally erupted, they entered the fray with enthusiasm and both displayed outstanding dedication and bravery toward the war effort and were decorated numerous times. The two men adopted or developed an attitude of fatalism and both often remarked that destiny guided their lives and that this destiny was directly connected to the fate of their beloved country—Germany.[15] They were both extremely forceful in their political and social convictions and were generally in agreement on most crucial post-war German issues and attitudes such as the Versailles Treaty, the Weimar Government, the organized Church, the Socialists, Bolsheviks, and, above all—the evil of world Jewry.

The two became leading speakers in their various *voelkisch* parties and possessed the ability to attract and often mesmerize large audiences with sensational and marathon-length speeches. It was said that only Hitler could outlast Streicher in lengthy oratory. Both were men whose extreme emotionalism regarding political and social issues often led them to illogical or irrational decisions and actions. This weakness cost them political reversals and frequent court penalties, such as fines and imprisonments. It is interesting to note that Streicher was not considered an agitator during the war. On the other hand, Hitler was not promoted beyond the rank of corporal because of his constant harangues criticizing the unenthusiastic attitude of his comrades regarding the war effort. Yet until late 1918, neither seems to have been particularly emphatic about his anti-Semitic convictions. Shortly after the war, however, both became well-known in local circles for their outspoken racial beliefs. At that time they also began developing to varying degrees the major symptoms that characterize the emotional disorders clinically observable in most anti-Semitic personalities.[16]

After the war, however, Streicher became increasingly and often totally illogical in his political speeches and newspaper articles. Eventually his emotionalism over racial topics so dominated his behavior that he was often blind to the matter of practical politics. Contrarily, Hitler, who was also a rabid anti-Semite, did not allow his emotions over this issue to cloud his decisions regarding day-to-day political questions. In the final analysis it was this ability—or inability—to control emotions that proved to be one of the important factors which altered the destiny of their political careers and ended the parallelisms in the lives of these two men until the closing days of World War II, when each prepared to enter his individual "Valhalla" heroically by marrying his mistress as the impending collapse of Germany ended their warped aims and ambitions.

Immediately after publicly announcing that he had joined Hitler's ranks, Streicher threw himself energetically into the task of organizing NSDAP groups in his district. The Nuremberg branch was founded officially on October 20, 1922, the same day he announced his allegiance to Hitler. Streicher assumed the chairmanship of this group and named Ferdinand Buerger, an ex-DW colleague, as vice-chairman.[17] Streicher delivered the keynote address at the first meeting and outlined some of the basic party objectives:

> The goal of National Socialism is a complete reformation of Germany; a revolution, not a slow, well-behaved, quiet build-up. We will fight to the extreme. The question of the Jews is, and will remain, the central purpose of our fight. The *Werkgemeinschaft* failed because of this (moderation). The German problem cannot be solved without solving the problem of the Jews.[18]

Eight days after the founding of the Nuremberg NSDAP a large public meeting was held in the Nuremberg Colosseum where Streicher spoke before a capacity audience. He urged all his followers from other *voelkisch* parties to join with the National Socialist movement and he claimed that the first Franconian branch already had approximately 1,000 members.[19] In this and subsequent NSDAP meetings in Franconia there were virtually no vocal dissidents. A local branch of the party militia *(Sturm-Abteilung)* (SA) had been formed at Hitler's direction.[20] These burly, brown-shirted brawlers proved very effective in preventing disturbances at Franconian Nazi party meetings. Their force was felt at the occasion of Streicher's founding of the NSDAP branch at Augsburg on November 4th. Some dissenters, mostly Communists, attempted to disrupt the proceedings and were roughly expelled from the assembly hall by over one-hundred SA men who efficiently swept through the audience.[21] These para--military party troops also proved effective in creating disturbances and disrupting meetings of rival political Franconian groups such as the Communists and Moderate Socialists.

Within a few months after joining Hitler's movement, Streicher proved himself very successful in organizing local Nazi groups in Franconia. By the end of 1922 he was credited with forming NSDAP branches in Hersbruck, Lichtenfels, Erlangen, Forcheim, Ipsheim, Amburg, and Regensburg, in addition to Nuremberg and Augsburg. By early 1923, he had also assisted in forming local Nazi groups in Hassfurt, Pappenheim, Straubing, Bayreuth, Uffenheim, and Gunzenhausen.[22] Streicher's achievements as a party organizer were due in part to the constantly deepening crisis which developed in Germany during these months. The French invasion of the Ruhr Valley precipitated a crippling general strike. A disastrous nationwide spiral of inflation began which obliterated the savings of millions of German citizens. The Weimar government was at its nadir of popularity. Almost all classes of people had reasons to be disenchanted with the republican regime in Germany. Political groups which opposed the national government had little trouble finding recruits to swell their ranks. Under the impetus of the economic collapse and the national humiliation of the French invasion, Nazi party membership grew from less than 10,000 in December, 1922, to over 70,000 by early autumn, 1923.[23]

Streicher's organizational success was also due to his ability to attract large crowds to his meetings. As mentioned previously, anti-Semitism was an increasingly popular subject in Bavaria in those years. By the time Streicher began his work for the NSDAP he had changed his speaking technique somewhat. Instead of the earlier disorganized harangues he now combined his racial attacks with references to the interests of particular audiences. For example, when he addressed an audience in Nuremberg composed mainly of workers, he spoke:

> I see thousands of workers, poorly dressed, passing me after a hard day's work—carrying a pot of soup. They speak of their hard life and unbearable misery. But other people also pass me by—clad in valuable fur coats, with fat necks and paunchy stomachs. These people do not work. . . .The whole German people work, but the Jews live at the expense of the German workers. . . .The only victor of the World War was the international Jew. . . .We know that Germany will be free when the Jew has been excluded from the life of the people.[24]

The following month he spoke in the large hall of the Cultural Society in Nuremberg. Posters announcing the meeting stated that its purpose was to protest against the ever-increasing destruction of the middle classes. A police report stated that the hall was filled to overflowing and that when Streicher appeared he was greeted with "stormy applause." After a preliminary complaint about unfair press reporting, he moved dramatically into his major theme for the evening.

> The middle class is the source of all creative and state-supporting forces, which must be protected under all circumstances. Once this middle class has been destroyed, the state must collapse in its foundations.[25]

To illustrate his point, Streicher referred to ancient history. He spoke about the fall of the Roman Empire and claimed that it was not the Germanic tribes, but the Jews who were responsible for the collapse of that great civilization. He went on to state that the Jews took advantage of the hospitality of the Romans by first grasping all local businesses and then carrying off all movable wealth:

> ....Then they moved on. That is how it happened, that this rich Roman Empire, where every citizen was firmly established and lived well, drifted more and more toward an economy with big landlords and that the middle-class disappeared completely with the years.[26]

Streicher usually spiced these "special interest" speeches with at least one sensational story based on sexual or sadistic crimes by Jews. This hysterical sensationalism was perhaps the principal reason why crowds of people, faced with the drabness of everyday life and the worries of unemployment, flocked to listen to the irrational fanaticism of the zealous anti-Semitic orator. In one of his more lurid stories he brought up the case of a local Jewish lawyer who had recently been accused of murdering two working-class girls. Although the lawyer, named Rauh, was later acquitted, Streicher insisted that the girls had been raped by Rauh, then poisoned with mercuric-chloride pills, sold by a Jewish pharmacist. In dramatic fashion, Streicher then intimated that this was part of the Jewish murder ritual, but "since he was denied free speech—and was recently sentenced to jail for telling the truth—he could not speak further about this despicable crime."[27] The police reports on this meeting concluded that Streicher's speech was received with "fanatical applause," and that "the speaker made a fascinating impression." The report stated further that Streicher "speaks extemporaneously and succeeds in winning the support of masses of the audience and that he appears as a highly spiritual and capable leader who is a popular *Volksredner* (public speaker) in the real sense of the word."[28]

It seems evident that the officer who wrote the complimentary phrases in the above report was receptive to the themes and oratorical style used by Streicher. He may have also been favorably impressed by the enthusiastic response of the audience. Streicher had the ability to generate such enthusiasm meeting after meeting. On the other hand, his words and mannerisms also provoked negative reactions in varying degrees among members of opposing political parties and among some fellow *voelkisch* constituents. A few weeks after he began his career as NSDAP organizer in Franconia, the animosity of a Moderate Socialist Party city councilman named Giermann surfaced with a public threat to Streicher. In an open letter to Nuremberg NSDAP headquarters, Giermann condemned the National Socialist movement and threatened to "march against Streicher's handful of Nazis with 50,000 workers."[29] Nothing came of this threat but in a speech, Streicher jeeringly praised Giermann's "courage" and added that he regretted the councilman's lack of enlightenment.

In December a "palace revolution" against Streicher was initiated by Walther Kellerbauer, former radical *voelkisch* colleague and sometimes editor of the *Deutscher Volkswille.* Kellerbauer accused Streicher of planning that newspaper's extinction in order to deprive him (Kellerbauer) of a livelihood.[30] An argument ensued which developed into bitter animosity and caused a split among Nuremberg's Nazi leaders. Joining Kellerbauer were Ferdinand Buerger, deputy chairman, and Wolfgang Pressl, prominent member of the executive committee. These three men sought to wrest the leadership of the Franconian NSDAP movement from Streicher. They issued a formal complaint to Munich headquarters, demanding Streicher's ouster on the grounds of his lax living habits and his embezzlement of party funds. During November, 1922, rumors were spreading in Nuremberg that Streicher's personal moral behavior was becoming increasingly scandalous.[31] Streicher referred to these rumors in a speech in the Nuremberg Colosseum on November 23.

He claimed that these were all lies and that the rumor-mongers would be sought out and punished.[32] A police report later stated that these rumors had been investigated, but no concrete evidence of wrong-doing could be found.[33]

Kellerbauer and his colleagues demanded that Streicher be made accountable for money collected at local party meetings. Over Streicher's objections, Hitler sent Major Walter Buch, chairman of the party's investigation and mediation bureau, to check into this matter. After a few days, Buch reported to Hitler that he could find no discrepancies in Streicher's party financial records. No information is available to ascertain whether or not Buch's audit was thorough and impartial. The end result of the complaint and investigation was that Streicher was absolved of all charges and reaffirmed by Hitler as chairman of the Franconian National Socialist movement.[34]

CHAPTER IV

THE YEAR OF THE PUTSCH

The year 1923 witnessed a series of crises which shook the foundations of the young German Republic. Serious problems began in January, when French troops occupied the Ruhr industrial area over a World War I reparations dispute. In reply to this action the Weimar government officials ordered a policy of passive resistance against French efforts to speed up deliveries of coal, iron and other products. This led to a crippling general strike which accelerated the momentum of an inflationary spiral already underway. Before the year's end the German mark became worthless, bringing about the total collapse of the German economy. Millions of middle-class families lost their jobs, and farmers and merchants struggled to exist on the barter system.[1] The Weimar republican regime was generally blamed for these dire circumstances, and as this chaotic year progressed, radical political parties flourished in popularity and numbers, openly hostile to the beleaguered central government.

In the early months of 1923, Streicher was busy participating in meetings of local Nazi groups. He made speeches throughout Franconia and began organizing "German Days." These were actually rallies which brought many Nazi groups together at mass meetings. The largest of these held that year was in Nuremberg and was attended by over 100,000 people.[2] This was the first of large-scale Nuremberg Party-day rallies which grew to spectacular proportions after the Nazis seized political power in Germany.[3] Besides devoting much time to consolidating his grip on the leadership of the Franconian National Socialist movement, Streicher began a campaign to gain full political control of the Nuremberg city government. A Dr. Hermann Luppe was the mayor of the city. A moderate Social Democrat and an able, experienced administrator, Luppe had been generally accepted as a political leader by most Nuremberg citizens. Streicher opened a quarrel with Luppe when he denounced the mayor in a speech, claiming that he had robbed the poor, because he had purchased a coat, in 1920, from a used-clothing store where items were donated for needy people.[4] From this inconsequential charge, Streicher expanded his verbal attacks against Luppe during ensuing months to include virtually every aspect of his character, activities, and office.

The accusations usually were in the form of grossly exaggerated and personally insulting half-truths and were mostly proven groundless in subsequent court hearings. In the early years of the feud Luppe was at a disadvantage. He was not a native Bavarian and spoke with a north German dialect. Although he had proven to be an efficient and honest mayor, he experienced difficulty in establishing friendly rapport with some Nuremberg citizens, notably the working classes. As the economic crisis deepened during the year, increasing numbers of discontented and frustrated citizens of all classes were seeking reasons or solutions for their problems. Streicher took advantage of the distressing economic circumstances in his vitriolic attacks on Luppe. After listening to these harangues, many Nurembergers began to believe that "something must be wrong in the mayor's office."[5]

Luppe, however, was intelligent and was determined not to be discredited by false charges. He countered Streicher's attacks in every way possible. In January, 1923, Luppe demanded that Streicher be dismissed from his teaching position. Since the previous November Streicher's teaching practices had been questioned by certain of his political enemies who allegedly remarked that he often stressed his racial views and was otherwise unqualified as a school teacher. At least one critic claimed publicly that Streicher belonged in a lunatic asylum, not a school-room.[6] Luppe's complaints resulted in an investigation which was launched in February by government school inspectors. The reports of the inspections offer interesting details concerning Streicher's teaching methods and habits.[7]

One of the earliest of these noted that the teacher (Streicher) was ten minutes late and that the pupils conducted their morning prayers without him. The report stated that in the absence of the teacher one of the girls stepped forward and began to conduct the lesson in arithmetic. Streicher reportedly arrived a little later and went on with the arithmetic lesson. He then posed problems "taken from daily happenings and according to the daily situation."[8] The reading lesson was criticized in the report because "the teacher's introduction took nearly the whole hour and was a senseless talk around sometimes only the pictures." The general criticism of Streicher's teaching methods in this account stressed his poor lesson preparation and his tendency to stray off into "meaningless oratory." The report, signed by an inspector named Grim, ended with a statement that there was no trace of anti-Semitism in Streicher's teaching that day.[9]

Throughout the year, the most frequent complaint against Streicher as a teacher was his unauthorized absenteeism. The first incident of this nature was noted by the same inspector who had filed the above report and who appeared somewhat partial and condescending to Streicher. It happened that Grim observed Streicher's classroom activities on a Friday. He stated that the words "Off Tomorrow" were written on the blackboard. The wording of the report reveals that the inspector was somewhat fearful of Streicher's hostile nature:

> I knew that there was a party meeting in Munich...but not wanting to antagonize Mr. Streicher I just asked him if I was correct that there was flag-inauguration on Saturday or Sunday in Munich.[10]

Grim added that Streicher finally admitted his desire to attend the Munich meeting but that an official from the Ministry of Culture had already rejected his request for a leave because "it was for political purposes." Grim then apparently agreed with Streicher that "an exception could be made in this case, because only two hours of lessons were to be taught on Saturday."[11] He gave Streicher verbal permission to be absent on Saturday but reminded him to arrange for a substitute teacher. Streicher did not do this, nor did he return to his classroom the following Monday and Tuesday.[12]

This infraction played into the hands of Luppe and others who were pressing for Streicher's dismissal. The *Fraenkische Tagespost*, a newspaper known to be friendly to the Nuremberg mayor, carried an article in February entitled "How Long Still?"

> ....(Streicher) uses his meetings to arouse his listeners to violence against the Jewish population; to insult the City Council and our Mayor, Dr. Luppe....Either Julius Streicher is mentally sick, in

which case he belongs in an institution instead of in a school as a teacher, or he is sane, in which case he should be responsible for his actions. How long is the (Government) court going to wait until they do something?[13]

The following month another newspaper, the *Nuremberg Anzeiger*, carried on this attack by asking in an article how Streicher, a known agitator, could be tolerated as an educator of young people. It was also stated that the poor children subjected to his influence should be pitied and that the local government should act to remove this "disturbing influence" from the classroom.[14]

In early March, a full report of the investigation of Streicher's teaching activities was forwarded by the Bavarian government authorities to the Nuremberg School Board. A public hearing was conducted and the final decision was indicative of the leniency and almost sympathetic understanding that Streicher usually received from judges and other governmental officials. The first charge against Streicher centered about the free speech law, which allowed all public employees freedom to express their opinions, but only within certain limits. Luppe's attorneys argued that Streicher was unfit to teach because he could not stay within the limits of this law.[15] As proof it was noted that Streicher had been convicted for his violation the previous year when he insulted the Jewish religion. The judge, however, sided with Streicher as he dismissed this charge with the following rationale:

> The court is confident that teacher Streicher has learned enough from his experiences. . .and his previous conviction should restrain him in the future. . . .Therefore because of this past incident it (the court) feels that the conviction in itself was enough punishment. . . .[16]

The most serious charge had stressed Streicher's recent unauthorized absence. He had defended this act by stating that he had written a request on Saturday for leave the following Monday and Tuesday. He had also argued that Grim had agreed to this request verbally. At the hearing, Grim stated that he "could not remember exactly" all the details of his conversation with Streicher that day. Also, Grim said that Streicher's written request was forgotten by the teacher who was supposed to deliver it and thus the appropriate official did not receive it until after Streicher's classes had been left unattended for two days.[17] The result of this confused evidence was that the Nuremberg school authorities were rebuked for poor supervision. Grim was reprimanded for his part in the affair and Streicher was merely "sentenced to a warning."[18]

Streicher renewed his attacks on Luppe after learning of his "exoneration" by the government school authorities. In a speech on April 11, he ridiculed Luppe as a "dupe of the Jews," and accused him of planning to demolish the Hans Sachs monument to please his Jewish bosses.[19] Luppe responded to this obvious fabrication by sending a copy of this speech to Dr. Huber, president of the Franconian government. Enclosed in the same envelope was a plea by Luppe that Streicher was undermining the Nuremberg city government and that he should be suspended immediately as a teacher.[20] Huber rejected this plea on the grounds that Luppe had already filed a suit against Streicher in a city court on the same charge and thus nothing could be done until the civil case was completed in Nuremberg.[21] Luppe was not satisfied with this answer and continued to demand Streicher's immediate dismissal as a teacher. The government office of the Interior Ministry informed Luppe in early June that "steps were being taken to investigate Streicher's continued insults of Nuremberg authorities." Huber, however, must have realized that an extremely strong case against Streicher would be necessary in order to convince the local courts that effective punishment was in order. In communicating his sympathetic feelings on the Streicher problem to Luppe, Huber also revealed his desire to remove Streicher from the classroom as soon as sufficient evidence to warrant dismissal was made available:

Relieving Streicher as a teacher would not stop his continuation of the insults. It would, on the contrary, due to his free time, give (him) more opportunity for agitation and insult....To dismiss Streicher from the school is not yet possible because enough facts are not in our possession.[22]

While Luppe pressed in vain for immediate government action against Streicher as a school teacher, he was again attacked in speeches and newspaper articles by the Nazi leader. In a speech at a party meeting in May, Streicher accused the mayor of tax fraud and general dishonesty. He also said that Luppe was trying to make it impossible for the NSDAP to hold meetings in the Nuremberg Central Hall. After a long harangue, he finally read a resolution asking for the removal of Luppe as mayor. This was approved and passed unanimously by Nazi members present at that meeting.[23]

The next month Luppe continued to urge official disciplinary action. In letters to Dr. Huber he expanded his charges, stating that Streicher's immoral personal behavior was creating a scandal in the local school system.[24] Luppe made direct references to a citizen's complaint charging that illicit relations had taken place between Streicher and the wife of a physician, a Dr. Jung, of Ipsheim. This complaint was based on a rumor that was subsequently investigated by police authorities and proved to be without foundation. According to the police investigation, nobody could be found to state positively that there had been sex relations between Streicher and Mrs. Jung. The report of this inquiry stated that Mrs. Jung was an admirer of Streicher and this was not unusual inasmuch as he was a popular figure in the eyes of many women. The report concluded with a notation that Dr. Jung was also an ardent follower of the Nazi leader.[25]

Even though the above rumor was unproven, it would not have been surprising if Streicher had "taken advantage" of the wife of one of his followers. Throughout his adult life he was frequently observed making indecent advances to wives of high-ranking Nazi officials.

Complaints against Streicher's teaching habits continued throughout the year. Inspector Grim reported that he had heard criticism from the parents' association regarding the behavior of Streicher and a teaching colleague, Else Huith. Both were accused of not taking their teaching seriously and also insisting that their students use the Nazi "Heil" greeting when addressing their teachers or classmates.[26]

In addition to the above charges, the school principal also filed an official complaint. He noted that Streicher often left his classroom to talk politics in the hallway with other teachers. The principal further criticized Streicher for inviting eight young workers to the school in early February. He supposedly told his class that these men had "escaped" from the French occupied Ruhr area. Then he described the deplorable conditions which had driven them from their homes and then asked the children if they would be willing to help these refugees in their hour of need. He repeated this in ten different classrooms and received cash donations from the children which totalled 43,000 marks.[27] According to Streicher's account to the principal, the pupils were so sympathetic to these men that in the afternoon they voluntarily set a large table loaded with food for the eight refugees. The principal concluded his report with the comment that while he admired Streicher's concern for these unfortunate men, this act must be considered a violation of the rules because Streicher had not requested permission before he brought visitors to the school.

August and early September were weeks of school vacation. Streicher was busy most of this time organizing the first Nuremberg Party-day Rally. He also attended many meetings in which plans were discussed for the coming "people's revolution." With the nation's economy paralyzed in the chaos caused by the runaway inflation, leaders of militant political parties and leaders of the Bavarian government sensed that the disintegration of the Weimar regime might be near. These dissident factions were immersed in plans to move against the federal government.[28]

At the Nuremberg rally in September. Hitler alluded to the coming revolution. In a speech entitled "The Time is Five Minutes Before Twelve," he repeatedly warned that change was necessary and imminent and that all listeners should be prepared for the political upheaval ahead.[29] Hitler was referring to his plans for a national revolution which would result in a Nazi take-over of political power in Germany. At the same time, Gustav von Kahr and other political leaders in Bavaria were finalizing their plans for a revolt in the form of secession from the Weimar government.[30]

These revolutionary plans both culminated in failure on November 8 and 9 in a series of events known as the Munich Beer Hall *Putsch*. This affair was later celebrated by National Socialists as one of the important milestones in the development and growth of the Nazi party.[31] While there is wide disagreement to be noted between various historical accounts of the abortive *Putsch*, Streicher's activities during the two days are well documented with the exception of a few minor incidents.

Streicher received a telegram from Hitler on the morning of November 8 containing a terse message to report to Munich immediately. Without doubt, Streicher sensed the urgency of the order because he contacted his school principal, Krauss, at noon and announced that it was imperative that he leave for Munich within the hour.[32] Krauss reminded Streicher that leaves of absence were not granted for political reasons, but Streicher argued that this was a matter of national importance and he would go with or without official permission. Krauss finally consented to grant the leave on condition that Streicher be in his classroom the next day.[33] Streicher, still unaware of the specific reason for the urgent order, drove with friends that afternoon to Munich. When he arrived there he read in a newspaper that a large meeting was to be held that night in the *Buergerbraeukeller*, a large beer hall in Munich. Unable to locate Hitler Streicher could only learn from Nazi headquarters that important things would be happening at the beer hall meeting that evening.

This meeting had been scheduled initially by Bavarian political and military leaders in order to gain support for their government to separate Bavaria from the German Republic. Hitler had been invited to join forces with them because of his large civilian and para-military following. The Nazi leader arrived at the beer hall after the proceedings had begun. First he had the building surrounded with SA troops. Then he burst into the crowded room, jumped on a table and fired a pistol-shot into the ceiling. With this, he announced that the national revolution had begun and it was he, Hitler, who was to be the leader of the new government. He managed to coerce the leaders of the secession movement into a side room to discuss his proposal. A timely entrance by General Ludendorff helped Hitler convince the secessionists to join the Nazi revolution.[34]

When Streicher arrived at the beer hall later that evening, the leader of the secessionist group, von Kahr, was just announcing that he and his colleagues were joining the Hitler *Putsch*. Streicher then learned that a large group of revolutionaries, principally Nazis, were to march the next morning from the beer hall to downtown Munich and seize key military, police, and government buildings. Later that evening, Hitler commissioned Streicher to organize and carry out propaganda speeches before the march. Streicher's high-ranking party position with Hitler is clearly evident in the following copy of his signed letter authorization hurriedly published in leaflet form and distributed throughout Munich during the night of November 8:

> Mr. Streicher is commissioned by the provisional national government to organize and lead the speaking program. The transportation section should consider it of primary importance to cooperate with Mr. Streicher and furnish him the necessary vehicles. All speakers of the party are subordinated to Mr. Streicher and will receive their instructions from him.[35]

On the morning of the 9th, Streicher spoke to huge crowds from a truck in various places in Munich. According to reports, he repeatedly announced that a new government had been formed, that Jews and imposters would be hanged and that the stockmarket would be closed. Then he assured his listeners they had nothing to fear because Adolf Hitler "will give you bread and butter."[36] He later returned to the beer hall where a crowd of about 600 men had gathered and were milling around. Hitler appeared nervous and vacillating. Streicher was reported to have organized the lines and started off the march at the head of the column. Hanns Hoffmann, German author, states that while Hitler stood around, evidently indecisive, and perhaps considering whether or not the march should be cancelled, Streicher strode forward and cried *heraus fahren* (start to march) and began marching at the head of the column. Then Hitler started to move silently behind him.[37] As the marchers crossed the bridge over the Isar River they were met by armed police and soldiers. Although words were exchanged, the Nazis were not halted until they reached the *Feldherrnhalle*, a monumental edifice in downtown Munich. Here the march ended when gunfire erupted. Sixteen marchers were killed, but Hitler and Streicher were among those who scrambled for safety. There is no valid information to indicate the source of the first shot. It is generally assumed, however, that Streicher was somewhat instrumental in causing the gunfire to begin. One marcher, Robert Kuhn, agrees with two other witnesses that Streicher sprang out of the formation and tried to convince the police to lower their carbines just before a small-arms shot rang out.[38] On the other hand two German authors,

Konrad Heiden and H. R. Berndorff, state that Streicher leaped out of the ranks and tried to snatch a policeman's carbine and then the first shot rang out.[39]

The volley of gunfire which scattered the ranks of the Nazis ended Hitler's dream of a forceful seizure of political power in Germany. For Streicher's political career, however, the abortive *Putsch* was to prove beneficial. News accounts of his role in the *Putsch* catapulted him to prominence as a leading Nazi zealot, and his activities before and during the march placed him more than ever in a favorable position with Hitler. In later years, when other party officials complained to Hitler about Streicher, they were quickly silenced by a reminder of his heroics during the Munich march: "Perhaps Julius Streicher is an unpleasant character to some of you, but he stood by me at the *Feldherrnhalle* and for that I will never forsake him as long as he does not forsake me."[40]

Streicher was arrested on suspicion of high treason that evening while he was returning to Nuremberg. The next day he was released "for lack of sufficient evidence." On Sunday, the 11th, he was seen speaking in behalf of Hitler from his own car in the streets of Nuremberg.[41] It seemed now that he was too excited about recent political events to return to the classroom. The next day he succeeded in obtaining a fourteen-day sick leave from his school principal, Krauss. Streicher's wife, Kunigunde, had appeared at the school in the morning and pleaded that her husband could not attend to his school duties because he was suffering from nervous exhaustion.

On November 26, Streicher asked for an extension of this leave because he said he was still not strong enough to return to teaching.[42] This request was accompanied by a physician's opinion, which stated that Streicher's illness "consists of a functional nervous disorder of the neurasthenic kind." The physician recommended a full rest of eight weeks as necessary for total recovery.[43]

Streicher's political activities in Munich brought renewed demands for his dismissal as a teacher. Another public hearing was held in early December to consider the latest complaints which had been lodged by Luppe's attorneys. The charges were prefaced by a statement that Streicher should be suspended as a teacher because he had been grossly neglecting his school duties and had allegedly used the time of sick leave for political agitation purposes. It was also noted that the government had suspected him of treason because of his actions during the Munich march. The major complaint, however, was that he had been seen recently speaking at political meetings even though he was on sick leave.

At a hearing in a Nuremberg civil court, Streicher protested the charges vehemently. He denied that he had done anything treasonous, explaining in detail that he had had no advance knowledge of what was to transpire in Munich when he went there. He also argued that after he had arrived at the beer hall, Kahr and other high military and political officials announced before thousands of people that the new national government had already been formed under Hitler. Thus, he reasoned, when he spoke about the new government from the truck on the morning of November 9, he had no idea that this was not a true fact.[44] His defense against the treason charge was stated in an earlier petition protesting his brief arrest on the tenth. In explanation of his allegedly treasonous words on the morning of the ninth, he was quoted as stating: "My friends and I were all absolutely convinced of the legality of the new government and therefore thought that we were within the law in what we were doing."[45]

Despite Streicher's arguments, the judges could not exonerate him completely on the treason charge. This was perhaps because Hitler and other participants in the Munich march had already been arrested and jailed pending trial on charges of high treason. The court ruled against Streicher and a directive was drawn up which officially suspended him as a teacher until further notice. A copy of this document was delivered to him a few days after the hearing.[46] This was followed by a notice of the decision to the Nuremberg School Board with instructions that during Streicher's suspension his salary would be reduced by one-third, and his living expenses and local pay supplements would be withheld.[47]

The day after he received notice of his suspension, Streicher wrote to the government school officials denying the charges against him regarding his sick leave. He stated that he had been examined again on December 10, by a doctor who had again stated that there was no doubt about his sickness and that his leave was "based on facts."

Furthermore, he noted that his appearances at the Nuremberg meetings during his sick leave were as a guest, not as the main speaker. He said that he had no intention to speak at either meeting but that in the first instance he spoke only to quiet the crowd, and the second time he spoke only "a few short words to show his opinion."[48] In this letter, Streicher also explained that he had refused all formal invitations as a speaker and had not given any political addresses during his sick leave. He also defended the charge that he was "too involved in politics" with the following statement which illustrated his ability at cleverly worded alibis using historical references as well as his view that the attempted Nazi revolution could be equated with honorable and patriotic duty:

Walter Rathenau has said five years ago that within 20 years the German people will only be an historical thought. . .that what was once called Germany will be a desert. . . .Is it not the duty of every German to try to prevent that this prophecy comes true?. . .It seems unnecessary to remark that this work of reviving the feeling of honor for the fatherland is a patriotic duty.[49]

Some phrases in this letter indicated that he was somewhat resigned to his suspension. He stated that he knew that his work after school during "these days of destiny" conflicted with some rules of the school, adding that whoever wants to help the German people "also has to sacrifice, even if it means losing his job." And finally, just above his signature, he closed the letter with a Luther-like statement of unalterable conviction: "I do not feel guilty—what I did was to follow my conscience."[50]

Streicher's activities in Nuremberg immediately after the attempted *Putsch* pose an interesting question regarding his personality. According to police reports, he acted entirely out of character. The excitement of the recent political happenings in Munich was reflected in the Nuremberg streets on the afternoon of November 10. Mobs of people were milling around, discussing the defeat of Hitler's *Putsch*. Streicher's car was stopped by the throngs in the early evening. He stood up, waved his arms in a quieting manner, and spoke:

German men and women, behave as befits Germans! Do not make it difficult for these men (the police). Do not cause a spectacle as in Munich, where German blood was spilled by German men.[51]

Streicher then began to sing the national anthem, *Deutschland ueber alles,* and the crowd joined with uncovered heads. The police report on this event concluded that at least four officers agreed that Streicher had a calming effect on the crowd that day, and that Streicher gave the chief inspector binding assurance that he would not talk in public in the near future without police permission.[52] The question of why he reversed his usual pattern of behavior to act in a calming and cooperative manner remains a matter of conjecture. He may have been actually afraid of the police after recently witnessing the bloodshed in front of the *Feldherrnhalle* or else he might shrewdly have realized that the Nazi movement was temporarily discredited and it was time to regain respect for the party in the eyes of the law. Kahr had outlawed the NSDAP and its affiliates in Bavaria on November 10, and a number of leading Nazis were either arrested and imprisoned or were being sought by the police.[53] The latter conclusion seems more likely because Streicher's war record indicated his lack of fear under fire. Also, throughout his political career he occasionally displayed the capacity to conceal his customary crude and antagonizing personality and at times in matters not directly related to anti-Semitism he was known to act with impunity regarding matters of political timing and strategy. This quality in Streicher was pointed out by one of his close personal acquaintances of long standing who stated that Streicher could be described as three-quarters crazy and one-quarter "foxy." In other words, the acquaintance said, while Streicher usually acted abnormally hostile, aggressive and erratic, he was also capable of very shrewd thinking and behavior.[54]

Leading figures in the November 9 march, besides Hitler and Streicher, included ex-general Erich Ludendorff, SA leaders Ernst Roehm and Hermann Goering, Hitler's aide Rudolf Hess, and Hermann Esser, an active Munich NSDAP speaker and organizer. Streicher, Roehm and Ludendorff were among those arrested immediately. The ex-general and Streicher were freed pending further evidence. Roehm was jailed to await trial. Goering, Hess and Esser escaped and soon left Germany. Hitler fled to the nearby country house of a friend, Ernst Hanfstaengl, where he was arrested on November 11, by a small contingent of state militia and then imprisoned in the fortress Landsberg am Lech to await trial for treason.[55] He was locked in a cell by himself and was allowed virtually no visitors during his first weeks there.[56] He was able to learn, however, that there had been an upheaval in the Bavarian government. Kahr and his regime had been ousted and a new government formed. The new prime minister, Heinrich Held, and the new minister of justice, Franz Guertner, appeared eager to cooperate with the defendants in the trial, which was scheduled to begin as soon as possible.[57]

During these days of Hitler's imprisonment some of the leading National Socialists were trying to continue the activities of the party despite its prohibition.[58] Some men, such as Esser, Drexler, and Alfred Rosenberg came together in Salzburg, Austria, where they published propaganda leaflets and newspapers which were smuggled into Germany.[59] In Nuremberg, Streicher was trying to keep the movement alive. It was reported that when he appeared in public he did not stress the racial issue as he usually did, but was making overt attempts to win back followers to the Nazi cause by agitating against present governmental policies. To win the working class, he attacked government attempts to increase the working day beyond eight hours. To attract farmers, he spoke against unfair mortgage laws on farm land. Minor government officials lent a sympathetic ear when he castigated the Kahr administration for reducing the "normal staff" of the civil service.[60] Prime Minister Kahr, obviously worried about growing political dissension in the state, moved to silence the Nuremberg leader. On January 18, 1924, he issued orders that Streicher be arrested and taken into "protective custody" because he (Kahr) feared that civil disorders might break out as a result of his inflammatory words.[61]

Some interesting incidents of this arrest and subsequent confinement are revealed in a diary kept daily by Streicher during this period. He recorded that four criminal investigators came to his residence about noon on January 18 and notified him that Kahr had ordered his arrest. These investigators appeared apologetic and repeated that the arrest had not been ordered by the Nuremberg Police Office. Streicher wrote that after the initial surprise, he soon became calm, and that his wife Kunigunde "smiled strangely."[62] Lothar, the elder son, became very excited while the younger son, Elmar, struck out at the one investigator who tried to be friendly. Streicher was taken to a local police station where he dictated a protest which demanded that he be informed of the specific reasons for his arrest. He recorded in his diary that he spent that night in a jail cell, where he read a book entitled *Atlantis, Earth and Bible*, before trying to sleep.[63]

Coincidentally, a junior police officer on duty that night was a man named Benno Martin, who later became head of the Nuremberg police and who ultimately gathered evidence which was used to topple Streicher from political power in 1939. Martin stated later that he had always been treated respectfully by Streicher because of a trivial incident that happened in the Nuremberg jail that night in January 1923. Apparently it was cold where Streicher was trying to sleep. He had asked for and received a third blanket from Martin who had seen nothing outstanding in this act but concluded that despite Streicher's arrogant mannerisms he usually appreciated small acts of kindness or understanding such as this and did not forget them.[64]

Next morning Streicher was taken by train to the fortress Landsberg am Lech. There he was placed in a cell-block with other Nazis being held in "protective custody." It is obvious from his description of a "cool reception" by about one-half of these fellow party members that Streicher was not too popular in their circle. The diary described the dull routine of prison life. Almost every entry complained of the bitter cold in the cells. In the daytime the prisoners were allowed to talk together, to play cards or chess, and to take routine walks. At night each was locked in an individual cell.

However, Hitler, also imprisoned here, was not allowed to mingle with the other Nazis at Landsberg during these weeks. He was kept in solitary confinement with an armed guard constantly on duty in front of his cell, and the peep-hole in his cell-door was covered with a piece of paper. Coincidentally, the prison dispensary was located just across the hall from Hitler's place of confinement.

On January 21, Streicher was ordered to take a physical examination at the dispensary. He noted in his diary that he wanted to call out a greeting to Hitler as he approached his cell, but he kept silent because he had been warned that any attempt at verbal communication was strictly against orders.[65]

But on January 25, Streicher went to the dispensary again, complaining of a severe cold. This time there were two armed guards in front of Hitler's cell door. Streicher wrote that he was determined to see and talk to the famous prisoner. He said he paced in front of the guards, talking about the weather, and when he had distracted their attention he jumped to the cell door, lifted the paper from the peep-hole and shouted: "Heil Hitler, here is Streicher!" The guards quickly pulled him away from the door. He was reported for this infraction and later punished by losing some yard privileges for a few days.[66]

During this prison term, Streicher's wife sent frequent letters and parcels. He noted in the diary that he suffered a severe case of bronchitis. His wife and sister were allowed to visit him on February 1, and they brought him medicine, food and flowers. He made a special request to be able to have himself photographed so he could send his picture to his father as a birthday present.

On February 4 he was permitted to send a letter to a Dr. Kelber accepting an offer by the Franconian "people's group" to be a candidate in the next Bavarian *Landtag* (parliament) elections. On February 11, Streicher noted that many of those in "protective custody" were allowed to cast their ballots in local elections. The final diary entry was dated February 24, 1924, when his wife and son Elmar surprised him with a visit on the day of his release from Landsberg.[67] They returned with him to Nuremberg. Nothing was noted in the diary that the much heralded trial of Hitler and other Nazis began on the same day.

News of the coming legal proceedings against Hitler gained wide interest. The new government consented to full radio coverage of the trial. Reporters from all parts of Germany as well as from several foreign countries were in attendance when the trial began on February 24, 1924. When it ended about six weeks later, Hitler received a sentence of five years in jail, but he had actually transformed defeat into triumph. He had discredited the former political and military leaders of Bavaria and had impressed the German people with his

69

nationalistic fervor and his eloquence. His name appeared for the first time on front pages of newspapers all over the world.[68]

Streicher had nothing to do with Hitler's trial. A few days after he returned home he resumed publication of his newspaper, *Der Stuermer*, which had been banned since the attempted *Putsch*. The first issue of the *Stuermer* had appeared in April 1923, after a quarrel between Streicher and other leaders of the Nuremberg NSDAP. At a party meeting on April 14, 1923, Walther Kellerbauer, Ferdinand Buerger and others had accused Streicher of embezzling the group's funds and leading an immoral life. At a meeting four days later, Streicher charged his accusers with the same transgressions. This meeting was poorly attended and consequently not many members heard his side of the story. Two days later he published these counter-accusations in a six-page leaflet entitled *Der Stuermer*, with the headline: "Streicher's Answers to the Accusers and Slanderers."[69]

The first *Stuermer* was one-half the size of a normal newspaper and was double-spaced. The heading took nearly one-fourth of the first page. Under the title in bold type was the phrase "Special Edition in the Struggle for the Truth." Almost the entire issue was devoted to Streicher's denunciation of Kellerbauer, Buerger and other "former party members who went sour." The final section of this polemic was entitled "Why?" Here Streicher charged that the reason these men became "traitors" was because of a "strong attraction toward the Jews." At the bottom of the last page was a single line in bold type: "Friends—think of Hitler."[70]

The following week's edition began a five-week series of attacks on Dr. Luppe. Streicher often wrote leading articles in the first person, directly against Luppe, accusing the mayor of such things as misusing public funds, failing to help the poor, or causing the widespread unemployment. The most frequent charge was that Luppe "was owned by the Jews."[71] In early July, Streicher announced the aims of the *Stuermer* in somewhat vague terms:

> In the Bavarian-German manner, you must believe the truth about these scoundrels! Wake up and combat half-heartedness and weakness in our city. Help strengthen our hearts for the coming 'Fight of Delivery'. . . .This is what the *Stuermer* wants![72]

70

From its inception the *Stuermer* called itself "a paper in the fight (or struggle) for the truth." As its title implied, it was a "fighting publication."[73] This type of paper has been described by some historians as one which

...rises and falls with the rising and falling power of a political movement and the mobilization of the masses for fight.... Everything that is the usual substance of a newspaper....is subordinated to the political fight....[74]

It was not the intention of the *Stuermer* to publicize information about local news events such as social happenings or athletic contests. Streicher's publishing purpose was identical to that later described by Joseph Goebbels, Nazi propaganda chief:

For us the goal of the publisher is printed propaganda. It forms conclusions about political happenings. It does not leave it up to its reader to form his own conclusions. It openly follows the goal of political influencing....(The reader's) thinking and feeling is to be pulled in a certain direction....[75]

By mid-summer Streicher was concentrating on the theme which he obviously felt was the most important in contemporary political thought. This theme, "the Jew and his crimes," continued with few alterations, the same for the next twenty-two years. In a typical example, during 1923 Streicher wrote a leading article headlined: "Who is the Villain?" He began by discussing the acute economic problems of the times. Then continued:

Is the cause of these problems the French?, the English?, the Russians?, the Americans? No—it is a common group—the Jews—who aim to control the world.[76]

The last section of this long article was headed "Down With Capitalism." This was aimed at the workers, and for added effect Streicher addressed them in the familiar *du* form. Except for the anti-Semitic aspects of the article, the emphasis of Streicher's arguments reflected the views of Marxian Socialism. In summary he encouraged the workers to go forth and do battle against the devil—capitalism. He concluded: "When capitalism is defeated—then also the Jew will go under."[77]

Other Nazi leaders were often as virulent as Streicher in their anti-Semitic attacks, but they usually used more subtle reasoning than he did. Streicher's *Stuermer* tirades were always lacking in educated phraseology. He used banalities in childish language to reach even the lowest classes of people. His shocking attacks on individuals attracted many who enjoyed "gutter sensationalism." Some critics have intimated that Streicher wrote as he did out of necessity; that low-class journalism appealed to the largest number of readers; and that Streicher was willing to do anything to make the *Stuermer* a financial success. They argued further that since the paper was owned privately and received no financial support from the party, it had to sell in large numbers to keep alive.[78] There is, however, little other evidence to support this argument. Even in later years when his publishing business flourished and his profits were high, Streicher's rabid style of journalism in the *Stuermer* did not vary much from his earlier newspaper endeavors.

CHAPTER V

HITLER'S LOYAL PARTY COMRADE

The National Socialist movement suffered a severe setback with the failure of the *Putsch*. The NSDAP and most of its press organs were outlawed by the Bavarian government. Some Nazi leaders had fled Germany and others were in jail or free on bail awaiting trial for treason. Alfred Rosenberg, editor of the party newspaper, the *Voelkischer Beobachter*, claimed that Hitler had issued a document from Landsberg prison naming him as interim party leader to be assisted by Max Amann, Hermann Esser, and Julius Streicher.[1] The radical political views and behavior of these four men were unacceptable to many of the more conservative-minded National Socialists. Some former Nazis questioned the validity of Rosenberg's claim, while others seemed reticent to accept or follow the dictates of Hitler while he was in jail. Ex-general Erich Ludendorff was especially reluctant to consider Hitler's wishes regarding the party's future. Considerable animosity had developed between the two men since the *Putsch* had ended in a fiasco. Ludendorff was piqued because he had not been consulted in advance of the attempted revolt. Hitler, in turn, resented the fact that the old soldier's bravery at the *Feldherrnhalle* had put him to shame. He voiced this resentment to some of his followers who had visited him at the Landsberg prison:

> I depended on Ludendorff—that was my greatest mistake! He forced us into this unnecessary massacre and then, like a hero, walked right through the police lines. If I had tried it, I would simply have been shot down like a dog. That's why I ran away in the automobile. Now Ludendorff is a hero, and I am nothing but a coward.[2]

While Hitler castigated himself in jail some former party officials, with varying aims and ambitions, sought to form successor organizations to the NSDAP. Because of the oncoming Bavarian *Landtag* elections, all these factions united temporarily under the banner of the *Voelkischer Block*.[3] The dominant section of the *Block* was the National-Socialist Freedom Party *(Nationalsozialistische Freiheits-*

partei) (NSFP), which was formed in December, 1923, when Ludendorff and others organized a merger of some prominent south Bavarian *voelkisch* groups with several northern Nazi local parties, headed by Gregor Strasser, a pharmacist and leader of a moderate northern wing of the National Socialist movement.[4] In principle, the *Block* endorsed most standard NSDAP policies and most leaders preferred loyalty to Hitler, but many were more moderate and more parliamentarian in outlook than the imprisoned leader.[5] Some "old line fighters" did not agree with these moderate principles but during the election campaign the fight against external foes overshadowed any differences with the *voelkisch* ranks. However, this unity was soon to be proven as superficial and short-lived.

Streicher was a candidate for a Bavarian *Landtag* seat, but his campaign activities were interrupted when he was subpoenaed to appear in court in Nuremberg on March 5, 1924, to face slander charges lodged by Mayor Luppe. In the subpoena Streicher was accused of making false and slanderous public statements which continually offended Luppe.

The nature of the defamatory remarks listed in the charges against Streicher were in keeping with his previous attacks on the mayor:

> Luppe descends from Jews.
> Luppe is not qualified to be a mayor.
> Luppe's election was arranged by way of a 'horse trade.'
> Luppe is not a patriotic German.[6]

At the first day's court session, Streicher displayed certain theatrical tendencies as he dressed and acted as a patriotic and sincere German in an obvious attempt to gain the sympathy of the court. He entered the courtroom in a gray, military-style jacket decorated with his most prized World War I medal—the Iron Cross, First Class.[7] His countenance was solemn and his initial responses were made in measured and subdued tones. He stated that it was his political conviction that the Jews prevented the national rise of Germany, so consequently he felt he was not quarreling with Dr. Luppe as a person but rather with the political system of which Dr. Luppe was the highest local representative.[8]

In the early days of the trial, Streicher and his attorney,

Dr. Kelber, established procedural tactics which often clouded the principal issues and forced Luppe to act as the defendant in the case. Rather than attempt to deny the charges against himself, Streicher elaborated on old and new allegations against the mayor and his associates. More than two days of the first week centered about the old "coat affair."[9] This was a renewal of a previous charge made by Streicher that Luppe was a dishonorable public servant because he had purchased a coat from a used-clothing store established to sell only to needy people. Both Kelber and Streicher spent hours attempting to prove that not only Luppe but other members of his administration were guilty of "robbing" needy families by profiteering on items from this store. Luppe's attorneys took pains to produce many witnesses, including the store manager, to testify that these charges were untrue.[10]

The next day, Luppe's attorney, Dr. Suessheim, opened the proceedings by offering as evidence various issues of the *Stuermer* to prove that Streicher had maliciously slandered the mayor. Streicher retorted quickly that his newspaper always spoke the truth about rogues and Jews. Suessheim, whose name indicated he was Jewish, then fell victim to an indirect attack when Streicher glared at him and talked about dishonest Jewish jurists. He referred to the case of a Jewish lawyer, named Rauh, who had recently been exonerated of a murder charge. When an exasperated judge asked what that had to do with this case, Streicher answered that it was important to note that Jewish jurists were not to be trusted because in the Rauh case the attorneys and judges were Jews and for this reason the guilty man was acquitted.[11]

Dr. Suessheim ignored Streicher's vicious inferences. Instead he argued that he could prove that Streicher had continually tried to defame Luppe by slanderous and false public statements. For these reasons, Suessheim continued, Streicher was guilty of violating the law and should be punished to the maximum extent, which in this case would be two months' imprisonment plus paying the costs of the proceedings. He concluded, rather weakly, that Streicher's punishment should be severe because Luppe's reputation as an honest politician had been endangered.[12]

Streicher's attorney, Dr. Kelber, then entered his final defense plea concluding that Streicher should be acquitted because he did not intend to slander, but only to criticize the system Luppe represented.[13] This plea was followed by some statements by Dr. Krafft, second attorney for the defense, who noted Streicher's outstanding effort in re-instilling national pride in thousands of workers. In his own final defense plea, Streicher declared that he considered himself a representative of idealism trying to defend Germany against all enemies and concluded that the future would prove his political opinions were correct. His last words, however, indicated that he knew that his defense had been weak. He stood stiffly looking directly at the judges and said that any punishment he received from this court would mean nothing to him because in his conscience he knew he was innocent.[14]

At the conclusion of the trial in mid-March, Streicher was found guilty as charged and sentenced to one month's imprisonment with the provision that this part of the sentence would be waived if the defendant fulfilled terms of good conduct until April, 1927, and paid a fine of 1,000 marks for the benefit of poor children. The court also granted Dr. Luppe permission to publish this sentence in three newspapers at Streicher's expense and ordered that all available copies of the most objectionable *Stuermer* numbers be confiscated and destroyed.[15]

At the time of the sentencing, Streicher appeared jubilant. As he left the court building, a crowd of admirers were waiting and greeting him noisily. He returned these greetings with a broad smile and "Heil" salutations. Luppe and Suessheim appeared dissatisfied with the light sentence. They immediately filed for an appeal hearing. Streicher, perhaps to show his contempt for Luppe, instructed his attorneys to file a similar appeal request.[16]

Streicher's light sentence in this case again evidenced the sympathetic attitude toward the anti-Semitic movement usually shown by German jurists during those years. The judges' decisions may have also been tempered by the public support that Streicher received. Many well-wishers greeted him enthusiastically each day as he entered or left the court-room.

Streicher lost no time returning to his political pursuits after the trial ended. The very evening after the sentence was pronounced, he led an election rally at nearby Fuerth. Since he was a candidate for a state legislature seat, he had been able to secure police permission for this rally while the trial was still in progress. Posters announcing this event had been printed and displayed in prominent places since early March.[17]

Streicher had ordered that this event be advertised as an "all girl rally." He scheduled meetings such as this occasionally perhaps in order to show his appreciation for his sizable, enthusiastic female following or perhaps to encourage women to participate actively in political affairs. Interestingly, this was in direct contradiction to the Nazi axiom that the place for the German woman was in the home and not in the world of business or politics. Joseph Goebbels, who later became Hitler's propaganda minister, summed up the male chauvinist principles of the National Socialist party:

> The mission of woman is to be beautiful and to bring children into the world. This is not at all as crude and unmodern as it sounds. The female bird pretties herself for her mate and hatches the eggs for him. In exchange, the mate takes care of gathering the food, and stands guard and wards off the enemy.[18]

While Streicher encouraged other men's wives and daughters to disregard the publicly stated Nazi-party directives regarding the "acceptable" behavior of women, he evidently concurred with the axiom in his private life. His wife always remained at home in the background, never appearing with him in his business or political activities. However, this example of double standard seemed in keeping with some of his known behavioral characteristics. He usually followed organizational rules or policies except when they were in contradiction to his own emotional desires or convictions. Because of his egocentric nature, he must have craved the self-satisfaction of being the center of attention in a hall filled with women. While it is impossible to estimate the practical political value of holding campaign rallies limited to women and girls, it can only be assumed that a large percentage of those voting for Streicher in his election contests were females.

Since launching his political career, Streicher had successfully developed a wide following of ardent and admiring women and girls. This popularity was perhaps engendered by his self-assumed role as protector of German women's "aryan virtue." He had developed this role by repeatedly insisting in his speeches and *Stuermer* articles that Jewish men were instructed by their scriptures to commit adultery with German females or rape them at every opportunity. In all of the diatribes, Streicher included "warnings" of this nature and stated that he was dedicated to preserve the "purity of aryan blood."

At the Fuerth meeting approximately 800 females greeted him with loud "Heils" and presented him with baskets of flowers when he appeared on the stage.[19] Streicher began a two-hour speech by discussing the Luppe lawsuit, stating that the trial gave him great satisfaction because he was able to "tell the truth about Luppe." He then engaged in an impassioned tirade on the race question. In a long story filled with fantastic but untrue "facts," he referred to Jews as "Negroes with three kinds of blood," and stressed repeatedly that everyone should do everything possible to prevent "the bastards" from increasing. He added that German girls who go out with Jews should have their heads shaved and that the German man who goes out with a Jewess should have his private parts cut off. At the end of the harangue Streicher asked everyone to "put oil on the fire," which he said "has finally started to get rid of the Jews." To guarantee a large "fire" he concluded, "all you have to remember is to vote for the right man in the coming elections."

This meeting was described in an official police report which noted that Streicher's speech was followed by loud and prolonged applause. The proceedings reportedly closed when a party official from Nuremberg, Herr Wiesenbacher, entered the hall and told the audience that the two best Germans were Adolf Hitler and Julius Streicher and it would be appreciated if everyone left a small offering in the collection plates at the exits. The report concluded that nothing illegal had transpired at the meeting and that at all times "good order" had been kept.

During this campaign Streicher demonstrated that his political popularity and authority extended from the radical to the moderate factions of the *Voelkischer Block*. On March 25 he spoke to a gathering of "hardline," racist-oriented former Nazis at Langenzenn in the early evening and was cheered tumultuously at the end of a one-and-a-half hour speech.[20] He appeared later the same night at nearby

Burgfarrnbach where he had been invited to a political meeting promoting "moderate" *voelkisch* candidates for the coming elections. Streicher entered the crowded hall while a candidate for re-election to the Nuremberg City Council, Herr Teichmann, was speaking. The audience greeted the newcomer so noisily that Teichmann could no longer be heard. Almost immediately the chairman of the meeting turned the podium over to Streicher who then spoke for an hour—mostly about the injustices of the Luppe trial.

The Bavarian *Landtag* elections, held on April 6, resulted in a considerable victory for the *Voelkischer Block* candidates who captured one-fifth of all seats. The majority of the *Block* representatives were moderates whose principal sponsor was Ludendorff.[21] Streicher and Hermann Esser headed the small contingent of radical *voelkisch* members who had been elected.

Esser had become leader of a Munich-based political group called the Greater German People's Union *(Grossdeutsche Volksgemeinschaft)* (GVG). This party had been founded in February, 1924, by two lesser-known Nazis—Arthur Dinton and Franz Schwarz. It was openly pro-Hitler and oriented to radical and activist Nazi policies.[22]

Since his banishment to Landsberg prison in November, 1923, Hitler was instinctively avoided by many people of conservative inclinations. Many of these were members of the moderate faction of the *Voelkischer Block*, striving with Ludendorff and Strasser to bring respectability to the *voelkisch* movement. While not openly opposing or criticizing Hitler, they also did not base their political endeavors on his reputation or his total political philosophy. In fact, many of these men felt that Hitler's name was more of a liability than an asset in this attempt to create a new political image.[23]

At least one German historian, Konrad Heiden, asserts that Streicher and Esser were the only Nazis totally loyal to Hitler during these months.[24] Because of this near fanatic loyalty, and because of Streicher's uncontrollable racist outbursts, the two radicals soon became very unpopular with most *Landtag* representatives. At one early session, Esser irritated many moderate *voelkisch* members in a speech stressing "the contemptuousness of those who pretend to be National Socialists yet do not admit to the leadership of Hitler."[25] Equally irritating to all *Landtag* members was the patented answer often used by both Streicher and Esser to questions directed to them on the floor. In emotional tones they would shout: "We are nothing, but Hitler is everything!"[26]

At the organizational meeting of the newly-elected *Landtag*, Streicher was asked to serve on a standing committee. He responded by launching into a long tirade on the subject of "Jewish crimes." The chamber soon resounded with hoots and catcalls and members began leaving their seats. Streicher ignored the chairman's plea for order, stating that he had constitutional immunity to say what he pleased. Raising his voice he continued this anti-Semitic tirade until he concluded with the words:

> Most of you are not aware that the Jews have caused untold misery in our fatherland. We true National Socialists will never allow any other problem (to have) priority over the Jew-problem. This work is much more important to me than the trivial details you think are important. My on-going fight against the Jews leaves me no time to serve on your trivial committee.[27]

By late May, leaders of the moderate faction began attempts to oust the two radicals from the *Voelkischer Block*. Strasser had stated at a political meeting that "the clown Julius Streicher" should be expelled from the movement.[28] On another occasion, Ludendorff and others referred to Streicher and Esser as "two dunghills who should be removed from the party."[29] These insulting remarks brought a scathing rebuttal from Streicher. In a Munich speech he retaliated:

> Among the first to be purged from the *voelkisch* movement should be the traitors Strasser and Ludendorff. Not only are they guilty of trying to water down the real National Socialist program, they are also guilty of trying to steal Hitler's movement from him.[30]

From his jail cell at Landsberg, Hitler stubbornly refused to heed any complaint from *voelkisch* moderates that Streicher and Esser be removed from the movement. His adamant insistence on keeping these two "old fighters" in good standing and high political ranking was probably based as much on shrewd reasoning as on personal loyalty. He knew that dissident elements such as Streicher and Esser were apt to create division and dissension in the movement. The divisiveness would thus prevent a strong and unified movement against him from developing. He had learned, through newspapers, that his political position was being threatened by some of the leading *voelkisch* moderates. Hitler had complained to one visitor at Landsberg that Ludendorff and others were "trying to steal my movement from me."[31] His animosity toward the potential leader plotting against him was evidenced in early summer when Ludendorff and Strasser went to Landsberg to pay him a visit. They were told by a guard: "Herr Hitler is too busy to receive visitors today." Shortly afterwards Hitler repeated a maneuver he had used earlier to thwart an attempt against his political leadership. He sent a letter to the rightist press announcing his resignation as leader of the National Socialist movement.

Although this act seemed to play into the hands of Ludendorff and his colleagues, the old general became furious because he saw this as a repeat performance of a similar maneuver in 1921, when Hitler's resignation forced the capitulation of Drexler and other members of the party's executive committee. Determined not to be intimidated in like fashion, Ludendorff countered Hitler's move by accelerating his efforts to gain hegemony over the various *voelkisch* factions. He issued an appeal in Bavaria that personal differences should be forgotten or compromised for the sake of party unity and stated that he (Ludendorff) would be willing to lead this "united front."

In response to this appeal, Streicher wrote a personal letter to the general stating that the latter's activities were highly objectionable—that he (Streicher) and others "had fought the *voelkisch* cause" for a long time "while you (Ludendorff) had at best lost the World War."[32]

Several attempts were made to mollify Streicher and to win his support for the NSFP, the recently formed party of Ludendorff and others in the *Voelkischer Block*. In mid-July, a political meeting was scheduled for the purpose of settling the differences between Streicher and leaders of the NSFP. This meeting was announced by Dr. Stoecker, one of the original members of the German Workers Party *(Deutsche Arbeiterpartei)* (DAP), which was the founding organization of the NSDAP. Stoecker also remarked that if this happened, the *voelkisch* cause would be strengthened immeasurably.[33] In answer to Stoecker's announcement, Streicher immediately ordered large posters to be published stating that there was no truth to Stoecker's "rumor" and that he (Streicher) was organizing a Nuremberg branch of the GVG in opposition to the NSFP and that he was not bothered by any frag mentation of the *voelkisch* movement because his ways were "the true Hitler ways." The posters, signed by both Streicher and Esser, also announced that there would be an organizational meeting of the local GVG that evening, July 17, in the Hercules Hall in Nuremberg.[34]

At this first meeting of the local GVG, both Streicher and Esser were the featured speakers. They were greeted by an enthusiastic audience of approximately 2,000 people of both sexes. A report from the police files states that many former members of the Nuremberg NSDAP of all social classes, including the aristocracy, were in attendance. Esser began by explaining that the goals of the GVG were essentially "Hitler goals" and the major purpose of organizing GVG groups was to keep the National Socialist movement alive until Hitler was freed from prison. When Streicher took the podium he continued the theme opened by Esser regarding the need for total party unity. He said that this could be possible only by rigid adherence to the leadership principle *(Fuehrerprinzip)*. This term had been used frequently by Hitler in urging the necessity for all National Socialists to render total obedience to their leaders. After stating his own personal allegiance to Hitler, Streicher then changed to more ominous tones. He told his listeners loudly that it was he (Streicher) who was organizing this group and that he was to be the "unquestioned leader," and further, that if anyone did not like his policies he could leave; or if he (Streicher) did not like any member's actions he would be expelled without explanation. Near the end of this speech he stated flatly that he would never let the leadership "slip from his fingers." He closed this section of his speech with the words:

There better not be anyone else trying to take the lead from me. Our organization is like a train, but who runs this train is up to me to decide. I am in the locomotive and I blow the whistle.

Streicher's demand for absolute and unquestioned control of this political group was met with little or no resistance. At this GVG meeting and those that followed during ensuing weeks, he enjoyed large and enthusiastic audiences. His dictatorial pronouncements were usually followed by noisy applause and his audiences seemed willing to submit to strong, authoritative leadership. It was also indicative of the acceptance by many Nurembergers of Streicher as the leader of the local *voelkisch* movement.

At some Nuremberg GVG meetings Streicher digressed from his standard anti-Semitic themes and dropped his overbearing attitude. Adopting the practice of a conventional politician, he would address himself to the problems of various professional or occupational groups. For example, he scheduled a meeting in late July for which special invitations had been tendered to civil service employees.[35] He opened his address with an "official" report on *Landtag* activities. Then he expressed his sympathy to the civil servants who had lost their jobs because of the recent government policy of reducing expenses by cutting some employees from the payroll. He reminded his listeners that he was fully aware of the financial misery of many minor officials. He said he had seen the stacks of petitions and letters begging for some supplemental income or for some work. He emphasized that unfeeling government officers had left most of these pleas unanswered. He closed this speech with a promise that if it were in his power he would make every effort to satisfy these justified grievances and requests. Although Streicher did not explain how he would do this, his speech brought a loud and prolonged applause.

By late summer, 1924, open hostilities between leaders of the NSFP and Streicher erupted in a series of public charges and counter-charges. This internal *voelkisch* feud intensified with the publication of a special pamphlet by leaders of the moderate faction. This was in the form of a small leaflet distributed free to passers-by at street corners in Munich and Nuremberg. Its opening section noted that it was necessary to bring public attention to the conflict Streicher was causing in the *voelkisch* movement. The first grievance noted was that Streicher purposely scheduled political meetings in Nuremberg on the same evenings that regular NSFP meetings were scheduled.[36] Streicher's tactic may have been unethical, but it proved so effective that it later became standard Nazi procedure to wait until an opposing political group announced its meeting and then schedule a Nazi meeting for the same time. Introductory sections of this attack on Streicher also complained that he consistently refused to apologize to some NSFP members he had slandered publicly. Next, some pointed questions were directed to Streicher:

> How can he (Streicher) assume that he is the plenipotentiary of Hitler and the 'Leader in Franconia' after Ludendorff has declared. . .all former authorities annulled?. . .How can he justify his race fanaticism when he himself is associating intimately with the brother-in-law of a very well-known Jew, the diamond dealer Bornstein?[37]

The body of the pamphlet was devoted to further castigation of GVG members and principles and explanations of the beneficial aims and objectives of the NSFP.

In dealing with adversaries, Streicher customarily succeeded in placing them on the defensive by glossing over their accusations and attacking them vigorously in return. He answered this pamphlet in a special issue of the *Stuermer*, and then repeated his words in a speech at a Nuremberg GVG meeting. He told his audience that he had recently received and read the NSFP publication, and when he had looked at the "watered-down" goals of "this so-called people's group" he had almost fainted. He castigated their half-hearted stand against the Jews and Freemasons. He further accused the NSFP of yielding to the pressures of Jewish money and the Freemasons' anti-nationalism. Concerning the charges directed at him in the pamphlet, Streicher brushed them aside, stating that he was responsible only to his conscience and he would answer reproaches like these only before a court of law.[38]

In retaliation, the NSFP newspaper, the *Voelkisches Echo*, published an article entitled "The Dictator Who Fainted." It opened by acknowledging the recent speech, then continued caustically:

> Now that Streicher has opened battle against the NSFP and specializes in personally slandering its leaders, we are sorry to realize that his nerves are so delicate. . .for the juicy blows are yet to come. . . .But while he continues the fight and renews it daily, he must accept the fact that we shall defend ourselves.[39]

Walther Kellerbauer, erstwhile colleague of Streicher, but

now editor of the rival *Voelkisches Echo*, complained that Streicher had instructed his audiences not to read the NSFP newspaper and to do everything possible to prevent others from reading it. He further accused some Streicher followers of disrupting a recent NSFP meeting in Marktbreit and beating the chairman with steel rods until he was unconscious. Interestingly, Kellerbauer did not request that his readers not read the *Stuermer*. Instead he continued in defensive tones to state that Streicher was trying to destroy him personally:

> I consider it my duty to paint the person and deeds of the Great Julius as they are, not only for the sake of our movement. . .but also for the enlightenment of the people. The activities of this agitator are (to be considered) dangerous. . . .I also wish to defend my personal honor, the name of my wife and my very existence against the slanders, attacks, and attempts to destroy me by Streicher and his followers.[40]

Kellerbauer followed this statement with an unsubstantiated complaint that one of Streicher's followers had tried to shoot him in February, 1924. Then he charged both Streicher and Esser with breaking up the unity of the *voelkisch* movement during Hitler's absence. Noting that there were no basic differences in the programs of the NSFP and the GVG, he seemingly lamented that earlier cooperation between the two groups was destroyed because the GVG party had been founded in Nuremberg. He concluded that this act violated an agreement, made earlier in 1924, that the Danube River would be the dividing line between the geographic areas of the two groups. Kellerbauer's allegation that such an agreement had been concluded lacks substantiation. There is no available document to this effect nor any other oral or written reference to it. Further, for obvious reasons, Hitler would not have sanctioned such an arrangement, and it would have been out of keeping with the nature of either Streicher or Esser to agree to a limitation of their political plans and ambitions.

There is evidence that Streicher was viewed by his opponents in the *voelkisch* movement as an uncooperative but key political ally, even though violent and repugnant as a person. Another NSFP newspaper, the *Deutsche Presse*, accused him of "doing all possible" to split the ranks of the

Voelkischer Block during plenary sessions of the *Landtag.*[41] As proof, the article related an occasion where Streicher allegedly refused to support a proposal by *Block* leaders to establish the eight-hour working day in Bavaria. It claimed that Streicher had agreed earlier that this measure favored the workers and that he (Streicher) would support it. It was not stated that Streicher spoke against the proposal. But it was stressed over and over that Streicher was to blame for its failure to win approval because he did not openly speak in favor of it. This article indicated that without Streicher's open cooperation, the *Voelkischer Block* was politically impotent in the *Landtag.*

The article in the *Deutsche Presse* concluded with vague remarks about Streicher's "questionable" handling of money and his immoral personal life. A report from the Nuremberg police files elaborated somewhat on these remarks. It noted that leaders of the NSFP, in a special meeting, had discussed problems dealing with Streicher. As if grasping at straws, these men had framed a formal appeal to Hitler, begging that Streicher's authority be limited. Since Hitler had already officially removed himself from political affairs, this action indicated that these men recognized the fact that Streicher would heed the words of only one person—Hitler. As evidence of questionable financial dealings they noted that Streicher's personal expenditures, as well as his deposits in the Middle Franconian Bank and the North Bavarian Bank, far over-balanced his known income. Therefore, the appeal reasoned, Streicher must be embezzling money collected at political meetings.[42]

Included was an allegation that Streicher's immoral personal life was an embarrassment to the *voelkisch* movement. This allegation referred back to Streicher's relationship with Dr. and Mrs. Jung. It repeated that as a friendly gesture Dr. Jung was helpful to Streicher and had loaned him his car to attend meetings. Then Mrs. Jung was seen frequently riding with Streicher and accompanying him to public places in Nuremberg. The story concluded that Streicher's immoral conduct was proven by the fact that Dr. and Mrs. Jung were divorced shortly afterwards.

These two charges evidently fell upon deaf ears inasmuch as there is no record that Hitler received the NSFP appeal document or gave any consideration to it.

Streicher retaliated to the attack in the *Deutsche Presse* in a lengthy speech during a *Landtag* session. Speaking on the theme "Loyalty to Hitler," he accused Ludendorff, Drexler, Strasser and others of working openly to undermine Hitler's authority in the National Socialist movement. He stated that he (Streicher) was the true Hitler representative in the *Landtag* and that these men were against him and trying, even in parliamentary sessions, to disgrace him and oust him from the movement. In attempting to prove this statement, he argued somewhat ridiculously that no *voelkisch* member had supported his bid to serve on a committee.[43]

As was his custom, he did not endeavor to discuss any substantive issue of politics or party ideology, but rather launched into an attack on the personalities of his political adversaries. For example, he questioned the sincerity of Anton Drexler, founder of the Munich *voelkisch* party. Although Drexler was not even present, Streicher levied pointed questions at him:

Is it true, Mr. Drexler, that you...are a salesman for a Jewish shirt manufacturer in Berlin? Is it true, Mr. Drexler, that you tried to betray Mr. Hitler...in 1921?[44]

A few days later he spoke in the same vein against Ludendorff at a political meeting in Nuremberg. After reiterating the shortcomings of the old general, he challenged his audience with a trite political ploy: "And if the time should come when General Ludendorff opposes me (in Nuremberg), by whom will you then stand?" Mechanically the listeners answered: "We will stand by Streicher!"[45]

While Streicher's open feud with leaders of the NSFP continued, his political power in Nuremberg seemed to increase. Perhaps emulating Hitler and his para-military SA organization, Streicher had formed an armed bodyguard called the *Landsturm*, which became known as the official police unit of the Nuremberg GVG.[46] There is very little information available concerning the details of the type of people involved in this organization or the amount of time they spent in this activity. It was a short-lived group used by Streicher in the absence of the SA, which had been outlawed during these months. Among the few references to this armed troup is a Nuremberg police report of a GVG meeting in late

August which noted that approximately seventy *Landsturm* security men were in evidence. They were described as being clad in white ski-caps, red windbreakers, and white arm-bands stamped with the letters GVG.[47] More than likely members of this group were ardent political followers of Streicher and were paid a small percentage of the receipts collected at meetings they attended.

In September, Streicher expanded the Nuremberg GVG further with the formation of local *voelkisch* women's clubs. These organizations were known as auxiliaries of the GVG. Members were required to pledge loyalty to Hitler and Streicher upon joining.[48] Since no reliable documentation is available, it can only be assumed that because of Streicher's popularity with females (as stated earlier) these groups enjoyed a large membership. They probably functioned as any other women's political auxiliary, mainly in fund-raising and political propaganda activities. Streicher also succeeded in forming new GVG local parties in Bamberg, Rahl, and Regensburg that month.[49]

During the later months of 1924, Streicher became mildly involved with local Communist groups and individuals. This was initially exposed in a description by police of a Nuremberg GVG meeting in September. An official report noted that a long, heated discussion resulted from Streicher's announcement that he was attempting to reach a closer understanding with local Communist groups. Some GVG members began questioning this radical change in *voelkisch* policy. The report concluded that because of strong objections, the leadership (Streicher) promised a stronger stand against the Communists.[50] Despite this promise, Streicher held a meeting the following month in conjunction with about one hundred local Communists. Streicher spoke about an eighteen-year-old boy named Elmer Ansel, who had recently hanged himself. He claimed that "the Jew Kromwell," who had been Ansel's employer for three years, was the actual cause of the suicide because he had swindled the young man.[51] At the end of his speech, Streicher invited a Communist leader named Gerber to speak to the audience. Gerber agreed with some of Streicher's viewpoints regarding the greediness of Jews, adding that this showed the "impossibility of the capitalist system." At the end of further remarks on his Communist ideas, Gerber invited Streicher to the next local Communist party meeting where he said the NSDAP was to be discussed. Streicher accepted the invitation and commented that he felt Gerber's views were made "from the deepest feelings in the heart but still were rather disordered in thought." The meeting was closed with the audience singing the "Hitler-song" and the "Internationale."

The true motives for Streicher's association with Communists at this time are unclear. He may have been attempting to win more converts for the GVG from the ranks of workers and others who opposed the republican form of government. He also may have been trying to arrange a truce or compromise in order to gain allies against his favorite political target—the "capitalist Jew." This latter conjecture is suggested by Streicher's conversation with Gerber after the above meeting had closed. He asked the Communist leader if he would be willing to meet with him in the presence of two witnesses on each side so that "some kind of political compromise" might be reached. Gerber, however, failed to respond to the invitation.

Streicher was not as consistent in his views and actions toward Communists as he was toward Jews. During his months as a leader of the Nuremberg GVG, he had associated with them sometimes at political meetings. In later years he went out of his way occasionally to do special favors for some Communist political prisoners.[52] On at least one occasion, he arranged for the marriage of a Nuremberg Communist while the latter was serving a prison sentence at Dachau.[53]

There is no indication that at any time in his political career Streicher was in any way sympathetic to Communist doctrine. While he considered many individual Communists as good German citizens, he remained totally opposed to their political ideologies. Typical of this attitude is the following excerpt from a speech in the mid-1920's:

Next to the Jews, the Communists are our worst enemies. . . .We must strike them all down like snakes before we reach our ultimate victory.[54]

Streicher's contacts with the Communists in the brief period beginning in late 1924 brought no known criticism from NSFP leaders. However, for other reasons, the NSFP passed a resolution in late October expelling both Streicher and Esser from the "official" Bavarian *voelkisch* movement. The resolution declared that both of these men had brought too much dissension into the movement with their "continuous unpatriotic heckling." When Streicher was told about the resolution he jeered: "How can I be expelled from something I never belonged to?"[55]

This action by the NSFP had little effect on Streicher's political activities. A few weeks later he held a meeting of the GVG in Nuremberg attended by approximately 2000 people.[56] As if indicating his contempt for the NSFP, he made no reference to the recent expulsion resolution. Instead he concentrated his attacks on Dr. Luppe. No action had yet been taken by the courts on the appeals petitions filed at the conclusion of the trial earlier that year.[57] In his speech, Streicher again charged that the mayor was dishonest and only "a tool of the crooked Marxists and Jews."[58]

He also charged that the present city council had withheld money from the needy war widows so they could give it to Luppe and the Jews. At the conclusion of this tirade, he mentioned the coming elections for city council seats. Announcing his candidacy for city council, he asked for support for himself and other GVG candidates in the coming elections.[59]

The elections were held on December 17, and resulted in Streicher and five other GVG members winning seats on the Nuremberg City Council.[60] The first meeting of the newly elected body was scheduled for January 1, the date that the mayor was traditionally installed. Luppe had barely begun to speak to the councilmen about their rights and duties when he was rudely interrupted. Streicher rose and declared that he and his friends refused to be welcomed by a chairman who "has called members of the council psychopaths." This declaration referred to a charge that Luppe had allegedly made about Streicher during the recent campaign. The mayor was unable to quiet his heckler and soon all members of Streicher's group began to shout insults at the other members of the council and the mayor. The audience, made up mostly of GVG members, joined in the shouting. Epithets such as "traitors to the workers" and "servants of the Jews" drowned out every attempt by Luppe to bring the meeting back to order. Streicher was said to have shouted the loudest.

In the midst of this confusion, the session was closed less than a half-hour after it had started. In subsequent months some of Streicher's colleagues were dismissed from the council for unethical practices. Streicher, after the first few sessions, attended very infrequently.

Streicher's record as a member of the Nuremberg City Council and the Bavarian *Landtag* shows that he had no sincere interest in the proper functions of these bodies. He never offered positive contributions to either of these parliamentary groups nor agreed to serve on any functional committees. This raised the question of his real motive for seeking these positions. Initially, the monetary factor may have been some inducement. He received monthly stipends of 450 marks as a *Landtag* representative, and 50 marks as city councilman. These amounts totalled approximately 65 percent of his known income.[61]

Secondly, he may have sought these positions to further his political goals. As a *Landtag* representative his political constituency may have been broadened. He may have also felt that his personal prestige might be enhanced and he would have an opportunity to air his political views before an official state body. As a Nuremberg city councilman, he may have thought he would be in a better position to undermine Dr. Luppe and possibly topple him as mayor of the city.

A third motive may have been his desire to further the interests of his newspaper, *Der Stuermer*. His experiences in the campaigns and in these elected positions could provide valuable propaganda material for editorial content. More important to *Stuermer* interests perhaps was the possibility that circulation would be increased because membership in these public bodies would add respectability and public recognition to the newspaper's proprietor and editor.

By the end of 1924, the *Stuermer* had become an effective political propaganda instrument. Since its reappearance in March it was enlarged in volume but still consisted of only six pages. The title and subtitle remained the same, but under this heading there were added the words "Julius Streicher, Editor." At the bottom of the front page between two heavy black lines the *Stuermer* slogan "The Jews are our Misfortune" appeared for the first time.[62]

This phrase was not an original innovation of Streicher. It had first been used by the renowned 19th-century German historian, Heinrich von Treitschke, in his *Preussische Jahrbuecher, 1879-80.* As in this case, most of the phrases and arguments used in the *Stuermer* to discredit Jews were copied by Streicher from earlier anti-Semitic writings.

On the *Stuermer* front page the lead articles were usually begun in the left column of the front page and continued on inside pages. The right side of the front page began to feature large, ugly cartoons signed by "Fips," a man whose proper name was Philipp Rupprecht. This cartoonist designed and created that caricature known later as the "*Stuermer* Jew." With variations, the faces featured a sinister expression with dark, beady eyes, an ugly, hooked nose, and protruding lower lips.[63]

In 1924 and 1925, these cartoons appeared only occasionally, but after November, 1925, Rupprecht joined the *Stuermer* staff and became the regular illustrator of the leading articles, which were usually repulsive and unfactual stories about the crimes of the Jews. Rupprecht later contributed cartoons that made up a "comic sheet" on the last page. As early as 1924, these illustrations were labeled pornographic by many critics of Streicher.[64]

A review of hundreds of *Stuermer* issues reveals that the cartoons were not pornographic as the word is understood in the Western world today. There were no pictures of totally nude persons or acts of a sexual or lascivious nature. Only in rare cases were sex acts suggested or portrayed. One such example shows a young blond woman struggling with a fat man who is depicted as a Jewish doctor. She is striking him while he is attempting to disrobe her. Her dress is torn partially and one of her breasts is exposed.[65] In another example, in an issue during World War II, a young German soldier is standing in the doorway, staring in disbelief at a bed where a young blond woman is lying in bed next to a "*Stuermer* Jew." Under this frame is the caption: "This is what the Jew does to your women while you are at the front!"[66]

In most instances, however, cartoons with sexual connotations focused on crimes allegedly committed by Jews against non-Jewish women. Typically the cartoon would include the victim (usually a blond girl) and one or more men with "*Stuermer* Jew" features. The girl would be lying in a pool of blood, or in a casket, and the men would be lurking in the background, whispering or rubbing their hands. It would be made evident, by picture and word, that the girl had been raped and murdered in a brutal manner, or else she had committed suicide out of fear of rape. There would be other verbal indications that tragedies like this occur regularly because Jews are "sexually perverted."[67]

Aside from occasional cases where other Nazi enemies, such as Bolsheviks or masons, were lampooned, the theme of the cartoons was always anti-Semitism. Jews were portrayed in all conceivable ways as a despicable, greedy race, with plans and ambitions to rule the world. The sexual aspect was used mainly to add sensationalism to this theme.

Rupprecht's cartoons were not confined to the *Stuermer*. His work was also published in two other Bavarian newspapers, the *Fraenkische Tagespost* and the *Fraenkische Tageszeitung*, and later also in the Spanish Falangist newspaper, *Arriba*.[68]

The main contents of the *Stuermer* were articles written by Streicher or members of his staff. Even though several new reporters were now contributing articles, the journalistic style had not improved since the previous year. Streicher insisted that his writers imitate his type of simple but sensational phraseology. Perhaps to insure that this was carried out, Streicher remained editor, or co-editor, most of the years of the *Stuermer's* existence. During the first fifteen years, this position was shared intermittently with Karl Holz, a radical *voelkisch* ruffian, who spoke and acted as a prototype of Streicher. The editorship was shared out of necessity because during these years one or the other of these men were usually involved in a court procedure or serving a jail sentence.[69] Major articles, in early years, dealt almost exclusively with castigation of Streicher's political enemies such as Kellerbauer and Luppe, and the ongoing anti-Semitic campaign. Between these articles were inserted slogans such as "You Get to Know the Jewish Problem Through the *Stuermer*," "Only Go to German Doctors and Lawyers!"[70]

In writing about his political enemies, Streicher used defamatory and mostly untrue phrases, as described in the case of Dr. Luppe. Further, he usually brought his principal theme, anti-Semitism, into these attacks. An example was his accusation, brought out in the trial, that Luppe was a descendant of Jews, and that Luppe worked for Jewish interests.[71]

A survey of *Stuermer* anti-Semitic articles shows Streicher's purpose had not changed since mid-summer, 1923—to prove to readers that the Jew was the root of all political, social, and economic evil in Germany and in the whole world. Parallel to this theme was the patent insistence that this evil must be feared, hated and eventually destroyed.

During the 1920's, political problems attributed to Jews were usually linked to one of Streicher's specific political targets, such as the Weimar government. One such attack entitled "Who Are the Real Villains?" appeared in 1925:

> The Jews are the real villains. They stabbed Germany in the back in 1918, so that they could end the war and control our government...as they are now doing in Berlin....[72]

Stuermer articles discussing economic and social problems normally included arguments to prove a distorted theory about the parasitic nature of Jews. A typical passage is from a 1927 article entitled "Deadly Enemy of Humanity:"

> The Jews are not settlers...they do not build villages...they cannot support themselves. You see the Jew where he can grab the fruit of work, the property of non-Jews. You can see the Jew as a thief, usurper, and a parasite.[73]

To prove the depravity of Jews, Streicher always insisted that they were a biologically inferior race. He referred to them as "sub-humans, worse than Negroes." He warned continually that any non-Jewish woman who had intercourse with a Jew would have the germ of this sub-human permanently implanted in her bloodstream.[74] In later years, articles of this type became so bizarre that the Nazi government ordered certain issues confiscated and destroyed.[75]

The *Stuermer* carried many detailed accounts of rightist political meetings. Streicher's speeches were always printed verbatim, with favorable comments, both on the topic and audience enthusiasm. Rival *voelkisch* party meetings were usually reported, but always in derogatory tones and with critical comments. As a rule, activities of other rival political groups, such as the Social Democrat and Communist parties, were ignored. National political events of special interest to Streicher, such as a Nazi Party-day Rally, usually merited a special edition which included larger headlines and more pages than normal issues.[76]

Included in almost every issue of the *Stuermer* was a section in the inside pages devoted to letters from the readers. Generally the letters were those of admirers of Streicher and sympathetic to the anti-Semitic cause. The contents were mainly some form of compliment about the good work being done by the *Stuermer* or some complaint about misdeeds done by Jews. A typical example was a letter from one Jean Adam, who reported on his experiences in Switzerland. He wrote that Jewish landlords in Basel and Zurich terrorized Christians by buying their houses and then throwing the Christians out into the street. He also complained that Swiss Jews continually "deflowered Christian girls."[77]

Continuing the policy adopted since its inception, the *Stuermer* contained little of the material which is generally included in standard newspapers. It published no news of national and local business events, serialized stories, news of social happenings (except for propaganda purposes), or reports on sports activities. News concerning world or foreign affairs was also omitted during the early years of the *Stuermer*.

The subject of anti-Semitism comprised 60 to 75 percent of the total space in the *Stuermer*. This was exclusive of the advertising section. It was normal practice for *Stuermer* writers to attempt to add "authenticity" to their stories by documentation from so-called "Jewish literature" which Streicher had collected in his personal library.[78] However, contemporary Jewish scholars exposed the fact that these citations were not taken from books written by Jewish authors, but from anti-Semitic literature dating back to earlier centuries. One basic source of this literature was a book entitled *Judaism Discovered*, written by Johann Eisenmenger and published in 1700. Eisenmenger, a German scholar, had quarreled violently with a Dutch rabbi over the question of Christians converting to Judaism. As a result, he swore to gain revenge on the rabbi and on the Jewish religion.[79] With his *Judaism Discovered*, Eisenmenger sought to discredit the Jews and to prove that they regarded the entire Christian religion with hatred and derision. To accomplish this, he blasphemed the Jewish religion by re-interpreting Jewish holy writings in a pseudo-scholarly fashion. In one example, he paraphrased and interpreted one passage of the *Talmud* to make it sound as if all Jews were instructed to take part in a murder-ritual at least once a year.[80] Although Eisenmenger's views were proven false shortly after publication and later banned by the Holy Roman Emperor, his interpretations have served as the basis of much anti-Semitic literature in modern times.[81]

In addition to the above-mentioned editorial content, slogans, and cartoons, the *Stuermer* contained an advertising section. This had begun, in modest fashion, at the bottom of the last page, where the *Stuermer's* early publisher, W. Haerdel, advertised certain books for sale.[82] The first full-page ad-section appeared in April, 1924, on the last page. All the ads were small and seemed to be oriented to the lower-middle class. Advertisers were independent stores and small businesses such as stores selling clothing, shoes, music, confectionaries, and furniture. At the bottom of the page were two blank application forms for *Stuermer* subscriptions.[83] Later in the year ads included announcements of GVG political meetings and some appeals from workers seeking employment. These were mostly from *voelkisch* people who had lost their jobs because of their political opinions and advertised that they were seeking employment with a *voelkisch* firm.[84]

Most early *Stuermer* advertisers seem to have been members of the Nazi party or at least sympathetic to its racial doctrines. In addition to advertising their own products, business firms began promoting the NSDAP and anti-Semitism. Some ads were decorated with the swastika emblem. Others claimed the proprietor was a member of the National Socialist party. Some establishments advertised Hitler shirts, Hitler pictures, and Hitler writing pads.[85] One restaurant ad noted that it did not welcome any Jewish guests. All NSDAP meetings were advertised with cordial invitations for everyone but Jews to attend. Ads for the Nazi newspaper and magazine, the *Voelkischer Beobachter* and *Saar-Deutscher*, appeared regularly.[86]

With few exceptions, the ad-section of the *Stuermer* was limited to two pages or less. It contained only small-sized ads of individuals, small businesses, or political activities and organs. Ads for nationally-known businesses or heavy industry did not appear until 1933. There is no evidence that the *Stuermer* staff made any effort to solicit ads from large and prosperous firms. Streicher seems to have ignored the normal business practice of developing a solid monied advertising clientele to serve as the principal financial support of the newspaper. Instead, he seemed to view the *Stuermer* advertising section as a means to popularize his political beliefs and to strengthen his following by offering low-cost ads (three-fourths one RM per column inch) to a large number of small businesses and individuals sympathetic to his political beliefs.[87]

In the early years of publishing the *Stuermer*, Streicher experienced periodic financial difficulty but somehow always managed to satisfy his creditors. In 1924 the price of the regular edition was 20 pfennig and the maximum circulation that year was approximately 6,000.[88] Outside subsidies were needed because sales income and advertising revenue did not balance publishing costs. Some Bavarian industrialists were rumored to have paid Streicher to discredit Jewish competitors, and some large landowners allegedly paid handsomely for Streicher's fight against proposed Socialist land reforms.[89] Another method allegedly used by Streicher to increase his income was to blackmail non-Jewish as well as Jewish businessmen by threatening to print scandalous articles about them unless they paid him large sums.[90] While this allegation was never proven to be factual it merits some credence because an official police report noted that Streicher employed approximately twenty private investigators in 1924.[91] It is a feasible assumption that most of these investigators were used to gather the defamatory information that was used in this blackmail enterprise.

Toward the end of 1924, Streicher was informed by his circulation manager that many Jews had bought up large quantities of *Stuermer* issues in order to curtail its circulation. Streicher later admitted that after he learned this he saw to it that *Stuermer* anti-Semitic articles maintain their radical and aggressive themes. On at least one occasion, in the presence of others he boasted that it was this type of Jewish "help" that enabled the *Stuermer* to stay alive in the early years.[92]

CHAPTER VI

A BRIDGE TO THE NORTH

Hitler was released from Landsberg prison in late December, 1924. Arriving by auto in Munich, he found conditions greatly changed since the previous year. The wheelbarrows filled with paper money were no longer visible. The hordes of unemployed loiterers had virtually disappeared from the streets and political proclamations on signboards were crowded out by advertisements for all types of consumer goods.[1] Since food and jobs were more plentiful, interest in political matters had dwindled and the desire for radical political change seemed far less urgent now than in the previous year. These factors contributed largely to the severe setback suffered by the *voelkisch* movement in the December 7 *Reichstag* elections. Total votes for *voelkisch* candidates dropped from 2,000,000 the previous May, to 900,000, and the number of *voelkisch* candidates elected dropped from thirty-two to fourteen.[2] Political observers saw these election results as a definite sign that the movement was headed for oblivion.[3] Hitler, however, was not totally disheartened because he began planning quietly to rebuild and to rejuvenate his National Socialist party.

The Nazi leader spent the holiday season loitering in various cafes. He talked with his friends cautiously because his prison release had been probationary and he knew that he was under close scrutiny by the police.[4] By government decree, he was not allowed to make any speeches, to put up any posters, to hold any meetings, or to promote the interests of the NSDAP, which had also been outlawed.[5] The only possible way for Hitler to re-enter the political arena in Munich was a repeal of all these bans from the Bavarian government, which was now under the leadership of Prime Minister Heinrich Held.

Early in January, 1925, Hitler persuaded a former political patron, Dr. Franz Guertner, to arrange an audience with the Prime Minister. At the outset of this meeting, Held received Hitler in a cool and formal manner. Hitler began talking smoothly, apologizing for the "mistake of November, 1923." He continued that the National Socialist movement, under his leadership, would henceforth remain strictly within the law.[6] Later in the conference, Held questioned the recent rightist attacks against the Catholic Church which had been initiated by Ludendorff. Hitler seized upon this opportunity to discredit Ludendorff and, at the same time, to appear as a champion of Christianity:

> I have all due respect for General Ludendorff's military genius, but I must deeply deplore the fact that he is not equally gifted as a politician. I beg you to believe that the National Socialist movement is in no way identified with Ludendorff's stand against the Catholic Church. . .my party stands for positive Christianity. Our only enemy is Jewish Marxism, against which your party is also waging a decisive battle.[7]

Hitler concluded his pleadings with a promise that in the future the National Socialists and the Catholics would stand together in the "common battle against Jews and Marxists." By the end of the interview, Held appeared relaxed and positively impressed by the sincerity of his visitor's words. He politely dismissed Hitler with the assurance that the government would act on Hitler's request to repeal existent bans against the NSDAP "as soon as possible."

During these days of behind-the-scenes political maneuvering, Streicher had been in close contact with Hitler. Many years later, he claimed that he (Streicher) was the first person visited by the Nazi leader upon his release from prison.[8] Although this statement remains unsubstantiated, there is reliable evidence that Streicher was well informed by Hitler about the pending negotiations with Held. A police report described a GVG political meeting in Nuremberg, January 21, where Streicher was the featured speaker. Addressing an audience of close to 1000 people, Streicher began by levelling some vicious charges against Jews in public office. Then he berated Mayor Luppe for allegedly throwing him (Streicher) out of the first city council meeting. Next he launched into the main topic of his speech, which dealt with the requested re-legalization of the NSDAP. He reiterated Hitler's pledges to Held that in the future the National Socialist party would cooperate with the government in upholding the Catholic Church, and in waging a battle only against the common enemy—Jews and Marxists.[9] He then chided the Prime Minister for his vacillation in granting the release Hitler had petitioned. After speculating on some possible reasons for this delay, Streicher ended his speech with the pointed question: "Is it possible that this request is still not granted because Luppe has good friends in the Prime Minister's office?"

There is no reason to believe that Streicher's Nuremberg speech would have affected a Bavarian government decision, yet it is interesting that the next day an announcement came from Held's office that all restrictions against Hitler and the NSDAP were tentatively removed.[10]

The fact that Hitler had made his peace with the Catholic Bavarian government increased the complaints of Ludendorff and other moderate *voelkisch* leaders, who were outspoken enemies of the Church. In addition to publicly criticizing Hitler for betraying National Socialist principles regarding the Church, these leaders continued to insist that the radical GVG leaders, Streicher and Esser, be ejected from the *voelkisch* movement.[11]

Hitler largely ignored the complaints regarding his departure from established *voelkisch* Church doctrine. He was, however, out-spoken in his defense of Streicher and Esser. Since his release from prison, he had determined that the GVG was the logical nucleus around which the National Socialist movement was to be rebuilt. His two trusted colleagues controlled most of what remained of the true Nazi movements in Nuremberg and Munich. In addition, a leading member of the Munich GVG, Max Amann, now headed the firm that published the official Nazi newspaper, the *Voelkischer Beobachter.*[12]

On February 25, 1925, this party organ reappeared for the first time since late 1923. It featured a lengthy editorial by Hitler, entitled "A New Beginning." In this article, Hitler answered those who still objected to Streicher and Esser. In reference to these two "loyal comrades," Hitler stated that he did not consider it the task of a political leader to attempt improving upon the quality of the "human material lying ready at his hand."[13] Also included in this issue of the official party newspaper were several announcements that Hitler was holding an important political meeting on the evening of February 27, at the same place the ill-fated *Putsch* had originated—the Munich *Buergerbraeukeller.*[14]

The occasion of Hitler's first public speech since his trial created a stir of excitement in *voelkisch* circles. Although the meeting was not to begin until 8 PM, the first visitors began lining up at the doors of the beer-hall in mid-afternoon. At 6 PM the police closed the hall. Three thousand persons had found room inside and another 2000 had to be turned away.[15] When Hitler finally appeared he was greeted tumultuously. As the noise subsided he began to speak quietly of his recent prison experiences. He then spoke louder about "some traitors" who had been working against him during his confinement. As he continued through the text of his speech, his voice became increasingly shrill, and when he reached the climax of his message he shrieked:

> I will allow no one to circumscribe my authority! As long as I am the leader of the party, I will make all the decisions. . . .After a year you shall judge for yourselves! If you are with me then—fine. If not, I will resign. But until then, I alone am the leader.[16]

This reaffirmation of his insistence on strong leadership stirred the audience into frenzied action. Leaders of various rival *voelkisch* factions rushed to the platform to shake Hitler's hand and publicly demonstrate their loyalty to him. Some witnesses said later that this part of Hitler's speech "swept away all doubt—that most listeners believed sincerely that all quarrels between various *voelkisch* factions were ended."

After this interruption, Hitler reverted to moderate tones. He stated that in the future there could be only one enemy—the Jew as a person and Marxism as a concept. But he added that under the guise of one enemy, several might be recognized. In other words, he would brand as "Marxists" anyone whom he wished to fight, including the state.[17] He concluded his speech with menacing and ominous words:

> Either the enemy will march over our corpses, or we over his. May the swastika banner be my shroud if next time the battle lays me low![18]

This statement was brought to the attention of Bavarian government officials, who then accused Hitler of violating his recent promise of moderation. He was asked how he intended to march over the corpses of his enemies and remain "strictly within the law" as he had vowed to Held. Since Hitler had no ready answer to this question, he was told by the Bavarian

Minister of the Interior that a decision on some form of punitive action would be announced within a few days.[19]

Seemingly unperturbed by this news, Hitler motored, on March 2, to Nuremberg with Streicher, who had arranged three political meetings there for that evening. These had been announced simply as NSDAP "reorganizational" meetings.[20] It is likely, however, that Streicher envisioned these meetings as accomplishing more tangible results than merely their advertised purpose. The Nazi party treasury was badly in need of funds, therefore it would be to his advantage if gate receipts would provide enough money for him to make a handsome contribution for Hitler to take back to Munich. Undoubtedly he also hoped for a large turn-out so that he could impress his leader with proof of his (Streicher's) successful efforts in developing and maintaining a large and enthusiastic core of Hitler followers in the Nuremberg area. In addition, he must have realized that Hitler's appearances with him that evening would add to his prestige with local party members. He could take full credit for the fact that Hitler had chosen Nuremberg as the first city, outside of Munich, to visit after his release from Landsberg.

Events at the three meetings must have been gratifying to both Streicher and Hitler. A police report noted that approximately 4700 persons crowded into the three halls and paid the "high admission price of one mark."[21] The report continued that all halls were filled to capacity by 6 PM even though proceedings were not scheduled to begin until 8 PM and later. As the two leaders made their appearance at each meeting place, the crowds both outside and inside the halls broke into spontaneous and tumultuous greetings. All three audiences seemed keyed to a high emotional pitch and responded with shouts of approval and loud applause to almost every phrase uttered by the speakers.

The same general format was followed at each meeting. Streicher took the podium first, and after welcoming those in attendance stated his unconditional subordination and loyalty to Hitler. In each address, he included attacks on Dr. Luppe in his opening remarks. At one meeting he ended this section of his speech with the statement: "Luppe must be fought first of all because he is the tool of Jews and the head of Marxism!" This remark usually brought a loud and prolonged applause. In a display of political showmanship,

Streicher would then bow his head and wait until the hall was quiet. Continuing in reverent tones, he then said: "Now let the soul of the child speak, for children tell the truth." Two little girls, between five and seven years of age, would approach Hitler and recite a poem, lauding his greatness, and then present him with a bouquet of flowers. After this, Streicher delivered some remarks concerning NSDAP goals, noting that he felt obliged to make these statements since he, as a member of the Bavarian *Landtag*, possessed parliamentary immunity and thus could speak more freely than Hitler. In each of these dialogues he included a virulent anti-Semitic threat. For example:

> One of the basic goals of the new party is to keep the blood of the Aryan race pure. . .we must fight with all strength against the alien race of the Jews. Merciless war is to be declared. . .(against those) who plot to conquer us. . . .[22]

He concluded each of his speeches with warm words of welcome to Hitler, whom he then introduced as the next speaker. Each time the Nazi leader took the podium, the audience applauded wildly and began singing the "Hitler-song." Hitler spoke informally and rather vaguely about his future plans for the NSDAP. In his second speech he digressed into reflections on the name of his movement. He noted that he had received complaints regarding the words "Socialist" and "worker" in the party title. He explained that the first word was necessary because of the social goal of the party, which was the social brotherhood of true-blooded Germans. He stated further that he insisted on retaining the word "worker" because this was a "word of honor, not designating classes, since a worker is anyone who is ready to serve his fatherland with his hands or his head." Hitler climaxed his last speech that evening by proclaiming his admiration for Streicher:

> . . . .I must relate something that I will always carry in my heart. On November 9, 1923, at one o'clock, when the *voelkisch* soldiers faced death. . .a man stepped up to me, his chest bared to the guns, ready to die for his banner. This same man was the first to come up to me after my release from prison and put himself unconditionally at my disposal; this man is Julius Streicher and I will never forget his action that day.

Then, as if speaking to Streicher's moderate *voelkisch* enemies and critics, Hitler concluded:

> Even though Streicher may have his faults, a man who acts as he does is loyal!...To these people who still have doubts about Streicher, I shout: 'Ask yourselves whether you were ever willing to give up your life for the movement!'[23]

These words may have been stated over-dramatically on this occasion, but Hitler's sincerity could not be doubted. He referred to the November 9 heroics of Streicher frequently throughout ensuing years in supporting Streicher when other Nazi leaders urged his banishment from the National Socialist party. Before stepping down from the platform, Hitler announced that as a reward, he was appointing his "true friend Streicher" as official *Gauleiter* (district party leader) of Franconia.[24]

The evening of March 2, 1925, must be considered a landmark in Streicher's political career. Never before or after this time could he be considered closer or more valuable to Hitler. Since the ill-fated *Putsch* the circle of important associates had largely melted away from the Nazi leader. For a short time after his release from prison, Hitler could look to only a few trusted followers, such as Streicher and Esser, to help him re-invigorate his movement.

In his plans to rebuild his party on a national basis, Hitler was determined to expand his movement northward, out of Munich. He realized that Streicher controlled the largest and most active group of hard-core Nazi followers in this direction. Until more northern groups could be organized and developed by trusted leaders, Streicher remained Hitler's most valued colleague outside Munich.

After Hitler's appearance in Nuremberg, he returned to Munich where he was informed subsequently that the Bavarian Minister of Interior had issued a ban on his (Hitler's) public speaking for an indefinite period. Hitler reacted furiously. He claimed that the newspapers had misinterpreted his speech and he issued a violent protest to the government officials, but this proved futile. Within a few days many other German states, including Prussia, Wuerttemberg and Baden, also outlawed Hitler's public activities. In frustration, he withdrew to a lodge in Berchtesgaden, where he continued his writing and attempted to direct the affairs of his little party.[25]

The official silencing of Hitler seriously impeded the rejuvenation of the NSDAP. The Nazi leader was much more gifted as a speaker than as a writer. With his pen alone he found it impossible to prevent rival National Socialist factions from developing, especially in distant places. Yet, when crucial issues arose which threatened his leadership position, Hitler managed to emerge victorious. In March, the choice of a candidate for the April presidential election created a dilemma. A strong northern *voelkisch* faction endorsed the lord mayor of Duisburg, Karl Jarres, as the candidate of the rightist parties. Somewhat surprisingly, Hitler proclaimed Ludendorff as his choice.[26] This move proved to be a master stroke of political ingenuity. In nominating Ludendorff, Hitler publicly displayed his respect for the old soldier, while at the same time Ludendorff's defeat (which appeared certain) would document his political impotence. Above all, this move forced sub-leaders to make a choice between his candidate, Ludendorff, and Jarres. This ploy also enabled Hitler to identify positively the core of his loyal followers.

As expected, Ludendorff suffered a disastrous defeat in the elections, polling only 211,000 votes out of the approximate 27,000,000 votes cast.[27] As a result of this disclosure of Ludendorff's political weakness, Hitler's stature increased in some *voelkisch* groups. As no candidate obtained a clear majority, a second election was held a few weeks later. This time Hitler abandoned Ludendorff and supported Field-Marshall Paul von Hindenburg, who was the eventual winner.

Perhaps because of the mutual animosity which had developed during the past year between Ludendorff and Streicher, the *Stuermer* did not mention that Hitler supported the ex-general in the first election. However, after the results were tabulated, Streicher published a long polemic on the "obvious inadequacies" of Ludendorff.[28] In the days before the second election, at least three articles were published in the *Stuermer* relating some of the past glories of Field-Marshal Hindenburg and advising readers to "vote with Hitler—for Hindenburg."[29]

By mid-1925, it appeared that the center of gravity of the NSDAP was shifting from south to north Germany. Gregor Strasser had founded seven new district Nazi groups and had held 180 meetings in the Berlin area during the past six months.[30] These new northern groups, known collectively as the Strasser faction, continually issued demands to Hitler. Among other things, they renewed the insistence that Hitler disassociate himself from the southern radicals, meaning Esser, Streicher, Rosenberg and others.

Rosenberg had returned to his job as editor of the NSDAP newspaper, the *Voelkischer Beobachter*, while Esser was still one of Munich's outstanding Nazi speakers. Both of these men sided with Hitler in fighting the Strasser faction openly. The greatest dispute between the two groups was the question of the so-called "Princes Compensation." Since November, 1918, large land holdings of ruling families were being held by state governments, pending a final settlement. Left-wing parties were leading a movement to expropriate these holdings. Hitler had taken the opposite view—that this property legally belonged to the noble families, and if it were not returned to them they should receive a fair and equitable compensation. The Strasser faction sided with the left-wing parties in this argument.

Streicher did not involve himself in this quarrel. Aside from a few short *Stuermer* articles stating that he sided with Hitler in this matter, he concentrated his efforts on anti-Semitic attacks, local political questions, and personal affairs. This was in keeping with his customary political practice. To him, no political issue over-shadowed the Jewish question, and local political affairs were always more important than national issues.

In April, Streicher scheduled a NSDAP meeting in Nuremberg and advertised the title of his speech "The Corruption of the November Republic." This title proved to be misleading because Streicher did not mention the national government directive prohibiting him (Streicher) from publicly discussing affairs of the mayor or the Nuremberg city council. He had recently been denied a permit to hold a meeting where his speech topic was scheduled to be "What Goes On In the Luppe-City Council?" This time he had secured a permit by changing the speech title. However, he did not change the original speech content.[31]

During his address, he complained bitterly about the recent denial to hold a meeting simply because of the advertised speech title. He said that certain government officials had warned him that this was a forbidden topic—that divulging city council affairs was illegal, and that he would be subject to arrest and prosecution if he violated the government order. Voicing his disagreement with this order, he stated that he had the right to speak on all incidents which concern the German people because he was a *Landtag* representative. He then delivered a lengthy polemic about the evils of world Jewry. After this, he defiantly launched into the topic of Luppe and the city council:

> The leftist members of the city council are merely tools of Mayor Luppe, who himself is a tool of the Jews. . . .All of us who oppose Luppe in the council are constantly ignored and mistreated and we cannot get any help for the poor war widows. . . .

He continued speaking in this fashion about this topic without interruption until he concluded some thirty minutes later.

Fifty extra state police officers had been ordered to supplement the regular law enforcement contingent at this meeting. Despite the numbers of police present, no attempt was made to stop Streicher after he began discussing the forbidden topic. This incident was illustrative of the favoritism shown Streicher by many police officials during those years. The officer-in-charge indicated his sympathic attitude toward Streicher in his rationalization for not taking action at the meeting. His official police report was evidence of this attitude:

> . . . .such drastic measure (stopping the speech) would have been out of proportion with the significance of the affair. . . .Besides Streicher had obeyed the Government prohibition for the entire first part of his speech.

Perhaps influenced by the recommendations of the officer-in-charge at the meeting, the Franconian government did very little to punish Streicher for his flagrant violation of the recent prohibitive decree.[32] After this, however, Streicher was frequently denied permits in Nuremberg to hold political meetings. Each time this happened, Streicher repeated his complaint that the denial was unfair because as a *Landtag* deputy he had constitutional immunity which, in his opinion, allowed him to speak as he pleased.

In the early months of 1925, Streicher took increasing

advantage of this *Landtag* fringe benefit. This was evidenced by his increasingly slanderous public attacks against Luppe and by his flagrant violation of city ordinances against the public discussion of forbidden topics. Until early summer, Luppe had been attempting to bring Streicher to court for the appeals trial in the treason case and to levy new slander charges against him. Each of these attempts had been blocked because of the *Landtag* immunity enjoyed by Streicher.[33] However, some of Luppe's friends eventually managed to lodge an official state complaint against Streicher. The matter was brought to a vote on the *Landtag* floor on June 17, 1925, one of the many days Streicher was absent. A majority voted that day to repeal Streicher's right of parliamentary immunity.

With this development, Luppe again pressed the Government Disciplinary Office to set a date for the appeals trial. He was informed that the court could not hear the case until November or December because of pending unfinished business and because of the coming annual vacation period.[34]

A week after the vote to repeal Streicher's right of parliamentary immunity, a *Landtag* meeting was scheduled to debate a bill dealing with an increase in taxes for educational purposes. Streicher made a surprise appearance at this session. Because of his preoccupation with local affairs, especially his publishing business, he had neglected his *Landtag* duties since late 1924. At this meeting, Streicher asked for the floor as soon as the call to order was announced. He spoke for over one hour but made no reference to the recent *Landtag* vote denying him the immunity privilege.[35] This omission was typical of Streicher's practice of not admitting publicly to any defeat or setback unless it could be twisted to his political advantage.

Streicher began this *Landtag* speech in his usual fashion, castigating the Jews. He rambled for over one-half hour on this topic. He reminded his listeners that the Jews consider themselves the master race, while they view the Germans as cattle. Then he referred to the French Negro soldiers who were part of the Rhine occupation force. These, he said, were a different race. In a rare reference to the deity, he stated that God had made a distinction of the races. He concluded his vague point by stating: "The motto for the future should be—not all that has a human face is the same!"

Alluding to the intended topic of discussion for that *Landtag* session, Streicher next addressed himself to the Bavarian Minister of Public Worship and Education. He criticized the existing school system because it allowed Jews to influence German youth. He said that the Ministry should create "pure German schools and academies" where the aryan youth could be educated in the proper manner. Raising his voice, Streicher demanded that German schools be reorganized with a strong emphasis on teaching racial doctrines.

Continuing his discourse on education, Streicher stated that the present system of differentiating between Catholic and Protestant children in confessional schools was antiquated:

> To my mind, a good German is also a good Christian. Instead of continuing a system which divides Christian children and teaches them different religious beliefs, we should unite our teaching and our educational goals. Let them all learn together that our worst enemy is the Jew.

Aside from the fact that Streicher had indicated, for the first time, an ecumenical movement within the Christian religion, the speech offered nothing beyond his usual racist views, and fell on the deaf ears of virtually all *Landtag* members, who either left the hall or sat whispering among themselves until Streicher had finished.

The repeal of his parliamentary immunity was not taken lightly by Streicher. Almost overnight he ceased his campaign of slanderous and illegal attacks on Dr. Luppe and the Nuremberg city council. He did not mention this subject in his *Landtag* speech and he avoided direct reference to these topics in his political speeches for the duration of the year. Until the Luppe appeals trial began in late November, *Stuermer* articles mentioned Luppe only infrequently and then in statements which could not be construed as slanderous.

During late summer and early autumn, 1925, Streicher concentrated his efforts on reorganizing and expanding the NSDAP in Franconia. As in earlier days, he proved to be very successful in these efforts. To stem the effectiveness of Streicher's reorganizational campaign, the northern Nazi faction, headed by Strasser, formed the National Socialist Working Association, *(Nationalsozialistische Arbeitsgemeinschaft)* (NSAG). The formation of this organization was described as "a direct attempt to curb the growing power and influence of Streicher, Esser, and other southern radicals." The northern group began publishing the National Socialist Letters *(NS Briefe)*, with which they hoped to unfetter Hitler from these "unprogressive advisors" and thus enable him to endorse wholeheartedly the northern National Socialist party line.[36] However, this party line was more radical in some respects than the goals of the southern Nazis. Strasser and his colleagues advocated such leftist reforms as public expropriation of landed estates and seizure of controlling interest in all vital industries.[37]

In early September the NSAG held a meeting in Hagen, which resulted in a renewed demand for the dismissal of Streicher and Esser. In addition, the NSAG stated its firm opposition to the NSDAP's participation in all elections.[38] In response to the Hagen resolutions, Streicher scheduled a meeting later that month in Furth, and invited only loyal Hitler followers. An orchestra group and several vocal soloists entertained the crowd until Streicher arrived at 8:30 PM.[39] He was received with applause and loud "Heil" greetings as he made his way to the podium. After welcoming the audience, he began speaking about the growing Nazi party. "More and more," he said, "the *swastika* is appearing on houses, roofs, and walls even in small villages." He explained that these were signs that the roots of the National Socialist movement were growing deep in cities as well as in rural areas. Then, in an obvious challenge to the Strasser faction he warned that anyone in the party who attempted to undermine Hitler's leadership and not follow true Nazi goals would be judged without mercy. Revealing his own concept of the party's main objectives, Streicher emphasized that the Hitler movement was built on a religious foundation. With this statement Streicher again reiterated his political ideology—that anti-Semitism was the keystone of the National Socialist movement. He then digressed into one of his usual racial polemics.

Streicher was followed to the podium by a Dr. Buttmann, who had recently switched allegiance from the Strasser to the Hitler faction. He spoke briefly about his disillusionment with the northern group and stated that he now knew that "the Hitler way is the only true way." He ended with an apology for his "past mistakes" in fighting with Streicher and Esser.

Shortly after Buttmann's brief address, Hitler arrived at the hall. Since this meeting was closed to all persons except party members it was considered a private affair and the official speaking ban could be ignored. He mounted the speaker's platform in the midst of tumultuous applause and after quiet had been restored, he began to talk about the on-going inter-party feud. Gesturing toward Streicher, he said he felt confident that his faithful followers possessed the moral strength to overcome the present opposition from the so-called National Socialists in the north. He continued that since they had opened the fight, he would take the challenge and end the differences in peace on all sides. He then pointed out that Buttmann was just one example of how "they would all soon come to their senses." He closed his speech with the assurance that it was possible for *voelkisch* members to be enemies today and comrades tomorrow. A police report stated that the meeting had been orderly and ended at 11:30 PM after Hitler and Streicher left amidst loud cheers and applause.

During the early autumn months, Hitler had made no official response to the activities of the Strasser faction. In mid-October, however, he took the northern leaders by surprise when he issued a directive prohibiting dual memberships in the NSDAP and NSAG. Strasser immediately sent an apologetic note to Hitler, stating that he only wanted to strengthen the party program and in no way intended to challenge his (Hitler's) leadership or his final program-making authority.[40]

Hitler obviously doubted the sincerity of this message. The following week he left Bavaria with Streicher to witness two Strasser-sponsored NSDAP meetings in Essen and Dortmund. In addition to gaining first-hand knowledge of this group's activities, Hitler perhaps also hoped to win some leaders and members of this faction to his side. However, he was to be denied this opportunity. The police stopped Hitler at the Prussian border and refused him permission to attend these political meetings. Because of this he sent Streicher ahead as his official representative. At the Essen meeting Streicher was received coldly and was not invited to the podium. The next evening, at Dortmund, an open street battle with Communists took place in front of the hall before the meeting began. The featured speakers at both meetings were Strasser and his protege, Dr. Joseph Goebbels, an intellectual who was often called "the brains behind the Strasser movement." Both men directed their addresses to the proletariat class, advocating anti-capitalistic reforms. Streicher was invited to speak at the Dortmund meeting. There is no record of what he said, however his words must have been displeasing to northern leaders. Goebbels perhaps reflected the general reaction to Streicher's speech that evening. He noted in his diary that Streicher spoke "like a sow."[41] Streicher left the podium and the meeting with boos and hisses ringing in his ears. Although unrecorded, his report to Hitler must have reflected his hostile treatment at the Prussian meetings.

Relations between the rival Nazi factions were strained further when Strasser held a meeting of the NSAG and secured a majority vote to replace Hitler's NSDAP program with party platforms of vague leftist policies.[42] Hitler made no public reply to this mutinous action. As if conducting a war of nerves, he remained quiet for almost three months.[43]

During this crucial period, Streicher could offer little help or support to Hitler. His party activities were forced into the background by legal proceedings which occupied him until the end of the year. The second Luppe-Streicher trial, which included appeals from the earlier treason trial as well as new slander charges, finally began on November 17, 1925, at the Nuremberg Palace of Justice. Dr. Suessheim and two other lawyers represented Luppe, while Dr. Krafft appeared as Streicher's legal representative. The case was tried before a jury—probably because Luppe and his attorneys had insisted on a jury trial because of the suspected partiality of the judges toward Streicher.

The district attorney opened proceedings by reading the plaintiff's charges, which consisted basically of the same complaints that initiated the earlier trial. Streicher was then given the opportunity to answer. Resorting to his customary tactics, he did not attempt to explain or deny his alleged indiscretions. Instead he again launched into a verbal tirade against his adversary, Luppe.[44]

After this, the mayor took the witness stand and stated his

reasons for bringing this law-suit. He concluded his statement by noting that the work in the municipal council had been hindered for a long time by a hostile faction led by Streicher.[45]

Throughout this trial, Streicher usually raised the same issues and used the same tactics as in the previous trial. When proven that he had made a false statement or when he was forced into a defensive position, he generally resorted to a vulgar tirade. For example, when Dr. Suessheim furnished positive proof on one occasion that Streicher had lied, he (Streicher) rose to his feet and shouted:

....How can anyone consider seriously any evidence from a lawyer who is a Jew and who uses the spittoon in his office for a urinal?[46]

According to a newspaper account, the most exciting event of the trial occurred when Adolf Hitler appeared as a surprise witness to testify in Streicher's behalf. Taking the stand, Hitler declared that Streicher's fight against Luppe was approved as official NSDAP action. To substantiate this statement, Hitler attempted to explain that the struggle against Luppe was symbolic of the National Socialist struggle against the corrupt German government system. The presiding judge remained passive as Hitler then answered some inconsequential questions posed by Dr. Suessheim. Hitler left the witness stand and shortly afterwards departed for Munich amidst loud "Heil" greetings from a crowd gathered outside the building.[47]

Streicher's belief in the justification of his case seemed to be reinforced by Hitler's court appearance. Even after the trial had adjourned for the day he acted somewhat transfixed, as if Hitler's approval surpassed any other judgment and eclipsed any possible consequence. In tense but quiet words he remarked to his attorney:

Hitler's words today have justified my actions completely. I do not care about a sentence anymore. . .and if I were in Luppe's place I would go home and shoot myself dead![48]

After seventeen days of testimony, final pleadings began. The district attorney stated he accepted Streicher's fight as a political fight. However, it had been proven conclusively that he had exceeded the bounds of legality and decency many times in his continual slanderous and false attacks on Luppe. He concluded that Streicher should receive the maximum sentence of six months' imprisonment without probation. Luppe's attorneys added little to the final pleadings. In general, they reiterated the views of the district attorney.

The next day Dr. Krafft spent seven hours repeating and emphasizing points previously mentioned in the vain attempt to prove that Streicher's allegations against Luppe were justified. In a lengthy address to the jury, he pleaded that Streicher's unfailing patriotism should be a key factor in their final deliberations.[49]

On December 17, the jury announced its verdict. Streicher was found guilty as charged and the presiding judge, following recommendations of the jury, sentenced Streicher to two months' imprisonment without probation. In addition, Streicher was to pay for the costs of the proceedings including Luppe's attorney fees. The mayor was given permission to publish, at Streicher's expense, the results of the trial in the *Fraenkischer Kurier* and several other local newspapers. Also the most offensive (to Luppe) issues of the *Stuermer* were to be confiscated from libraries and destroyed.[50]

Streicher made no formal response to the sentence. He voiced his displeasure, however, to his attorney as they left the courtroom. Further, he quietly instructed Dr. Krafft to file perjury charges against Luppe as soon as possible.

A few days after the conclusion of the Luppe trial, Streicher was in court again as defendant in another slander trial. This had been initiated by two Nuremberg attorneys named Dr. Gallinger and Dr. Kohn, who charged that Streicher had publicly and falsely accused them of sexually assaulting a stenographer employed in their office.[51] Several witnesses testified that on October 14, 1925, they had attended a political meeting where Streicher had accused Gallinger and Kohn of this crime. Evidence supporting the case against Streicher also included a September, 1925 issue of the *Stuermer*. This carried a front-page article entitled "The Secret of the Jewish Law Office," which detailed sordid accounts of the alleged assault. The stenographer, Mrs. Klein, as well as the two attorneys, swore under oath that Streicher's charges were untrue. It was further proven that

Mrs. Klein never worked alone while her employers were in the office. In a counter-charge, the plaintiffs accused Streicher of collaborating in this lie with Mrs. Klein's husband, an NSDAP member who was estranged from his wife.

Streicher's defense was weak. He claimed that he did not write the offensive *Stuermer* article and, as editor, he had obliterated several defamatory lines, but that the printer had included them by mistake.

As a rebuttal the prosecuting attorney pointed out the recent guilty findings in the Luppe case to emphasize that Streicher must now be classed as a habitual slanderer. At the conclusion of this trial, the court found Streicher guilty of defamation and slander and sentenced him to two months' imprisonment without probation.[52] Because of pending perjury charges against Luppe, Streicher's prison sentence was detained for approximately ten months.[53]

Streicher's political activities were virtually halted during the last six weeks of 1925. Involvement in the two slander suits had left him no time to hold meetings or attend to regular party business. In many respects the Franconian NSDAP movement seemed to have lost its momentum. *Stuermer* issues during this period focused on the trials and made no mention of local political activities or membership increases in the parties Streicher had organized.[54] When the news of Streicher's prison sentences was published, many people felt that the leadership of the Nuremberg area Nazi movement would be weak for an extended period. Since the previous March, when Hitler had publicly announced in Nuremberg that Streicher was to be the Nazi *Gauleiter* in that area, there had been no challenge to Streicher's leadership position. As local party head, he had authorized only Karl Holz to act for him on political matters. Holz, however, was not an imaginative or popular leader. In addition, while Streicher was occupied with legal proceedings or serving a prison term, Holz was usually very busy with editorship of the *Stuermer*.

In a bold move to capitalize on Streicher's absence and to extend their influence southward, the Strasser faction scheduled an NSAG meeting in January, 1926, in the heart of Streicher's territory—Nuremberg.[55] Willy Liebel, a local NSAG member who was usually in disagreement with Streicher, was placed in charge of arranging the details of this event. As a meeting place Liebel chose the Colosseum, traditional site of Streicher's large and important political activities. In order to attract a large audience, Liebel flooded the town with posters inviting everyone "who was sympathetic to the *voelkisch* cause." Somewhat surreptitiously he advertised the event as a celebration in honor of the founding of the "German-*Voelkisch*-Officers' Association."[56] Ludendorff was scheduled to deliver the first official address of this newly formed organization, which appeared to some observers as merely a ploy to popularize the NSAG by venerating Ludendorff and other army officers who were mostly members of that party. Liebel also published notices that Hitler had been invited, and "in all likelihood" would assist in the first installation of the association's officers.

Liebel's promotional efforts proved very successful. A police report noted that approximately 2500 persons paid one mark each to attend. Although Hitler did not attend, he named Streicher as his representative. Liebel, as master of ceremonies, opened the meeting and then introduced the important guests by name. Interestingly, the report stated that the loudest and most prolonged applause followed the introduction of Streicher. Eventually Liebel turned over the meeting to Ludendorff, who, for unknown reasons, insisted on speaking from his seat.

In summary, his speech was a dry monologue centering on the need for unity among various *voelkisch* parties. Audience response to his words reflected the boredom of the meeting's atmosphere. In contrast to the scattered and unenthusiastic applause that followed Ludendorff's speech was the display of genuine admiration accorded Streicher as he rose to leave the hall. As the *Gauleiter* walked toward the exit door, a majority of the crowd stood and applauded loudly until he disappeared from view.[57]

Two weeks after the attempted NSAG intrusion in Nuremberg, Hitler moved toward a showdown with the northern group. For the first time since his release from prison, he called a meeting of all top Nazi leaders from north and south Germany. This was scheduled to be a secret party conference at Bamberg, in northern Bavaria. Ostensibly, Hitler chose this site because it was geographically closer to northern Germany than Munich. More crucial to Hitler's political purpose, however, was the fact that Bamberg was part of Streicher's *Gau* (political territory) and solidly pro-Hitler in political sentiment.

Invitations listed a tentative program beginning on Saturday and Sunday, February 13 and 14, with welcoming ceremonies, mass parades, receptions, and group caucuses.[58] Business sessions were scheduled to begin on Monday. This meeting was dominated by Hitler, who spoke at length on the inadequacies of the leftist measures promoted by the Northern "revolutionaries." At the same time he described a series of decrees designed to tighten the organizational centralization of the rejuvenated Nazi party. When he finished speaking he refused to debate any of the controversial points he had discussed. Instead he forced an immediate vote by those present to choose between rejection of his leadership or acceptance of his dictatorial decrees.[59]

Streicher and the other southern representatives, composing the overwhelming majority present, stood and cheered loudly after Hitler had finished. The northern leaders were left stunned and confused. The conference ended in total victory for the southern Nazi contingent. No one had disputed Hitler's emphatic reaffirmation that his leadership and program were immutable. Also very significant in the long run was the subsequent capitulation of Goebbels, who soon became a leading force in Hitler's Nazi movement.[60]

In addition to the above gains, the Bamberg conference resulted in a general upsurge in efforts to rejuvenate Hitler's National Socialist party. A few days after Bamberg, Streicher led a demonstration of strength in Munich which signalled that inter-party opposition would no longer be tolerated. The NSAG had previously scheduled a rally there. Hitler, Streicher, and a group of southern Nazi stalwarts entered the meeting hall just as the program was beginning. While Hitler remained standing in the rear, Streicher led a small contingent of followers to the platform. There he shouted to the startled assemblage that this meeting was illegal and constituted a breach of faith to Hitler. Brandishing a fist, he threatened that blood would flow if proceedings were not halted. The meeting broke up immediately and about one-half the persons present left the hall. Hitler then came forward smiling and acknowledged the *"Heils"* of those who had remained.[61]

The following week, Hitler issued a series of decrees

designed to tighten the line of organizational centralization in the party and to curtail the trends towards regional and local autonomy that had developed. Throughout the early spring months, various party districts were ordered to hold congresses to acquaint sub-leaders with Hitler's Bamberg policy statements. Further, all local party leaders received instructions to expand their membership rosters.[62] In accordance with this latter directive, Streicher scheduled an NSDAP meeting in Nuremberg on March 20.

Posters and newspaper advertisements announced that this meeting was open to NSDAP members and others interested in the Hitler movement. The main speakers were to be Streicher and Goebbels, who was to make his initial public appearance in Nuremberg. The scheduled discussion topic was: "What Does Adolf Hitler Want?" A police report stated that a very large crowd of 1200 to 1400 persons of both sexes filled the spacious Hercules auditorium well before the program began and greeted the arrival of Streicher and Goebbels with stormy and prolonged applause.[63]

Streicher was the first speaker and began discussing a recent nationwide plebiscite regarding the question of expropriation of estates from the landed aristocracy. Hailing the defeat of this measure, Streicher argued somewhat illogically that the reason it failed was because the sponsors of the petition were supported by some land-hungry Jews. Then he defended Hitler's position of fighting in favor of the nobility. He said that these people had inherited this property legally, therefore no one had the right to take it from them. Streicher concluded his rather brief speech with one of his typical anti-Semitic polemics.

Before leaving the podium, Streicher introduced Goebbels warmly as a "new and valuable asset to the Hitler movement." Goebbels responded to this introduction with a Nazi salute, a broad smile, and an extremely friendly handshake. To the audience it seemed that any differences which might have existed between the two men were now totally forgotten. Privately, however, Goebbels' low opinion of Streicher had not changed since the previous October, when he had compared Streicher's speech to the noises of a sow. On March 12, 1926, eight days before this political meeting, Goebbels referred to Streicher in a diary entry as a disreputable "bum-brusher."[64] On the other hand, Streicher must have resented Goebbels more than ever because he was one of the new leaders who was crowding him (Streicher) out of Hitler's inner circle.[65] The personal relationship between Streicher and Goebbels typified the rivalry and animosity which constantly existed between Nazi leaders who looked only to Hitler for their political existence, and whose public display of friendship was a charade played for the sake of outward party unanimity.

After Streicher's introduction, Goebbels took the stand and spoke in eloquent tones about a wide range of topics; from an evaluation of the Dawes Plan and Locarno Treaty, to problems of the itinerant factory worker. His main theme, however, was Hitler, whom he portrayed as a fearless demigod—the only one capable of recreating a strong and united Germany. The police report noted that Goebbels' speech was followed by enthusiastic applause, and that this concluded the evening's program, which had been orderly and interesting.[66]

Throughout the spring months, Streicher concentrated his efforts on the NSDAP membership campaign and his anti-Semitic program. Since Bamberg, he held political meetings two and three evenings each week. While there are no reliable statistics to evaluate the results of this membership drive, the vigor of these endeavors was reflected in the sums of money collected as admission fees. During these months, Streicher's local political operations provided more funds to the national party treasury than any other Nazi district in Germany.[67]

During the months of spring, 1926, Streicher again revived the Jewish murder-ritual myth in *Stuermer* headlines and lead-articles. Lists of missing children from each Franconian village and city were published in successive issues. Repetitious and unsubstantiated articles then pointed out that these children were doubtless kidnapped by Jews and chained in dungeons awaiting the annual Passover season's Jewish blood ritual.[68] *Stuermer* anti-Semitic attacks varied only occasionally from the general theme of earlier issues.

In a few exceptions to the practice of repeating his previously published stories that spring, Streicher related that a Jewish doctor, named Marcuse, had presented a proposal to the Bavarian *Landtag* to repeal the law against abortions. Emphasizing that he agreed with Hitler that abortion was a criminal act of murder, Streicher wrote that Marcuse's proposal only added proof that Jews want the bodies of German girls made available to them legally.[69] In another issue, Streicher castigated the recent popularityof short hair styles for women. He wrote a long editorial charging that the Jews had promoted this hair style so they could purchase the shorn hair to make into expensive wigs. He ended this bizarre article stating: "The man who goes with a short-haired girl is not a German man!"[70] Gauged by the growing popularity of the *Stuermer*, it seemed as if an increasing segment of the German population enjoyed reading this type of radical and repetitious newsprint. Since early 1924, *Stuermer* circulation had increased from 6,000 to 10,000 average weekly issues.[71]

The culmination of the early 1926 Nazi reorganizational campaign came in May at a national NSDAP membership meeting in Munich. The membership meeting was scheduled annually only to satisfy the requirements of German laws governing associations.[72] This gathering, however, proved more than the usual perfunctory affair. Hitler managed to gain sweeping approval of a by-law which, among other things, legalized his power to expel individuals as well as groups from the party.[73] For the first time, the position of a *Gauleiter* was formally included in the organizational structure of the party. Hitler also announced a variety of measures to gauge the performance of the individual *Gauleiters*. Among these measures, the collection of money and money management ranked high as a basis of evaluation. In discussing this subject, Hitler noted Streicher's record as a leading provider of party funds. He said: "If all of my *Gauleiters* were as efficient as my old fighting comrade, Julius Streicher, then half of my worries would disappear immediately."[74]

Shortly after the May meeting, Streicher, obviously flushed with pride at Hitler's praise, unwittingly bragged to some Munich party officials that his success as a fund raiser was due to his ability to supplement his regular source of receipts from political meetings with large private contributions. As an example, he noted that he had recently received a large sum from a wealthy party comrade whose wife was his (Streicher's) mistress.[75] Eventually this information reached the ears of Hermann Esser, who was presently *Gauleiter* of Upper Bavaria and Swabia. Esser, perhaps goaded by Hitler's recent stress on the importance of money, opened a feud with his erstwhile friend, Streicher, over this matter. He complained to Hitler that without Streicher's interference, he (Esser) could have extracted even more money from this source. Hitler, displaying his partiality to Streicher, chastised Esser for overstepping the bounds of his authority. As punishment, Hitler forbade Esser to address him henceforth in the familiar *du* form.[76]

Hitler's efforts to re-establish his authority and to reconsolidate his movement at Bamberg and Munich had proven eminently successful. By July he felt his position strong enough to hold a mass rally to demonstrate publicly the restored unity of the NSDAP. The *Voelkischer Beobachter* announced that a national "Party-day Rally" would be held in early July at Weimar, in Thuringia, one of the few states in which Hitler was still allowed to speak in public.[77] This rally was to be the first since September, 1923, when Streicher had originated the mammoth-scale "Party-day Rally" in Nuremberg.[78] Because of his experience in organizing and staging the Nuremberg rally, Streicher was asked by Hitler to give the *Gauleiter* of Thuringia every possible assistance in planning for the Weimar event.[79] Accordingly, Streicher was busy throughout June in this endeavor. While others arranged parade routes, housing facilities, and meeting places, Streicher concerned himself mainly with printed material such as programs, time-tables, and lists of regulations.

Paradoxically, Streicher who was usually contemptuous of rules and regulations, demanded the strictest adherence to his time-tables and long lists of regulations which governed the most minute detail of the rally. On the cover of the program, Streicher warned all participants that the precise time-table for all events would be strictly followed; that all regulations were to be obeyed unconditionally; and that special guards, in uniform and in plain clothes, were authorized to eject anyone who did not conform to all the rules.[80]

The Weimar rally was attended by approximately 5000 uniformed storm-troopers and an equal number of National Socialists out of uniform. Events of the afternoon and evening of July 3 were highlighted by demonstrations of enthusiasm, welcoming arriving dignitaries, and torch-light parades.[81] The next day, ceremonies began at 6 AM and continued until early evening. Streicher was one of the featured speakers to address the entire assemblage in the late afternoon. His speech lasted less than one-half hour and centered on the growth and development of the Nazi party since Hitler was released from prison. Streicher then introduced Hitler, who delivered the keynote address of the rally.[82]

Hitler thanked Streicher and capitalized on his words to emphasize the major point of his address. He noted that the party membership had increased from 27,000 to 35,000 in the past six months. The principal reason for this remarkable gain, Hitler said, was that the party was no longer weakened by dissident groups and feuding members. He emphasized the important contributions of Streicher and the Franconian Nazi groups in bridging the geographical gap between Munich party headquarters and northern Germany. Referring to the Bamberg conference, Hitler stated that the "new image" of the unified party had become possible because that conference had succeeded in welding the northern and southern *voelkisch* groups together and because he had insisted that all leaders and members of the movement must recognize him (Hitler) as the absolute and unquestioned leader. Hitler continued for an additional forty-five minutes, discussing rudimentary elements of his concept of leadership——the *Fuehrerprinzip.*[83]

At the conclusion of his speech, Hitler left the rostrum amidst the loud and prolonged cheers of his followers. Streicher was the first to shake his hand and remained standing beside Hitler as he accepted the congratulations of many other party leaders. The entire audience seemed charged with excitement and enthusiasm. The sea of faces reflected an unwavering belief in the charismatic Hitler and all that he represented.[84]

CHAPTER VII

THE WAITING YEARS

The successful rally at Weimar was considered by Hitler and his close associates as a critically important step in the overall development of the Nazi party. On the national level, however, events that occurred at the Weimar assemblage were considered insignificant. Most political observers viewed the rally as little more than a documentation of Hitler's charismatic power over a small group of right-wing radicals. With a membership of 35,000, the party was an obscure minority amidst the approximate 15.6 million voting Germans.[1] The possibilities for large-scale growth seemed remote for a party which was based on negative goals, such as racial hatred and destruction of existing governmental institutions. By mid-1926, the German Republic showed positive signs of economic and political stabilization. Unemployment was declining, real wages and salaries were increasing, and at the head of the government stood the nationally respected war hero, Field Marshal Paul von Hindenburg.

At Weimar some of the Nazi delegates in caucuses had mentioned these changes and noted that perhaps now the party needed a more positive program to gain mass support. Some discussions centered about suggestions for changes in propagandistic direction and programmatic emphases. Hitler evaded direct response to these questions, stating merely that any substantive decisions in these matters must be postponed until the proper time. "For now," he said, "we can only consolidate our strength—and wait."[2]

Streicher and other southern delegates returned to their homes with no new directives or different party policies. Aside from renewed enthusiasm for Hitler, these local leaders were left virtually to their own devices in their designated tasks to carry on party work and expand their memberships. Streicher did not alter his schedule of endless local meetings where he continued emphasizing the same general topics—the greatness of Hitler, and the evil of Jews.

Somewhat remarkably, Streicher continually attracted large crowds at these meetings. Police reports note that empty seats were seldom in evidence. In most cases, the front section of the hall would be filled by a group of Streicher's loyal followers who attended most of his meetings, and cheered him at every opportunity. Aside from an ever-present scattering of political opponents and hecklers, the balance of those who attended occasionally, or for the first time, consisted mainly of young persons, students and workers under twenty-five years old, or older men who had lost savings and other holdings during the economic collapse of 1923.[3] These people may have had jobs, but they apparently were still disillusioned or lacked faith in the existing institutions, especially the Weimar government. They all seemed to be searching for something other than their present drab existence.

Streicher's success as a popular political speaker during this period cannot be attributed to the intelligent or enlightening quality of his speeches. Even his closest followers must have been bored by many of his monotonous repetitions. However, he had a facility for theatrics which even some Communists found entertaining. Perhaps purposefully, Streicher always managed to create an element of drama at some point in his speech. In hushed or thunderous tones he would relate some lurid or sensational story about his enemies—usually Jewish people. During these dramatic moments audiences reportedly became alive—breaking out in smiles, whistling, or shouting *"Heils!"*[4]

Undoubtedly, there were other reasons why large numbers of Streicher's listeners between 1926 and 1929 found pleasure in this gutter-sensationalism. A few may have been amused by the element of ludicrousness. Others, perhaps because of their own harsh existence, appear to have enjoyed listening to the degradation and belittling of other humans. These people evidently liked this appeal to their baser instincts and were drawn to the swastika because of the coarser aspects of National Socialism. For the next few years, the style and themes of Streicher's speeches and the format of his political meetings were virtually unchanged. With the exception of a few unusual or outstanding variations in these activities, further description of them is pointless and will be minimized or omitted altogether.

The first of the exceptions occurred a few days after Streicher returned from Weimar. At a Nuremberg NSDAP meeting he spoke on "Hitler's Storm Army In Weimar."[5] Paying only lip-service to this topic, he devoted most of his speech to a prison term he was soon to serve. He began by berating the *Landtag* for voting to uphold a recent court order sentencing him to prison for three and one-half months. For the balance of his speaking-time he dwelled on the injustice of the "Jew-filled" legal system and repeatedly professed that he was innocent of doing anything other than telling the truth about certain "enemies of the state." This meeting adjourned shortly after the conclusion of Streicher's speech.

The court order which Streicher discussed at that meeting noted that he had been found guilty in the two recent trials and sentenced to a total of four months in prison.[6] Further, the order stated that an ensuing investigation into perjury charges against Luppe had revealed some minor legal discrepancies, but not of "such consequence as to constitute perjury." Concluding, the order cited these discrepancies as the reason for reducing the sentence to three and one-half months, to be served from August 23 to December 8, 1926. The judges' rationale for reducing the original sentences is not clear and probably was due only to their bias in Streicher's favor. Understandably, the plaintiffs and their attorneys were highly critical of his unjustified leniency. Luppe complained to Dr. Huber, the president of the Franconian government, that the court had no legal grounds for reducing Streicher's sentences. In addition, Luppe wrote that Streicher should have been ordered to serve extra time because he had violated his parole conditions countless times since the first trial.[7] Huber evidently did not wish to interfere in the court's decision. There is no record that he answered Luppe, or that Streicher's reduced sentence was discussed further in official circles.

Shortly after the announcement of the court order, demonstrations and newspaper articles began appearing in Streicher's behalf. Some of these demonstrations were in the form of mass protests which, because of their nature and size, were considered highly unusual by local authorities. The imprisonment of political agitators happened routinely and normally without widespread protest or commotion.[8] The demonstrations in Streicher's behalf were probably organized by some of his own close associates. However, the enthusiasm with which thousands of people participated in them was indicative of his popularity. In one instance, the police reported a mass-protest meeting which took place in a large hall in Nuremberg on August 15. Announced only twenty-four hours earlier, the meeting was attended by an overflow crowd of more than 2000 persons. After several speeches condemning the threatened imprisonment of their leader, the Nuremberg National Socialists unanimously approved a resolution demanding the immediate suspension of Streicher's sentence. After the meeting, some members of the audience participated in a torchlight march to a nearby square, where a few extemporaneous speeches extolling the virtues of Streicher were delivered.[9]

In addition to the *Stuermer*, which mentioned little else during those days, many other Nazi newspapers came strongly to Streicher's defense. Among these was the official party organ, the *Voelkischer Beobachter*, which in a typical article pleaded that Streicher's sentence should be suspended because "he has throughout his whole life served the State and the German people."[10]

These attempts failed to bring any official indication of a last-minute sentence suspension. In fact, it is unlikely that Streicher was anxious to be relieved of his punishment. The mass-protests and newspaper headlines had suddenly thrust him into the limelight as a martyr to the Nazi cause. As a political opportunist, he capitalized on this means of gaining renewed and additional popularity. He appeared at most of the demonstrations and spoke only after the strong urging (perhaps staged) of the crowds. As a general theme, he stressed the injustice of his forthcoming punishment, but always added that he was willing to pay this price because it would offer clear evidence that Jews controlled the courts as well as the local and national governments.[11]

Taking fullest advantage of this martyr image, Streicher planned extensive "farewell" ceremonies for August 20. Advertised in the *Stuermer* as Streicher's last public appearance for four months, the program was planned to produce strong emotional impact.[12] Events began at 11 AM, in the Lorenz-Church, where a certain Pastor Weigel delivered a eulogy about Nazi heroes who had fallen and those who were then suffering hardships on behalf of the party. The Pastor then consecrated the Nazi flags of a Nuremberg SA company. Following this, a parade consisting of Hitler youth groups, uniformed SA units and hundreds of party members, was led by Streicher through the downtown streets of Nuremberg.

Evening festivities shifted to the spacious Hercules Auditorium. A police report noted that the crowd seemed highly enthusiastic and that the entrance doors were barred at 6 PM because the hall was already over-crowded with approximately 4000 persons.[13] At 8 PM, amidst loud cheers, Streicher, accompanied by Hitler, led a group of dignitaries to the stage. It was generally known that the personal visit to a *Gau* by Hitler was one of the highest possible honors attainable by a *Gauleiter*. To many Nuremberg Nazis, his appearance with Streicher this evening was the most impressive of the day's events. After the meeting was opened with some remarks by Pastor Weigel, Hitler addressed the audience briefly, noting that by government decree he was not permitted to speak publicly, but as party leader addressing party members, he felt within the law in expressing support and appreciation for his "friend and old fighting comrade, Julius Streicher."

Following Hitler's address, Streicher took the podium and spoke for a little over an hour. At his dramatic best, he began by thanking all those present, especially Hitler and Pastor Weigel, noting that the latter was an outstanding churchman and that he was the first in Nuremberg to join the Nazi movement. He then mentioned the flag consecration and said that this ceremony would enable him to enter the prison with an easy mind. Most of his talk, however, centered on the injustice of his sentence. Perhaps attempting to emulate Martin Luther, he intoned that although he had been unfairly judged, he would rather suffer in prison than "recant a single word" against the enemies of the true German people. He concluded his speech with the announcement that in his absence, Karl Holz would take over local party leadership, and that his orders should be obeyed promptly. After a few more speeches and some songs, the meeting ended.

On the evening of August 23, Streicher was driven by friends to the Nuremberg city jail where a group of his loyal supporters had gathered. Shouts of encouragement and "*Heils*" filled the air as he left the auto and entered the prison gate. His time in jail seems to have been spent in relative comfort. This was evidenced by an article in a Socialist oriented newspaper, *Die Bombe*, that complained about Streicher's preferential treatment. The article claimed that the prisoner was treated as a guest, "occupying a room and not a cell." It also stated that Streicher was allowed visitors at all hours and that his meals were served to him in his room with "all the beer and wine he desired."[14]

Stuermer editorials, by Holz and others, offer no details of Streicher's prison life. They only stressed that their leader was being punished unjustly and was bearing his martyrdom like a good soldier. The Stuermer carried numerous articles written by Streicher in jail, but these were mainly polemics about current political and racial injustices.[15]

Regardless of his treatment, Streicher may well have considered his imprisonment as a sanctuary from ongoing legal attacks against him. On August 30, the Franconian office of the Bavarian Interior Ministry, at Luppe's urging, brought more legal action against Streicher in the Nuremberg Provincial Court.[16] In a lengthy plea, the plaintiff cited all of Streicher's past legal transgressions and convictions and sought to prove him unworthy as an educator. The purpose of the complaint was to cancel Streicher's remuneration as a suspended teacher. In arguing Luppe's plea, the prosecuting attorney pointed out that Streicher's family would suffer no hardship if this were done because his monthly gross income from the Stuermer was now averaging over 15,000 marks.[17] After hearing the opening pleas, the judge halted the proceedings because, he said, a matter of this nature could not be settled in the absence of the defendant. He then announced that the case was postponed until some unspecified future date.

In early September, Streicher was notified that he was named as defendant in two additional legal proceedings. One was another suit filed by Mayor Luppe, charging further slander in recent Stuermer articles. This case was scheduled for September, but it was later postponed because Streicher was not available for trial.[18] The other case stemmed from an article published in Die Bombe, entitled: "Streicher Unmasked as a Seducer of Girls."[19] Subsequent findings revealed that the title and contents of the story were apparent falsifications intended to discredit Streicher. According to the article, Streicher was guilty of raping the twenty-one-year-old wife of a certain Kurt Hennsch, of Munich. Because criminal procedures were pending against Streicher, Franconian government President Huber ordered the Nuremberg police to investigate this matter and report at a court hearing on September 29.[20] Although he could not appear at this hearing to defend himself, Streicher was completely exonerated. The police produced a sworn statement by Mrs. Hennsch that the charge was untrue and that it had been falsely made by her husband whom she was divorcing and who had a jealous and vindictive nature.[21]

There is no evidence to indicate whether or not Streicher was seriously concerned about these court proceedings. In all likelihood he concentrated more on writing *Stuermer* editorials and articles and discussing local political matters with his visitors. It is also likely that he concerned himself with the possibility of receiving an early release from prison. Some of his Munich Nazi colleagues supported this possibility consistently by writing a number of articles in the *Voelkischer Beobachter* demanding his early release.[22] Despite these demands, Streicher was held for the full term of his sentence and released at 8 PM, December 8, 1926. A police report noted that a crowd of over 1000 well-wishers had gathered to celebrate his return to freedom.[23] Evidently pleased at this reaffirmation of his popularity, Streicher smiled broadly at this reception and returned some of the handwaves and *"Heils."* He was then escorted to the lead car of a motorcade which eventually drove through the downtown section of Nuremberg. Streicher stood in the open car and acknowledged the greetings of some 2000 people who stood at the curbs, shouting and waving. After a stop at a downtown hotel, where he ate and talked lengthily with Holz and other colleagues, Streicher eventually made his way home to be reunited with his family.

During his days at home, Streicher did little other than sleep, eat, and brag about his recent political exploits. As a rule, he spent very little time with his family. There are no indications that he ever concerned himself with household affairs or bothered with family outings or vacations. His wife, Kunigunde, had no influence on his political ideas or activities. Devoted to her motherly duties, she concentrated her attention on her two young sons, Lothar and Elmar. She seemed to be completely attuned to Nazi party doctrines regarding the role of women in German society.[24] She was rarely seen outside her home and evidently never spoke out in public about her political views. A shy woman, she had little in common with her husband who, because of his dictatorial temperament, probably dominated and intimidated her. This distressing relationship with her husband, coupled with the oft-publicized stories of his marital infidelity, must have caused her a great deal of unhappiness and mental anguish. Most likely, it was this constant strain that brought on a complete mental breakdown in the late 1930's.[25]

After the year-end holiday, Streicher returned to his routine political and publishing work. Now his political activities rarely extended beyond the Nuremberg area. Aside from a few special events, such as Party-day Rallies and *Gauleiter* meetings, he had less and less to do with national party affairs. There were several reasons for this. Hitler's close circle of top party aides now included men such as Goebbels and Strasser, who were more intelligent and politically knowledgeable than Streicher. Because of his fanaticism and volatile nature, members of Hitler's new inner circle were generally hostile to Streicher and on several occasions urged Hitler to get rid of the Nuremberg *Gauleiter*. Hitler, however, was steadfast in his loyalty even though he admitted at least once that he realized the limitations of Streicher's political abilities. In mid-1928 he dismissed a bitter complaint against his "old comrade" somewhat indulgently by stating simply that he did not wish to forego Streicher's work within the bounds of his capabilities just because "everybody is not fond of his disposition and his facial features."[26]

Although Streicher may have displayed ambitions in earlier years to become a national leader in the *voelkisch* movement, there is no evidence that he resented his exclusion from Hitler's inner circle after 1926. The acceptance of this fact may have been due to the freedom permitted him by Hitler to conduct political affairs in Franconia virtually as he pleased. Most likely he found contentment in this role because it provided him many opportunities to satisfy certain psychological needs, especially those related to ego-gratification and undisciplined or unrestrained behavior.

From a practical standpoint, Streicher had become so involved in day-to-day business that he had little or no time for affairs outside his *Gau*. At least two days each week were taken up with promotion and publication functions for the *Stuermer*. Besides numerous discussions with individuals or

small groups about party matters, he organized and participated in at least two local political meetings each week.[27]
The balance of his time was fully occupied with legal affairs,
mostly court cases dealing with personal slander or misconduct on his (Streicher's) part.

The list of Streicher's enemies, both inside and outside the
party, was now virtually countless. Since entering politics he
had built his reputation mainly by vilifying thousands of
persons individually and the Jewish community collectively.
As a natural consequence, he was, in turn, subjected to
endless verbal and legal attacks. As a rule, he considered these
as petty nuisances and displayed an almost arrogant personal
insensitivity to charges of libel and slander and made few
attempts to deny them. For inexplicable reasons, however, he
reacted in the opposite manner when charged with illegal or
illicit sexual behavior. He argued that charges of this type
were vicious attempts at character assassination and denied
them with vehemence.

In defending his innocence, Streicher often pointed out
that he was never found guilty of sex offenses with which he
was formally charged. Interestingly, in each of the legal cases
of this nature Streicher was exonerated because his alleged
victim, or partner, denied complicity in the affair. His
opponents, however, scoffed at Streicher's claim of innocence
They claimed that most women would deny complicity in
illicit sexual relations, even if true, in order to avoid
embarrassment or to protect their reputations.

The argument was perhaps factual in the Madame Douchet
affair which was the most celebrated case against Streicher
for sexual misconduct. It was first reported in *Die Bombe* in
December, 1926 and shortly afterwards reprinted in another
opposition newspaper, *Nuernberg-Fuerth Morgenpresse.*
Briefly, the articles related that as a soldier in 1916, Streicher
had attempted to rape a teacher, named Madame Douchet, in
the French village of Atis. The charge was based on a signed
affidavit by a war veteran named Georg Schmidt, who
allegedly witnessed the attempted crime and helped prevent
it.[28]

Immediately after the articles were published, Streicher
filed a slander suit against the two newspapers. At a
preliminary court hearing in late January, 1927, Streicher's
attorney insisted the charge was false, and on his request the

case was postponed to provide time for his client to prove his innocence.[29] In the meantime, Streicher had sent one of his party subordinates, named Ertl, to France to locate the woman in question. Eventually Ertl returned with a written statement from Madame Douchet absolving Streicher of all guilt. This statement was signed, but it was not notarized, and may well have been a forgery. In overruling defense attorneys' objections, the court accepted Ertl's sworn assurances that the statement was valid. It proved to be the decisive evidence in favor of Streicher.[30] At the conclusion of this hearing, the court levied a fine against the newspapers. In a final hearing the next month on charges levied by Streicher against Schmidt claiming unlawful personal injury, the court found the war veteran guilty of perjury and sentenced him to one year in prison.[31]

For weeks after the conclusion of these hearings, newspapers capitalized on the scandal and its outcome. For example, the *Nuernberg-Fuerth Morgenpresse* published a series entitled: "What is Going on in the Nuremberg Palace of Justice?" These articles pointed out several reasons why Streicher should have been found guilty. They repeatedly accused Streicher and his friends of bribing the French teacher or forging the statement allegedly signed by her. Inasmuch as either of these two accusations may have been correct, they were perhaps justified in hinting that the court showed partiality to Streicher.[32] On the other hand, the *Stuermer* capitalized on the affair and turned it into "another righteous victory" for Streicher over Jews who had supposedly paid Schmidt 300 marks to defame Streicher.[33]

Months before the Madame Douchet affair was settled, Streicher became embroiled in a feud with the Nuremberg *Landsturm*. This group, formed in 1924 by Streicher as his bodyguard and police unit of the GVG, lost its official function in 1925 when the local SA company was organized. Although most members joined the re-formed NSDAP, some *Landsturm* leaders, claiming that they did not wish to lose their group identity, refused to merge with the SA unit.[34]

In mid-1926, hostilities erupted when Streicher, in a *Stuermer* article, castigated them for not joining the SA.[35] In retaliation, the *Landsturm's* leader complained to Munich party headquarters that Streicher was pocketing their dues payments.[36] This quarrel dragged on until October, 1927, when Streicher ended it by issuing an official directive which effectively dissolved the group. In summary, the directive outlawed simultaneous membership in the *Landsturm* and the NSDAP.[37]

The *Landsturm* incident might have ended sooner if Streicher had not been engaged in more important matters throughout the summer months of 1927. In early May, Nazi headquarters had announced that the national party-day congress would be held August 20, 21 and 22 at Nuremberg. Planning sessions began a few days later with Hitler presiding. He announced that the prime objective of the congress, or rally, was to demonstrate the strength and solidarity of the National Socialist movement.[38] In discussing his plans, Hitler reportedly stated that his overall goals for the rally could best be achieved at Nuremberg because it had a highly organized local party and that the enthusiastic group of National Socialists there would provide rally visitors with an illusion of Nazi success and popularity that could not be found in any other city.

Streicher stated in a *Stuermer* article that Hitler had chosen Nuremberg as the congress site because the 1923 rally had been such an outstanding success. He claimed boastfully that this gave him great satisfaction because it was he (Streicher) who had suggested to Hitler that Nuremberg would be the ideal city for that rally.[39] An American writer, Alan Wykes, confirms this claim. Wykes states that Streicher told Hitler (in 1923) that Nuremberg was the ideal city to hold the rally because "the National Socialist life breathes in the ancient walls and gable and moat."[40]

Streicher and two other party officials assumed responsibility for the extensive preparations required for this rally. It was estimated that the three-day affair would attract 160,000 visitors to the city. Streicher was mainly concerned with logistics problems such as transportation, housing and food supply.[41]

The most spectacular event of this rally was the massive torchlight parade of some 30,000 uniformed Nazis through the streets of Nuremberg and past a downtown hotel where Hitler saluted the columns with a raised torch. Thousands of spectators paid as much as 20 marks for seats to watch this parade.[42]

Perhaps the most interesting aspect of all the events was

the content of some of the speeches. For example, Arthur Dintner, Thuringian party leader, outlined for the first time a systematic anti-Semitic doctrine that foreshadowed the Nuremberg racial laws of 1935. Other speeches predicted the alliance of Germany and Italy and urged withdrawal from the League of Nations. Streicher's speeches were among the least interesting. At the opening session of party leaders he delivered a brief welcoming address.[43] Later that day, he spoke as the fifth and final speaker on the afternoon program. The relative unimportance of this speech is evidenced by the fact that Hamilton Burden, an American author who chronicled these events, did not even mention that Streicher spoke that afternoon. In a *Stuermer* article, however, this speech was printed verbatim. It was mainly an anti-Semitic tirade in which he praised Dintner's words but said nothing else that Streicher had not discussed many times previously.

Hitler's appearances and speeches were considered by party members as the high points of all events. His messages during this congress focussed on attracting national attention to the more positive aspects of National Socialist goals. These included the need for German moral regeneration, the importance of a strong, unified federal government system and total elimination of unemployment. Interestingly, Hitler did not emphasize the Nazi anti-Semitic policies in any of his speeches.

Hitler's final address preceded the brief closing ceremonies of the third day's program. Most Nazis left for their homes with renewed enthusiasm for their party. They generally agreed that the Nuremberg rally was an overwhelming success.[44]

In early January, 1928, Streicher was faced with a legal attempt to force him to leave Nuremberg. This action was instigated by Dr. Luppe, who as head of the Nuremberg School Board had been pressing intermittently for the conclusion of the disciplinary procedure initiated against Streicher after he had been temporarily suspended from his teaching duties for absenteeism in late 1923.[45] On previous occasions, Luppe had formally requested that the Nuremberg disciplinary court for non-judicial officials render final judgment in this matter. In his petitions, he noted that the only solution satisfactory to the local school board would be the outright dismissal of Streicher as a teacher. Various court officials had set these petitions aside for over four years. Although Streicher's popularity may have had something to do with these delays, Luppe was informed repeatedly that it would be a waste of the court's time to seek such stringent punishment on the grounds of a few days of unexcused absence.[46]

The January hearing was granted because Luppe had altered his previous pleas. He no longer insisted that Streicher be permanently dismissed. Instead, he cited numerous reasons why Streicher should be transferred to a school system some distance from Nuremberg.[47]

Streicher acted dumbfounded as he heard the reading of this plea. He was obviously not prepared for an eventuality as serious as this. It was one of his rare court appearances without an attorney. In his own defense, he could only utter disjointed phrases concerning his innocence and his need to stay in Nuremberg. Later he listened helplessly as his hated adversary, Dr. Suessheim, reviewed his (Streicher's) outstanding war record. As if rubbing salt into a wound, Suessheim also quoted passages from favorable reports on Streicher's classroom activities and added that these talents should not be wasted. Concluding that political circumstances prevented Streicher from using these gifts effectively in Nuremberg, Suessheim recommended with emphasis that the only viable solution was to transfer Streicher back to Mindelheim, where he had taught before moving to Nuremberg in 1909.

Perhaps the most interesting aspect of this legal procedure was the total lack of sympathy shown Streicher by court officials. On the second day of the hearing, the verdict was rendered by the panel of judges. Following Suessheim's recommendation, the jurists ruled that Streicher be transferred to the Mindelheim school district. In addition, the court ruled that Streicher pay a fine of 500 marks for publicly insulting Luppe, his superior school administrative officer. Streicher was visibly upset by this ruling but managed to stifle a strong urge to condemn the verdict and the judges who rendered it.[48] On the advice of his attorney, Dr. Krafft, he simply notified the court that he could not comply with the order to be transferred away from Nuremberg and that he would appeal this sentence to the State Ministry for Education and Culture in Munich.[49]

Streicher's appeal was heard on May 23, 1928, before the disciplinary court for non-judicial officials in Munich.[50] The verdict showed clearly that officials of this court were biased in Streicher's favor. Because of his refusal to be transferred he was to be discharged as a school teacher and his salary was to be discontinued. However, the court ordered that he receive the full pension to which he would be entitled if he were retiring at the time of his discharge. The order also stipulated that in case of his death, his survivors would be entitled to full support.

The pension, as ordered by the court, amounted to 3374 marks annually. This lifetime income, together with the support clause for his survivors, was a better arrangement for Streicher than his temporary, partial teaching salary which since his suspension had fluctuated between 3000 and 3500 marks.[51]

Shortly after publication of Streicher's disciplinary sentence in January, a palace revolution against the leadership of the Nuremberg National Socialist party was initiated. Although never mentioned, the timing of this revolt suggested that it was planned in anticipation of Streicher's transfer from Nuremberg. At a clandestine meeting in early February, some 80 Nuremberg Nazis organized a movement to oppose and/or prevent the continued party leadership of Streicher or "any of his henchmen."[52] The group was composed of men, such as former *Landsturm* members, who disliked Streicher for a variety of reasons. The spokesman at this meeting was a former deputy party leader, named Kaefer, who for unknown reasons had been recently demoted by Streicher. In listing grievances, Kaefer insisted that Streicher misused party funds because he refused to account for money collected at party meetings. Kaefer reminded his listeners that the annual election of local party chairman was scheduled for next month, and urged everyone present to enlist support for the candidacy of a certain Conrad Weber, who was a relatively obscure local party member. To make the fight against Streicher more effective, Kaefer said, an opposition newspaper, the *Deutsche Volkszeitung*, would soon begin weekly publication.

This newspaper, which first appeared in late February, existed only for a few months. It merits attention because it illustrated the feelings and major frustrations of some of the more intelligent and independent-minded Nuremberg National-al Socialists who organized revolts against Streicher during the decade after the Munich *Putsch*. It also reveals that Hitler may have followed a policy of non-intervention in these insurrections, leaving Streicher to his own devices to prove his ability to weather storms within the local Nazi party.

The *Deutsche Volkszeitung* opened its campaign by charging Streicher with dishonest handling of party funds.[53] Articles in the first two issues accused him of persistently pocketing most of the money collected at meetings and bleeding money from the national party treasury by submitting forged bills for such items as flag material used at the Party-day Rallies. In most cases little attempt was made to back these accusations with records or figures. Instead they were based on speculation and the fact that Streicher stubbornly refused to account for any of these funds in question. One incident, which seemed to be in keeping with Streicher's undisciplined nature, was cited to typify his uncompromising attitude in this regard. When asked about the distribution of certain local party receipts, Streicher allegedly retorted: "What I do with the money is none of your damned business!"

Subsequent editions of the *Deutsche Volkszeitung* continued to express frustrations related to Streicher's questionable money practices. The only other major complaints centered about his unsavory colleagues and his disreputable moral habits. It is notable that his fanatic anti-Semitism, which became an embarrassment to many party officials, was not criticized. Instead, Streicher's paranoid attitude concerning the Jewish question was apparently adopted also by some members of the group bitterly opposed to him. The following excerpt from a *Deutsche Volkszeitung* editorial reflects the radical and unreasoning anti-Semitism prevalent in some Nuremberg Nazis who may have been initially indoctrinated in racial fanaticism by Streicher but who later became disenchanted with his political leadership:

> Like a wild river floods fertile fields and meadows through a broken dam, so the Jew came from the east; flooded our home-city and settled in all streets and businesses. . .with cold, cruel greed he stole all he could from trusting citizens. . . .With sadistic pleasure he satisfied his lust in wild orgies with blonde women and girls in Nuremberg. . . .[54]

Almost every edition of the *Deutsche Volkszeitung* included questionable statements to the effect that Hitler supported the fight against Streicher. One week before elections were scheduled for local party officers a circular, signed by one of the editors of this newspaper, was mailed to all Nuremberg party members. In soliciting support for the movement against Streicher it proclaimed, in bold print, that opposition to Streicher was sanctioned by Hitler because he now realized that Streicher was unfit as a Nazi leader.[55] While these claims were not substantiated, they pose an intriguing question: Why did Hitler not come to his *Gauleiter's* defense in the face of these obvious untruths? Perhaps, as suggested earlier, he remained silent purposely to test or evaluate Streicher's political strength in Nuremberg at this time.

The election, or re-election, of officers was held annually by most local Nazi parties. To many observers these were not taken seriously, but were considered as formalities to comply with the law and to add a degree of legitimacy to office holders who had been hand-picked by Hitler. Under an existing government statute entitled "German Laws of Associations," all political groups were to hold at least one membership meeting annually and these meetings were to be conducted along democratic lines and were subject to official censure or prohibition.[56] However, since there was no outside supervision, these democratic exercises actually amounted to little more than demonstrations of the political control possessed by the incumbent leaders.

According to police witnesses, the annual election of the Nuremberg NSDAP in mid-March left no doubt about the absolute control of the Streicher faction over the local party. The police report noted that SA guards checked the credentials of each person entering the meeting hall on election night.[57] All persons known to be antagonistic to Streicher, as well as all former *Landsturm* members, were refused admission on the grounds of faulty membership cards. A Nazi city councilman, named Gradl, acted as election official. After reading the names of the present officers, Gradl asked for a show of hands to approve re-election of the entire slate. Only three men failed to raise their hands. Gradl than called these three to the stage where they were subjected to an embarrassing body-search by SA guards and forced to remain there while another city councilman, named Nagel, hurled a tirade of personal insults at them. Following this, Streicher made a short "acceptance speech," in which he thanked everyone for supporting the party leadership. He concluded this brief address with a warning that in the following year, any sign of disloyalty by any member would result in immediate dismissal from the party.

The precautionary screening measures employed at the Nuremberg meeting suggest that Streicher felt that an undisputed election was of critical importance. He must have realized that this show of strength was needed to reaffirm Hitler's faith in his (Streicher's) political abilities. Also, only a decisive victory would bring on the collapse of the organized opposition group and possibly silence its abrasive organ, the *Deutsche Volkszeitung*. With these problems out of the way, Streicher could now devote all his energies to the political work ahead—that of running the campaign for the national and regional political elections scheduled for May 20.

According to *Stuermer* accounts, Streicher left local party matters in Holz's hands between April 1 and May 20, and concentrated on campaign activities throughout Franconia. Besides planning and organizing countless political programs, he participated in an average of five campaign rallies each week.[58] He appeared in the dual role of *Landtag* candidate and local sponsor for Bavarian Nazis running for *Reichstag* seats. It is not clear why Streicher did not run for a *Reichstag* seat himself. Perhaps he felt that at this time it was more important for him to stay close to home and take care of his many political and publishing affairs. But since the decision on the final slate of candidates was up to Hitler, it would also seem that he might have thought it wiser to keep the uninhibited Streicher out of the *Reichstag* at this time.

Two candidates, both ex-army officers, Franz von Epp and Walter Buch, often came from Munich and appeared at rallies with Streicher. These men were inexperienced speakers and had difficulty holding the attention of the audiences. While the presence of Epp and Buch added dignity and prestige to the rallies, it was Streicher who provided the necessary ingredient of showmanship. By clever use of lighting effects, music, and flags, he generated and maintained audience enthusiasm. The programs were usually concluded with one of Streicher's long speeches, which always featured some sensational anti-Jewish story, related in a dramatic fashion.[59]

With few exceptions, Franconian audiences responded favorably to Streicher's brand of anti-Semitism. An example of one of these exceptions was a meeting on May 12, at Fuerth. According to a police report, approximately 200 workers had gathered at the rear of the hall and began waving little red Communist party flags and interrupting Streicher as he spoke. Eventually physical violence erupted between these hecklers and some SA men and the meeting was dissolved by the attending police.[60] A *Stuermer* article capitalized on this disturbance in order to illustrate the rowdy and undisciplined nature of Communists.[61]

After the election results were tabulated, Streicher had reason to be highly pleased with his campaign efforts. Nationwide, the Nazis suffered disastrous defeats at the polls. Altogether, the party received only 810,000 votes and 12 seats in the *Reichstag;* a loss of nearly 100,000 votes and two seats in comparison with the NSFP showing in December, 1924.[62] Franconia, however, was one of the few districts where Nazis scored a genuine political victory by accounting for over 100,000 votes, or one-eighth of all votes cast for the party in Germany. Streicher was re-elected to the *Landtag* by a wide margin, while his campaign partners, Epp and Buch, were among the 12 Nazis who won *Reichstag* seats.[63]

Streicher's easy victory as a *Landtag* delegate provides an interesting insight into the attitude of Franconian voters. Streicher's *Landtag* record was very poor since he had attended only a few sessions during his past two-year term. He probably ran for a *Landtag* seat because it added prestige to his name and also provided a steady income of some 60 marks monthly.

In analyzing the motives of voters who supported Streicher in the *Landtag* elections, two key factors—anti-Semitism and fear of an agricultural depression—emerge as the dominant issues. There is a strong possibility that anti-Semitism was historically more deeply rooted and widespread during these years in Franconia than in any other electoral district in Germany.[64] Stressed over and over again by Streicher, this issue became very much alive and perhaps dominated the minds of thousands of Franconian voters as they entered the polls on election day in May, 1928.

Analysis by party statisticians revealed that people in areas such as rural Franconia were almost totally dependent on farming for their economic life, and had not benefited materially by the recent industrial boom as much as city dwellers.[65] More tradition-bound by nature than their urban counter-parts, this rural population had little confidence in the republican government. Their concerns were summarized in a *Voelkischer Beobachter* article by a reporter who had conducted a series of post-electoral interviews in the Franconian towns of Langenzen and Veitbronn:

> ....These people are greatly concerned that the prices of agricultural products will become so cheap that it will not pay to plant crops. . . .The feeling here is that the government cares only for large industries and railroads and has no concern for the situation among farmers. . . .[66]

It was only after the election that Hitler and his advisors realized that they had seriously underestimated the possibility of a wide base of support in the rural districts. Considering these as political backwaters, they had been concentrating most money and efforts on urban centers where Nazi election losses were recorded as the heaviest.[67]

Responding to this lesson, Hitler soon embarked on an organizational revolution. He ordered the so-called "urban plan" discontinued and initiated sweeping changes so that organizational efforts could be concentrated more on outlying farming communities.[68] Primarily because of financial reasons, he cancelled the annual Party-day Rally, and in its place scheduled a leadership conference in Munich to explain and promulgate his organizational reforms.[69]

Streicher was one of the principal speakers at the opening session of the conference on August 2.[70] Taking his cue from Hitler's opening address, Streicher spoke first about the need for the party to follow up its rural triumphs. He could not resist repeating the already well known election results in the rural areas of Franconia. Although he had never previously displayed open concern for farmers, he now talked as if he had always been aware of their problems and fears. He concluded with the statement that he fully agreed with Hitler's new organizational plans and that he (Streicher) was pledging himself to "work unceasingly" in this direction.

In the course of the three-day conference, Hitler's new plan became an organizational reality. Perhaps as a reward for his successful campaign work, Streicher was named to an ad-hoc executive committee. This group held several long sessions framing recommendations for realignment of *Gau* personnel and boundary lines. However, as soon as he was assured there would be no recommendations for changes in Franconia, Streicher lost interest in the tedious deliberations of this committee.[71]

Following the Munich conference, Streicher began directing more of his publishing and political efforts towards the farming communities in his *Gau*. The *Stuermer* initiated a series of articles dealing with current, local agricultural problems. There was little originality in these articles, however most of the pertinent information was in the form of references to agricultural magazines or other newspapers.[72] Streicher also revised his schedule of speaking engagements to include more appearances at political meetings in rural areas.

In the early weeks of this rural campaign, he spoke in vague terms, attempting to prove that the major cause of all agricultural economic problems was the "greedy Jew."[73] These arguments, however, failed to generate much enthusiasm because many of the men in the audiences seemed to be seeking more specific answers to their mounting agricultural problems. For example, at one meeting in the town of Iphofen, attending police noted general disgruntlement when Streicher glossed over a question from a young man concerned with falling livestock and grain prices.[74] By December, the declining *Stuermer* circulation and reduced attendance at meetings indicated that the rural population was losing interest in the Franconian *Gauleiter*.[75]

Streicher was facing a dilemma which was new to him. A large portion of his rural audiences was now preoccupied only with problems concerning agriculture and sought specific answers or information dealing with these problems. It became evident even to Streicher that these people found little satisfaction in the racial diatribes which had always before appealed to rural and urban crowds prone to prejudices. Streicher was at a disadvantage because he had no background in agriculture and could say very little about the problems facing farmers. Also, there were very few Jews connected with farming and farm business, and consequently Streicher had been unable to convince many villagers of his favorite argument—that the Jew was the cause of their misfortune.

In February, 1929, Streicher stumbled across information which enabled him to overcome the above disadvantages and gained him considerable national publicity as a protector of small farmers. By a routine investigation, a *Stuermer* staff member learned that a Jewish man, August Bauernfreund, conducted a large meat packing business in the Wuerzburg area. Streicher jumped at the lead, and within days obtained several signed affidavits from Wuerzburg farmers charging that Bauernfreund, by monopolistic and illegal practices, was driving local livestock producers to financial ruin.[76]

As might be expected, Streicher capitalized on the Bauernfreund case to the fullest possible extent. By April, *Stuermer* circulation in rural areas increased again and Streicher was speaking to capacity audiences at political meetings in rural areas in spite of admission fees as high as one mark.[77]

In early June, Streicher made one of his rare *Landtag* appearances to speak about new developments in the Bauernfreund case. He levelled the sensational charge that two highly placed officials in the Bavarian Ministry of Agriculture, Dr. Fehr and Dr. Niklas, were implicated in the illegal operations of Bauernfreund, who Streicher now called the "sausage Jew." He noted that Fehr was formerly a member of the board of directors of the packing firm and claimed that both Fehr and Niklas were currently receiving free gifts from Bauernfreund in return for illegitimate licenses and other favors.[78]

After Streicher's speech the Bauernfreund case became national news. While most newspapers made light of Streicher's claims and emphasized the denials of the accused men, Nazi newspapers turned the story to their own political advantage.[79] All public mention of the case died out within a few days however, when the injured parties obtained a court injunction ordering a cessation of charges until legal proceedings could be arranged to establish the truth.

Although this matter dragged through several courts for over two years and Streicher was eventually found guilty of malicious slander,[80] the Bauernfreund story was a vital factor in the success of Streicher's rural campaign. It provided ample material for the countless sensational articles and speeches which brought overflow crowds to party meetings in many rural areas. In turn, these meetings fostered interest in the National Socialist movement and most likely contributed to the record number of new members attracted to the party in 1929.[81]

The unprecedented increase in party membership in 1929 was attributable only in part to the above described political campaign in rural areas. A more important factor was the economic depression which by late summer was beginning to affect all segments of German society. To a considerable extent the NSDAP was a direct beneficiary of the slumping German economy. The increasing unemployment and growing paralysis of retail and wholesale trade had precipitated a notable spread of fear, especially among lower-middle-class members who were as fearful of the loss of social status as they were about future economic hardship. By the tens of thousands, people of this class flocked to join the Nazi party because it combined familiar appeal to traditional values with promises of immediate relief.[82]

While the depression was taking root, many Nazi leaders were optimistically preparing for the third Nuremberg Party-day Rally, scheduled for early August. Streicher was deeply involved during the spring and summer months in a series of planning sessions held in Nuremberg preparing for this rally which was planned as a spectacular theatrical production on a scale dwarfing all past Party-day Rallies.[83] The newly appointed Nazi propaganda chief, Goebbels, was placed in charge of the overall program, while Streicher was to direct all local logistics arrangements.[84]

Although the program was to be far more elaborate and was to involve many more people than the previous rally, Streicher apparently had little difficulty fulfilling all his designated responsibilities adequately. He managed this organizational work with little or no interruption in his local publishing and political endeavors.[85]

The rally opened at 11 AM on August 2, in the main hall of the Nuremberg *Kulturvereinshaus*. With Hitler and other party dignitaries present, Streicher, as official host, began proceedings with a brief welcoming address.[86] This was followed by a number of speeches by other Nazi officials.

The most important of the new issues discussed that day was the coming referendum on the Young Plan, which was a governmental proposal to accept a generous offer by former enemy nations to reduce Germany's World War I reparations indebtedness.[87] The National Socialists denounced the proposal and sought its defeat at the polls.

Streicher delivered the last speech of the afternoon session. His topic as usual was anti-Semitism. For emphasis, he singled out the Bauernfreund case and stressed its significance in awakening the local rural population to the menace of the Jews.[88]

The 1929 Party-day Rally drew to a close later that evening with Hitler's final address, which again stressed the need for party unity and membership growth. There was no question that Goebbels and other planners had succeeded in staging a theatrical extravaganza that had outshone all previous Party-day affairs.[89] The rally's lasting historical importance, however, was not that it surpassed all previous attempts in terms of record crowds and propagandistic intensity. More importantly, it symbolized a crucial milestone in the history of the National Socialist movement. As the final program ended with the mass singing of the national anthem, Hitler, Streicher and other Nazi leaders probably sensed that this rally marked the end of the years of waiting and heralded the beginning of the final struggle for political dominance over Germany.[90]

CHAPTER VIII

THE RISING BROWN TIDE

Shortly after the Nuremberg rally Hitler announced in the *Voelkischer Beobachter* that he had committed the Nazi party to cooperate with other rightist political groups in a campaign to oppose promulgation of the Young Plan.[1] Opposition to this plan was based mainly on the concept that rejection of the plan would reflect dissatisfaction with the Weimar government and also reflect German reluctance to recognize the huge World War I reparations debt. Although most National Socialist leaders were agreeable to work towards defeat of the Young Plan, many, for other ideological reasons, were also opposed to an open alliance with rival right-wing groups, led by wealthy businessmen, industrialists and large landholders.[2] Streicher, while disavowing the Marxist brand of Socialism, had consistently championed the cause of the poorer class "victims" of the moneyed strata of German society. Like other party militants he was probably stunned to see the picture in the newspaper of Hitler, side by side with one of the nation's leading capitalists, Dr. Alfred Hugenberg, head of the German Nationalist Peoples' Party *(Deutsche Nationalistische Volkspartei)* (DNVP).[3]

Most party functionaries, including Streicher, apparently had no knowledge of the underlying motives prompting Hitler to form this partnership. Yet, Hitler's authority was so well established that he had no difficulty engaging his *Gauleiters* and other leaders overnight in this political effort.[4] Streicher's reaction was typical of many others who were inwardly opposed to Hitler's sudden and unexplained move. In a speech at a political meeting a few days later, Streicher refrained from criticizing Hitler but at the same time expressed the expectation of a valid explanation:

> He (Hitler) must have his reasons to join hands with these strangers to our cause. . . .He has always proven to be a true and wise leader. . . .We must not ask questions. . .but wait to hear what he has to say. . .he will, no doubt, explain everything when the proper time comes. . . .[5]

Within a week, Streicher was called to Munich to attend a *Gauleiter* briefing session on the Young Plan referendum campaign. Hitler opened this session by urging everyone present to do "all possible" in this national effort. Then, in strictest confidence, he revealed the financial and political benefits to be realized by the NSDAP from this campaign whether or not it succeeded.[6] Besides providing the party with badly needed funds Hitler said he hoped to win nationwide political respectability for the Nazi movement and gain more backing from the industrial and banking community, as well as more support from the wealthier segments of the middle classes.[7] Even after Hitler's explanation, Streicher showed no great enthusiasm for this referendum campaign. Nevertheless he made some sincere efforts to cooperate in the overall attempt to defeat the plan.

In late September, Streicher began to align some of his publishing and political efforts with the nation-wide Nazi anti-Young Plan campaign. The overall strategy was directed from Munich headquarters where staff writers provided published themes to be followed and emphasized weekly in each *Gau*. The *Stuermer* reprinted most of these publications and Streicher discussed some parts of this information in his speeches.[8] During this campaign, Streicher made only token attempts to follow the Munich campaign schedules. His speech titles and opening statements were usually taken from the weekly themes. However, police reports on two of these meetings stated that his discussions were little more than racial polemics. Using vague references, he attempted to prove that the Young Plan was conceived by an organization of international Jews scheming to bring on the ruination of Germany.[9]

Perhaps the most interesting aspect of the Young Plan referendum was that it provided a clear indication of the relative weakness of all right-wing political parties, including the Nazis, in mid-October, 1929. German voters opposing the plan numbered approximately four million, or only 10.02 percent of the electorate in the balloting conducted on October 16.[10] Nazi publications did not disclose serious concern over the defeat or the overwhelming display of support for the Weimar government it clearly indicated. Instead, Hitler capitalized on the referendum, using it as evidence that his *Gauleiters* and other party leaders would have to expend more energy to broaden support for the NSDAP.[11]

The Young Plan referendum failed as dismally in Franconia as it did throughout Germany. As suggested by the above police reports, Streicher's arguments against the plan were probably weak and appealed only to certain confirmed anti-Semites. In addition, his schedule of meetings was interrupted in the middle of the campaign by an enforced court appearance, and he became preoccupied with local elections near the end of the referendum campaign.

In early November, Streicher and Holz were subpoenaed to face trial on charges of slander and blasphemy of the Nuremberg Jewish community.[12] The charge stemmed from some recent *Stuermer* issues, featuring front page allegations of the Jewish murder ritual in words, as well as ghastly cartoons. Among other claims the articles stated that the Jewish holy book, the *Talmud*, sanctioned these bloody rituals.

On the witness stand, Streicher repeatedly confused relevant issues by random exhortations about his political and racial beliefs. The trial lasted ten days and ended in convictions and prison sentences for both defendants. Holz, because he authored most of the articles, was sentenced to a prison term of three months and fifteen days, and Streicher, because he was editor of the *Stuermer*, was to serve a two-months prison term. In addition, the court ordered that all remaining copies of the offensive *Stuermer* issues be confiscated and destroyed. Before leaving the courtroom, Streicher's attorney filed appeals for both sentences.

After the trial, Streicher held most of his political meetings in the immediate vicinity of Nuremberg. Elections for city councilmen were scheduled for mid-December, and Streicher headed a list of seven National Socialists seeking council seats.[13] Since 1925, he had won re-elections to this office with little or no effort, however this year he felt the need to campaign actively. This may have been because Mayor Luppe had initiated a series of newspaper articles, in late October, publicizing Streicher's poor record as a councilman for the past five years.[14]

Some political opponents questioned Streicher's motives for seeking an office which was apparently of no interest to him. Luppe brought out the charge that Streicher was only interested in the 1300 marks in annual salary this position provided. Streicher ignored questions and charges such as these. However, in a speech at a Nuremberg NSDAP meeting in early December, he explained his reason for continued absenteeism from council sessions:

> We tried at first to bring honesty into the city government by removing Luppe as mayor. . .but we were outvoted. . . .Since we continued to be outvoted there was no purpose of wasting time at those meetings.[15]

In this speech Streicher also stated that he hoped the coming election in early December would produce a Nazi majority in the council so that the "mess in the city hall could be cleaned up." Other than the vague and unlikely hope for a Nazi majority, Streicher offered no other reasons why he should be re-elected to city council.

Based on the intellectual quality of Streicher's campaign, political observers had reason to believe he had little or no chance for re-election. Yet, after the votes were tallied, Streicher was easily the leader of the four Nazis who won seats on the city council.[16] This outcome suggests that in the minds of many of those casting ballots, the issue was not a matter of qualification for the office but rather a matter of favoring the Nazi cause as well as expressing agreement with Streicher's racial views.

The easy Nazi victory in the Nuremberg City Council elections reflected a new wave of National Socialist voter appeal evidenced throughout Germany in November and December. In the last weeks of 1929, communal and provincial elections were held in most districts and the Nazis scored unprecedented victories at the polls. The size of the vote (for National Socialist candidates) exceeded the party's most optimistic expectations.[17] Post-election analysis revealed that the Nazis not only increased their rural support, but showed remarkable relative gain in urban areas. This new support in the larger cities, however, did not come from the working class districts, but from the same group joining the NSDAP in record numbers—the lower middle class, which feared the adverse social, as well as economic consequences of a serious depression.[18] This fear had been heightened with the October 29 Wall Street crash and the immediate adverse repercussions in Germany, such as the closing of the largest banks and cancellation of hundreds of factory orders.

Streicher did not seem to recognize that the new wave of

Nazi popularity resulted largely from the critical economic circumstances. At least he made no mention of it in *Stuermer* articles or in political speeches in late 1929. In his remarks about Nazi electoral victories he usually referred to the growing awareness, among the German masses, of outstanding Nazi leadership, or the party's realistic programs and ideology.[19] In a special issue of the *Stuermer* the day after the city council elections, he bragged that he had never doubted that he would win handily. He stated further that if there were "six more Streichers" in Nuremberg, the Nazis would control city hall.[20]

Streicher's words indicate that he may have become somewhat intoxicated with a sense of added self-importance. There were also indications that after his latest electoral victory he may have become determined to attempt elevating his political image. This would not have been unusual during this period. Documented evidence indicates that some Nazi leaders were embarked on an image-building program during these months and that several of them felt that the newspaper had become the main status symbol for the *Gau*.[21]

Streicher's subsequent actions disclose that he shared this feeling. A few days after the Nazi electoral victories were announced, he moved to establish a monopoly of all National Socialist newspapers in the Nuremberg area. Since mid-1923, Willy Liebel, former local leader of the Strasser NSDAP faction, had been publishing a weekly Nazi newspaper in Nuremberg, entitled *Die Flamme*. Liebel's editorials and articles were never hostile to Streicher or critical of the *Stuermer*. In their personal relations, both men had mended their past political differences and seemed to be on friendly terms. Yet, a week before Christmas, Streicher suddenly ordered Liebel to stop publication of the *Flamme*, and ordered SA guards to be posted at newsstands to threaten anyone who tried to purchase the paper.[22]

After Streicher's unexpected action, Liebel, already badly in debt, sold the *Flamme* to Gottfried Feder, long standing associate and former advisor to Hitler, and presently a member of the *Reichstag* as well as the *Reichsleitung*, which was the national party leadership staff. Since Feder outranked him in the Nazi hierarchy, Streicher was now faced with a greater problem than before. He had been covertly jealous of Feder's influence over Hitler, who in earlier years had not only appropriated much of Feder's political philosophy, but also his style of moustache.[23] This jealousy probably increased Streicher's determination to oust Feder from the newspaper business in Nuremberg as soon as possible.

Perhaps unwittingly, Feder goaded Streicher further by stating in the first issue of the new *Flamme* that Hitler had given his blessing to the purchase and also agreed with the *Reichsleitung* that the *Flamme* should be known as the "NSDAP mouthpiece of Franconia," and be entitled to carry the official party-emblem—the swastika, on its front page.[24] There was no evidence besides Feder's words that Hitler indeed had done so.

After this first issue of the new *Flamme*, Streicher disregarding Feder's superior rank, moved directly to drive his new competitor out of business. First, he issued a threat in the *Stuermer*, urging readers to boycott all merchants who advertised in the *Flamme*. Then he warned all news-vendors that if they carried the *Flamme*, he would stop their supply of the *Voelkischer Beobachter*, over which he (Streicher) held a sales monopoly. As a final measure, he ordered SA personnel to be stationed at all newsstands to note any violations of his warnings.[25]

By mid-March, Feder, who despite pleas had received no support from Hitler in this affair, was on the verge of bankruptcy, and was forced to discontinue the *Flamme*.[26] Streicher's ruthless tactics with Hitler's silent consent not only solidified his image as the highest Nazi authority in Franconia, but also served as a warning to other ranking Nazis who might have been inclined to meddle in Nuremberg-area political and publishing affairs.

Perhaps encouraged by his success in the *Flamme* affair, Streicher continued concentrating on extending his personal fortunes by devising and implementing programs and schemes to benefit him financially as well as politically. The first of these was directed toward increasing the circulation and advertising income of the *Stuermer*. With no prior publicity, Streicher attempted to implement a rather flimsy scheme at a large NSDAP meeting in Nuremberg.[27] As each of the approximate 2200 attending members entered the hall they were handed one red, and one green leaflet, or coupon. Streicher opened the meeting with a few introductory remarks and then began issuing instructions on the use of the coupons. The red handouts were marked on one side with a swastika, and on the other side with the following sentence: "A National Socialist has just made a purchase from you!" The green handouts were marked on one side with the words, "*Der Stuermer*," and on the other side with the following paragraph:

> The Social Democrats and Communists are buying from Jewish department stores and cooperatives, and thus destroy the German businessman's existence. National Socialists buy only from the German businessman and because of this you should support the weekly *Stuermer!*

Streicher urged everyone to take a supply of these coupons at the door and always leave one of each at the store wherever a purchase was made. He also warned his audience that it would be considered an act unbecoming a true Nazi if anyone took these coupons and failed to use them properly.

Except for demonstrating Streicher's resourcefulness, the coupon plan amounted to virtually nothing. Initially, only a few persons attending the meeting received or asked for a supply of the leaflets. In the next *Stuermer* issue, Streicher urged all members to pick up a quantity of the coupons at certain Nuremberg business-places.[28] For two successive weeks after this, *Stuermer* notices complained that stacks of the coupons were still available.[29] Following this, no further mention was made of the coupons.

Seemingly undismayed by the failure of the coupon scheme, Streicher next turned his attention to plans for the construction of a Franconian NSDAP headquarters building. He disclosed his preliminary ideas in an April *Stuermer* issue. The principal reason stated for this decision was that a choice building lot had been donated to the local party by a wealthy member in 1928, and that it was time to make use of this lot.[30] Although not mentioned at the time, Streicher's later remarks suggest that his decision may have been prompted by the desire to elevate his political image, especially since he had recently heard Hitler announce his plans to remodel an old mansion in Munich into a sumptuous party headquarters to be known as the Brown House.

In May, Streicher scheduled an NSDAP meeting in Nuremberg to elaborate on his plans for the local headquarters building. He announced during his speech that he had appointed a building committee to engage an architect and to approve preliminary sketches.[31] He stressed, however, that since he was paying for most of the architect's fees, he (Streicher) reserved the right of final approval on finished blueprints. He then talked about the need for the proposed building, noting that present party office facilities and staff needed to be expanded greatly to keep up with the rapid growth of party membership and activity. In addition, he said, the Franconian National Socialist movement, next to the Munich movement, was the most venerated in Germany and deserved an official home in keeping with this standing.

Next, he launched into some of his promotional schemes to finance the building. In proposing these, Streicher seems to have followed the tendency of many self-centered Nazi leaders, who valued the fulfillment of their personal ambitions far more than the welfare of their followers. Many local party members were undoubtedly hard-pressed to make ends meet at this time, yet Streicher contrived and insisted on a variety of schemes to bleed as much money as possible from them to finance his prestigious building. The first of these plans was the building-stone project. He said that he had located piles of building stones at a nearby abandoned quarry. These stones were to sell for 50 pfennig, one mark, and 5 marks, and each party member was expected to buy at least ten of them and sell at least ten more to friends and relatives with the understanding that all the stones be donated to the building project at a future ground-breaking ceremony.

Streicher then introduced the next scheme, feigning concern that National Socialists needed to devote more time to cultural development. This would now be possible, he said, because negotiations had been completed to rent the Intime Theater in Nuremberg on Sunday mornings and Monday evenings for special showings of "good German plays and movies." Tickets were to sell for between 50 pfennig and 2 marks, and Streicher said that he expected all members to "show their loyalty" by bringing their friends and buying seats for 2 marks.[32]

In the last money-raising scheme presented that evening, Streicher announced that Hitler was scheduled to speak in Nuremberg in July. Tickets for that meeting would be sold in advance and each member was expected to purchase at least two tickets at 2 marks each. As a special inducement, Streicher added, members who sold three or more tickets would be admitted free.[33]

Before stepping down from the podium, Streicher referred briefly to the appeals trial scheduled for the following week. This was in connection with the sentences levied against Holz and him the previous November for slanderous *Stuermer* articles against the Jewish religion. Streicher spoke about cases of missing children who he claimed had doubtless been victims of the Jewish blood ritual during the past Jewish Easter season. He expressed hope that the judges in the appeals trial would be aware of these atrocities in reconsidering the November sentences.

On the request of Streicher's attorney, Dr. Krafft, the appeals trial was conducted in the superior court in Munich.[34] This request was based on Streicher's assumption that Munich courts were generally the most sympathetic to National Socialist members. This assumption, however, proved largely incorrect. Neither the defendants nor Dr. Krafft could produce new evidence to alter the facts of the case. After three days of hearings, the panel of three judges upheld the findings of the lower court. In imposing the sentences, however, the judges yielded to a plea by Dr. Krafft that Holz and Streicher serve successive prison terms so that Streicher's political and publishing affairs might be carried on without interruption under competent leadership. Holz was sentenced to serve from June 10 to August 25, and Streicher from August 25 to October 25, in the Stadelheim prison.

It developed later that the date of Streicher's prison term would interfere with important political events. In mid-July, German Chancellor Heinrich Bruening dissolved the *Reichstag* and set national elections for September 14, 1930. Hitler moved at once to take advantage of this opportunity to capitalize on the mood of resentment and uncertainty sweeping the nation. As evidenced by the nearly three million unemployed, the depression was becoming more severe and people of all classes were heaping blame and criticism on the Weimar government. The Nazi organization launched a massive campaign to saturate both the cities and rural areas with National Socialist propaganda to win votes for *Reichstag* seats.[35]

As in the 1928 national elections. Streicher was named campaign manager for the Franconian district. On July 27, he was called to Munich to attend a two-day national campaign planning conference directed by Hitler. As in the Young Plan referendum, direction of the entire campaign was to remain centralized. All district managers were instructed to conduct their campaign activities according to directives to be issued each week by the *Reichsleitung*, which would make final decisions on all matters ranging from the size of posters to major propaganda issues to be stressed.[36]

Stuermer accounts of Streicher's activities in this campaign are not clear regarding the degree to which he conformed to the weekly party directives. His election rallies were always well attended and the enthusiasm of the crowds was even greater than in previous campaigns.[37] In Nuremberg, and other cities, however, he often encountered strong opposition from the Communists when appealing to uncommitted young voters as well as to blue and white collar workers disenchanted with the traditional parties. This opposition, led formally by the Communist party *(Kommunistische Partei Deutschlands)* (KPD), was viewed by Streicher as a direct challenge to his efforts, and led to frequent physical clashes.[38]

In keeping with his volatile nature, Streicher seized on every chance to best the local Communists in displays of brute force. As campaign manager he must have at least encouraged the gangs of Nazi ruffians that engaged in street brawls with KPD members almost daily. On several occasions he lured KPD leaders into holding joint meetings by challenging them to debates on various campaign issues. Most often, these meetings ended in physical violence.

A typical example of these was a joint meeting reported by Nuremberg police held at the Herkules auditorium on August 13. A crowd of over 2000 persons, mostly between the ages of twenty and twenty-seven years, attended this meeting.[39] The police report estimated that approximately one-half of the audience supported the Nazis while some one-third supported the Communists. The remainder of the crowd seemed undecided in their political preference. According to pre-arranged agreements, Communists and Nazis were to speak for one hour each, followed by an open forum conducted by a joint panel of opposing leaders. Almost as soon as the program opened, Streicher and a group of his followers who were seated near the front of the hall, began hurling insults and contradictions at the Communist speaker. These interruptions continued until objects, such as beer mugs, were flying at the Nazi hecklers. Soon, Streicher strode to the platform, seized the speaker by the coat lapels, and began shaking him and shouting in his face. The police broke up the scuffle and ordered everyone out of the hall.

It is questionable whether Streicher's crude behavior succeeded in winning many votes from intelligent or sensitive people. Consciously or not, he was recruiting the support of those who admired, or were willing to submit to crude and ruthless leadership. Perhaps attempting to emulate Hitler, Streicher adopted the custom of carrying a riding whip to symbolize not only his personal authority, but his favorite political axiom: "What counts is will, and if our will is hard and ruthless enough we (the Nazi party) can do anything."[40]

Streicher's campaign activities were halted on August 25, when he began serving his two-months prison sentence. Perhaps due to the coming elections, there was no series of large protests and ceremonies as there had been in the weeks prior to his 1926 jail term. There was, however, one spontaneous demonstration which seemed to display genuine affection and loyalty towards Streicher. It was apparent from this that he had lost little of his grass-roots appeal among the solid core of his local followers.

At 4:30 PM Streicher was escorted to the prison by Nazi dignitaries and friends in a long caravan of autos. A large crowd of men and women, gathering since noon, was waiting near the entrance gates. As Streicher approached a loud cheer arose and women strewed flowers in the path of the cars.[41] Hermann Esser, as official representative of Hitler, delivered a farewell address, which may have reflected the feelings of many of those present:

> The only thing that may reconcile him (Streicher) with his fate in his cell is the certainty of being a hero and martyr of one of the mightiest movements in world history, and the conviction of having pushed this wonderful movement one more step ahead through this sacrifice. . . .

Just before entering the prison gate, Streicher turned to the crowd and spoke a few somber words of farewell. Many women and some men wept openly as they attempted to cheer and shout farewells. The women showered Streicher with flowers and everyone began singing the battle hymn of Nazi martyrs—the Horst Wessel song.

Perhaps the worst aspect of this prison sentence for Streicher was that he could not share in the celebration following the landslide victory in the elections on September 14. That evening most Bavarian Nazi officials gathered at an election headquarters in Munich to await results. Some time after midnight, as final results were being announced, Hitler appeared in person to lead the celebration. The Nazi vote had jumped from 810,000 in 1928, to 6,400,000; and the number of *Reichstag* representatives from 12 to 107.[42]

Aside from the important overall political implications of this stunning victory, it is significant that with this election, Franconia lost its position as the leading district of Nazi electoral support. In the May, 1928 *Reichstag* elections, Franconia had led all other electoral districts in percentage of votes cast for Nazi candidates with 8.1 percent.[43]

In the September, 1930 elections, the percentage of votes cast for Nazis in Franconia was approximately 35. While this gain was remarkable, many other districts registered even greater gains.[44] Of all electoral districts, Franconia ranked in the middle, between a high percentage figure of 44, and a low of 21.[45] The change in voting pattern between 1928 and 1930 can be partially illustrated by comparing results in Franconia and the four leading districts in the May, 1928 election:

Percentage of Votes Cast for Nazis

District	May, 1928	September, 1930
	Percent	Percent
Franconia	8.1	35.1
Upper Bavaria-Schwaben	6.2	27.1
Weser-Ems	5.2	33.0
South Hannover	4.4	39.9
Schleswig-Holstein	4.0	44.0

In attempting to analyze Franconia's drop from its position as the leading Nazi-supporting electoral district, some observers may have considered Streicher's untimely departure to prison as a pertinent factor. However, this consideration was not valid, because after three succeeding *Reichstag* elections after September, 1930, the percentage of votes cast for Nazi candidates in Franconia remained virtually the same as in September, 1930. It seems most likely that Nazi campaigns were more successful in some districts because of other factors, such as nationalism and economic problems, which interested a broader segment of voters than anti-Semitism—always the central issue in the Franconian campaigns.[46]

Streicher's release from prison on October 25 was marked by incidents resembling a comic-opera. The *Stuermer* and the *Voelkischer Beobachter* carried announcements that a large celebration was planned to welcome Streicher as he left the prison at 4:30 PM.[47] However, the jail warden, evidently wishing to avoid commotion, attempted to frustrate these plans by ordering the prisoner to be released at 10 AM in the morning. When informed of this, Streicher became irate and refused to leave until the scheduled hour. After a bitter but fruitless argument he attempted a sit-down strike which ended at noon when guards unceremoniously evicted him from the prison.[48] Not to be outdone, Streicher hid in a nearby house as crowds gathered in the streets during the afternoon. He telephoned some of his friends and informed them of his release but asked them to proceed with the celebration as planned. Later, he joined the caravan of Nazi dignitaries as it approached and got into the lead-car, carrying Hitler, and was driven near the prison gate where he greeted everyone and delivered a two-hour speech on the injustices of the Bavarian legal and prison systems. After this, Hitler addressed the crowd briefly, eulogizing Streicher as a hero and a martyr.[49]

Streicher returned to Nuremberg the following day and quickly resumed his busy round of political activities. On October 30, he was the featured speaker at an NSDAP meeting attended by some 2500 persons. Apparently seeking sympathy, he spoke about the harsh treatment of inmates at the Stadelheim prison in exaggerated and probably untruthful remarks. He stated that he was allowed visitors only one day a week; that he was forced to spend all of his time in a small cell, except for skimpy and tasteless meals and for exercise periods, where all prisoners walked in a circle and were punished if they stepped out of line. He ended this discussion on a gleeful note, joking about the way he had "outsmarted" the prison warden on the day of his release.[50]

Among further remarks, Streicher mentioned the recent elections, noting that Hitler was pleased not only with the election results, but also with the fact that thousands of new members were joining the party now because of its recent rise to prominence. Holz then made some concluding remarks, closing the meeting with a request for generous donations to the Nuremberg party headquarters building fund.

By the end of 1930, Nazi party members totalled nearly 400,000, and new membership applications were still pouring into Munich headquarters so rapidly that special clerks were working a second shift to process them.[51] Hitler sensed that many of these new members were only "emotionally attracted" to the party and might soon lose interest if the NSDAP could not present them with immediate solutions to their economic and social problems. He expressed fear that the party would not be able to attract a sufficient following to win control of the government if it could not hold the bulk of the members enrolling now. The *Reichsleitung* was set to work formulating a plan to utilize the talents of party members associated with various groups or segments of German society.

The plan they developed featured a process that became known as *Gleichschaltung*.[52] This was to be organized nationwide as a major effort to hold the interest of enlisted members and also to win new members and followers. It called for capable leaders, considered experts in each of many varied economic and social groups. These leaders were to be appointed by the appropriate *Gauleiter*, who was also to oversee and coordinate the mushrooming network anticipated in the plan.[53] In most districts, the *Gauleiter* position and function expanded as this new bureaucratic structure grew. This, however, was not to be the case with Streicher, who would "not let himself be squeezed into the limited confines of a bureaucrat." He was one of the new *Gauleiters* who had not become nominal governmental president of his district.[54] With few exceptions he avoided most *Gleichschaltung* bureaucratic and organizational work and concentrated his efforts, with increasing fanaticism, on his anti-Semitic crusade.

One of these exceptions was Streicher's appearance in mid-February, 1931, at a meeting of the Erlangen branch of the National Socialist Student Association.[55] This meeting was part of a nationwide drive initiated by the *Reichsleitung* to extend party influence into the national union of German student groups by accelerating the growth of its Nazi affiliates, such as the Nazi Erlangen Student Association.

In a typical display of Nazi dramatics, a flag-consecration ceremony opened the proceedings. Streicher, the featured speaker, addressed the young men in a sincere manner, praising the students who came to Nuremberg's aid "in the hour of need" when leftist mobs threatened to take over the city after the World War. He then spoke with empathy about the frustration of university students preparing to graduate with little chance of a successful future. Next, he discussed the greatness of Hitler, noting that he alone was able to lead the German people to dignity and freedom. The speech continued in this vein for little over an hour and was received with a standing ovation by most of the students. By his restrained—almost dignified—manner of speech and his moderate remarks on Jews, Streicher seemed totally out of character. This may have been an isolated instance of his conforming to Munich directives. More likely, it was one of the few speeches where his instincts were correctly reacting to the interests and intelligence of the particular audience.

In April, Streicher was asked to speak before a large group of coal miners in Essen, at a meeting in which Nazi organizers were attempting to promote certain candidates for official posts in a coming union election.[56] According to a police report, he spoke about two hours on the Jewish question. Towards the end of his speech, Streicher mentioned that Walter Rathenau, the late foreign minister, had also been a Jew and that it was a good thing he was dead because he had betrayed the German people. Streicher's reputation as an agitator and slanderer must have preceded him here, because several police officers stood near the front of the hall listening intently to everything he said. As soon as he made the remark about Rathenau, two policemen came to the podium and ordered him to stop speaking. Before stepping down, Streicher protested this action and said it was discouraging to see police officers who were not capable of understanding what was being said. Following this meeting, the police filed slander charges against Streicher. However, the Bavarian *Landtag* refused a request by the Prussian Ministry of Justice to prosecute this case.[57]

In May, Streicher came into minor conflict with Munich headquarters over his lack of cooperation in *Gleichschaltung* organizational efforts. This was evidenced in some correspondence between Gregor Strasser, the head of the *Reichsleitung*, and Streicher. On May 6, 1931, Strasser had reprimanded Streicher on the grounds that Franconia was the only *Gau* in Germany that had failed to submit a list of experts recommended to become leaders of affiliated special interest groups.[58]

Streicher answered this reprimand on May 27 with the promise that he would furnish the list at his first opportunity. He complained that he was experiencing difficulty finding the properly qualified personnel.[59] While this may have been true, Streicher did not attempt to apologize for his tardiness or even show concern that his local problems might be impeding the progress of the overall program. When he finally sent Strasser the requested list two weeks later, on June 9, it was incomplete. He had no recommendations for three positions, and three men were recommended to double in filling six other positions.[60]

Streicher's letter of May 27 is interesting in other respects. It helps explain the almost complete lack of surviving Streicher correspondence. He may have been so busy with political affairs or with writing anti-Semitic articles that he found no time for letter-writing. In the opening paragraph to Strasser, he mentions this weakness, but attributes it to laziness:

> You already told me to my face that you consider me extremely lazy as far as writing letters is concerned. I always welcome such frankness, especially when it is true. Now...this letter, as an exception, confirms the rule....[61]

This letter also points out that Streicher was capable of trying soft-soap tactics, even on his known political enemies, in order to cover his mistakes or inadequacies. Rather than express regret that his tardiness may have caused an inconvenience, Streicher, in pseudo-poetic fashion, attempted to ingratiate himself with Strasser, who was still recuperating from a near-fatal skiing accident:

> . . . .I was in the vicinity of Oberstaufen recently and was reminded of the days when the terrible news of your accident was reported. . . .So many people had already given up hope! The fact that you survived. . .proves that you were born under a lucky star. May you soon regain your robust freshness. . . .

These words could not have been sincere inasmuch as the two men were long-standing political enemies and had frequently denounced each other publicly. On prior occasions Strasser had referred to Streicher as a clown and Streicher had accused Strasser publicly of being a traitor.

While Streicher disdained the bureaucratic details of the *Gleichschaltung,* he needed no prodding to assist in its promotional work as long as it held special interest for him, or dealt directly with anti-Semitism. A typical instance of this occurred in mid-July, 1931, when Streicher expanded his anti-Semitic efforts to include special news-articles and programs for children. The timing of these new efforts coincided with the recent reorganization of the Hitler Youth group *(Hitler-Jugend)* (HJ). The newly named HJ leader was Baldur von Schirach, a rising young Nazi official, who credited Streicher with arousing his interest in a National Socialist political career.[62] Under the reorganizational plan the HJ program was broadened to attract a younger group of children from ten to fourteen years old. Streicher had always shown interest in German youth. He may have displayed an affinity for young people when he chose teaching as a profession. According to the German historian, Arnd Mueller, Streicher enthusiastically supported the founding of the HJ, and it was he who suggested the title of the group to Hitler.[63] Without waiting for an invitation, he voluntarily began to assist Schirach by instituting programs to indoctrinate young minds in the anti-Semitic facet of Nazi ideology.

These programs were initiated and announced with little fanfare in a July, 1931 *Stuermer* issue.[64] An inside page carried an article announcing the *Reichsleitung* reorganization plan for the HJ. The article included a brief biographical sketch of Schirach, and concluded with a statement that the

Stuermer and its publisher would make every effort to cooperate with this new plan by "becoming more attentive to the needs of our youth." The same page of this *Stuermer* issue included an article entitled "What is the Intention of the Jew?" It was the first of a long series of *Stuermer* anti-Semitic articles aimed at children.[65] Written in terms understandable to adolescents, this article opened with a description of the facial features of the "*Stuermer* Jew." This was followed by a general discussion about alleged Jewish treachery. The bulk of this article (and those that followed) was devoted to "case histories" which most likely were fabricated stories of Jews committing base crimes against children. These stories contained warnings that Jews were untrustworthy, corrupt and vicious. The major thrust, however, was to instill fear of Jews in the minds of the youthful readers.

The following passage, in condensed form, illustrates the gist of one of these *Stuermer* "case histories":

> . . . .Heinz saw his kitten on the porch of a large house. . . .His mother had warned him to stay away from that house because a Jew lived there. But Heinz could not resist going after his kitten. . . .While he was on the porch the door opened. . . .The man, who was a dirty Jew, pulled Heinz inside. . . .Just as the Jew raised his knife to stab Heinz and drain out his blood, Heinz darted out of his grasp. . . .He found his way outside. . . .Later Heinz told his mother that he would never go near a Jew, or a Jew's house again. . . .[66]

Stories of this nature were probably written by Streicher himself, and they continued to appear intermittently in the *Stuermer* through 1934. After this, a writer named Ernst Hiemer joined the *Stuermer* staff and was responsible for most of these articles. Later, Hiemer compiled and edited a number of "case histories" and they were published by Streicher as a children's book, entitled *Der Giftpilz, (The Poison Mushroom)* which was circulated widely in Germany during the Nazi years.[67]

The back page of the same July *Stuermer* issue included an announcement that an NSDAP meeting would be held Friday evening, July 24. Parents were invited to bring all their children over ten years old, to be admitted free.[68] This meeting was advertised as the first of a series of Friday night "special meetings" which were to continue for the balance of 1931.

The thrust of the presentations was the same as the *Stuermer* case histories—to instill the fear of Jews in children, who usually comprised approximately one fourth of the audience.

The July 24 meeting was typical of most of these "special meetings." According to a police report, the meeting was attended by some 2000 persons, of whom approximately 500 were children of adolescent age.[69] Streicher opened the proceeding with an anti-Semitic story, told in simple language. He then retired behind a black curtain which was drawn acrosss the stage. An organ began playing a selection of religious music. After this the house lights dimmed and the curtain opened. The stage was shrouded in black cloth and Streicher, dressed in a black costume and eye-mask, sat at a table under a spot-light. He rose slowly and began intoning passages from the *Protocols of the Wise Men of Zion*, which was allegedly a secret tract, written by Jews, to describe how the world eventually would fall under Jewish domination.[70] Streicher paraphrased some of the passages and explained them in terms that children would understand. The police report noted that Streicher's performance as high priest of Judah was impressive; some of the audience, especially the children, seemed to shudder and their faces seemed to reflect an expression of deep fear. At the end of his so-called sermon, Streicher removed his mask and walked down the aisle, waving and smiling at the children that were present.[71]

Streicher presented these "special meetings" in different locations in his *Gau* each Friday evening except for certain interruptions, such as the Munich conference for *Gauleiters* and SA leaders in mid-September. The major purpose of this conference was to reorganize the territorial jurisdiction of the SA in order to prevent mutiny by dissident leaders and factions.[72] Since September, 1930, two open revolts had been initiated in Berlin by Walter Stennes, former SA leader for eastern Germany. Hitler had dismissed him in April, 1931, but Stennes had joined with other disgruntled ex-Nazis and reportedly continued to foment agitation against present SA and other party leaders.[73]

According to *Stuermer* accounts, Streicher seemed disinterested in the discussions at the conference and had little or no voice in the final reorganizational decisions. However, he reportedly expressed resentment with another Franconian delegate, Wilhelm Stegmann, a wealthy landowner and ambitious Nuremberg-area SA commander. Stegmann allegedly made some insinuating comments in Munich about Streicher's handling of SA funds and also interrupted Streicher several times during the routine report on NSDAP affairs in Franconia.[74] Stegmann's actions in Munich initiated a feud which later developed to revolutionary proportions in Nuremberg.[75]

A few days after his return from Munich, Streicher announced in a *Stuermer* article that Hitler was planning a gigantic SA demonstration in mid-October, in the city of Brunswick. The announced purpose of this event was to maintain the spirit of the party's national congress, or rally which had not been held for two years. In actuality, however, Hitler intended the October demonstration to be a display of strength to impress, and possibly intimidate rival political parties and their supporters.[76] Streicher, perhaps on Hitler's orders, traveled to Brunswick several times in early October, to assist in preparations for this demonstration. This work involved the usual planning for housing, eating, transportation facilities and timetables.[77]

The Brunswick demonstration on October 17 featured a massive, colorful parade of over 100,000 uniformed SA and SS men, marching past Hitler at the saluting base.[78] The swollen ranks of the brown tide of parading Nazis symbolized the strength of the National Socialist party, whose membership was approaching the half-million mark by this time.[79]

CHAPTER IX

ON TO THE LAST ROUND

The formidable para-military display at Brunswick was undoubtedly disturbing to peace-loving citizens who witnessed the endless columns of brown-shirted, swaggering storm troopers parading past Hitler.[1] At the same time, the thousands of National Socialists attending the Brunswick demonstration must have experienced a renewed feeling of confidence in the future of the party.

The air of self-assurance instilled in the Nazis was more than a temporary exhilaration. As the new year approached various other party successes sustained and even boosted National Socialist confidence. In various provincial elections held late in the year the Nazis registered overwhelming gains. For example, in Hesse the Nazi candidates received double the vote in late November that they registered in the September, 1930 elections.[2]

At the beginning of the new year Streicher's confidence in the future success of the NSDAP was expressed in a cartoon which was featured on the front page of a special New Year's *Stuermer* issue.[3] The sketch provides an interesting insight into Streicher's political ideology at this time. It illustrates that he undoubtedly equated the recent meteoric rise in the party's strength solely in terms of anti-Semitism. The cartoon depicts two prize-fighters in a boxing ring. One of the men is slumped on a stool in one corner and is caricatured as a battered and fatigued "*Stuermer* Jew." The other boxer is portrayed as a strong and determined nordic-type young Nazi. He is standing over his dazed opponent waiting for him to get up and finish the fight. As an indication that a final Nazi victory is close at hand, the cartoon is entitled "On to the Last Round."

Judging by Streicher's behavior in early January, he may have been under a delusion that he personified the young boxer in the cartoon, engaged in the last round of the fight and throwing caution to the winds as he moved in to destroy his opponent. At political meetings in early 1932 his anti-Semitic speeches became so frenzied that he repeatedly disregarded police warnings and continually transgressed legal restrictions. At an open meeting in Fuerth on January 7, he launched into a diatribe about the Jewish murder ritual and was stopped twice by police with warnings that this was a forbidden topic. Within ten minutes after the second warning, he brought up the subject again and the police not only stopped him but also halted the meeting.[4]

The following evening, at Rothenburg, Streicher opened his speech with a denunciation of the "stupid police authorities in Fuerth" and again launched into the topic of the Jewish murder ritual. On this occasion, members of the previously alerted Bavarian state police stopped him immediately and dismissed the meeting with a warning to Streicher that further violations of this nature would result in more drastic action.[5]

Obviously unconcerned with this warning, Streicher spoke with increased fanaticism at Schwabach on January 17. In his opening statements, he denounced the Jews with exceptional venom, spewing terms such as "Jordan Waders," "Jericho Pilgrims," and "Galician Garlic Pencils." He then mentioned the names of several police and civil officials who were beholden to Jewish money. At this point police again stopped him and dismissed the meeting.[6]

Two days later, Streicher received an official notice from the president of the Franconian government that he was forbidden to speak in public until March 1, 1932. The notice cited repeated violations of legal statutes and continued disregard of police warnings as reasons for this censure.[7]

Streicher reacted to this order in surprising fashion, offering only mild objections and appearing somewhat embarrassed. In a brief *Stuermer* article he mentioned the speaking ban without detailing the events leading to it. He only noted that if attending police had listened carefully to his words, this "misunderstanding" could have been avoided.[8] In a telephone conversation with the Nuremberg police office on January 20, he agreed that he would obey the order, but requested that it not be mentioned in every permit issued for NSDAP meetings.[9] This was customary in many provinces of Germany in those years. The police agreed to Streicher's request on condition that he make no attempt to disobey the order. Both parties lived up to the terms of this verbal agreement.

The contrite attitude displayed by Streicher after imposition of the official speaking ban contrasted sharply with his hostility and belligerence which led to it. This attitude differed from his normal behavioral pattern. Usually when subjected to punishment by the authorities, he appealed the sentence, pretended martyrdom or criticized the sanctioning officials. In this case he may have recognized that the punishment was perhaps more lenient than it might have been under the circumstances. Streicher may have also realized that he had misjudged Dr. Huber and other Franconian officials, expecting them to close their eyes to his legal transgressions in order to curry favor with the political party that in his opinion would soon control Germany.

In addition, it is possible that Hitler's attitudes and actions during January had some influence on Streicher. On January 6, the Nazi leader received a telegram from Berlin inviting him to participate in some top-level government discussions. According to the historian Konrad Heiden, Hitler erroneously interpreted this telegram to mean that the Weimar administration was finally yielding to Nazi pressures, and that he (Hitler) and his party would soon attain control of the government. Heiden notes that after Hitler read the telegram he indicated this interpretation with a purr of triumph, exclaiming: "Now I have them in my pocket!"[10]

While this incident was not mentioned in the newspapers, Streicher may well have learned of Hitler's exuberance by word of mouth. Coupled with Streicher's existing confident attitude about the future of the party, this news may have added to the impetuous *Gauleiter's* urge to attack the Jews as viciously as possible without concern for the "triviality" of provincial legal restrictions.

It is interesting that Streicher began this series of speeches on January 7, the same day that Hitler defiantly rejected a proposal by Chancellor Bruening to cooperate in the postponement of the coming presidential elections.[11] In subsequent negotiations, Hitler's defiance melted away when his attempt to dislodge and replace Bruening as Chancellor was rebuffed unceremoniously by President Hindenburg. By January 19, the date of the imposition of Streicher's speaking ban, Hitler was nervously debating whether or not to openly oppose Hindenburg as a rival candidate in the coming elections.[12]

After considerable vacillation, Hitler finally agreed to become a candidate in the presidential elections scheduled for March 13. Even before this announcement was made, the propaganda chief, Joseph Goebbels, had designed a massive saturation campaign, which was outlined in a conference of Nazi leaders in Berlin, on February 24.[13] Streicher attended this meeting accompanied by Holz, who was to handle Streicher's speaking assignments until March 1. After his arrival, Streicher learned that he was to share the responsibility of this campaign in Franconia with a hated rival, Willy Liebel. The next day, Streicher protested to Hitler about Liebel's appointment. However, Hitler appeared unconcerned, telling Streicher that there would be plenty for everyone to do in the days ahead and that the *Reichsleitung* handled matters such as this.[14]

This presidential campaign lasted a little over two weeks and featured the linking of Hitler's name with Germany's emotional and material desires. In Franconia, a master-schedule of campaign activities drawn up in Munich was followed closely. This schedule was worked out in detail for each district, providing for rally locations and dates, as well as local and outside speakers, speech-topics, poster design, and size. Local campaign leaders were assigned speaking duties and were involved in minor organizational affairs, such as making arrangements for music, hall decorations and program printing.[15]

Streicher was able to resume public speaking on March 1. During the twelve days which remained in the campaign he appeared at more than twenty afternoon and evening meetings, usually as the featured speaker. One exception to this was a massive campaign rally at the Nuremberg Hercules-Auditorium where he acted as official host to Hitler and provided only a preliminary introduction to the Nazi leader who was the principal speaker on that occasion.[16] Throughout the early weeks of his public appearances after the speaking ban was lifted Streicher was careful to stay within the law. Police reports on two of his early March rallies noted that Streicher seemed conscious of legal limitations.[17] As always, however, his speeches eventually turned into anti-Semitic attacks.

In similar fashion *Stuermer* front-page cartoons and articles continued to concentrate on anti-Semitic themes. On two occasions, Hitler was included in the major cartoon, shown as a conquering hero, surrounded and out-numbered by Jewish criminals. *Stuermer* campaign coverage, on the other hand, appeared on the inner pages. Yet while there were only synopses of speeches by Hitler and some other officials, Streicher's speeches were reported verbatim.[18]

Despite unprecedented party campaign efforts, Hitler did not win on March 13. However, the Nazis made considerable inroads, especially among the middle-class voters, and kept the front-running candidate, Hindenburg, from gaining a majority.[19] Nationally, the Nazi vote had increased from six and one-half million in September, 1930, to nearly eleven and one-half million. This total gave Hitler approximately 32 percent of the votes cast in Germany.[20] The national average was exceeded somewhat in Franconia, where 36.6 percent of the voters supported Hitler.[21] This figure, however, was only one percent more than the votes cast in Franconia for the Nazis in September, 1930.

The result of this election emphasizes the consistent pattern of Franconian voters. The percentage of votes cast for Nazis in *Reichstag* elections after September, 1930, remained virtually the same, at approximately 35 percent. This fact suggests that Franconian support for Nazis in national elections did not rise beyond this percentage figure mainly because the central issue in the campaigns was always anti-Semitism. In the presidential campaign, however, Streicher was silenced until March 1 and anti-Semitism was only one of many topics covered by visiting speakers, who saturated Franconia with a broad spectrum of Nazi propaganda. Yet, the percentage of votes cast for the Nazi ticket still remained almost unchanged. This phenomenon suggests that there may have been a plurality of 60 to 65 percent of Franconian voters who, for various reasons, consistently refused to support the National Socialist party or its leaders.

Because no candidate received a clear majority of ballots cast on March 13, a runoff election between the two leaders was scheduled for April 10. The Nazi campaign again was preceded by a leadership conference which was held on March 19 and 20, in Berlin.[22] Many leaders, including Streicher, appeared discouraged, and Hitler bent all of his efforts toward instilling in them a new spirit of optimism. Although there is no record of a meeting between Streicher and Hitler, a revised campaign organization list issued the second day of the meetings suggests that they may have discussed Streicher's previous complaint about sharing the Franconian campaign leadership with Liebel. On the new list Liebel's name was deleted and Streicher was named as sole chairman, with Holz designated as his assistant.[23]

The NSDAP's campaign strategy for the runoff election was essentially unchanged from the earlier blueprint of activities with the exception that leaders were advised that more meetings would be scheduled in larger towns and cities. It was felt that campaign workers could concentrate their appeals on middle-class voters who had cast ballots previously for Hindenburg. Streicher again worked tirelessly but did not follow Munich's directives too closely. A review of four *Stuermer* issues during this campaign finds him again obsessed with anti-Semitism in his speeches. He spoke mostly in urban centers but seemed to direct his appeal solely to working-class voters. In each of these four speeches he referred to the misery of workers in Russia and blamed this on the evils of Communism, accusing both Lenin and Stalin of Jewish parentage. Following these remarks, he usually noted that Hitler would fight the Communists, whereas Hindenburg coddled them.[24]

Although the Nazis again expended all available energies in this campaign, Hindenburg emerged the victor with a comfortable majority. Hitler had increased his vote by more than two million, mainly at the expense of the Nationalists, who had withdrawn their candidate. In percentage figures, Hitler's vote had increased to 37.3 percent nationally, while in Franconia the voters again exhibited their consistency by supporting the Nazi ticket with approximately 36 percent of the votes cast.[25]

During this second presidential campaign, Nazi SA and SS forces had caused an extraordinary amount of civil disruption and bloodshed. Mainly because of this misbehavior, the newly invigorated Bruening Government persuaded Hindenburg to issue a decree on April 14 dissolving these groups as organizational entities and prohibiting the display of their uniforms.[26] Although this edict was to remain in force for only three months it not only placed considerable limitations on Nazi political activities but also served to increase discontent and dissension which was already existent in certain SA circles for a number of reasons.[27] One of the leading dissidents at this time was SA Commander Stegmann, of Nuremberg, who had been quarrelling intermittently with Streicher about many SA matters, especially the disbursement of funds, which Streicher had controlled for years.[28]

Almost immediately after the second presidential elections, Streicher became involved in plans and campaigns for the upcoming Bavarian *Landtag* elections. After Hitler's failure to capture the presidency, many Nazi leaders became determined to achieve as much political power for the party as they could by winning parliamentary majorities in elections scheduled for April 24 in Prussia, Bavaria, and several other states. In fact, the *Reichleitung* had been laying plans for these elections even before Hitler had decided to become a presidential candidate.[29] Streicher was notified in January to prepare a list of names recommended as viable *Landtag* candidates from Franconia. Typically procrastinating in administrative responsibilities, he had not prepared the list until April 12, when he was called to Munich to attend a Bavarian *Gauleiter* meeting to finalize the official slate of Nazi candidates and to work out campaign strategy. In addition to his own name, Streicher recommended his close colleague Holz, and two Nazi city councilmen, Gradl and Ertl.[30]

The Munich meeting was headed by Strasser, who found it impossible the first day to complete the official Bavarian list to the satisfaction of all *Gauleiters*. On the second day Strasser announced that there would be no more arguments about the choice of candidates; that the *Reichsleitung* would make the final decisions which could be appealed only to Hitler.[31]

Acting somewhat out of character, Streicher made no objections or comment when he learned that Holz's name had been omitted from the official slate of candidates. During the next ten days, however, he again immersed himself in energetic political campaigning, both for himself and his fellow Nuremberg candidates. According to *Stuermer* accounts, there were only slight variations in the strategy of this campaign compared to the two that had immediately preceded it. Except for the fact that after the Jews the incumbent Bavarian Government was the major political target, Streicher's speeches and *Stuermer* articles in this campaign contained nothing that he had not mentioned in the previous campaigns.[32]

Results of these elections proved generally disappointing to the Nazis. Although the number of their deputies increased in all cases they still did not approach a majority in any state legislative body. Significantly, the Nazis did not poll a percentage of votes in any state equal to the national average in the second presidential election. At 32.5 percent, Bavaria ranked highest in National Socialist vote among all other states involved in this election.[33] The percentage of electoral support for Nazi candidates in Franconia was only slightly higher than the Bavarian average. Streicher, however, again proved his political popularity by emerging with the most Nazi votes in his district. In addition, both of his Nuremberg nominees, Gradl and Ertl, won seats in the Bavarian parliament.[34]

After these elections Streicher was able once again to concentrate on his local publishing affairs. For the first time in many months he managed to spend at least one half of each working day in his newspaper office. Because of Streicher's many enforced absences, the entire *Stuermer* staff was organized to function with or without him present. Unlike most newspaper owners, the *Gauleiter* left the bulk of the administrative affairs of his firm to others, while he concerned himself with writing and editing.[35] Interestingly, unless specific inferences were included, Streicher's contributions were indistinguishable from other *Stuermer* copy. This was because Streicher had established a style of writing which he used constantly and which he insisted all *Stuermer* writers imitate. Perhaps to insure literary consistency, Streicher did not allow the authorship of *Stuermer* articles and editorials to be revealed.

Until 1932, the format, editorial style and general content of the *Stuermer* remained much the same as previously described with only a few changes noticeable. Beginning in 1929, as the political popularity of the Nazi party increased, anti-Semitic articles and editorials became more vitriolic and radical. Despite his many law-suits and jail sentences, Streicher seemed more determined than ever to prove the validity of some of his more sensational charges, such as the Jewish murder-ritual.

Also during this period the political horizon of the *Stuermer* broadened somewhat. There was less coverage of personal vendettas with individuals and more space allotted to national Nazi party activities and national political news. Many articles during this period dealt with the struggle to eliminate dissident party factions, such as the Strasser wing, and to unify the Nazi movement under the single leadership of Hitler. Events such as the Bamberg conference and Nuremberg rallies also received broad coverage as did the many elections after mid-1928. Throughout 1929, the depression was mentioned frequently, but in these articles no attempt was made to analyze the real causes or implications. Instead, increasing unemployment and falling prices were discussed in terms of blaming the problems on inept German government officials or corrupt Jews.

After the Nazi party effectively entered the national political scene in early 1932, the *Stuermer* began publishing some articles lambasting prominent national political figures, such as Chancellor Bruening or his successor, Franz von Papen.

The *Stuermer* ad-section remained virtually unchanged throughout the 1920's until the depression set in and the Nazi party began to increase rapidly in popularity. While the numbers of business-ads remained fairly constant, more emphasis on bargain prices and more appeal to *voelkisch* sentiments became evident. Comments in the ads were included noting the Nazi affiliation of the proprietors or stressing the "good *voelkisch* quality" of certain goods or services. By early 1930, this section was expanded by increasing numbers of personal ads by unemployed Nazis seeking employment in *voelkisch* establishments. Also in evidence consistently were ads by young women seeking companionship with men of proper qualification, especially membership in the SA or SS. As Nazi party membership and activities expanded rapidly during these months, *Stuermer* political announcements increased approximately fourfold and included such events as election rallies, Hitler Youth activities and speeches by nationally known party officials.

The deepening depression served to improve the financial situation of Streicher's publishing business. *Stuermer* circulation expanded from approximately 20,000 copies per week in the late 1920's to some 25,000 by mid-1932. During this period income from the paper's advertising customers increased modestly. In addition, sales of other Streicher publications, such as children's books on *voelkisch* racial beliefs, rose markedly.

After a few weeks respite from the political scene in Spring, 1932, Streicher seemingly regained the energy he had expended during the flurry of political campaigns earlier in the year. Beginning in mid-May, he organized ten to fifteen NSDAP meetings each week and participated as the main speaker in at least three of them.[36] In these speeches he attempted vigorously to re-instill the spark of enthusiasm that now seemed lacking in many local party members. In the recent campaigns many glowing predictions and promises were made by all Nazi speakers but the party had failed to achieve its ultimate goal in any of the elections. While there was nothing actually new that Streicher could say to reinstate high party morale among local members he prefaced his usual anti-Semitic harangues in three consecutive May meetings with the phrase: "Now is the time for us to regroup our forces; strengthen our faith in Hitler, and organize ourselves for the final battles which lie ahead!"[37]

Aside from the few vague references in his speeches about possible high-level political changes coming in Germany, Streicher seemed generally unaware of the political turmoil going on behind closed doors in Berlin during these weeks. He appeared stunned at the news that Chancellor Bruening resigned on May 30 and was replaced by Papen. He also voiced surprise to hear that the new Chancellor dissolved the *Reichstag* on June 4 and scheduled new elections for July 31.[38]

By June 8, however, Streicher was made aware of recent high echelon party developments while attending a leadership conference called by Hitler to outline strategy for the coming elections and to select a slate of candidates for the *Reichstag*.[39] Although he had previously expressed no desire to become a member of this parliamentary body, he learned that his name was included on the initial list of over 500 Nazi candidates.[40]

Streicher's participation in this campaign was similar in most respects to his efforts in earlier ones that year. He was perhaps the only *Reichstag* candidate who totally ignored the official strategy calling for a temporary soft-pedalling of anti-Semitic attacks. The overall campaign efforts of the Nazis, however, were intensified greatly this time because in early June Hitler had managed the repeal of the ban against public activities of the SA and SS.[41]

When the election results were announced it seemed to many Nazis that a great victory had been achieved. With 13,745,000 votes and 230 seats in the *Reichstag*, the NSDAP was without question the strongest party in Germany.[42] However, more sobering facts later dampened this initial exuberance. In percentage figures, the Nazis had garnered 37.4 percent of the total vote, which indicated practically no relative gain since the second presidential election.[43] And even with the record number of 230 seats, the Nazis were far short of a majority in the *Reichstag* and, by themselves, could not control the legislative branch of the Government.

In percentage votes, Franconians again remained consistent in supporting the Nazis with slightly under the national average, at 37.1 percent.[44] Streicher was declared an easy winner but his personal victory was somewhat clouded by the news that SA Commander Stegmann, one of his most bitter political rivals, also succeeded in this election.

On September 12, Streicher attended the only meeting of the *Reichstag* deputies elected in July. In this strange session the Communist delegation opened proceedings with a motion for a vote of no-confidence in the Papen government. Following party orders, Streicher joined the entire Nazi delegation in voting to support the Communist proposal. This action resulted in the immediate dissolution of the *Reichstag* and meant that there would be yet another election that year.[45]

While Nazi cooperation in this move was ordered by Hitler, and the *Reichstag* dissolution may have been beneficial to his overall political strategy, it did nothing to appease the drive for action by certain SA factions. Already angered and frustrated in August by the party's continued inability to achieve political power by the democratic process, many activist SA leaders had been urging "substantial military actions" to take over the Weimar government by force. By mid-August, the SA's frustration exploded into numerous localized revolts against certain Nazi party leaders.[46]

One of the worst of these local revolts erupted in Franconia and was led by SA Commander Stegmann, whose dissatisfaction with Streicher's leadership was of long standing. Stegmann's actions developed into the most serious challenge yet faced by Streicher, and, with few exceptions, was to demand his full attention during the final six months of the Nazi ascendence to power.

Stegmann initiated open hostilities with Streicher in early August with the publication, in Nuremberg, of a newspaper called *Der Nazi—Spiegel*.[47] The first edition of this newspaper declared that its intended purpose was to expose the corruption of Streicher. Among his charges, Stegmann alleged that Streicher continually embezzled party funds. This allegation, however, was made as a sweeping statement with no specific proof offered. In one of many complaints listed against Streicher, Stegmann voiced his resentment that in recent years the Nuremberg SA had become nothing more than Streicher's bodyguards, poster-hangers and rally ushers. In summary, all of Stegmann's charges and demands, true or false, served as supporting evidence that the local SA should be freed from Streicher's jurisdiction.

Streicher retaliated in the *Stuermer* with articles charging that the SA commander was unworthy as a Nazi and SA officer rank.[48] This newspaper feud continued until after the *Reichstag* dissolution. Stegmann returned home from Berlin, called a meeting of the local SA and opened it with a declaration of his freedom from subordination to the *Gauleiter*. At the end of a short speech, Stegmann threatened all present with expulsion from the SA if they followed Streicher's orders instead of his own.[49]

Not to be outdone, Streicher spoke at a Nuremberg NSDAP meeting a few days later and threatened to expel from the party all SA members who disobeyed his orders. He added that he expected every SA man to march in the parade which he had organized for the following Sunday, September 28.[50]

Despite this latest ultimatum, the rank and file of the local SA chose to support Stegmann. In effect, the entire local SA company refused to march in the parade as ordered by Streicher. The majority of these men were not expelled from the party but were later subjected to a special party headquarters investigation where they testified that their decision not to march was not based on feelings about Streicher as *Gauleiter*. Instead, they explained, they were guided by the principle that the SA should act independent of any civilian party official except Hitler.[51]

By early October the Streicher-Stegmann feud had divided

the vicinity of Nuremberg into two hostile Nazi camps and many instances of bloody fighting were reported by the police.[52] In one skirmish, Stegmann was reportedly caught by several Streicher "henchmen" and forced into a basement where he was beaten into an unconscious state.[53] The serious nature of this situation in Nuremberg was reported in national newspapers with expressions of glee by some political opponents of the Nazis.[54] With campaigns now underway for the November 6 *Reichstag* elections both Streicher and Stegmann were ordered by party headquarters to put their differences aside for the sake of Nazi unity.

Streicher seemingly heeded this order and throughout most of October and early November devoted all his energies to the campaign as he had done four times previously that year.[55]

The results of this election were bitterly disappointing to the Nazis, who lost two million votes and thirty-four seats in the *Reichstag*.[56] Despite these nationwide losses, the Franconian campaign, spearheaded by Streicher, proved effective. Returns in this district showed the consistent Nazi support of approximately 35 percent, which was two percent above the national average of total votes cast for the Nazi candidates.[57] Again, both Streicher and Stegmann won seats as *Reichstag* delegates.

The account of Hitler's success in overcoming the Nazi's discouraging political reversal and emerging as German Chancellor is well known and need not be repeated here. In the weeks following the election Streicher played no part in the developments leading up to Hitler's appointment and remained largely uninformed of political developments in the nation's capital.

In Nuremberg, the Stegmann revolt had broken out into something like a civil war by January, 1933.[58] Streicher had demanded Stegmann's resignation as an SA officer and Nazi party member. Stegmann not only ignored this demand, but stepped up his attack on Streicher in the *Nazi Spiegel* and in special meetings. Street fights turned into skirmishes between armed gangs. After several men on both sides were killed, Nuremberg police arrested over 20 Nazis on suspicion of murder. In one incident, an SA gang, attempting to capture and perhaps kill Streicher, stormed his office building, but Streicher was saved by timely police intervention. Streicher then appealed to Hitler, who took the time on January 24 to fly to Nuremberg. With customary loyalty to his old party friend, Hitler fired Stegmann and berated the remaining SA officers for disobeying their *Gauleiter.*[59]

With order restored in Nuremberg, the Nazi leader returned immediately to Berlin where he resumed his frenzied negotiations for six more days until Monday, January 30, 1933, when he was named Chancellor of Germany.

CHAPTER X

ASCENSION TO POWER

Streicher was at his desk in the *Stuermer* office that important Monday when an old party comrade of his, now an SA officer, burst in with news of Hitler's appointment as Chancellor. Perhaps because he now mistrusted all local SA personnel, Streicher made no response but placed a telephone call to Nazi headquarters in Berlin. Hans Lammers, Hitler's executive secretary, answered the call and confirmed the news somewhat reluctantly. Lammers was one of the many ranking Nazi officials openly critical of Streicher's crude behavior and fanatic anti-Semitism. When Streicher asked about possible arrangements for a victory celebration, Lammers replied that all such plans would be relayed in due time to the Nuremberg SA office and Streicher could get his instructions there.

Slamming down the receiver, Streicher ordered Holz and others in the office to round up as many loyal local party members as possible and arrange transportation immediately for Berlin. Arriving in the capital city at dusk, Streicher hurried to the Kaiserhof Hotel where he managed, after a considerable struggle, to see Hitler only a few minutes for a friendly embrace and brief congratulations. He left the hotel just as the massive torchlight parade was beginning to move. Fighting his way through the crowds, he reached the starting point of the parade at the *Tiergarten* just in time to take his place at the head of the large Nuremberg column of marchers. Tens of thousands of Nazis, wearing swastikas or in uniform, as well as thousands of *Stahlhelm* men marched to the blare of martial music, passing under the Brandenburg Gate, down the Wilhelmstrasse and past the presidential palace where they paid homage to Hindenburg. From there the paraders seemed to gather more enthusiasm as they approached the chancellery building. As each new marching unit spotted the new Chancellor the triumphal cry: '*Heil*, *Heil*, *Sieg Heil!*' rang out incessantly.[1]

It was long past midnight before the revellers in the Berlin streets ceased celebrating. Streicher spent most of the night with Nuremberg party comrades joining in the festivities. He remained in Berlin for two more days attempting in vain to see Hitler. Until recent months Streicher never had to wait more than a few hours to gain an audience with the Nazi leader. But now he found that Hitler was inaccessible to him. If Streicher had been a person endowed with even a small amount of political awareness, he would have realized at this time that his usefulness to Hitler was extremely limited; that he could contribute nothing to the weighty decisions now facing the Nazi leader. But since perception of this nature was beyond Streicher's scope of sensibility, he could only curse loudly at the recalcitrant Lammers after his last attempt to bluster past the guard outside Hitler's office door ended in failure.

In addition to his newly acquired state responsibilities, such as cabinet meetings, Hitler also engaged himself in long conferences with his enlarged inner circle of Nazi advisors, planning new party strategy. It was evident to these planners that propaganda tactics and themes would have to be altered drastically to develop the new Chancellor's political foothold into full control of Germany. Hitler was determined to achieve his dictatorial goals despite the legal restrictions of the German constitution and lack of parliamentary and cabinet majority. He had already won approval for new elections to be scheduled March 5 and had stated that this would be the final election in Germany.[2]

In the early campaign strategy meetings Hitler's advisors agreed that millions of new voters might be won over if the racial issue were soft-pedalled. Joseph Goebbels, party propaganda chief and campaign director, who was an ardent anti-Semite, was enthusiastic on this point. He urged Hitler to adopt this soft anti-Semitic line at least temporarily. He also joined cabinet member Frick and finance advisor Schacht in attempting to convince Hitler that chances for success in the election would be better if Streicher were ousted from the party and the *Stuermer* banned from further publication. Hitler, however, replied that this was no time to discard old fighting comrades. The Nazi leader added that winning this election was crucial, but it was only a springboard to the next step, and then Streicher's help might be needed again.

Even though Hitler remained adamant in his refusal to silence the radical anti-Semitism of Streicher, he conscientiously adopted the recommended mild racial approach throughout this campaign. The tone of these campaign speeches was set early, on February 1, in his first radio address as Chancellor. Concealing his racial prejudices, he said nothing offensive or alarming about the Jewish people or their interests. In further speeches he made a few references to his anti-Semitic views but these were couched in subtle inferences or mildly standardized racial phrases.[3] In addition to revising his public image regarding the Jewish question, the Nazi leader changed his former public attitude on the opposition right-wing party, the DNVP, led by the influential industrialist Alfred Hugenberg. Intermittently hostile and friendly to this group, Hitler as well as his advisors calculated that support from this party and its para-military subsidiary, the Steel Helmets, might be a crucial factor in gaining the substantial majority necessary to affect constitutional changes to give the Nazis dictatorial powers.

Streicher was evidently unaware of the change in the party line concerning the Hugenberg party. When he returned to Nuremberg late on February 2, he expressed surprise and anger at the news that awaited him. Following orders from Berlin party headquarters, Holz and other local Nazis had organized a huge torchlight procession and rally in coopera-tion with leaders of the Nationalist-Steel Helmet party. The event was billed as a celebration to recognize Hitler's political ascendency and newly formed partnership with Hugenberg's party. Hastily printed leaflets announced the event as a rally to honor the "Cabinet of the National United Front."[4]

Despite his initial complaints, Streicher took his place at the head of the Nazi marchers when the rally began at 8 PM. The torchlight procession ended at the Nuremberg market place where a hastily erected platform was draped in both Nazi and Steel Helmet party flags. Although he had in past years shown consistent hostility to members of the local Nationalist party, Streicher managed to conceal his animosity as he greeted Steel Helmet leaders when they mounted the platform with him. A large mass of jubilant people filled the market place but almost automatically a solemn and dignified atmosphere swept through the crowd as the Nazi band began to play the German prayer of thanksgiving, *Wir treten zum Beten (We Have Entered to Pray)*. Assuming the posture of a religious leader, Streicher led the singing reverently, with bared head, from the podium.

As the first speaker, the *Gauleiter* paused solemnly until

the musicians were seated and the audience had settled to listen. He began with the words: "Men of the SA and SS! Soldiers of the Steel Helmets! Fellow Germans!" Next, he intoned lengthy phrases congratulating the ascension of the coalition "Hitler-Papen-Hugenberg cabinet." But before reaching the mid-point of the brief, half-hour address, he shattered any hope held by some listeners that his cordiality toward the Steel Helmets was sincere. His countenance seemed to darken as he launched into one of his typical anti-Semitic tirades. He concluded almost as suddenly as he had begun: "For me, coalitions can come and go but the Nazi movement is the only party representative of true Germans! The struggle will not stop until all Jews will be put in their proper place!"

At the end of Streicher's words, bedlam erupted and the next speaker, a Steel Helmet leader, did not attempt to begin his speech. Applauding raucously, a contingent of the *Gauleiter's* followers roared repeated *"Heils,"* then began singing loudly the *Horst-Wessel* song and raising fists at those in the crowd who stood stunned and silent. Within minutes the audience began to melt away.

During the following two months, Streicher was involved in the March 5 Nazi election effort, but to a lesser degree than in previous campaigns. This was evident by the record of his absences from the sizable number of campaign events conducted in northern Bavaria this time. This change in his political behavior was due to several factors. Berlin had issued stern orders that all events promoting Nazi candidates be cleared before scheduling and that speakers follow the official party line according to Berlin directives. Streicher's undisciplined behavioral characteristics were well known, and since the initial directive called for a soft-pedalling of the anti-Semitic issue, Nazi strategy planners refused Streicher permission to schedule a campaign meeting unless he promised, in writing, to refrain from radical or threatening remarks about the Jews.

The *Reichstag* fire on February 27 played directly into the hands of the Nazi leaders who had set a goal of a two-thirds parliamentary majority to assure constitutional changes in the near future. In placing the blame solely on the Communists, Hitler was able to obtain special emergency powers and mobilize SA and SS forces as well as many regular police

Julius Streicher—1930

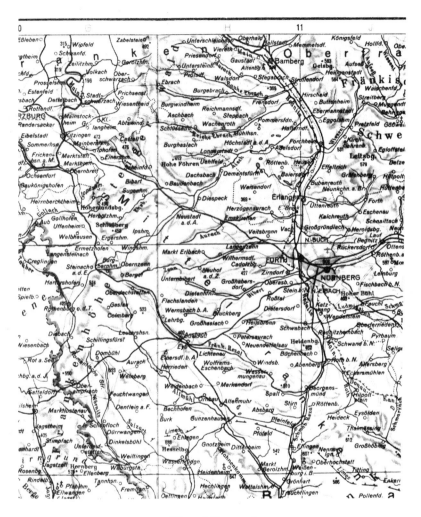

Map of Franconia

Der Stürmer

Sonderblatt zum Kampfe um die Wahrheit.

Nr. 1   Weitere Ausgaben erscheinen nach Bedarf.   1923.

Streicher's
Antwort
an die
Verleumder und Verräter!

Die „Fränkische Tagespost" vom 15. August 1913 führt Bebel's Worte aus dem Jahre 1903 an. Diese lauten:

„Wenn bei uns (Sozialdemokraten) ein Eitergeschwür auftritt, dann operieren wir vor aller Welt; wenn wir schmutzige Wäsche zu waschen haben, dann waschen wir vor aller Welt. Das ist ja gerade das Großartige in unserer Partei, daß wir diese Wäsche vor der ganzen Welt waschen und doch keinen Schaden dadurch erleiden, sondern nach erfolgter Wäsche größer dastehen, als je zuvor".

Wir Nationalsozialisten machen das gleiche.

Wer sie sind!

1. Ferdinand Bürger.

Im Oktober 1922 gründete ich die Ortsgruppe Nürnberg der „Nationalsozialistischen Deutschen Arbeiterpartei". Von den zur Gründung Erschienenen wurde Ferdinand Bürger einstimmig zum 2. Vorsitzenden gewählt. Bürger erbot sich, die parteigeschäftlichen Arbeiten ehrenamtlich zu übernehmen. Da die neugegründete O.-Gr. ohne Geldmittel war und heute noch nur von den Mitglieder-Beiträgen und Sammel-Geldern ihre Notwendigkeiten bestreitet und da Geldmittel in größerem Maße nicht zu erwarten waren, erklärte ich Bürger, daß wir ihm für seine Arbeit eine Vergütung zukommen lassen würden, sobald dies möglich sei. Gelegentlich frug ich Bürger, ob sich anfangs eifrig der ihm anvertrauten Sache annahm, wovon er lebe da er ja neben der Partei-Arbeit keinen anderen Beruf nachgehen könne. Bürger erklärte mir, er lebe mit seiner Mutter zusammen, die durch Näharbeiten genügend verdiene und ihn mitversorgt. Bürger erschien mir und anderen als Idealist. Dem die Bewegung, der er sich verschrieb, über alles gehe. Ich war beglückt, einen solch uneigennützigen Mitarbeiter in Bürger gefunden zu haben und nahm wiederholt die Gelegenheit wahr, auf die Opferbereitschaft Bürgers in Mitglieder- und Sprechabenden hinzuweisen. Bürger genoß meinerseits volles Vertrauen und auch das Vertrauen fast aller Mitglieder, die ihn auch bei der Neuwahl der Vorstandschaft einstimmig wiederwählten. Nach Bürgers Rückkehr aus Rumänien, wohin er sich im Dezember zu privaten Zwecken begeben hatte, stiegen innerhalb der Mitgliedschaft Zweifel über Bürgers Ehrenhaftigkeit und Ehrlichkeit auf. Es wurde berichtet, daß Bürger viel Bier trinke und für andere Zwecke bezahle. Seine Lebensführung machte immer mehr den Eindruck, als hätte man es mit einem Mann zu tun,

der über außerordentliche Geldmittel verfüge. Ich machte Bürger auf die aufsteigenden Zweifel aufmerksam und bat ihn, alles zu vermeiden, was den Glauben an die persönliche Ehrenhaftigkeit des 2. Vorsitzenden und des ehrenamtlichen Geschäftsführers erschüttern könnte. Bürger versicherte mir wiederholt, daß er sogar Mittags kalt esse und sich äußerst einschränke. Ich mußte bald darauf erfahren, daß Bürgers Angaben zur Verdunkelung bereits vorhandener Schäden dienten und daß ein böses Gewissen schon lange lastend belastet fühlte. Obwohl nach den Angaben Bürgers die Ausgaben für die Partei die Einnahmen weit überschritten, gestattete ich nun Bürger, sich kleine Beträge als Entlohnung aus der Kasse zu nehmen. Ende Januar gab mir Bürger auf meine Anfrage zur Antwort, er habe sich für diesen Monat 85000 Mk. entnommen. Von einem ähnlichen Betrag sprach er im Februar. Bürgers Angaben bestärkten mich auf's Neue im Glauben, es mit einem ehrlichen, nur aus Idealismus der Bewegung dienenden Mann zu tun zu haben. Um zugleich alle gegen Bürger schon gewordenen Zweifel zu zerstreuen, ordnete ich an, daß zwei von der Mitgliederversammlung ernannte sachkundige Prüfer die von Bürger geführten Bücher durchsehen sollten. Bürger hintertrieb diese Nachschau.

Mitte März wurden in einer Mitgliederversammlung 66000 Mk. gesammelt mit der ausdrücklichen Bestimmung, daß ich persönlich das Geld mit den in Raten an hilfesuchende Ruhrflüchtlinge verausgaben solle. Bürger, der das Geld zur Parteistelle zu bringen hatte, erklärte tags darauf, er habe noch 21000 Mk., es sei ihm über Nacht das Uebrige gestohlen worden. Bürger versicherte mir auf die Aeußerung meiner Zweifel hin, er dürfe umfallen und tod sein und sein Leben lang sein Glück mehr haben, wenn das Geld nicht gestohlen worden sei. Im Augenblicke dieses eigenartigen Schwures empfand ich den ersten Ekel vor Ferdinand Bürger, das Vertrauen war erschüttert, der Glaube an seine Ehrenhaftigkeit vernichtet. Auch die übrigen Vorstandsmitglieder betrachteten sich von Bürger für betrogen. Eine bald darauf einberufene

Weltverschwörer

Die enthüllten Geheimnisse der Weisen von Zion

Das große Rätsel

Der Reichsparteitag 1936 findet in einer Zeit statt, die gekennzeichnet ist durch Unruhen, Revolutionen und blutige Bürgerkriege. Eine gewaltige Erschütterung geht durch die Welt. Verschwörungen haben sich in allen Ländern gebildet. Ihre Fäden reichen hinein bis in die höchsten Stellen der Politik und der Wirtschaft. Politische Agitatoren sind fieberhaft tätig und versuchen die Massen auf. Ein großer Teil der Weltpresse schreit geheime Richtlinien bekommen zu haben. Es dreuen alles aber verstecht und ein bestimmtes Ziel wo Ziele Ziel heißt: Durch die Weltrevolution zum Weltkommunismus.

Wer nicht völlig mit Blindheit geschlagen ist, sieht die Gefahr ungeheuer und riesengroß am Himmel droben überall wittern sich die Zeichen der Zeit. Schon schlagen die Flammen hell in allen Ländern engeheitet kommunistischen Brandherden an und dort zum Himmer empor. In Brasilien brach vor nicht langer Zeit ein bolschewistischer Putschversuch aus. Er wurde mit Müh und unter großen Opfern niedergeschlagen. In anderen Ländern Amerikas treten die bolschewistischen Agitatoren offener und gewalttätiger auf dann in In der Vereinigten Staaten kam es anläßlich eines kommunistischen Rund-

Deutscher Volksgenosse!

Was hat es für eine Bewandtnis mit den Geheimnissen der Weisen von Zion? Woher kommen die Unruhen die Revolutionen, die Kriege in der Welt? Wer sind die Drahtzieher bei

Massenmorden in Spanien?

Auf diese Sonder Nummer und Du bist Willkoder geworden. Hilf mit an der Auflärung! Gib viele Sondernummer weiter! Schaffe sie darum, die die Judenfrage noch nicht kennen! Es soll das ganze deutsche Volk lebend werden Es soll auch der letzte deutsche Volksgenosse wissen worum es geht. Sorge auch Du dafür, daß dieses große Ziel erreicht wird!

Der Stürmer

Das auserwählte Volk

Den Satan, der die Menschheit quält - Hat nur der Teufel auserwählt

gebung die beiden größten amerikanischen Rabbinerschaften ihren Rundruf zu einer Revolutionsorde zur Bersammlung. Den Sinn Ursprungs brach die diplomatische

Beziehungen zur Conservation ab. Er war noch des Komerzagenten der Eurye der Regierung Uruguays unterwertet hatten. In anderen Ländern ist der Bolschewismus

Die Juden sind unser Unglück!

A *Stuermer* issue illustrating the *Stuermer* Jew

A *Stuermer* advertisement page, December, 1931

A Fips pornographic cartoon

Stuermer cartoon—Jewish murder-ritual

Der Stürmer hat recht

In der Neujahrsnummer 1932 brachte der Stürmer dieses Bild:

Auf zur letzten Runde

Stuermer cartoon—on to the last round

Stuermer cartoon—after Hitler's ascension to power

Ortsgruppe der NSDAP. Kreis X, Berlin

Stuermer enclosed bulletin boards

Der Stürmer

Deutsches Wochenblatt zum Kampfe um die Wahrheit

HERAUSGEBER : JULIUS STREICHER

| Nummer 17 | Nürnberg, im April 1935 | 13. Jahr 1935 |

Judenärzte
Frauenschänder und Mörder

Das Raubtier

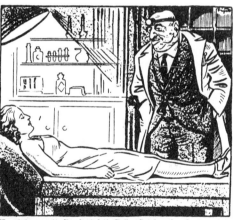

Wozu haben wir die Berufe, daß die Gojims sind in unsere Hand gegeben

Die Juden sind unser Unglück!

Stuermer cartoon—evil-minded Jewish doctor

units to "legally" harass or throttle efforts of Communist candidates. The direction of these para-military and police forces emanated from Berlin and was largely beyond the jurisdiction of any *Gauleiter*.

To some extent, however, Streicher conducted his political activities independently, as he often did. Without bothering to seek official permission, he organized and conducted one or two "unauthorized" election meetings weekly throughout February and early March. The themes of his speeches at these events did not vary much from his efforts in previous campaigns, except for the fact that he never failed to remind his listeners that the Communist party and the Jews worked hand in hand to achieve their destructive goals.

Despite the harassment and intimidation of the Nazis against their opponents in the campaign, they polled a disappointing 43.9 percent of the vote nationwide in the March 5 elections. The district of Franconia fared slightly better with a Nazi plurality of 45.7 percent. Whether justified or not, Streicher claimed a great deal of credit for the fact that the Communists managed only 5 percent of the votes in Franconia, which was the poorest showing for that party of all the nation's electoral districts.[5]

Throughout the campaign period, Streicher continued to be involved in his bitter controversy with Stegmann, who had not left Franconia after his dismissal by Hitler in late January. Stegmann's continued presence in Nuremberg created an unreasonable hatred in Streicher, who seemed to fear another massive SA uprising against him. Even though Stegmann was without position of authority, Streicher continued complaining about him to Hitler at every opportunity. In late March the *Gauleiter* caused Stegmann's arrest on charges of attempted murder. While this charge could not be proven, Stegmann was soon released but remained in the Nuremberg area as a threat to Streicher until June, when he was assigned to another SA post in northern Germany.[6]

During the week following the elections, the Nazis organized victory celebrations throughout Germany and began the process of taking over political control. In claiming an electoral mandate by a majority of the voters, the National Socialists had added the 8.0 percent plurality won by the Nationalist party to their own plurality of 43.9 percent. The signal for the formal NSDAP takeover in

Nuremberg was received in the early morning hours of March 9 from party headquarters in Munich where General Ritter von Epp had just been installed as National Socialist *Reichskommissar* for Bavaria. Streicher headed the official Nuremberg ceremony, beginning at mid-day. A motorcade of local Nazi dignitaries and columns of SA troops including a noisy band formed at a park on the outskirts of the city. Proceeding with loud martial music and incessant *"Heils,"* the parade wound through most of the main thoroughfares and culminated at the large central market square in the middle of the old city where a huge crowd had gathered around a hastily erected platform. Streicher climaxed the brief program of speeches and announcements with a brief address during which he proclaimed that this was the proudest day of his life. The *Gauleiter* then ordered all men present to remove their hats in honor of the new national flag. A huge swastika fluttered free while the crowd sang the German national anthem and the *Horst-Wessel* song. At the conclusion of the singing, church bells throughout the city rang out in funereal tones, as if portending the ominous days ahead.[7]

Streicher lost no time in demonstrating the inconsistency of his words and deeds. During his unusually brief and moderate speech he had stressed that the new regime would benefit all true Germans and would govern with "righteousness, law and order." Yet, a few hours after the church bells had ceased ringing, he led a group of Nazi ruffians to the printing offices of the outspoken anti-Nazi newspaper, the *Fraenkische Tagespost.* There he directed the illegal entry of the premises and destruction of all the printing equipment, including the presses. The next morning he led a similar assault on the offices of the Socialist-led metal workers' union.

For several weeks after the Nazi ascension to power, Streicher somewhat methodically conducted a campaign of vindication against those he felt had harmed or insulted him in past years. These vengeful activities resulted in severe property damage to some ten business establishments and more than a dozen men arrested by SA ruffians and imprisoned.

Mayor Luppe, with whom Streicher had been feuding for ten years, did not escape the *Gauleiter's* wrath. Ousted from his official position and city hall office promptly after Nazi rule was proclaimed in Nuremberg, the dignified elderly man was once again vilified by Streicher in the *Stuermer.* These inflammatory articles precipitated verbal attacks by groups of young Nazis who gathered in front of the mayor's home and shouted insults and threats almost nightly. On March 18, several SA troopers appeared at Luppe's door and arrested him in open view of a small crowd of onlookers. He was thrust roughly into an open police van and transported to a local police station where he was jailed on charges of treason by Streicher. The next night, Holz, Koenig and a few SA bodyguards accosted Luppe's wife, alone in her home. They demanded that she hand over all official city documents located there. Protesting that she knew nothing about such papers, the frightened woman stood by while Streicher's henchmen ransacked the house. Finding nothing pertaining to city business, the frustrated Nazis carried away almost all of Luppe's personal records. After more than a month of imprisonment, Luppe managed to regain most of these possessions. Under pressure of veiled threats from his jailers, Luppe agreed to forego applying for his rightful pension in return for his release from jail and permission to move out of Franconia.[8]

Streicher's vindictive acts were publicized in some newspapers, and political observers conjectured that these roughshod tactics may have played into the hands of some high-ranking party officials who had been trying to convince Hitler that the Franconian *Gauleiter* was a political liability to the party. Hitler may have heeded these arguments when he refused to broaden Streicher's base of legal authority. During the early months of National Socialist rule, when hundreds of party members were receiving promotions in the party or governmental appointments, Hitler seemingly ignored Streicher's request to be named Special State Commissioner of Franconia. He also failed in a later bid for the Nuremberg Police President's position. The principal persons responsible for blocking these appointments were Wilhelm Frick and the new Bavarian State Commissioner, Ritter von Epp.

Whether or not Streicher suffered any degree of humiliation at the rebuffs of his bids for additional offices is unknown. But if he acted as he usually did he would have registered anger and blamed his failure on Frick, von Epp and other Nazi officials. Then he would have complained to Hitler about these "untrustworthy culprits." Subsequent developments indicate that the new Chancellor may have felt somewhat rueful that he had followed advice which must have been disappointing to his "old fighting comrade." At a cabinet meeting on March 28, Hitler announced suddenly that he was naming Julius Streicher general chairman of a nationwide boycott of Jewish businesses to begin on April 1.[9]

The naming of Streicher to head the Nazi government's first official anti-Semitic act was reportedly a shock to members of Hitler's inner circle, who attempted in vain to convince their leader that a more reputable person would better serve the intended purpose of this event. In all likelihood, however, most of these objectors were not aware of all the goals of the boycott. The strategy behind it was a combination of Nazi duplicity and rationalization. Hitler had achieved legal authority for a dictatorship on March 23, with the passage of the Enabling Act. After this, the question uppermost in his mind concerned the Jews. He discussed privately, with Goebbels, a confusing assortment of reasons to conduct this boycott, but his publicly stated reason was that this was necessary to register an orderly protest against Jews "who created all the violence in Germany and spread lies throughout the world about the *Reich*."[10] Privately, however, Hitler most likely felt that he had contained his hatred of the Jews long enough, and that now was the time to brand them as enemies of the state. He remarked in one late March meeting that he was anxious to channel the enthusiasm for overt acts of Jewish persecution on the part of the rank-and-file anti-Semites into "meaningful political action."

The new Chancellor's motives for naming Streicher boycott chairman may have been triggered by a desire to reward the *Gauleiter* and perhaps bolster his diminished standing in the party. However, Hitler may have also felt that Streicher was the party member best suited to symbolize the depth and meaning of his (Hitler's) racial feelings. Streicher's anti-Semitism had often been praised by Hitler, who, on several occasions, had credited his old comrade as being the pioneer of the Nazi anti-Semitic movement.

Prior to April 1, 1933, Streicher was a relatively obscure political figure on the national level. After the Nazi ascension to power, however, he had managed to increase circulation of the *Stuermer* more than 50 percent partially because he claimed that it was an official party organ. Yet, his name was still unknown to the large majority of German people until the announcements by radio and press that Julius Streicher was to head the Jewish boycott.

Streicher was credited with organizing the boycott efficiently, with local committees named to carry out activities which were stated in moderate terms. The benign tone of Streicher's instructions is evident in the following relevant excerpts from his official Boycott Decree:

1. There is to be no violence. Businesses are not to be closed unless the owners wish to close them. Entry into Jewish business places by SA, SS or other deputies is strictly forbidden. The central mission is to inform the public that the enterprises are Jewish.
2. No business is to be subject to boycott unless it is established beyond doubt that the owner is Jewish.
3. No business place should suffer property damage and this will not be instigated.

This document was signed simply: "Streicher."[1 1]

With some exceptions, Streicher's instructions for disciplined and orderly behavior were observed by the teams of SA men assigned to carry out the boycott, which lasted until April 4. Throughout Germany, brownshirts placarded most Jewish stores and offices and stood outside reminding all who entered that they were about to patronize a Jewish business. Only a small number of cases of violence were noted and there was no confirmed report that serious personal injury had been inflicted on anyone. Yet, in some cities and towns, citizens were harassed and frightened as truckloads of SA men drove through the streets shaking their fists and shouting threatening slogans such as "Perish Judah!" and "Down with the Jews!"

The extent to which Streicher may have been responsible for the "orderly conduct" as well as the verbal abuses of SA boycott participants is undeterminable. Despite the consistencies in his printed instructions calling for disciplined behavior, the *Gauleiter* seemingly encouraged contradictory deportment in a radio address on the eve of the boycott. Appealing for complete support, Streicher reiterated his previous printed boycott messages in even tones until he neared the end of his address. Then, almost as if he could contain himself no longer, he burst into one of his usual discourses about the evil nature of all Jews. He ended this nationwide address with phrases easily interpretable as a battle cry for vengeful and violent action somehow to be carried out in an honest manner:

> I do not ask you whether you are Catholic or Protestant, but if you are Christian, then I say to you—Golgotha is still not avenged. . .those who are responsible for Golgotha are already on their way there. . . . The Jew is our eternal enemy. . .I stand at the head of this battle which will be carried on in such a thoroughly honest way that the eternal Jew will derive no satisfaction from it.[12]

Streicher's mental processes at this time may be partially understood by the manner in which he answered questions in the autumn of 1945 regarding his role in the boycott. When asked to explain the meaning of the above speech, which had been reproduced in the *Voelkischer Beobachter*, he expressed surprise that anyone could interpret his words as incitement to violent action. He explained that he only wanted to reveal the "truth" about the Jews so that everyone would understand the need to cooperate in the boycott. He said he thought his message was a clear call for "honest" methods, which would be legal and non-violent so that the Jews could not later claim they were martyrs of brutal treatment. When questioned further about his emphasis on honesty and legality, Streicher answered almost indignantly that he always conducted himself in this manner; that it was only certain Jewish businessmen who acted illegally by transferring their property to fictitious persons, called German "strawmen," even before the boycott began.[13]

During the years of Nazi rule under Streicher, Jewish enterprises and individuals would suffer extreme injustices and hardships in Franconia. At the same time, the *Gauleiter* would always try to pose as a "protector" of the Jews and a rigid observer of legal procedure. His repeated attempts to appear as the champion of firm but non-violent treatment of Jewish persons in Franconia is well documented in Nuremberg police reports and official party correspondence. The following excerpt from a June, 1933, letter to Chief Party Secretary Hess is a typical example of this questionable attitude:

> . . . .Because I am aware of the consequences of a clumsy action against the center of anti-Semitism I took the greatest care that there would be no stupidities. An example: on the second day after the seizure of power some SA people led a Galician Jew through the streets, followed by thousands who demanded his thrashing. I had him brought to me, then had him escorted. . . .to his freedom. . . .I told the SA leaders that I would throw out of the party anyone who attacked a single Jew. . .that a single beaten Jew could arouse the entire world against us. . . .[14]

Despite his declared intentions to conduct Jewish policies in a non-violent and sensitive manner, Streicher established harsh Nazi rule in his *Gau* within a few weeks after the end of the boycott. He expanded his authority as *Gauleiter* into an archtype of absolute political domination and soon became known as the leading racial persecutor and most powerful local party leader in Germany. He was aided in quickly subjugating the Jews and eliminating most political enemies from positions of authority by a flurry of racial legislation suddenly enacted by the Hitler government. On April 7, 1933, the first of these Nazi anti-Semitic laws was promulgated. This decree, entitled the "Law for the Restoration of the Professional Civil Service," called for the elimination of Jews and political opponents of the Nazis from civil service. Subsequent laws, following in rapid succession, denied Jews the right to teach in schools and universities, to practice law and to act as judges or jurors.[15]

In the execution of these edicts, Streicher began earning one of his infamous sub-titles: "The Hitler of Franconia." He seemingly attempted to emulate the leadership principle *(Fuehrerprinzip)* which was the hallmark of Hitler's political philosophy. He demanded unquestioned authority and rarely tolerated objections to his decisions. Ignoring Berlin directives to act in consultation with local and state committees, Streicher personally issued orders for the dismissal from office, or position, of hundreds of Franconian Jews and political dissidents as well as many personal rivals or enemies. He then selected the needed replacements for vacant positions from among political lackeys who would yield obediently to his whims.

Streicher assembled a large number of subordinates whom he ruled with the help of a small, loyal group that was around him consistently and was especially suited to carry out his orders. Chief among these was Holz, who remained as co-editor of the *Stuermer*, member of the Nuremberg City Council and official deputy *Gauleiter*. Throughout his many years as Streicher's top lieutenant, Holz had willingly assumed responsibility for the misdeeds of his boss and suffered twenty arrests and five prison sentences.

Ranking with Holz at the top of Streicher's inner circle was Hans Koenig, sometimes referred to as the "evil spirit of Franconia." Without the intellectual qualifications for high office, Koenig possessed a shrewd mind and fearless demeanor, having gained notoriety as a Nazi "muscle man." He was to prove most effective in intimidating business leaders to yield meekly to Streicher's subsequent "aryanization program." Koenig's weakness was his passion for seducing young artists at the city theater.[16]

The only other member of this group worthy of mention here was Max Fink, a grade-school teacher placed on the city council to deliver Streicher's orders and to clear Jews out of the schools. Although more messenger boy than bully, Fink possessed a devious mind and became the *Gauleiter's* chief confidante as well as frequent "front man" in a number of clandestine and unethical financial manipulations.[17]

With his organization of obedient bullies and lackeys, Streicher retained his dictatorial reputation for a number of years. Yet, his authority was not as absolute as it appeared to outsiders. From the beginning of the Nazi takeover, his power in Nuremberg was limited to a certain extent in the affairs of the city administration and the police force.

Hitler's choice as Nuremberg's mayor was Willy Liebel, a competent administrator and also an ambitious man. He proved more of a danger than a toady to the *Gauleiter*. Liebel was determined to make Nuremberg a model city and received Hitler's endorsement in this goal. This was the main reason he was able to side-step Streicher frequently in such matters as determining the selection of high-echelon city administrative officials. Even though there seemed to be on-going differences between the two men, Liebel managed to remain on speaking terms with Streicher most of the time. This outwardly smooth relationship may have been due to the fact that Liebel felt it politically expedient to placate the eruptive *Gauleiter* from time to time with compliments and lavish gifts. Outstanding among the gifts was the sumptuous Cramer-Klett villa, which reportedly cost the city over 300,000 marks. The mayor presented this property to the *Gauleiter* in 1935, as a Christmas present "to express the city's gratitude for cooperation." On a later occasion, Streicher's fifty-second birthday, the mayor gave him a rare 1543 edition of a book by Martin Luther, entitled "About the Jews and the Lies."[18]

Except for occasional favors and scattered instances of obedience shown the *Gauleiter*, Liebel ran the city's affairs largely unhindered. Prostesting strongly that he was not operating a welfare institution, the mayor frequently rejected Streicher's attempt to force a crony into a city hall position. In addition, Liebel agreed to the *Gauleiter's* anti-Semitic measures only if he thought the proposed policy sound and feasible. One case of the mayor's flat rejection concerned Streicher's request for special street cars for Jews. Liebel dismissed this request promptly, adding that it was a ridiculous idea.

Despite abrupt rebuffs of this nature, Streicher was unable to overcome Liebel's dominance of the city's administrative affairs. Occasionally the *Gauleiter* would complain to Hitler that Liebel was disloyal or incompetent and should be replaced by a party member more dedicated to true *voelkisch* principles, but these arguments fell on deaf ears as Hitler continued to support Liebel and he remained Nuremberg's mayor long after Streicher disappeared from the political scene. Liebel reinforced his standing with Hitler by lavishly praising him on every possible occasion. The relationship between the *Gauleiter* and the mayor continued, until the end of the decade, as it had started—a surreptitious rivalry between two men, with very few major disruptions or consequential occurrences.

But this was not to be the case in Streicher's dealings with the police force, where leadership was quite inconsistent, usually manipulated by SS Chief Heinrich Himmler. Streicher had made known his desire for the police president's position in early March. At that time Bavarian Commissioner von Epp

blocked the appointment and Himmler moved in as temporary police president until he could find a Nazi official he
thought capable of handling the job and curbing Streicher,
whom he considered a dangerous nuisance.[19]

Himmler's choice for Nuremberg police president was an
aristocrat, Erasmus von Malsen-Ponickau, who almost instant-
ly became a subject of Streicher's animosity. In the case of
Ponickau, however, most of the difficulties he experienced
with Streicher as well as with other Nuremberg officials were
caused by his own actions. His attitude was cavalier, even to
his fellow SS men, whose company he shunned because he
felt they were below his social station in life. He aroused
Streicher's anger early in April, when he refused haughtily to
consider the *Gauleiter's* request to transfer a police official
who had publicly attacked the party. He further raised
Streicher's ire by refusing to attend a party meeting and by
issuing orders threatening the arrest of SS men who obeyed
the *Gauleiter's* orders. Ponickau was almost without support
in his efforts to oppose Streicher openly and to establish his
own hegemony of power in Nuremberg. Rank-and-file party
members did not trust this haughty newcomer, and experienced police officers were unconvinced of his capabilities as a
police administrator. Because of his insistence on long morning
horse rides and afternoon naps, he was infrequently
in his office. In addition, Ponickau, a married man, was often
seen squiring new theater girls around the town.[20]

Most routine administrative work in the police office was
conducted by another Himmler appointee, Deputy Police
President Dr. Benno Martin, who was a career civil servant
with a ten-year record of outstanding police work. Martin
was an educated man, having authored a widely used
textbook on police methods. He had also passed the State
Jurisprudence Examinations with high marks. He was a
veteran of World War I and although not a party member
until 1933, remained in the good graces of Himmler and
other top-ranking Nazis. From the time he became Ponickau's assistant, Martin developed a friendship with Streicher,
who expressed on several occasions that he respected Martin's
ability and reputation for efficient police work.

By midsummer of 1933, observers in Nuremberg reported
that Martin and Streicher were frequently in each other's
company. They seemed to be drawn together because of

mutual dislike and disrespect for Ponickau. However, Streicher's open cordiality towards Martin was also based on the respect he held for the police official's professional record and for a kindness he had shown him (Streicher) almost ten years earlier. In January, 1924, Streicher had been in jail and complained of the cold in his cell. Martin was the officer on duty in that police office and he had provided Streicher with an extra blanket. Martin said that Streicher never seemed to forget that small incident and told other persons about it on frequent occasions in later years.

By August, 1933, a crisis between Streicher and Ponickau was triggered by Martin, who reported an alleged conversation between himself and Ponickau to Streicher. In an evident attempt to ignite an open feud, Martin reported that he had been told by his superior officer that "he would fight with all his resources against *Gauleiter* Streicher, and anyone sent. . .to represent him." Martin also confided to Streicher that he felt compelled to report that Ponickau had "a certain hatred" for the *Gauleiter*. Within a few days a well publicized eruption of hostility between Streicher and Ponickau took place during final preparations for the annual Nuremberg Party-day Rally.

The public confrontation between the *Gauleiter* and police president was triggered by Ponickau's loud reprimand of Martin, who had been conversing with Streicher in an automobile at the rally site. Suspecting that the two were plotting against him, Ponickau shouted at Martin in front of a large group of party men that he should leave Streicher's company immediately. At this treatment of Martin, Streicher approached Ponickau with threatening gestures and the denunciation:

> You are a degenerated *Schweinhund*. I'll beat you with my riding whip about the ears, if you continue to provoke me in my *Gau*. The police president for me is Dr. Martin. . . .You are the meanest rascal I have ever met in uniform. . . .Go home, and take care of your estate.

Ponickau did not attempt to answer Streicher, instead he took out pen and paper and copied down the insulting words and walked away. Interestingly, Hitler was a witness to this scene, but moved away as though he had seen nothing.

Ponickau later reported the incident to his superior in the

Bavarian government, adding that only the presence of Hitler had kept him from knocking Streicher down on the spot. He demanded Streicher's banishment from office for this insult and that Martin be fired immediately for insubordination. But events proved that Martin had chosen sides correctly. After a short investigation, Himmler relieved Ponickau from his position, ruling that he was wrong to give Martin an order "which could not be carried out."

Himmler's choice for Ponickau's successor was an SA officer, Hans Guenther von Obernitz, who assumed his position on September 1, the day that the 1933 Nuremberg Party-day Rally opened. The new police president was more interested in party military and political affairs than police work and consequently left most of the operations of his office up to Martin, who had remained at his former post. Obernitz's first act was to order that all old (experienced) officers be fired and replaced by SA men, but Martin was able to stall this order in a tangle of red tape and keep the police force virtually intact. The new police president managed to avoid serious conflict with Streicher. However, he soon provoked the criticism of his superior officer, SA Colonel Hofmann of the District Police Office, because of allegedly encouraging illegal SA activities. Obernitz, who consistently subordinated police duties to SA activities, flagrantly ignored threats of censure by Hofmann and deliberately refused to carry out his orders. The feud between these two SA officials became so heated that eventually Obernitz commanded Martin to draw up an order for the arrest of Hofmann if he entered Nuremberg.

While nothing serious developed from this command, the feud was ended in late June when Hitler ordered the eradication of top SA men in the Roehm *Putsch*, a brutal scheme by the Nazi leader to nullify the overambitious and defiant leadership of the SA. Obernitz learned that he was among those slated for execution and, in desperation, begged Streicher for help. The *Gauleiter*, perhaps sensing that Obernitz's future loyalty would be useful, succeeded in intervening through Hitler, having Obernitz's name removed from the death list. The police president was relieved of his position but was subsequently named SA regional commander where he remained loyal to Streicher until the end of the decade.[21]

After Obernitz left the police office, Martin assumed command as deputy until he was officially named police president on September 30, 1934, remaining at that post until promoted to a higher SS position in 1942. From the time he began his police duties in Nuremberg, Martin proved to be a highly skilled political tactician. He outlasted his two predecessors and slowly built an almost impregnable power base in the police office. At the same time he was able to ingratiate himself with Streicher while keeping him from intervening in police affairs except in a few instances. To maintain his position, Martin knew he needed the *Gauleiter's* full cooperation and so he became "Streicher's man" publicly. At the same time, he realized that the support of Himmler as well as Hitler was necessary in case Streicher became unmanageable. As part of his survival strategy, Martin joined the Nazi party in August, 1933, and shortly afterwards became an SS officer, nominally under Himmler's direct jurisdiction.

When he received his official appointment from Himmler, Martin was instructed, in the hearing of others, to "get along with Streicher." It seems certain that he also was instructed secretly by the SS chief to maintain close surveillance on Streicher at all times and to compile a confidential dossier on the *Gauleiter's* unethical or illegal activities. Whether Himmler's instructions were in the nature of routine police procedures or whether he was plotting the *Gauleiter's* political demise at this early date is uncertain. Yet, Martin proved unusually adept at playing this type of double-game. His success in this role attests to his ability as a crafty police officer. But also to his advantage was his ability at certain social talents, such as winning the admiration of a person like Holz for outstanding drinking capabilities or entertaining Hitler on his visits with charming stories or attentive listening. One technique used by Martin was to prepare for Hitler's favorite subject of conversation—operettas—by reading up on an obscure operetta just before Hitler arrived.[22]

While Martin usually managed to keep Streicher from intervening in police affairs, there were a few occasions when this proved impossible. One such occasion was the well publicized beating that the *Gauleiter* allegedly inflicted on a Nuremberg citizen named Steinrueck, who was locked in a jail cell. This occurred in early July, 1934, in the turgid climate immediately after the Roehm *Putsch*. Streicher appeared extremely nervous, possibly worried about his own fate. While he was sitting in a restaurant with Martin, Holz, and Koenig, news came of Steinrueck's arrest for having allegedly said: "It would have been better to have killed Streicher than those in the SA." Streicher demanded that the man be brought immediately to the restaurant, but Holz and Martin talked him out of it, only to have Streicher spring to his feet and insist that they go to police headquarters. Arriving there, the *Gauleiter* ordered the cell door unlocked and he entered to accost the accused prisoner.

Accounts of the extent of Streicher's violent action inside the jail cell are somewhat contradictory. According to later testimony by Steinrueck and an attending police officer, Streicher began beating his victim mercilessly with his riding whip and while Steinrueck did not raise a hand to hit back, Streicher continued beating him until he fell unconscious to the floor. Included in this testimony was the statement that Martin did not witness the scene "having been called away." Martin, however, filed a report the same night which led to an investigation by the Bavarian state attorney. Included in it was a medical report by a physician who had examined Steinrueck soon after Streicher left the jail. The doctor minimized the results of the beating as only minor bruises on the body and head.[2][3]

Findings of the state attorney's investigation were brought into the open in 1940, during a formal party hearing on charges against Streicher for overall misconduct as *Gauleiter*. In the matter of the Steinrueck affair, the state attorney had found that Streicher was guilty of illegal and brutal assault. This jurist added that because of the preponderance of contrary evidence, the initial reports of the attending physician and Martin were discounted. Conclusions of the investigation stated that Streicher had acted as a sadist, beating the helpless Steinrueck without mercy into a state of unconsciousness, then bragging about it to his colleagues with the remark: "Now I am relieved, I really needed that!"

In defending his actions in this affair, Streicher did not deny making this comment, but vehemently insisted that he only struck the prisoner once or twice to "teach him a lesson" because of the serious threats he had made and because he had acted like a coward in the jail cell. Although severely questioned, Martin refused to change any details of his initial police report. He repeated that he had been present when the scene occurred and that Streicher had struck the prisoner only a few times. At this hearing Martin also volunteered the statement that he had talked later to the prisoner and found him to be a person of lowly character.[24]

Despite Martin's reputation as an upright police officer, his capability for devious conduct seems to have surfaced in his handling of the Steinrueck case. It is almost certain that he altered the truth in his report and most likely persuaded the attending physician to do the same. His account of the beating was inconsistent with that of all other witnesses and the only one to support Streicher's version of the assault. Admitting to bias against Steinrueck's character, Martin nevertheless released him, dropping all charges. Also, it was known that the attending physician, Dr. Anton Wegner, was a personal friend of the police president and could have easily been persuaded to report only minimal injuries to the prisoner. While Martin was secretly accumulating incriminating evidence against Streicher, he probably felt in this case he should still curry the *Gauleiter's* favor. On the other hand, he may have wanted to protect his professional reputation by covering up the brutal results of his own failure to protect his prisoner. Despite the questionable handling of the Steinrueck affair, Martin remained consistent in his version as stated in his original police report and he repeated this story at five subsequent criminal trials after World War II and again reiterated it emphatically in a 1970 interview related to this study.

Perhaps the most important result of the Steinrueck beating was the more stringent limits placed on Streicher's power over the Nuremberg police office. Following his initial report on the affair, Martin was called into the district SS office for questioning. His defense emphasized that he had been unable to prevent the assault because Streicher was his superior. In subsequent official memos to both Martin and Streicher, Himmler rejected this excuse stressing that the *Gauleiter* had no legal jurisdiction over the police president. Censuring both for the occurrence of this violence upon a "citizen of pure blood," Himmler threatened Streicher with "severe consequences" if his illegal meddling in police affairs continued.

Although Streicher usually disregarded threats or orders from any Nazi official except Hitler, he may have sensed that open conflict with the SS chief in this matter was unwise. This seems evident inasmuch as the *Gauleiter* made no further overt attempts to override Martin's authority after mid-1934. At the same time, the police president seemed to exercise caution in dealing with Streicher and avoid testing his patience. He followed a policy of general non-interference with the *Gauleiter's* activities until the last year of the decade. Despite this outward attitude of cooperation, Martin was able to maintain surveillance on Streicher by obtaining his agreement for the need to post day and night police guards outside his office and residence.

Streicher's acceptance of the limits placed on his political authority by both Martin and Liebel was perhaps also the result of his preoccupation with his major interests, which were the local party organization and his anti-Semitic publications. His base of operations was Nuremberg, which had dominated the surrounding rural areas since medieval days. Provincial Franconia was a complex of hundreds of small villages, traditionally strongholds of conservatism and rigid religious conformity. Pinpointed throughout the countryside were larger communities which had been organized as Nazi provincial centers, headed by an NSDAP *Kreisleiter*, a title coined for lesser party leaders directly subordinate to the *Gauleiter*. In Franconia Streicher had been almost solely responsible for the organization of these rural party centers as well as for the assignment of the various *Kreisleiter*, who in most cases adopted the bellicose attitude and tactics of Streicher.

With the Nazi assumption of power, it was no longer necessary for the *Gauleiter* to concentrate his efforts on meetings and speeches to attract party members and support. Instead, Streicher now kept a close check on his *Kreisleiter*, constantly calling them in to his Nuremberg office for instructional or informational sessions. Business affairs at these meetings were usually dominated by problems regarding Streicher's rigid policy against the encroachment or political interference in his domain by other Nazi agencies such as the SA, SS or the district governmental office at Ansbach. Except on rare occasions there were no serious problems involved in maintaining adherence to National

Socialist rule in the rural areas and Streicher spent little time outside Nuremberg until he retired to a farm near the village of Pleikershof after 1939. Throughout the agricultural hinterland of Franconia, the government of Hitler had been accepted by small farmers with the same outward unconcern and calm as their forefathers had displayed at the ascension of Emperor William II or the establishment of the Weimar Republic.[25]

Under Streicher's jurisdiction, Franconian villagers were not disrupted from their passive modes of existence and generally were allowed to pursue their agricultural interests without political interference. Since Jews hardly ever conducted business outside the larger cities, villagers rarely came in contact with them and were largely unaffected by the odious Nazi racial laws. Streicher's anti-Semitism did not seem important to the average Franconian farmer who, typically, was concerned mostly about the prices of agricultural products, which after 1934 moved upwards steadily. Overall satisfaction with their life-style during the Nazi pre-war years was indicated in later interviews with dozens of Franconian farmers in *Bierstube*, small village drinking establishments. The villagers stated no major objections to pre-war Nazi governance and generally spoke favorably about their relationships with Streicher.

In view of Streicher's known behavioral characteristics, it is not surprising that he would have gotten along well with these small farmers, and possibly showed them some partiality during the years of his political rule. The villagers were no threat to him and he may have realized the value of their support in ongoing differences with officials of the Bavarian government. Streicher's problems with these bureaucrats stemmed from his own volatile nature and from the chaotic organizational structure of the Hitler regime. In the Nazi system of governance, the authority of the *Gauleiter* was ill-defined and it usually varied according to the individual's aggressive capabilities. In addition, the powers of the *Gauleiter* were superimposed upon, or were overlapped by the powers of other officials in positions of the formal state government organization. In Bavaria, district political centers had been established in the 19th century as headquarters for the civil administration of the provincial areas. District headquarters for Streicher's Franconian *Gau* was Ansbach, while the formal head of the provincial government residing there was the district president, Colonel Hofmann, who had been named to that office on April 1, 1933.

While most *Gauleiter* had become nominal presidents of their provinces, Streicher said he had not sought this position because he did not like the "limited confines" of a bureaucrat. Without doubt, Streicher felt that his activities may have been hampered by the limits of the district president's authority. As matters developed, Streicher overrode the dominion of Hofmann, who from the outset tried in vain to restrain the *Gauleiter's* anti-Semitic policies. He also attempted to stop the Nuremberg NSDAP from forcing more party members on the town council. Hofmann not only incurred the bitter animosity of Streicher, but also was disliked by most local Nazis almost immediately after he assumed his new office.

In less than two years, Streicher was able to force Hofmann out of office and influence the naming of Dr. Hans Dippold in his place.[26] A former school administrator, the new district president was a former acquaintance of the *Gauleiter.* He became obscure as a president and almost totally dominated by Streicher's strong will. Dippold privately expressed deep personal hatred for Streicher and filed innocuous secret reports to the Bavarian government regarding problems caused by the *Gauleiter's* policies, yet frequently appeared frightened of him in public. One such instance was reported by the police attending a large ceremony. Dippold allegedly permitted himself to be called *"Arschloch"* by Streicher and offered no remonstrance. On another occasion, Dippold presented the *Gauleiter* with a riding whip as a present at a birthday party, then paled as Streicher grinned devilishly and shook the whip at him remarking that now he (Dippold) would have to behave or he'd feel his present on his buttocks.

Dippold remained district president from 1935 to 1940 and provided no evident deterrent in limiting Streicher's political activities during these years. On the contrary, the *Gauleiter's* ability to degrade the Bavarian district president in public served to strengthen his public image as the "dictator of Franconia." The fact that the meek Dippold was retained in his post until the end of the decade also lent credence to the unassailability of the *Gauleiter's* position.

The official Nazi head of the Bavarian government, General von Epp, an outspoken critic of Streicher, tried continuously to silence or to oust him from the party and his position. Since the Roehm *Putsch*, Hitler had elevated most state commissioners, including von Epp, to special positions as *Statthalter*, or regent, for their own states. In most political matters, von Epp ruled Bavaria with dictatorial powers, yet his efforts to banish Streicher proved futile. The best that von Epp could do was continually try to "get the goods" on the *Gauleiter* by sending various Munich officials to Nuremberg for occasional inquiries into alleged party or governmental abuses, but Streicher treated these investigators with contemptuous rudeness as he did Dippold.

Von Epp appealed periodically to Hitler, complaining of the confusion in the Bavarian governmental structure caused by Streicher's insolent disregard for regulated political authority. These appeals were echoed strongly in Berlin by Schacht, minister of finance, who understood the serious economic consequences if Streicher's Nuremberg anti-Semitic policies were to spread throughout Germany. Beginning with the April 1 boycott and the dismissal of all Jews from public or professional positions, Streicher had stepped up his racial persecution by threats and actual punishment to persons who worked for Jewish firms or did business with them. Harassment of the Jews in the form of increased economic restriction was intensified by the ever-present *Stuermer*, spouting radical anti-Semitic polemics. In late 1934, one *Stuermer* headline announced the "scientific finding" that blood corpuscles of Jews were different and the leading article included the recommendation that laws for severe penalties for intercourse between Jews and non-Jews be enacted.[27]

Hardships created by early economic pressures against the Jewish community as well as the embarassment from the flow of degradation from the *Stuermer*, and other anti-Semitic publications, were reflected in the diminishing Jewish population. By mid-June, 1933, 700 of Nuremberg's 8,266 Jews had already left the city. Yet these figures would have undoubtedly been higher except for the *Reichsfluchtsteuer*, a Nazi-imposed tax on citizens (especially Jews) desiring to leave Germany. The tax was levied at the rate of one-fourth of the total value of all assets of individuals or immediate families, and payable in cash before receipt of the emigration permit. To prevent any chance of minimizing this tax, the provincial revenue office kept close track of any irregular transfers of capital as well as legal documents such as promissory notes.[28]

The total demise of Jewish business establishments in Nuremberg occurred over a period of approximately six years, yet in some cases failures or closings of Jewish firms were recorded less than one year after the April, 1933 boycott. A typical illustration of early collapse of a merchandizing enterprise in Nuremberg was documented by Hugo Gutmann, business manager of the Hartmann, Ltd., Company, wholesale dealer in office equipment. Gutmann related the "snowballing" of business losses suffered under the rule of Streicher. While the four-day boycott did not result in serious trade reverses, the ban on advertisements by Jewish firms in National Socialist newspapers was costly. Then, Gutmann stated, the majority of Hartmann's regular customers were eliminated by a Streicher edict prohibiting governmental and civil service offices from purchasing supplies and equipment from Jewish firms. Because of the sharp drop in sales and the slanderous anti-Semitic publicity, most of the leading manufacturers of office machines and furniture withdrew Hartmann's sales' franchises. By the end of 1934, with only inferior merchandise to offer its customers, the firm was struggling to make ends meet but then closed its doors for good when a vicious Christmas boycott, initiated by Streicher that year, drove away the few customers who still tried to do business with the Hartmann Company.

The rather rapid collapse of the Hartmann firm might be viewed as merciful when compared to the many cases of Nuremberg Jewish business owners who endured years of Streicher's rule only to be swindled out of their businesses and properties later under the *Gauleiter's* "aryanization" program. The full impact of this series of illegal appropriations was unleashed in 1938 and virtually wiped out the balance of the remaining Jewish propertied inhabitants in Nuremberg. These criminal acts also resulted in the political ruination of Streicher and will be discussed in detail subsequently. However, the initial phases of what some former Nurembergers called "creeping aryanization" began in early 1934, with a Hitler edict entitled "Law for the Organization of National Labor." This was intended as a measure to disenfranchise labor unions and to provide employers with more authority over their employees.[29] Yet, Streicher twisted the meaning of this edict and proclaimed that according to his interpretation, the law meant that no Jew could be manager of a Jewish business. Then he ordered that Jewish owners were to appoint a National Socialist party member as business manager who would have the powers to make independent business decisions.

Streicher's ridiculous interpretation of this edict was called to the attention of Schacht, who, without consulting Hitler, notified Nuremberg businessmen and Streicher of the correct meaning of the law. Schacht also emphasized that no governmental or party official had authority to force management changes on any business establishment without the written permission of the Economic Ministry Office in Berlin.[30] Knowledgeable observers theorize that Schacht, almost single-handedly, provided the principal obstacle against Streicher's ambitions to begin the systematic and total economic ruination of Nuremberg Jews as early as 1934. This theory is substantiated by the fact that the full fury of the Nuremberg aryanization program broke out about the same time that Schacht was dismissed by Hitler in early 1939.

While Streicher was blocked in his attempt to utilize Hitler's January 20th edict as legal authority to implement a full-scale aryanization program at an early date, there was little protection provided Jews from isolated, unauthorized harassment, dubbed "creeping" aryanization. These illegal acts were usually perpetrated by SA men, subordinates of von Obernitz, who, by late 1934, was under Streicher's domination. On some occasions, gangs of six to ten brown-shirted bullies would appear at the main entrances of a Jewish store and block customers from entering or leaving for several hours at a time. Similar SA gangs would engage in blocking delivery services to another Jewish establishment and throw the merchandise into the street or beat up the driver. A favorite form of annoyance was to challenge all customers entering a Jewish store and examine their identification cards or to threaten civil servants that they would be reported as disloyal Germans not deserving of public employment if they purchased anything. Between 1933 and 1938, SA bullies also tormented Jewish businesses by spitting and cursing at their customers as they left the stores or seizing packages recently purchased and tramping on them or throwing them in the street.

While extensive and generally brutal personal abuse of Jews in Franconia did not begin until late 1938, sporadic unpunished acts of violence against them began almost as soon as Hitler was named Chancellor. The majority of these cases involved private SA beatings in larger towns. However, there were several instances recorded of Jewish persecution involving extreme forms of degradation and viciousness as well as death. As early as mid-March, 1933, Himmler ordered the arrest of a number of politically prominent Franconian Jews. This group, numbering approximately twenty, was sent to the concentration camp at Dachau where all suffered beatings while some were forced to eat their own feces and to drink their own urine. Nine of these men were killed there and their bodies were returned home with bullet holes in the back.[31] An eyewitness at Dachau said later that these prisoners had been tricked by a guard who ordered them to pick up debris near the fence, then shot them in cold blood alleging they were trying to escape.

An occasion of SA anti-Semitic crime in July, 1933, was initiated by orders of Obernitz, who ordered his men to arrest approximately 300 Jewish persons, some of whom were elderly men and women. These people were herded together in a field and forced to crawl on their hands and knees and eat the grass that had been recently soiled by horses and cows. Another form of SA persecution in the early years of Nazi rule involved arresting non-Jewish women seen with Jewish men and shaving their heads and parading them in the streets and on theater stages with sandwich-board signs over their shoulders stating their names and that they had had sex relations with a Jewish man, whose name was also on the sign.[32]

A case of sustained small-town violence in the early Nazi years occurred in Guenzenhausen, which stood alone in Franconia as a rural community with a relatively large Jewish population. Anti-Semitic disturbances here began in April and May, 1933, with the breaking of windows.[33] In August a peasant was attacked by an SA gang after he left a tavern owned by a Jew named Strauss. After suffering blows by fists and clubs, the victim was led through the streets with a placard fastened to his back with the words: "I drink my beer at a Jew's place!" At various times during the ensuing months, SA groups gathered in front of Strauss' tavern, shouting threats and breaking windows, and repeatedly forced Strauss to close his business for several days at a time.

In late March, 1934, tensions erupted when two SA leaders, named Baer and Kaiser, entered the tavern and physically abused a customer who happened to be a rural mayor. Later, Baer attacked Strauss' son, dragging him down a stairway and outside the tavern, where the SA mob beat the young man into unconsciousness. Baer later claimed that he had been "forced" into drastic action because the young Jew had spit at him. In an example of SA arrogance, Baer added in his report that he felt he had done his duty as a good SA officer because the police in Guenzenhausen were too cowardly to arrest criminals like young Strauss. Baer also alleged that the crowd had demanded the punishment of the "insolent young Jew."

After this beating, Baer had re-entered the house and arrested the elder Strauss and his wife and they were taken, with the unconscious boy, to the local jail. There, Frau Strauss protested that the family was innocent of any wrongdoing. Baer then struck her in the face with his fist several times and ordered everything in their house destroyed. Baer's men then ran amok in the town with the bestiality of a predatory wolf pack. Shouting insults to the words of caution by local police, the SA gang chopped up the furnishings in the Strauss home and indiscriminately "arrested" thirty-three Jews whom they beat with clubs and escorted to the jail. Baer seized one of these victims, named Rosenfelder, and asked him if he was a coward and when the shaken man answered in the affirmative, Baer beat him again, severely, and sent him home with orders to wait there for further questioning. The mob later gathered in front of Rosenfelder's house chanting anti-Semitic slogans and then broke in with an axe. Afterwards, neighbors found the house in shambles and Rosenfelder's sister at the side of her brother who was lying on the floor of a shed, dead of bullet wounds. The next morning another Jewish man was found dead of knife wounds.

An SA report was filed the next day omitting mention of the unwarranted brutality. Instead, the report stated that the Jews had begun the altercation by taunting some SA men drinking beer in Strauss' tavern. Then, because of Jewish threats, SA leaders ordered homes to be searched for illegal weapons. The SA fabrication continued that both Rosenfelder and the other Jew were found dead by suicide. However, a governmental investigation, held immediately afterwards, found the SA report unacceptable because of the severe contradiction of facts by eye-witnesses. Some local policemen also attested to the truth of the SA violence and provided substantiating evidence that suicide was impossible in the cases of both dead men.

The Guenzenhausen atrocity was denounced by Streicher, who acted as if he was horrified when he heard the news. He repeatedly claimed to Bavarian authorities that he had consistently forbidden personal abuses to Jews in his *Gau*. District President Hofmann brought charges of felonious assault against the town's SA company. Twenty-three SA men were tried in a Nazi civil court the next month with the result that most of them were found guilty of assault and battery and sentenced to a few months in jail. Strangely, Baer was not punished by a jail sentence but was stripped of his membership in the party and the SA. Further results of the Guenzenhausen affair included the firing of Hofmann, who Streicher managed to incriminate as the responsible authority. Arguing that the police president had bragged publicly that Hitler had given him the job of cleaning up the Franconian SA, Streicher claimed he had trusted that Hofmann was capable of this task and was sorry to see that he had failed.

A grisly epilogue to the March, 1934 violence in Guenzenhausen occurred some weeks after Baer was ousted from the party and the SA. Perhaps intent on revenge, he entered the Strauss tavern in mid-July and shot both father and son, killing the father. Leaving the tavern he shouted that he would kill twenty more Jews unless the jailed SA men were released. Arrested immediately by the police, Baer could not carry out this threat but was jailed until brought to trial. The ruling judge, an NSDAP member, found him guilty of manslaughter, then placed him on probation with the stipulation that he remain outside his home county until further notice.

These crimes in rural Franconia were among the earliest public fatalities of Jews at the hands of the Nazis and received widespread hostile publicity. Foreign newspapers condemned Hitler's anti-Semitic policies, claiming the brutal acts were reflective of the racial prejudice of the Nazi regime. In like manner, the flagrant miscarriages of justice in both of the trials were criticized as results of Hitler's recent racial laws. Most of all, however, the foreign press focused on Streicher as the direct cause of the Guenzenhausen violence because of his reputation as the Franconian dictator and as the owner and editor of the *Stuermer*, which was now circulated in some nations outside Germany.[34] While Hitler and other ranking Nazis appeared aloof of the criticism and seemingly dismissed the violence as a local problem, Streicher wrote many long articles, published in the *Stuermer* and most other Nazi newspapers, denouncing the violence and repeatedly stating that he was deeply embarrassed by it because of his "pledge" that no Jew was in danger in his *Gau*.[35]

Assertions by Streicher that he pledged no harm to come to Jews under Nazi rule were ringing hollow as early as mid-1934. Only very naive or gullible people could believe that the Franconian dictator did not favor punishing Jews harshly after reading one or two issues of the *Stuermer*. His promises of non-violent treatment to those he swore were his deadliest enemies seemed as an evil mockery of the truth to persons who were aware of the fate of the twenty Franconian Jews sent to Dachau in early 1933 or to those who witnessed the ongoing creeping aryanization in Nuremberg, or the atrocities committed by Obernitz in mid-1933. After the odious Guenzenhausen crimes, Streicher was not only being blamed in many newspapers throughout Europe for the bodily harm suffered by Jews in Franconia, but he was also being severely criticized for this violence by some National Socialist party officials. In the manslaughter trial of Baer, one minor SA officer filed a report which speculated candidly that perhaps the reason for Baer's violence was that he was only twenty-two years old and somewhat gullible as well as over-enthusiastic, conceivably indoctrinated in the hatred created in the Nuremberg area for many years, especially by Streicher, and possibly believing that he had acted as Hitler secretly wanted brave Nazis to act.[36]

The above suggestion that Baer's crimes may have been a

result of anti-Semitic brain-washing is of crucial significance here. This was the first known admission by an NSDAP member that serious crimes could emanate from the hatred of Jews preached by some party leaders. The officer's report also pointed a guilty finger at Streicher, who was the Nuremberg area's principal Jew-baiter, and the one most responsible for Baer's racial indoctrination. In larger context, the report also brings into view the important question of placing the blame for the later mass atrocities which befell the Jews. It is almost certain that the intensive anti-Semitic propaganda of Streicher and other Nazi leaders fostered deep hatred of Jews in the minds of countless young Nazis which, in many cases, sanctified overt expressions of brutal and criminal acts against Jews in Franconia as well as elsewhere in Europe. Yet, as mentioned previously, Streicher often tried to convince his readers and listeners of his genuine intention to protect Franconian Jews from bodily harm. In August, 1935, he repeated this oftspoken "pledge" but in more sweeping terms, warning all National Socialists to refrain from physically abusing Jews. Speaking before a capacity audience in the Berlin Sports-Palace, Streicher intoned this warning during a section of his speech concerning recent attacks against him in foreign newspapers that referred to him as the "bloody czar of Franconia." Professing his peaceful intentions, Streicher warned his audience against violent action against Jews:

Any party comrade who believes he can serve the high goals of our movement by beating up a Jew or by breaking his windows never was and never will be a National Socialist. Neither do I believe that the disgraceful activities. . . observed here and there were undertaken by National Socialists. They were not National Socialists who did that. They were provokers!. . .Anyone who believes he can approach the solution of the problem with such external action is too stupid to grasp the graveness of the situation.[37]

Streicher's references in this quote to the "high goals" and "grave situation" undoubtedly reflected his unique pseudo-philosophic viewpoint that the struggle against the Jews was an honorable battle, to be waged within parameters of legality. Many times, especially in *Stuermer* articles, he tried to create the impression that his anti-Semitism was tantamount to a religious crusade. More than any other Nazi racist, Streicher had concentrated his attacks on the philosophic and religious aspects of anti-Semitism. Again and again he focused his arguments on interpretations of Hebrew scriptures, although many of these were later proven to be forgeries or distortions of earlier Hebrew writings.

Hitler, who was among the listeners of Streicher's Berlin speech, was evidently aware that the *Gauleiter* was probably deluding himself when he voiced repeatedly his aim for the demise of the Jews without violence or bloodshed. Although Hitler often stated his admiration for Streicher's dedicated anti-Semitism, he also noted in one of his later table conversations that he (Streicher) might have shown too much tolerance toward the Jews. Perhaps referring to this non-violent approach to anti-Semitism, Hitler claimed that Streicher "idealized" the Jew, adding that "the Jew is baser, fiercer, more diabolical than Streicher depicted him."[38]

On the other hand, it seems inconceivable that a person of normal intelligence could conduct himself as Streicher did and be sincere in his intention that no bodily harm would result eventually. There is little doubt that in vilifying the Jews as consistently as he did, he aimed at convincing his readers and listeners that Jews were the mortal and dangerous enemies of "true Germans." In addition, as a Nazi, he should have been well schooled in the significance of propaganda as one of the most important stimulants of men's beliefs and actions. In view of these facts, it seems most likely that Streicher was lying, or "talking in thin air" in his pledges and warnings to keep Jews safe from harm. His attempts at the pseudo-philosophic approach to anti-Semitism may have resulted from his school-teacher training or from his admiration of the works of outstanding racist authors such as Theodor Fritsch or Houston S. Chamberlain. Further, Hitler's comment about Streicher's tolerance toward Jews cannot be taken seriously inasmuch as it stands alone opposed to the fact that Streicher's racial fanaticism was his main strength with Hitler. Despite consistent pressure by high-ranking party members, Hitler supported Streicher's anti-Semitic publications until his last days in power.[39]

Regardless of the paradoxical nature of Streicher's stated intentions concerning the treatment of the Jews, many of Hitler's advisors were convinced that the *Gauleiter's* radical anti-Semitism was to blame for the alarming economic losses and physical violence reported in Franconia since the April 1, 1933, boycott. While high-ranking party officials such as Schacht and Cabinet Minister Wilhelm Frick voiced disgust with Streicher over these events in Franconia, Hitler seemingly illustrated his approval of the *Gauleiter's* activities by awarding him titles and by honoring him on special occasions. At the tenth anniversary commemoration of the Munich Beer Hall *Putsch* on November 9, 1933, Hitler insisted that Streicher again take the honored position at the head of the large columns of party dignitaries following the footsteps of those who marched to the *Feldherrenhalle* where sixteen "loyal Nazis" had been killed by policemen and army regulars. A few weeks later, Hitler notified Streicher that for "outstanding services" he was "elected" to a seat in the *Reichstag*. The following February, Hitler bestowed on Streicher the title of Honorary SA *Gruppenfuehrer* (group leader).[40] One Nazi newspaper speculated that Roehm had recommended this decoration in an effort to strengthen the bond between the *Gauleiter* and the SA. This speculation, however, seems groundless because at the time of this honorary gesture, Hitler was already planning ways in which to weaken Roehm's political powers and connections.

On February 11, 1935, Hitler paid special tribute to Streicher by attending a large banquet in honor of the *Gauleiter's* fiftieth birthday.[41] A crowd of approximately 150 party members, including Hitler's personal entourage, feted Streicher at the banquet with gifts and words of praise. Hitler followed a number of local Nazis offering complimentary words and toasts. He began a rather lengthy commendation by presenting Streicher with an autographed photograph of himself. A newspaper account of this occasion noted that Hitler's words touched the emotions of Streicher and some of his close associates, who reportedly appeared enraptured and close to tears. Hitler began talking about his personal visit to Streicher's home earlier in the day, then read the inscription he had written on his gift to Streicher. It expressed the close and friendly bond between himself and the *Gauleiter*. Following this, Hitler continued in the same cordial terms:

....On this day of honor for Julius Streicher, I remember who stood faithfully by my side. It was trust like this that moved mountains....Streicher is a companion....and I know that there is a man here in Nuremberg who does not waver for one second and stands firmly behind me in any situation. . . .

Hitler's cordial expressions honoring Streicher were well publicized in party newspapers. It is possible that this public reaffirmation of close association between Hitler and Streicher may have influenced Bavarian officials at the State Ministry for Education and Culture at Munich to approve an honorary promotion for Streicher from *Hauptlehrer* (head teacher) to *Oberlehrer* (senior teaching master). At the same time the ministry ordered an increase in Streicher's school-teacher's pension, which had amounted to 3375 marks annually for a period of approximately twenty-seven years. As a result of this grant, Streicher would receive a slight boost in his annual pension as well as a windfall payment of some 2700 marks, representing back-payments for the alleged shortage of 105 marks a year for the entire twenty-seven years since he began his teaching career early in the century.[42]

Hitler's loyalty to Streicher seemed, in some ways, to be related to his open admiration for Nuremberg. At each visit to the Franconian capital Hitler spoke in warm terms about his love for the city and spent hours with Liebel and some local architects discussing his plans to glorify Nuremberg with great edifices in keeping with its "esteemed" position in the history of the NSDAP. He frequently called Nuremberg the "cradle of National Socialism." In his book, *Mein Kampf*, Hitler lauds the city as the place where Streicher was able to establish a "bridge," connecting northern Germany to the Munich base of the young Nazi party. He also referred to Nuremberg in the later 1920's as the center of the most dedicated party members and the best disciplined local party organization.[43]

As a self-proclaimed authority on German history, Hitler may have also held Nuremberg in esteem because of its prominence as a bastion of German anti-Semitism, dating from medieval times. As a free imperial city, since 1219, Nuremberg was governed by an elitist ruling class that conducted unspeakable crimes against Jews. These included large-scale massacres and maiming for amusement and also selling them as slaves. In 1498, a law was promulgated banishing all Jews from the city, and the exclusion remained in effect for over 300 years, until Napoleon's edicts removed the ban in 1813. Although Jews re-entered the city throughout the 19th century, their numbers were relatively few, amounting to less than one percent of the city's population by 1920. Hostile attitudes against this tiny minority remained under the surface until re-emerging after the end of World War I, when widespread latent anti-Semitism became evident with the popular acceptance of the anti-Jewish polemics preached by men like Streicher.[44]

There is little question that Hitler credited Streicher as principally responsible for the 20th century revival of Nuremberg's tradition-bound anti-Semitism. In addition to his previously described racist publishing endeavors, which included hate-filled children's books, Streicher organized regular schooling sessions in the mid-1920's for adolescent and teen-aged members of the *Hitler Jugend* (youth groups). At these sessions, as in meetings for adults, Streicher and other Nazi spokesmen repeated, over and over, sensational and sordid lies about Jews. It was therefore not surprising that the Nuremberg area was the scene of Nazi Germany's earliest flagrant demonstrations of racial persecution and regained its odious historical reputation as the capital of anti-Semitism.

Hitler's favoritism for Nuremberg was further demonstrated in his repeated selection of the city as the site of the spectacular Nazi Party-day Rallies. Streicher had been the principal organizer of the first Nuremberg rally in 1923, and since then rallies had been held there in 1927 and 1929. The next one of these party conventions, in 1933, was the first of an uninterrupted series of annual rallies which terminated with the last one, in 1938, before the beginning of World War II. The 1933 rally was also the first unrestrained spectacular demonstration of National Socialist "aryan" superiority. Widely publicized as well as filmed, this colossal affair attracted over 500,000 visitors, including news correspondents from North and South America, Europe and Asia, as well as delegates from South America, Asia, Scandinavia and Italy. Streicher played a major role in organizing this rally and was also among the list of Nazi officials who droned long-winded speeches at the various centers of activity throughout the three-day schedule of events.[45]

In the series of annual rallies that followed 1933, the

overall format was generally the same but numbers of participants were added each year and staging and lighting effects became increasingly sensational and spectacular.

CHAPTER XI

THE NAZI POGROM UNLEASHED

The Party-day Rally of 1935 transcended all previous Nuremberg extravaganzas in scope and dramatic effect. This was the first of these annual events to include full-scale military demonstrations and maneuvers. Wave after wave of tanks, armored cars and mechanized artillery thundered in large arenas, engaged in mock battle, or paraded in formation. Bomber and fighter planes, flying in precise patterns, roared overhead and later staged an air attack on a model village.

While this military display must have been viewed with apprehension by many visitors, the implication of renewed German militarism did not seem as ominous from a humanistic standpoint as Hitler's opening speech, which focused on the newly promulgated Nuremberg Laws. Formally entitled "The Law for the Protection of German Blood and Honor," these edicts defined and legalized the subjugation of Jews to the status of second-class citizens.

It was speculated in some newspaper articles that Streicher had influenced Hitler strongly in the formulation of these decrees and had actually authored important sections of the law.[1] Some of these articles also stated that Streicher had insisted to Hitler that the racial edicts be proclaimed in Nuremberg. However, there is no evidence to substantiate these speculations. On the contrary, Streicher was not consulted when the early drafts of the laws were being written and had little or nothing to do with Hitler's last minute decision to announce the promulgation of these racial decrees in his opening speech at the 1935 Party-day Rally at Nuremberg.

According to his own sworn statement, Wilhelm Frick, Nazi Minister of the Interior, was principally responsible for the framing of the September, 1935, Nuremberg Laws. Frick testified in 1945 that Hitler had broached the subject to him by confiding that he felt the time ripe for everyone in Germany as well as all the world's nations to realize his racial goals. Frick also stated that Hitler had ordered him to have these laws prepared only a few days before the opening of the Nuremberg rally because this would be the best possible setting to announce these measures.[2]

With such short notice, Frick assigned three Berlin party headquarters lawyers, headed by Bernhard Loesener, an expert on "racial law," to write several drafts for Hitler's consideration. Streicher was not consulted at this time. However, Frick stated later that Streicher had informed him the previous year that he felt a racial law should be enacted which would define persons born of mixed marriages, up to an eighth of Jewish blood, as Jews. Streicher also allegedly recommended at this time that any person found guilty of "defiling German blood by intercourse" should be punished by death and that Jews as well as part-Jews should be compelled to undergo sterilization.[3]

The Nuremberg Laws, as recited by Hitler on September 15, 1935, were considerably more moderate than the enactments that Streicher and some other party radicals had promoted. It was noted by some authors that these racists expressed resentment at the restraint shown in some of the key sections of the edicts.[4] Loesener, who was present at the reading of the laws, claimed later that he had watched Streicher closely during the reading and observed that Streicher appeared angry and unhappy and commented under his breath that he disagreed with this kind of piecemeal handling of the Jewish question.[5]

Publicly, however, Streicher made no adverse comments about the laws. Instead, he voiced satisfaction that the matter was being solved "piece by piece" in the best German tradition. Feigning dignity and sincerity, he boasted: "We don't smash any windows and we don't smash Jews. Whoever engages in a single action of that kind is an enemy of the State, a provocateur, or even a Jew."[6]

Some Nazis, such as Loesener, were evidently convinced that the Nuremberg Laws, as promulgated, worked to the advantage of the Jews. These men argued that in many cases the specific ordinances curbed the arbitrariness of persons like Streicher and established certain standards of legal procedure where none had previously existed. This argument may bear some validity. However, Loesener exceeded all reasonable bounds of credibility by insisting to observers later that he saw an improvement in anti-Semitic practices in the three years following passage of the Nuremberg Laws.[7]

There exists overwhelming evidence to indicate that the

racial decrees announced by Hitler on September 15, 1935 proved far more harmful than beneficial to Jews in Franconia as well as throughout Germany. Overnight, by federal statute, the Nazis stopped the sporadic and arbitrary harassment of Jews which had gone on since the spring of 1933 and enacted severe and consistent measures which were enforceable by threat of stiff prison sentences. In distinct terms, full-blooded Jews and "part-Jews" were defined and shorn of most rights normally accorded citizens. They lost the right to vote and to hold public office. Assigned to a separate and inferior status, the Jews were no longer allowed to call themselves Germans. Marriages or extra-marital relations between them and non-Jews were forbidden.[8]

The draft of the Nuremberg Laws proclaimed at the 1935 rally included a number of other restrictions which throttled the Jews in many ways. But perhaps more damaging than these measures was the fact that the legalizing of racial policies provided a precedent, or a point of departure, for many subsequent anti-Semitic laws. Among these was the censorship of Jewish activities in the fields of writing and entertainment, which went to extraordinary lengths. For example, Jewish writers were forbidden to discuss a large number of "prohibited" subjects. Some of these were often innocuous, such as a description of a German landscape. In similar fashion many words and phrases were forbidden because they were deemed as having double meanings. The word "blond" was banned because it was thought to be a surreptitious code word for Nazi. For the slightest infraction of the tedious censorship rules periodicals were suspended for days or weeks and their writers and editors usually lost their journalist licences and were arrested. Jewish cultural activities were also severely censored. Jews were forbidden to perform works by aryan playwrights and composers. Musicians who had once played Bach, Beethoven and Wagner now were restricted to playing East European Jewish folksongs.

Among the few Jewish survivors of Nuremberg was a man known simply as Kolb, who described in an interview two cases which illustrate the flagrant miscarriages of justice in Nuremberg in the weeks after passage of the racial laws.[10] One Jewish man, whose initials were D. L., received a four-year prison sentence because he allegedly had touched a German woman's bosom three times and had kissed her. The second case involved a prominent Nuremberg resident, Leo Katzenberger, who had for obscure reasons incurred the wrath of the *Stuermer*, which then demanded his punishment. Katzenberger was finally arrested and tried on a trumped-up charge of sexual relations with a woman, whose home he had been seen leaving after visiting with both her and her husband. During the trial, both husband and wife testified under oath that the families had been friends for years. But the couple was charged with perjury and their testimony discounted, Katzenberger was found guilty and sentenced to death and this verdict was announced publicly on poster columns as well as in the *Stuermer*.

When the Nuremberg Laws were first announced by Hitler, Streicher was undoubtedly dissatisfied with the moderate nature of some of the key sections. However, in most of his public statements he appeared to be in total agreement with the overall concept of channeling anti-Semitic practices into law. For more than two years prior to passage of the racial edicts, he had advocated in many speeches and *Stuermer* articles the need for German national laws to "protect the race." Shortly after the promulgation of the Nuremberg Laws he reaffirmed his public support for these legalistic anti-Semitic measures in a speech before a large audience at the Berlin Sports-Palace. Addressing the topic "The Meaning of the Nuremberg Laws," Streicher not only endorsed the new edicts but actually presented them as "the solution" to the Jewish question:

> In the Third Reich the Jewish question has been solved by law. Anyone today who resorts to individual action is an enemy of the movement. . . .Within the framework of the Nuremberg Laws the Jew can live with us in peace, but he too must leave us in peace. . . .But we shall take care that the laws are kept, that they are respected, and never shall we tolerate their infringement.[11]

In addition to urging and endorsing the new racial laws, he also evidently aimed at promoting a European-wide agreement for the ultimate development of international legal restrictions against Jews. In mid-May, 1935, Streicher had organized, in Nuremberg, the first large-scale rally of the Anti-Semitic World League. This event attracted anti-Semites from most all European nations as well as hundreds of NSDAP leaders and representatives of the army and national police. The Hercules-Velodrome was the site of the speaker's podium, but five other halls were used for the overflow crowds, where loudspeakers carried the words of the rally leaders. Streicher and a French racial agitator, Jean Boissel, were the featured speakers. Streicher's speeches contained his usual polemics and warnings about the eternal Jew and his goal to dominate the world. Boissel was almost as radical as Streicher in his anti-Jewish denunciations. An excerpt of one of his speeches indicates his opinion that the fight against Jews should be carried on internationally:

> Today I have come to you as a Frenchman, as a front-line fighter. . .in order to expose the enemy, who is our enemy and your enemy: All Juda! Four years we were engaged in combat. Our united armies should have moved out together to fight to the last drop the scourge of the world, the Jews![12]

Boissel's sentiments favoring international cooperation in the fight against Jews were echoed by other foreign leaders, including Sir Oswald Mosley, British Fascist leader, who could not attend the rally but sent the following excerpted telegram:

> Dear Mr. Streicher:. . .I very much appreciate your message in the middle of this, our tough fight. The power of Jewish corruption must be defeated in all major countries before Europe's future in justice and peace can be secured. . . .Your most devoted. . . .
>
> Mosley. [13]

The cautionary words of Boissel and Mosley seemed to focus on the major argument—fear of Jews—that Nazi racial propagandists had been emphasizing since the end of World War I. In the twelve years since the beginning of regular *Stuermer* publication, the theme of fear had always been the bulwark of Streicher's anti-Semitic polemics. With its ever-present by-line, "The Jews are our Misfortune," *Stuermer* articles incessantly presented grotesquely caricatured Jews and their "evil ambitions" as the greatest danger to German society.

Considered rationally, the effectiveness of fear as a major anti-Semitic propaganda weapon would have been almost nullified after the legalization of discriminatory practices against the Jews in September. Stripped of normal political rights, the Jews in Germany had overnight become second-class citizens, rendered almost impotent as an economic force. In months to come their Nazi masters would levy stringent emigration taxes which would hold most of them as increasingly impoverished and helpless prisoners.

Consistent with the unreasoning attitude of a confirmed historical anti-Semite, Streicher did not diminish themes of fear in *Stuermer* articles after passage of the Nuremberg Laws. Initially, he capitalized on the promulgation of these edicts by emphasizing that the legalization of racially discriminatory policies was proof that his long-standing struggle against the Jews was justified and righteous.

Streicher also wrote or approved the publication of *Stuermer* articles that emphasized the need for laws to further restrict the rights and actions of Jews. The following excerpt from a late 1935 *Stuermer* article typifies these illogical arguments:

> Jews are injurious and carriers of many sicknesses. . . .Where they settle and increase in numbers. . . .they cause the same reactions as a virus to a human body. . . .And as the human body tries to fight off a virus, or gain control over it, the non-Jewish people (in Germany) had no choice but to (legally) gain control over the Jews. . . .[14]

A number of *Stuermer* articles after the 1935 Party-day Rallies stressed the race-purity aspect of the Nuremberg Laws. From this viewpoint, Streicher and his writers were able to develop sensational stories dealing with sex-oriented racial fantasies. A January, 1936 *Stuermer* issue carried a front-page article of this nature which was entitled "The Alien Eggwhite":

> The alien eggwhite is the seed of a male Jew. . .it is taken in by the female and entered into her blood during the act of copulation. . . .One act of intercourse between a Jew and a German girl is enough to poison her blood forever. . . .She will never be able to have pure aryan children even if she marries a German man. . . . She will only have bastards, in whose body will live two souls. . .and they will be ugly children with unsteady character and the inclination to bodily suffering. . . .[15]

After the passage of the Nuremberg Laws, Streicher profited more than ever from his disreputable newspaper.

Stuermer circulation, which averaged 20,000 in early 1933, had increased rapidly after the Nazi takeover. By March, 1934, this circulation figure had expanded to 47,000, and by the following August to 80,000. Two months before Hitler announced the racial edicts at the 1935 Party-day Rally, *Stuermer* average circulation had reached almost 250,000 weekly copies. But by October, 1935, this number burgeoned to over 486,000.[16] Streicher testified in 1945 that the peak period of his publishing business was in the closing months of 1938, when approximately 600,000 *Stuermer* copies were reproduced and distributed.[17]

The rapid rise in *Stuermer* circulation up to mid-1935, as well as the exceptional increase in these figures after passage of the Nuremberg Laws, has been viewed by some observers as a direct reflection of the growing acceptance by German people of the Nazi racial doctrines as they developed.[18] While this viewpoint may be partially valid, there were other factors of more importance that contributed to Streicher's success in reaching almost one-half million readers with his *Stuermer* by late 1935. Initially, it is virtually certain that as the Nazis expanded their rule, news agencies and news-vendors were persuaded by various means to carry the *Stuermer*. Throughout Franconia, Streicher organized small groups of party members and SA men to visit public establishments such as restaurants, hotels, and barber-shops, and ask for the *Stuermer*. If the newspaper was not available, these men would feign anger and issue threats. Usually the owners would subscribe to the *Stuermer* without much delay. In the same manner, Streicher would be able to convince industrial firms to subscribe to hundreds of copies of his newspapers for factory cafeterias, restrooms and reception areas.[19]

After the legalization of the racial laws in September, 1935, the subject of anti-Semitism was included in the daily curriculum of most German schools, and many classes were instructed to read the *Stuermer* on a daily or weekly basis. *Stuermer* issues in the late 1930's often carried letters from young children relating their appreciation for this "newspaper of the truth" which they now read habitually in school.[20] In addition, all Hitler-youth groups which mushroomed rapidly after early 1933, were encouraged constantly to urge parents of the young members to subscribe to the

Stuermer. These orders emanated from the national head of the Hitler-youth movement, Baldur von Schirach, a strong admirer of Streicher.

Further, *Stuermer* circulation was also boosted by Hitler's endorsement of Streicher's scheme to have glass-enclosed bulletin boards erected from public funds to display publicly all pages of *Stuermer* issues in every section of all cities and towns as well as in farming villages. By governmental decree, some women were designated to clean the glass and post new *Stuermer* issues in these poster boards each week.[21]

It seems almost certain that the numbers of new *Stuermer* readers would not have been from the class of mature-minded, intelligent citizens. Many persons of this class have stated that the contents of this newspaper were so bizarre and ridiculous that they never gave it a second glance. Even though the Nazi government tolerated the newspaper at Hitler's insistence, most members of his inner circle considered the *Stuermer* an embarrassment. Some of these officials managed to have it banned from Berlin news-stands while that city hosted the 1936 Olympic games.

Most knowledgeable observers agreed that the *Stuermer* found its readers from among the uneducated adult population or from the growing numbers of gullible youths. In discussing the mental conditioning of young people in the Hitler era, the British author, Louis Bondy, alleges that because of its abundance of cartoons and its simple style of phraseology, the *Stuermer* was read widely by these children and teen-agers who turned into a generation of anti-Semites in the later years of Nazi Germany.[22]

Despite Streicher's growing reputation as a hate-mongering, fanatic anti-Semitic propagandist, he continued to enjoy a sizable following of admirers among the thousands of Franconians who were not members of the Nazi party and were probably apathetic about racial issues. His popularity among these persons was evidenced by comments during later interviews conducted by the author with Nuremberg citizens. Documentary evidence indicates that he experienced no difficulty recruiting non-Nazis as voluntary helpers during charity drives. To earn this loyal following, Streicher frequently displayed his concern for the less fortunate citizens among his constituency. *Stuermer* back pages usually carried messages from the editor about a poor farmer, a disabled war veteran, or sick elderly person, and followed with pleas for voluntary aid or job opportunities. In his speeches, Streicher often expressed compassion for the poorer families of Franconia. Since 1933, he had assumed leadership of the annual *Winterhilfswerk* (winter-aid program), a voluntary charity drive to help needy local families and persons. In a typical *Winterhilfswerk* campaign, beginning in October, 1935, Streicher opened proceedings with an address which included words that contrasted sharply with his usual anti-Semitic gutter language:

> . . . .We have assembled here to open the great undertaking of the *Winterhilfe* in the *Gau* of Franconia. The sound of music we have just listened to led us to the beautiful, the great, the lofty, led us to God. What we are undertaking is something great and lofty. . . .The *Winterhilfe* will therefore bring the blessings which we expect from it. . . .[23]

Following this address, Streicher turned the proceedings over to Mayor Liebel, who recited the results of the previous year's drive. Some of the statistics of the 1934-1935 *Winterhilfe* program deserve mention inasmuch as they reveal the remarkable success of this drive, headed by Streicher, in terms of the large amounts of money and material goods donated and distributed as well as the large numbers of persons working in this program and benefiting from it. Liebel noted that 26,500 persons volunteered their services the previous year as staff members and collectors. Monetary contributions amounted to approximately 2,700,000 marks. Some 170,000 persons benefited from the program, receiving aid in the form of food, food coupons, clothing, beds and coal.

Streicher's periodic gestures of compassion and good-will included the occasional defense of performers of the arts who had received unfavorable reviews in newspapers. Details of the methods used by Streicher are noteworthy because his actions in these instances again illustrate his flair for showmanship and his pedagogical tendencies. One case of this nature occurred in Nuremberg in October, 1936. Streicher had issued a "command invitation" to all local journalists to attend a popular stage performance at the cabaret Eden. Throughout the first half of the program the audience was reportedly puzzled by the sight of a young man seated at one side of the stage. During the intermission, Streicher took the microphone and called that person forward, asking him to read the review he had written the previous week criticizing harshly the performance of a stage actor who was an older man and a World War I veteran.

Streicher then lectured the audience on the difficult life led by stage artists who had to perform "with smiling faces" day after day even if they were burdened by personal problems. Turning to the reporter, Streicher ordered him back to the center of the stage, and with a blinding spotlight turned on him, the young man was asked to read the passage he had reported in his review as an example of the actor's bungled performance. After the reporter had stumbled through this reading, Streicher launched into a lecture to all press members in the audience, warning them of the harm done by unfair or hasty critical press reviews. He concluded by advising them that it would be better to remain silent on a questionable performance rather than report unfair negativisms which might cause worthy artists to lose their means of livelihood.[24]

Another incident of this nature occurred the following spring. Under similar circumstances, Streicher had lectured a group of critics of the performing arts and then forced them to attempt a dance routine on the stage, while the regular dancers sat in the seats of the audience, laughing. However, this occurrence was denounced by the Director of the Reich Association of the Press, Wilhelm Weiss. Reacting in vigorous fashion, the director castigated Streicher publicly for forcing dignified journalists to prove their artistic incompetence on the cabaret stages. Weiss questioned the educational value of such methods and warned that inasmuch as Germany was fighting hard for cultural recognition abroad, it was unwise for party officials to undermine the confidence of the German press in front of the whole world.

Despite objections such as Weiss's against Streicher's unorthodox attempts to inhibit free press opinions, the *Gauleiter's* actions in these cases may have initiated an edict proclaimed later in 1937 by Propaganda Minister Joseph Goebbels. This new Nazi law prohibited public critiques on all German artistic performances and ordered that, in the future, newspapers and magazines could publish only moderate "reflections on art," which would be censored after they were published, and, if found objectionable to Nazi party doctrines, could be punishable by removal of the journalist's employment license.[2 5]

By the mid-1930's, the Nazi government began campaigns of slander and abuse against the existing churches in Germany. Streicher, acting individually, initiated his own series of malicious attacks against some Catholic Church practices and clergymen in 1934. These aggressive acts developed into a bitter feud with high ranking Catholic officials and later provided sensational material for *Stuermer* front pages. Acting on rumors provided by *Stuermer* readers, Streicher began this feud by including derogatory remarks about some priests in his speeches and newspaper articles. These verbal attacks increased in intensity and eventually led to a long, official complaint to the Governor of Bavaria, von Epp, from the Archbishop of Bamberg, known by the name of Jakobus.[2 6] This long protest, written in November, 1936, began with a notation that a similar protest had been sent, in recent weeks, by the Archbishop of Freiburg to the Governor of Baden, taking exception to Streicher's defamatory remarks against Baden priests in speeches in Karlsruhe and other cities in Baden. Apparently, Streicher had accused several local clergymen of indecent behavior such as sexual relations with women of their parishes. Earlier in the summer, the archbishop wrote, Streicher had spoken at the University of Munich and had shouted in a loud voice: "International pig-priests, even if they are cardinals!" Streicher also allegedly related to his audience some tales told to him by his sister, detailing immoral talk to women by priests in confessionals.

The archbishop also complained about a ridiculous attack in the *Stuermer* against a priest because he had used the word "Jerusalem" during a church service. The clergyman explained in his letter that this word was always included in a traditional Catholic prayer and that this prayer happened to be offered by the priest during the funeral of an SA man on the day before the vicious *Stuermer* article was published. Streicher had evidently seized on this innocent occurrence to accuse the priest of deliberately attempting to undermine his anti-Semitic work.

The archbishop also related in his letter to von Epp that Streicher had publicly challenged the concept of conversion to another faith by the sacrament of baptism. Streicher's crude words regarding his opinion of this sacrament were quoted in the newspaper, *Fraenkischer Kurier:*

> Once I wanted to make clear to a highly educated gentleman that a Jew, if one baptizes him, is still a Jew. He didn't understand. So I told him: "Take a pig and pour water over it. You will see when it comes back that it is not a billy goat, but still a pig."[27]

Allegations from the archbishop to von Epp also included Streicher's endeavors to abolish denominational schools in Nuremberg and replace them with community schools. The *Gauleiter* supposedly voiced violent objections to the classroom use of the *Old Testament*, which he claimed was a danger to the education of German youth. Jakobus attempted to strengthen his petition to the Bavarian governor with a reminder that Streicher had violated an order by Hitler, dated in November, 1935, which warned all Nazi officials to refrain from meddling in questions concerning the Church and religion. In closing, the archbishop asked von Epp to pass his presentation on to Hitler for possible governmental sanction against Streicher's further abuses of the Church.[28]

Unfortunately, the archbishop's attempt in this complaint, as well as subsequent ones, to repel Streicher's attacks against the Catholic Church proved to be futile. There is no evidence to indicate that von Epp did anything about the lengthy complaint except refer it to SS Colonel Berckmuller, Director of the State Secret Police at Karlsruhe. This official apparently held little sympathy for the archbishop or his problems and consequently gave him no offer of relief. Instead, Berckmuller initiated an "investigation" into the charges of indecent behavior that Streicher had mentioned in his speeches and newspaper articles. The results of the secret police inquiries were sent to von Epp, with copies also mailed to Streicher's office. These reports subsequently provided material for further sensational *Stuermer* articles levied against Catholic Church personnel and practices. Comparisons of Berckmuller's reports and corresponding *Stuermer* articles reveal that Streicher and his writers embellished these accounts grossly, especially in the aspects of sexual promiscuity. In one case, Berckmuller reported that his men had obtained a "confession" from a young Jewish woman affirming that she had had sexual relations with a priest named Father Schatz, whom she had met through her elderly uncle.[29] The corresponding *Stuermer* article embellished this story with fictitious details of the sexual act and also added that the girl had been seduced many times in her younger years by her sixty-three-year old uncle, who was her legal guardian.[30]

A second case reported by Berckmuller implicated the Archbishop Jakobus, who had taken a fatherly interest in a teen-aged boy named Schuelle. This boy was group leader of a Catholic youth organization in Baden and the archbishop was helping finance his education for the priesthood. However, Schuelle had gotten into a quarrel with some boys in the *Hitler Jugend* and an ensuing *Gestapo* inquiry supposedly had uncovered evidence that he had committed incest with his two young sisters.[31] The corresponding *Stuermer* article related this story in dramatic fashion and added that the younger of the sisters had actually given birth to Schuelle's child at age thirteen. Further, that since the boy had been in jail he was allegedly exposed to some Jews, who had corrupted him so badly that he was belligerent and not regretful about the incest he had committed. The *Stuermer* account also suggested that the archbishop was having homosexual relations with Schuelle, since he visited him frequently in jail and made a number of telephone calls to inquire of his welfare while he was incarcerated.[32]

While there is evidence of a number of other attacks by Streicher against Catholic Church personnel, there is no indication that he impaired, to any great extent, the ecclesiastic operations of the Church in Franconia. However, it is probable that Streicher was indirectly responsible for later restrictions and persecution of diocesan clergymen. His unproven allegations and sensational *Stuermer* fabrications against the archbishop and others connected with the Church led the *Gestapo* to initiate and continue inquiries which oftentimes led to forced confessions which, in turn, resulted in further victimization at the hands of Nazi persecutors.

Somewhat surprisingly, Streicher rarely included Protestant church personnel in his anti-church attacks. His relationship with leaders of that denomination was often tenuous, but never went beyond a few inconsequential confrontations which ended in uneasy compromise. The local Protestant bishop, Reverend Meiser, and his two assistants, Pastors Schieder and Daumiller, were somewhat friendly with many

NSDAP members until mid-1933, when they became disillusioned with National Socialist church policy. After this time these men, especially Meiser, led a firm, but moderately voiced opposition to Nazi practices and to Streicher, refusing to be coerced into adopting the lines of the Nazi-initiated German Christian Church. Meiser was fortunate in having Police President Martin as a personal friend and confidante. Using diplomatic methods suggested by Martin, Meiser and his colleagues refrained from openly antagonizing Streicher or criticizing articles published in the *Stuermer*. In retrospect, the strategy of avoiding open journalistic conflicts or verbal battles with Streicher proved the wisest course to follow for Franconian Protestant clergymen. With few exceptions, they managed to carry on their ecclesiastical affairs unhampered by the Nazis for the duration of the Hitler period.[33]

By the mid-1930's, it proved to be futile for a non-Nazi to seek redress by legal means for libelous or slanderous attacks published by party members of Streicher's caliber. The Nazi system of jurisprudence was consistently biased in cases of this nature. One outstanding example of this type of legal bias involved a clash between Streicher and a Prussian nobleman, Count Henckel Donnersmark. A law suit was initiated by Donnersmark because of a front-page article published in the *Stuermer* in June, 1935. The article was entitled "From Jewish Ragpicker's Daughter to Countess." Based on a questionable story gleaned from a Jewish newspaper published four years earlier, the *Stuermer* account focused on a woman named Therese Lachman, allegedly a Jewess and a prostitute. She had supposedly married Count Henckel's father through trickery and then caused his mental degeneration and eventually brought disgrace to his old German aristocratic family.[34] Henckel complained in his petition to the court that his stepmother was an honorable woman and "not a Jewess."

Retaliating to the count's court petition, Streicher did not soft-pedal the issue or print a retraction. Instead, he authored an article in a July *Stuermer* front page repeating the earlier story and accusing the count himself of being "basically" Jewish since he had associated in the past with well-known Jews, such as Dr. Dernburg and Walter Rathenau. The *Stuermer* article added as further proof of Henckel's "Jewishness" that he was listed along with other Jewish men, as a sponsor of the German Society of Artists, a modern art museum which featured non-traditional works of art in styles of expressionism, cubism, and dadaism, considered by Nazis to be revolutionary and decadent in view of National Socialist principles.[35]

In September, 1935, Count Henckel filed a lawsuit in the Nuremberg Common Pleas Court against Streicher as publisher of the *Stuermer*, demanding public retraction of the harmful allegations against his father, his stepmother and himself. This lower court ruled that Streicher should publish retractions as requested by the plaintiff, Henckel. The next *Stuermer* issue carried a vague apology disavowing some of the statements previously published against the Henckel family. However, another article on the same page mentioned that the retraction was merely a formality and was not to be taken seriously by *Stuermer* readers.[36]

In 1936, Count Henckel brought Streicher to trial at the High Civil Court in Berlin, charging that spurious and slanderous *Stuermer* articles against him and his family had not ceased. The high-court trial ended again only in an order that the *Stuermer* publish another retraction. Dissatisfied, Henckel appealed and re-appealed the decisions of this court, but failed to obtain a ruling of any consequence against Streicher's abusive newspaper attacks. According to the judges, Streicher did not have to furnish proof that his defamatory articles were based on factual evidence. Instead, the rulings handed down in all of the trials were based on Henckel's inability to prove that the allegations published in the *Stuermer* were false. The count had been unable to furnish documentary proof that his father had not died mentally and spiritually degenerated or that his stepmother, whose birth records had been burned, was not Jewish.

After Henckel finally realized the futility of seeking justice in the Nazi courts, he began the practice of ignoring the disreputable contents of the *Stuermer*. Within a few weeks, the scurrilous newspaper attacks ceased as new targets of abuse were found.

The unearthing of fresh material for sensational *Stuermer* articles seemed to pose no difficulty. One of the most consistent sources used by Streicher and his writers were letters from readers. As an incentive, these contributors to *Stuermer* journalism were usually rewarded by a brief but flattering article of appreciation published in the back pages alongside a photograph of themselves. As a rule, the content of these letters indicated that the contributors were either children or below-average-mentality adults. And the nature of the information volunteered often suggested that the writers seemed to follow the example of irresponsible accusations, as seen regularly in the *Stuermer*. Others were evidently merely seeking recognition for their racist views, which were popular with the political leadership during those times.

Excerpts of one of these letters sent in early 1936 illustrates the low mentality of some of the *Stuermer* contributors. Letters of this type were usually reproduced on back pages with little or no acknowledgement and no following story:

> Dear *Stuermer:* In Herrington. . .there lives a farmer who obviously has already been in contact with Jews. . . .Some citizens recently witnessed him delivering a horse to the Jew N., in Kame. The horse tried over and over to run away because it must have smelled the Jew. A second horse had to take its place. . . .So, dear *Stuermer*, you can see that the horse was more intelligent than its master![37]

A second excerpted example is typical of the letters that provided a lead for *Stuermer* research and following racial denunciations in the prominent sections of the newspaper:

> Dear *Stuermer:* Recently here at Odenbach, the Jew F. was buried. . . .We learned later that many of our 'aryan brothers' attended the funeral. These must be the same characters that buy from Jews at night. . . .Now that their masks have fallen, we know who they are. . . .[38]

This letter was followed up by *Stuermer* staff members, who visited the town and obtained the names of all who had attended this funeral. Further "research" by means of listening to town gossip provided material for at least four *Stuermer* articles scandalizing some of the men who had paid their last respects to their Jewish friend.[39]

While letters from readers provided fresh material for *Stuermer* propaganda articles dealing with local issues, Streicher's main source of material for articles of nationwide interest was other newspapers. He regularly subscribed to at least six Jewish newspapers as well as to some two dozen daily papers from large German cities. For his attempts at the scholarly approach to anti-Semitism he usually referred to volumes in his large personal library collection of anti-Semitic literature. With this wealth of source material and an enlarged staff of writers virtually unfettered by journalistic legal restrictions, Streicher and his associates produced an ever-increasing number of publications as well as record numbers of regular issues of the *Stuermer* and other daily and weekly newspapers and magazines by 1936.

The burgeoning volume of Streicher publications in the mid-1930's paralleled the expansion of his publishing business operations. During the early 1930's the *Stuermer* had been printed by a Nuremberg firm owned by Wilhelm Haerdels, who died in February, 1934. That same month, Streicher bought the business from Haerdels' widow for 40,000 marks and changed the name of the firm to the Koenig Publishing House. In August, 1935, Streicher opened another publishing company registered as The *Stuermer—* Julius Streicher. However, he listed Max Fink as the sole legal representative with full power of attorney. In November, 1936, Streicher established a third publishing firm registered as the Publishing House of the German Health— Julius Streicher, and again listed Max Fink as holding full power of attorney.[40]

While Streicher had installed Koenig and Fink as the "frontmen" of the companies for the evident purpose of dodging legal and tax liabilities, he remained the sole owner of all of them and relied on Ernst Hiemer as his chief business manager for all of his publishing interests. Between 1934 and 1938, Streicher firms published a variety of newspapers, magazines and books, almost all focused on anti-Semitic propaganda. In addition to the consistent publication of the *Stuermer*, other newspapers included the local NSDAP organs, *Fraenkische Tageszeitung* and *Fraenkische Abendzeitung*. A typical issue of magazines published by Streicher firms was the initial effort of the third publishing enterprise. It was entitled "German People's Health," and it stressed methods of nature healing and discouraged the use of medicines that Streicher claimed were invented mostly "by Jews such as Louis Pasteur and Edward Jenner." This magazine also harped on the "scientific" theories of permanent blood infection of women through sexual intercourse with Jewish men. After less than a year's time this "health" magazine was discontinued due to lack of reader interest.

Books and pamphlets published by Streicher enterprises ranged from race-oriented picture books for kindergarten children to complex pseudo-philosophic treatises on the history of anti-Semitism. Almost all of these were crudely written and filled with lies and radical exaggerations. One example, published in 1935, was advertised by Streicher as a "picture book for young and old." It was authored by a nineteen-year-old girl, Elvira Bauer, who was evidently an admirer of Streicher. The book was awkwardly titled "Don't Confide in a Fox in Green Pastures or a Jew on His Oath," and the language in it was seemingly aimed at children in the second or third year of school. Primitive drawings in *Stuermer* style were sketched next to childlike verses describing Jewish children and adults in many stages of growth, concluding in the final stages of mature criminality or prostitution. At the end of this "book" was a picture of Streicher, labelled the "Children's Friend," accompanied by the following verse:

> A fighter was born to us in the State of Franconia,
> To him we must give thanks that our country stays healthy
> and free from the Jewish influence.
> He taught all the Jews what a healthy population is worth
> And let them feel the German spirit.
> What it means to be Jew and what it means to be German.
> This is our Streicher![41]

Through his political influence Streicher managed to force books such as this into schools as required reading material. The sales volume of this small book required the printing of four editions during the first year of its publication. Some *Stuermer* issues later carried pictures of classrooms where young children were learning to read using this book and others like it.

In addition to a large volume of business in the sale of children's books, Streicher's firms published many so-called serious works dealing with racial topics. These included works by the Berlin University racist lecturer, Dr. Peter Deeg, entitled "Jews, Jew Criminals and Jew Laws from the Past to the Present," "Court-Jews," and "Jewish Laws of Germany."

Other prominent German racists who authored books published by Streicher were Dr. Rolf Kummer, who wrote a large volume entitled "Rasputin, Tool of the Jews," and Dr. Richard Stock who wrote "Jews Through Five Centuries." Streicher also found time during this period to author some books of the same nature. One of these, published in 1937, was a crude attempt at scholarly writing entitled "Blood and Earth as the Source and Symbol of German Strength and Science."[42]

With the expansion of Streicher's publishing business, a modern chemigraphical department had been added to provide a new dimension in *Stuermer* illustrations. Using over-exposed prints of other photographs, staff artists could superimpose grotesque facial characteristics that usually resulted in horrid, frightening likenesses of persons Streicher chose to victimize in journalistic defamations. Among conspicuous examples of this *Stuermer* pseudo-art were likenesses of former New York Mayor La Guardia and ex-President Franklin Roosevelt, caricatured as evil-looking, thick-lipped, hooked-nosed "*Stuermer* Jews." Accompanying articles asserted that these Americans were Jewish and were working for the downfall of Germany as well as the ruination of the non-Jewish world population.

Another example of *Stuermer* trick photography was an illustration of the explosion and burning of the German dirigible "Hindenburg" at Lakehurst, New Jersey, in June, 1937. The smoke from the flaming wreckage formed a vague, but recognizable outline of a "*Stuermer* Jew's" face. The caption of this illustration as well as the headline article indicated that this tragedy was not an accident but the handiwork of malevolent Jews.

Perhaps the most infamous usage of *Stuermer* trick photography was the illustration intended to indoctrinate racial hatred in young children. In a typical example in a 1936 issue, a figure of an evil-appearing "*Stuermer* Jew" was superimposed on a photograph of a police dog and a two-year-old boy holding a copy of the *Stuermer*. Below this illustration was the caption: "Faithfully Watched Over by the *Stuermer* and German Shepherd."[43]

It has been mentioned in earlier chapters that Streicher's consistent racial propaganda must have created attitudes of hatred among some young SA men that led directly to atrocities against Jews in the early years of Nazi rule. In the same vein, it seems almost certain that a great deal of blame for the tragedies that befell many Jewish people in the later 1930's and during the war years was attributable to the Nazi racial education of children. In Franconia this education was enforced by Streicher and Max Fink, who had been installed by the *Gauleiter* as Franconian Superintendent of Public Schools. Racial education in many schools was spiced by many Streicher publications. The Nuremberg area was one of the first districts to insist that public schools teach in accordance with National Socialist doctrines. Special textbooks, such as the one by Elvira Bauer, were ordered as mandatory curriculum material. In many Franconian elementary schools teachers also used the *Stuermer* for anti-Semitic instruction and filled bulletin boards with grotesque illustrations from that newspaper. Some teachers involved young students in writing contests, offering prizes for the best letter to the *Stuermer*. These letters usually praised Streicher and his newspaper for bravery in the struggle against the Jews or boasted about the writer's firm belief that Jews and their intentions were all evil. An excerpt of one of these letters from a student at the elementary school in the Franconian village of Roth illustrates the degree of racial hatred instilled in his eight-year-old mind:

> ....We children in Roth contribute to this (struggle against Jews). Several of our class often go to the department store B.; when people want to go inside we shout to them: 'Fie upon you!' Then their faces turn all red and they go away. Does that not please you, *Stuermer*?[44]

In addition to special greetings to *Gauleiter* Streicher, this young boy included the following frightening verse:

> The Jew does not rest his muzzle mouth
> Therefore he must be taken to Dachau!

It may provide some measure of relief to modern-day members of the teaching profession that a fairly large number of cases were reported during this period where elementary and secondary-level teachers managed to keep Nazi racial propaganda to a minimum, or to avoid it altogether. On the other hand, there were a few cases reported where teachers actually insisted to pupils that they spy on their parents and inform school authorities of family attitudes hostile to the Nazi regime and its doctrines.

The process of racial indoctrination of school children was aided further by Streicher when he took time to spend hours at various Nuremberg area schools. During these visits Streicher proved his insidious propaganda effectiveness with young people. At first he gained the confidence of the students by talking to them in tones of a benevolent protector and showing interest in their classroom work. Oftentimes these visits would be well advertised and advance preparations for this "special event" at the school would include festive decorations, refreshments, and instructions to students to wear freshly laundered uniforms or school clothes. With news correspondents present, these visits by Streicher would later receive wide publicity in the *Stuermer* and other local newspapers. One of these well publicized occasions occurred in mid-May 1938, at the *Pilotystrasse* School for Girls. Accounts and pictures of Streicher's activities at the school were carried in the May 25 issue of the *Fraenkische Tageszeitung.* A lead article stated that over 400 uniformed girls in their early teen years listened attentively while the *Gauleiter* spoke to them for approximately one and one-half hours. Departing from his usual style of abusive language and radical anti-Semitic attacks, Streicher spoke to the girls as if he were their guardian and spiritual teacher.[45] According to the newspaper account, Streicher spoke about matters that were very important to growing young people. He stressed the dangers which lay ahead during their developmental years and emphasized proper behavioral standards to be followed at this stage of their lives. It was reported that all the girls felt that somebody who was able to lead their souls and to prepare their lives was talking to them. The *Fraenkische Tageszeitung* article reiterated the gist of Streicher's address and lauded it as very successful in winning the admiration of his young audience. The following excerpt of a passage near the end of Streicher's talk illustrates further his penchant for affecting the role of a benevolent protector by referring to Hitler and to his own racial mission in life in pseudo-religious tones:

. . . .There is a sharp difference between men who are priests or
true soul-leaders, and the popes, who never really render services
to the people entrusted to them. . .to find true happiness we
would be well off if we had fewer theologians and more priests of
action. Adolf Hitler is the greatest priest of our time. He leads us
on our way to God. . .he has given proof of his priesthood through
action!. . .The true hereditary sin is the sin against the blood. . . .

This newspaper account of Streicher's visit to the school was
accompanied by photographs of his visit to a classroom
where he handled some of the appliances in the Home
Economics Department. All photographs featured crowds of
smiling girls surrounding the *Gauleiter* admiringly, as if he
were a very famous person.

The adulation demonstrated by the school girls toward
Streicher seemed spontaneous and somewhat genuine. This
may have been due at least partially to special instruction
given them by their teachers or school administrators. They
may also have appeared joyful and enthusiastic in reaction to
the festive atmosphere of the day, created by the decorations, refreshments and half-day holiday granted for Streicher's visit. It is also possible that they reacted in a straightforward manner to Streicher, who appeared to them as a true
friend and protector. Even though his performance in the
presence of these girls would be considered incongruous and
hypocritical to most knowledgeable observers, it is possible
that Streicher actually believed himself sincere in his pious
and fatherly performance. This possibility is reinforced by
Jean-Paul Sartre, who states that most confirmed, historical
anti-Semites are convinced that they are apostles of the true
sentiments of the "real" nation.[46]

While Streicher may have gained the admiration of a
number of young people in the years following the passage of
the Nuremberg Laws, he had also acquired more and more
adult enemies, especially because of his increasingly vicious
racial attacks in the *Stuermer* and other publications.
Archival files contain dozens of copies of newspaper articles
and letters condemning Streicher's anti-Semitic journalism or
actually threatening his life. While most newspaper condemnations emanated from Jewish or foreign sources, the letters
were usually mailed anonymously from within Germany. The
following passage from an unsigned letter to Streicher in
June, 1938, is among the more serious warnings penned to

him during this period:

> . . .and if you think that you will live much longer you are mistaken. Whether you are sitting in your guarded house or accompanied, as always, by your body-guard hoodlums, you are going to feel the reward you richly deserve. . . .You swine! You will feel the sting of my bullet very soon. . . .[47]

Despite the drastic tone of some of these letters, Streicher did not seem too concerned about these threats. Rather than seek added protection or moderate his racial diatribes because of their warnings, he seemed to react by intensifying his anti-Semitic attacks. In late January, 1938, his racial fanaticism reached a climax when a leading *Stuermer* article blatantly demanded the death penalty for Jews found guilty of sexual involvement with "pure" German females.[48] Branding this breach of the Nuremberg Laws as a "desecration of the race," Streicher classed the violators of the Nazi racial edicts as murderers of the coming generation of aryan citizens. While this was not the first time that Streicher had suggested the death penalty as the appropriate punishment for transgressions of this nature, he had never previously blazoned his opinion this vociferously, as a front-page headline article. In an adjoining column he had also taken the liberty to imply that Hitler was in favor of death sentences for Jewish sex-offenders. To strengthen this argument, Streicher had quoted a few scattered sentences from Hitler's book, *Mein Kampf.* In the same *Stuermer* issue another article attempted to prove the weakness of some high Nazi officials who were allegedly being consistently duped by Jewish criminals. To substantiate this charge, Streicher committed the blunder of quoting a passage from a confidential letter by the Berlin Ministry of Finance to the Swiss Embassy.

After the earliest distribution of this *Stuermer* issue, Berlin Nazi officials, with the apparent approval of Hitler, ordered police throughout Germany to confiscate all remaining copies and ordered that further publication of the *Stuermer* be halted indefinitely.

The news of this official ban on Streicher's newspaper reached foreign capitals almost immediately. The next day, publications from cities such as Vienna and Prague featured leading articles expressing glee over the *Stuermer's* transgressions, adding the hope that the disreputable racist newspaper would remain banned permanently.[49]

However, this hope proved to be short-lived. Displaying continued loyalty to his "old party comrade," Hitler visited Nuremberg on January 28 to meet with Streicher. After listening to some assurances that the *Gauleiter* intended no harm to Hitler or to the government, and after Streicher agreed to dismiss two editors, Hitler repealed the prohibition against the *Stuermer* effective the next day.

The temporary ban on the *Stuermer* caused Streicher little, if any, monetary loss. His financial fortunes in the publishing business had reached a zenith by early 1938. That year his annual income from his three firms exceeded two million marks. This unprecedented prosperity was made evident by his extravagant living style and a number of costly investments. He had spent over 300,000 marks furnishing his palatial *Cramer-Klettstrasse* residence, which was fully staffed with domestic help, including a full-time chauffeur. He had purchased a farm near the village of Pleikershof, about twenty miles outside of Nuremberg. This property contained eighty hectares of land, (approximately 200 acres) at a cost of 250,000 marks. By mid-1938, the expenses for construction of farm buildings and living quarters on this farm amounted to over one million marks. He had also purchased a sumptuous resort villa at Bodensee (Lake Constance), bordering on Switzerland and Austria, at a reported cost of some 200,000 marks. In addition, he was reportedly supporting a mistress named Anni Seitz and contributing to the support of two young actresses named Betty Weidner and Fraeulein Aldor. Later testimony by a witness under oath indicated that Streicher had spent between 25 and 30 thousand marks between late 1937 and late 1939 to finance his extra-marital affairs.[50]

Streicher's conduct towards most of his party and business associates had always been overbearing, but it seemed that as he became more prosperous he bullied his peers more than ever. He seemed to delight in demonstrating his disregard for the feelings of even his closest associates at odd occasions. He placed these colleagues in untenable situations that were expedient to his own personal interests, however costly and embarrassing to his victims. One of these occasions took place in early 1938 during an evening at the Cramer-Klett house. He had invited eight or ten party colleagues for a few hours of sociability. Guests included SA Colonel Wurzbacher, District Inspector Haberkern, District Party Treasurer Hoellrich, as well as Koenig, Holz and Fink. Shortly after the men arrived, Streicher announced that this was a "he-man" affair and everyone should remove their gold wedding rings and place them in a bowl. Later, when the guests were preparing to leave, the bowl was found empty and Streicher brushed off questions impatiently, telling the men to go home and not worry about a small matter like a wedding ring. It was discovered later by Fink that the rings had been melted down and a gold key fitting a bedroom door was made of them which Streicher presented as a gift to his mistress, Anni Seitz.[51]

A similar incident on a larger scale occurred about one month later. Streicher issued a summons to some thirty party colleagues and well-known Nuremberg public administrators to report in the early morning for "exercises" in a vacant lot behind the Cramer-Klett house. This group included such eminent persons as the Nuremberg Police President, the Mayor of Fuerth, judges, state prosecutors, chief editors and publishing executives. The men reported at the appointed hour, dressed in sports overalls, prepared for a session of calisthenics. Streicher strode out of his house dressed in work-clothes, and in tones of an army sergeant, delivered the following brief address:

> You, my party comrades, are all workers of the brain. . . .So that you gentlemen. . .may get to know and understand better the workers 'of the fist,' we shall all work physically just like those workmen. We shall come here every morning at 6 AM and for three hours shall work with shovels and picks under the supervision of a worker. . . .[52]

Streicher then distributed shovels, picks and wheelbarrows, and while a workman with a cigar in his mouth gave orders, these executives began digging a large hole in the ground. After three hours of this strenuous work, Streicher served them mint tea and jelly sandwiches and ordered them to go home and prepare for their daily jobs, but to be sure to report at the same time the following day. Almost unbelievably, this routine continued for the next three months throughout the early summer's humid weather, until some

1500 cubic meters of earth had been moved and the appropriated workers had completed the excavation for a large swimming pool for Streicher. Perhaps as additional evidence of Streicher's unassailable political position at this time, no records exist of indignant or resentful comments by these victimized officials.

Streicher's somewhat ludicrous exploitation of his party and business colleagues in the swimming pool project provided Nuremberg citizens a topic for light-hearted banter about their Nazi rulers. The sight of thirty National Socialist dignitaries, sans uniform, bared to the waist, working in the mud with picks and shovels provided welcome comic-relief to many Franconians living in the hub of racial persecution in Germany.

As indicated in previous pages, Nuremberg was recognized throughout Europe as the anti-Semitic capital of Nazi Germany and Streicher was considered the person most responsible for this dubious recognition. Since the April 1, 1933 boycott, Nuremberg had been the scene of "creeping aryanization" and as a result of harsh, unfair measures, some Jewish firms had closed their doors while others had quietly sold their business interests and had emigrated or retired. On the other hand, there were some who had managed to circumvent Streicher's policies by successful appeals to Hjalmar Schacht's Berlin Offices of Finance and Economics. However, by late 1937, Finance Minister Schacht had fallen into irreconcilable differences with Hitler and his influence in helping maintain the Jewish economic community had virtually been eliminated.[53]

Perhaps because of Schacht's weakened position, Streicher received no reprimand from Berlin when he announced in mid-December that a "private campaign" against Jewish businesses and stores would begin immediately and continue throughout the 1937 Christmas season. Interestingly, a *Fraenkische Tageszeitung* article claimed that Streicher was prompted into this action when he noted the unusually brisk sales in Jewish department stores on the Sunday preceding the announcement.[54] As in previous boycotts in Nuremberg, SA pickets mistreated and threatened customers. They physically assaulted store employees and frequently confiscated or damaged merchandise purchased at these establishments. On one particular day, all employees were ordered not to fail to report for work at Jewish establishments. However, on that same day all customers were forbidden, on pain of imprisonment, to enter these stores or carry on any form of trade with Jews or Jewish business firms. To avoid tedious repetition it can be summarized that SA forces employed all usual forms of hooliganism and bullying tactics and succeeded in causing all Nuremberg Jewish businessmen to suffer drastic losses during the 1937 Christmas boycott.[55]

On April 26, 1938, the Hitler government had begun the first step in the total economic strangulation of the Jewish community with a law compelling all Jews to "register and evaluate their total domestic and foreign properties." The edict also prohibited them from acquiring, in any manner, further business enterprises without a specific permit. This measure signalled governmental sanction of the process which eventually stripped all German Jews of their material assets and which became known as the aryanization of Jewish property.[56]

The word "aryanize" was one of the many Nazi inventions new to the German vocabulary. Defined loosely as a "cleansing" process, it was used as the philosophic purpose of several National Socialist doctrinal programs. For example, the Nazi selective breeding experiments and sterilization procedures were part of the social aryanization scheme. Politically, the elimination of all opposing parties and the denial of the franchise to Jews followed guidelines of Nazi political aryanization policies. However, the word, or term was employed most broadly in the context of Nazi economic measures against Jews and Jewish business interests. In official terminology, the word broadened in its connotation rapidly in 1938, after the April decrees. By late November, it meant that any interest in a business firm or any real property owned by Jews would be taken over by non-Jews in some manner prescribed by Nazi law. However, the laws were not only loosely defined, they were also loosely enforced. Under the aegis of aryanization, countless cases of outright robbery and confiscation without remuneration were perpetrated by Nazi officials, usually of high rank.

The first recorded case of aryanization by means of forcing a Jewish businessman to sell out to "pure Germans" occurred in Nuremberg in late January, 1938. The firm in question was registered in the name of its owner, Walter Lessing. It was a well-established, large producer of galvanic coal. Lessing's factory manager was a man named Musclin, who became an ardent Nazi party member after February, 1933.[57] In late 1937, Musclin informed his employer that he had *Stuermer* backing and would like to purchase the firm. A few days later, Fink came to Lessing and insisted he sell to Musclin at the price of 100,000 marks. However, the value of the firm's assets had been estimated the previous year at 1,400,000 marks. Realizing his tenuous position in Streicher's *Gau*, Lessing went to Berlin and arranged for the sale of his business to a competing firm at approximately the estimated fair market value.

When the prospective buyers of the Lessing firm came to Nuremberg to finalize the sales contract, they initially conferred with "someone" in the *Gauleiter's* office and subsequently informed Lessing that they were no longer interested in the purchase. In January, 1938, negotiations to purchase the Lessing firm were conducted by Fink, and before the end of the month the assets of the Lessing company were transferred to Musclin's name for the amount of 500,000 marks, about one-third of the actual value. As a tragic sequel to this transaction, Dr. Lessing was too frightened to attempt emigration and died shortly after the sale and his wife committed suicide the following year, just as SS men were on the way to arrest her and send her to a concentration camp.

The April, 1938, Berlin directive which included the order for Jews to register and evaluate all their property came several months after Streicher had ordered similar measures to be undertaken in Franconia. However, the earlier Nuremberg edicts added a measure which encouraged local party members to seek out small Jewish businesses within their capabilities of management. Streicher had organized a Franconian Chamber of Industry and Commerce with a lackey of his, named Strobl, as head. This office became the clearinghouse for official aryanization procedures which soon ran rampant in the Nuremberg area. The Streicher edict ordered all non-Jews, preferably party members, to register their aryanization requests with Strobl's office, where they were to be processed. By mid-1938, Koenig had established himself as the processor of these requests.[58]

An example of an unusual early 1938 aryanization

takeover of a Nuremberg business, processed through Strobl's office, involved the *Kaufhaus Weisser-Turm* (White-tower Department Store). The owner, Theo Hartner, was not Jewish, but he was married to a wealthy Jewish woman, who owned a considerable number of shares in this store. During the Nuremberg boycotts against Jewish businesses the White-tower store was excessively molested by the Nazis. Under extreme pressure by Holz during and after the 1937 boycott, Hartner agreed to obtain a divorce in order to save his store. After he had done this, Holz and Koenig forced him to employ a party member named Leissing, as manager of the store. Leissing, a petty criminal, knew virtually nothing about the business but was installed in his position at a salary of 1250 marks a month. A few weeks later, Hartner was threatened again by Streicher's henchmen. They told him that he would be sent to Dachau unless Leissing received 40 percent of the store's profits in addition to the monthly salary. Again under threat, Hartner was forced to retire the following month and Leissing took over the entire business. This case was so flagrant that it was investigated the following year by a board of government Nazi examiners. Leissing testified that he paid Holz and Koenig at least one-half of the money he had received from the White-tower store. He was ordered by the examining board to quit the store and he later became an SS guard at a Nazi concentration camp. Hartner was reinstated as the store's owner and manager in 1939, but the establishment was almost totally destroyed a few years later by bombing.

The Hartner case proved to be exceptional since it was the only recorded Streicher-led aryanization swindle during this period where the business interest or property was returned to the rightful Jewish owner. In all other cases on record, Jewish businessmen and property owners were exploited by the Streicher gang in a variety of ways not yet "legalized" by the Nazi government and were unable to recover their losses. One scheme devised in Nuremberg featured the skimming of money from aryanization appropriations for "special services." A representative case of this type involved a Jewish-owned establishment, *Lederwerke Cromwell* (Cromwell Leather Works), valued in excess of 4.9 million marks. Under pressure by Strobl's office, a sale to a competing firm was consummated at the "stipulated" purchase price of 1.5

million marks. In this transaction, ownership passed permanently out of Jewish hands and Streicher's representatives collected some 206,000 marks for special services noted as consultation fees and sales commissions.[59]

Another variation of mid-1938 Streicher-style aryanization featured the actual purchase of the business or property by a Streicher henchman, followed by quick resale. A case of this type involved a cotton-goods establishment owned by a Jew named M. Stern. The value of the firm was 161,250 marks, but Strobl's office "stipulated" the value at only 1,244 marks. A Koenig "strawman" bought the firm at the "stipulated" price and immediately resold it for 30,000 marks with a side agreement from the buyer to pay Koenig 10,000 marks a year for the next three years as "special consultant fees."[60]

In addition to the active program of robbing Jews of their property as indicated above, a further wave of general anti-Semitic persecution was instituted in Franconia beginning in early summer, 1938. With the process of mandatory reporting and registering of their properties, Jews were subjected to brutal questioning and some physical abuse by SA and SS men. In early August, the Nazis struck a severe blow to the spiritual life of the Jews. Streicher and Liebel announced jointly the decision by city authorities to demolish the main synagogue on the prominent *Hans-Sachs Platz* in downtown Nuremberg. The reason for this decision was explained by Liebel in a speech. He rationalized that the structure's design was offensive to the architectural style of the city and that the demolition complied with a new law listing Nuremberg as one of the cities to receive restoration and improvement in the name of Hitler's *Reich*. [61]

Perhaps in order to further humiliate the local Jewish population, a large Nazi rally was organized in front of the synagogue on August 10, the day demolition work was scheduled to begin. In addressing the assembled crowd, Liebel explained the importance of Nuremberg in the development of the National Socialist movement and described his embarrassment when, on various Party-day Rallies, he was asked by out-of-town Nazi officials when this eyesore would be eliminated from the Nuremberg scene. While the gist of his brief talk focused on the contrived righteousness of the removal of the synagogue, excerpts of some of his statements are noteworthy in that they illustrate the mayor's condescending flattery to Streicher, who seemed to be the honored guest at this occasion:

My *Gauleiter!* Fellow countrymen! When the *Gauleiter* of Franconia, our Julius Streicher, placed his trust in me. . .I promised him. . .that we would do everything possible to make this city once again a truly German city, the treasure box of the German *Reich.* . . .I am proud to be able to tell you, my *Gauleiter,* we have created the legal prerequisites for the removal of this building. For a few days now, I, as the mayor. . . have become the owner of this lot. . .and have given orders that this blemish—this synagogue be destroyed. . . .[62]

In closing his address, Liebel asked Streicher to assume the "honor" of striking the first blow to initiate officially the demolition of the synagogue. After a short speech of acknowledgement, Streicher, amid cheers, mounted the seat of a heavy construction machine and maneuvered a heavy iron ball over the dome of the building and then dropped it with a crash while tears glistened on the faces of saddened Jewish persons standing hopelessly by in the distance. Although Liebel had promised in his address that the synagogue would be completely removed in time for the early September Party-day Rally, the historic building was so solidly constructed that the work dragged on until early November at a cost to the city of over 600,000 marks.[63]

The 1938 Nazi Party-day Rally was scheduled to begin in Nuremberg on September 5 and was to last for eight days. Well before the opening day, Streicher had been busily engaged, along with Mayor Liebel, finalizing the many arrangements necessary to accommodate an expected crowd of over one million visitors. Among Streicher's self-appointed responsibilities was the closing of all Jewish business places and the evacuating of all Jewish families located along the parade routes or near the various rally areas.[64] To commemorate the *Anschluss* (joining with Germany) of Austria six months earlier, the festivities were named the First Party-day Rally of Greater Germany. Among the trophies gathered by the Nazis after entering Vienna were the priceless Austrian crown jewels. These were presented to Hitler the day before the rally opened and were accepted by him "on behalf of the German people."

Rudolf Hess, Hitler's chief secretary, opened the formalities the next day with a brief address. Streicher was the second speaker and delivered one of his customary lengthy diatribes against the Jews and Marxists. Throughout the week of the rally, spectators were treated to the usual pattern of military maneuvers, speeches and Nazi group-displays, which were somewhat more ostentatious than in previous rallies. According to foreign newspaper accounts, the displays were "each bigger and more beautiful than ever before, " and the speeches grew "ever longer and never less hideously threatening."

Hitler's final speech focused on his next military victim, Czechoslovakia. He vented his personal hatred against this nation in long and bitter phrases. To some visitors the speech, which was accompanied by the animal-like responses of the huge crowd, continuously roaring *"Sieg Heil!" "Sieg Heil!"* was no less than terrifying. Hitler's threatening words climaxed this last and most extravagant rally only eighteen days before the Nazi invasion of the Czechoslovakian Sudetenland was to be launched.

In the weeks immediately following the Nuremberg rally, more anti-Semitic violence broke out in Franconia. Another synagogue, this time in the small town of Leutershausen, was burned and demolished. Then in mid-October, the *Gestapo*, under Himmler's orders, began rounding up 433 Franconian Jews who had previously immigrated from Poland. After arrest and brief imprisonment, these persons, along with thousands of others of Polish origin, were transported to Germany's eastern border and dumped there with orders never to return to Germany.[65]

The "illegal" aryanization practices initiated by Streicher in Franconia seemingly led the way to further anti-Semitic edicts promulgated by the Nazi government. In most instances, as new measures against Jews were announced by Berlin headquarters, the action to be taken was prefaced by reasons (however false) that supposedly justified the Nazi decision. In the case of the October edict forcing the deportation of all Polish Jews, the formal reason for the decision was that "true" Germans were being exploited by these Jews who (somehow) sent their earnings and profits to Poland.

A few weeks after the *Gestapo* had begun rounding up

Polish Jews, an incident in France provided NSDAP leaders with another "justifiable reason" for sweeping, violent anti-Semitic action. On November 7, Hitler and hundreds of other ranking Nazis were gathered in Munich preparing for the annual commemoration of the 1923 Beer Hall *Putsch.* That same day, a young Jew, Herschel Grynszpan, whose parents had been deported to Poland, went to the German Embassy in Paris to assassinate the ambassador and mistakenly shot a German counselor named Ernst vom Rath. Propaganda Minister Goebbels seized on this incident immediately, elaborating in a nationwide radio broadcast that this was another clear example of Jewish treachery.[66]

On the afternoon of November 9, vom Rath died, and after a brief consultation with Hitler, Goebbels opened a vigorous campaign of incitement against the German-Jewish population. He announced to a group of party officials that Rath's murder had already triggered anti-Jewish riots in several cities. He added that Hitler had agreed that if riots spread spontaneously throughout Germany, they were not to be discouraged. Goebbels followed this announcement with a message to SA leaders nationwide, to organize demonstrations against Jews, but to make them appear as impulsive acts by ordinary German citizens. That night, fires were ignited all over Germany, and glass from hundreds of thousands of shattered windows littered the streets. The viciousness of this pogrom, called *Kristallnacht* (crystal-night), could be evidenced by the following statistics: More than 7000 Jewish businesses destroyed, almost four thousand persons seriously injured, and nearly one-hundred Jewish persons killed.[67]

One of the oddities about *Kristallnacht* was that Streicher knew almost nothing of the action and took no part in the violence. Franconian SA Chief Obernitz received the order from Goebbels' office late in the evening on November 9. Obernitz later testified that he had gone to Streicher's home with the news and found the *Gauleiter* in bed, preparing for sleep. The SA chief allegedly asked Streicher for his consent to act on Goebbels' orders and received only a sleepy nod, indicating that he had no objections to whatever action would be taken that night.[68]

Accounts of the violence perpetrated in Franconia on *Kristallnacht* are somewhat contradictory. However, Fink's sworn statement of the report submitted to Streicher by

Holz, Koenig, and others on the morning of November 10, provides sufficient information to summarize fairly accurately the atrocities that occurred during the previous night. Apparently, most of the brutality was inflicted by SA men dressed in plain clothes. Violent action broke out around 10 PM when gangs of men began breaking windows in synagogues and Jewish stores, later setting them on fire. City fire department crews were on the scene, but worked only to keep the fires from spreading to buildings not owned by Jews. Within a few hours almost every Jewish synagogue or business establishment suffered smashed windows and destruction or looting of merchandise, fixtures and equipment.

The gangs then invaded the Jewish residential neighborhoods, breaking down doors and, in some cases, throwing Jews bodily out of windows or down flights of stairs. Holz and Koenig also stated that some Jews were thrown down stairs so forcibly that they lay dead where they landed. They also said that they had witnessed a few cases where Jews were beaten to death or had their throats slashed. The scene of the worst violence against Jewish homes and individuals occurred in the predominantly Jewish neighborhoods in Nuremberg's *Tiergarten* and *Luitpoldhain* districts. In these localities, piles of furniture thrown out of windows littered the sidewalks and in some instances were heaped in mounds and set afire. One family of three or four persons in the *Tiergarten* district was forced to walk nude in the streets. Violence of this nature was not confined to the city of Nuremberg. Later reports indicated that similar cases of brutal actions had occurred in most Franconian towns with comparatively numerous Jewish populations.

A report from Martin's police office listed damage on *Kristallnacht* in Nuremberg and Fuerth alone at 70 stores destroyed, 256 dwellings damaged, and nine Jewish persons killed. Estimates on the value of furniture, fixtures, and other personal property damaged or destroyed as well as information on numbers of seriously injured persons was unavailable, presumably because statistics were not recorded. Shamefully, Liebel ordered city hospitals closed to injured Jews. However, the small police hospital did what it could to treat the most serious cases of injury. Streicher reportedly issued a public statement the following morning to the effect that the Jews had brought on this damage themselves and German people should not sympathize with them.[69]

The vom Rath murder not only served as a "legitimate reason" for the atrocities committed on *Kristallnacht*, it was also utilized by the Nazis as justification to add further measures of reprisal against the Jews. Special assessment of one billion marks was levied for "economic and political damages" caused by the murder. This levy was to be paid by a 20 percent tax on all Jews in Germany whose property value exceeded 5000 marks. In addition, Jews were compelled to pay all costs for damages done to their own properties. Where insurance payments reimbursed Jewish property owners, the money was to be expropriated by the state.

Further Nazi reprisals "justified" by the vom Rath murder included edicts which "legalized" the near-total aryanization of Jewish businesses. New laws now stipulated that Jews were forbidden to participate in almost every kind of business and provided for trustees to be appointed to dispose of Jewish business holdings. Jews were also ordered to deposit their stocks and bonds with a recognized German bank. A later law ordered all gold, platinum, silver, jewels, and similar possessions to be surrendered to special purchasing agencies established by the federal government.[70]

As news of the latest anti-Semitic laws reached Nuremberg, Streicher bragged to his cohorts that he was glad to see that Berlin officials were finally following the examples provided in Franconia of proper handling of the Jews. Holz, echoing his chief's sentiments a few days later, stated that *Kristallnacht* had "signaled a completely new phase in settling the Jewish question," adding that since the *Gau* of Franconia had distinguished itself so outstandingly in the past with its actions against the Jews, the district must once again assume the leadership in anti-Semitic "achievements."[71]

According to the sworn testimony of Fink, Holz suggested to Streicher that it would be possible to implement the new *Reich* laws in such a way that Nuremberg's housing shortage could be relieved. When Streicher asked how this could be possible, Holz answered that since the latest racial laws implied that it was improper for Jews to own chattel property, the *Gau* party leadership could aryanize all Franconian Jews' houses, land and businesses and then send the former owners to concentration camps. Streicher reportedly agreed to this proposal half-heartedly, answering "if you think you can (do this), go ahead." Interestingly, Fink stated that Streicher concluded his agreement to Holz's proposal with the remark that he hoped to use some of the proceeds for a new school in the *Gau*.

With this off-hand assent by Streicher, Holz began, that same day, to implement the infamous Nuremberg property aryanization action. By a proclamation bearing Streicher's name, all Jewish persons owning real property were called to the local party's headquarters where they were forced into surrendering these assets at one-tenth the actual value or less.[72]

Methods used in Franconia to obtain signatures on the sale documents were varied, but usually followed a consistent pattern. First the recent aryanization laws would be read to the Jewish owner. This reading was followed by threats of bodily harm if the "seller" appeared hesitant. Then, if the desired results were not obtained, arrest, imprisonment, and oftentimes torture would come next. Firsthand reports to a surviving Jewish attorney by several victims of Nuremberg aryanization appropriations in November, 1938, provide details of cases in which Jewish owners resisted the initial approaches and threats. These persons had refused to sign deeds transferring their property to the Franconian NSDAP for ten percent of the actual value.[73]

One victim, whose name was not given, said that he had refused to sign the prepared deed and had gone to seek police protection. However, he learned that the police president was unable to intercede and the next night, the victim, an elderly man, was visited by several SS men who robbed him of his cash, then beat him until he was covered with blood. Later, he was placed in a cell with a Jewish lawyer, Dr. Walter Berlin, who was also bleeding from a beating. They were reportedly saved from immediate shipment to the Dachau concentration camp because a physician provided by Martin declared they were too badly injured to be moved. Later, these two men were kept together with several other elderly Jewish persons in the prison's gymnasium and forced to perform excruciating "exercises" until about two weeks passed by, when all of them agreed to offer their real estate to Streicher's representatives for 10 percent of the actual value.

Another victim, a woman named Martha Hutzer, offered testimony elaborating on the torturous exercises inflicted on Jewish prisoners during this period at the Nuremberg prison. She recalled the treatment of the elderly Jew, M. Friedmann, who had to lay across a stool, while another prisoner, Josef Heilbronner, was ordered to beat Friedmann's buttocks with a stick. When the guard growled that the blows were too mild, Heilbronner hit Friedmann so hard that the stick broke. Friedmann was released the following day after he agreed to sell his property at Nazi terms.

According to one victim, some Jewish homeowners were compelled by their tormenters to fall forward from an upright position, keeping their bodies erect and arms and fingers outstretched stiffly. Before all fingertips became bloody pulps from the cement floor, the transfer documents were placed before them and were usually signed. In the few cases where these measures failed, the Franconian prisoners were shipped to Dachau. There some of them were subjected to further methods of torture until they signed the necessary transfer papers.

By these illegal and brutal measures, the Streicher gang forced the transfer of 569 real estate parcels in less than two months. While specific figures regarding the monetary losses to former Jewish owners are not available, an approximation of the scope of this "robbery" was provided during a later investigation conducted into Streicher's affairs. Here it was estimated that the difference in its real value and sale price was 21 million marks.[74]

In addition to forcing Jews to sign over their properties at very low prices by threats and torture, Streicher and his hoodlums levied commissions on these forced sales. The commissions, frequently referred to as "donations," were usually handled through Strobl's office and paid by the buyer who, in turn, deducted the fee from the amount due for the aryanized Jewish property. Donations from real estate sales in Franconia were calculated at a rate of five to ten percent and were supposed to be handed over to the local Nazi party treasury. However, large numbers of these donations were deposited in special *Stuermer* accounts or given directly to Streicher, who distributed part of the money to his close colleagues and used the rest for personal expenses.[75]

In Franconia, the Jewish seller was often paid his share of

the "agreed" purchase price if he consented immediately to pay the additional commission fee in cash to one of Streicher's men, usually Koenig. In most cases, however, the final amount due the former Jewish owner was deposited by the buyer in a bank which, in turn, usually allowed the Jewish individual to withdraw nominal sums monthly for essential living expenses.

While the major sums of money in commission and "donation" fees were collected in Franconia from real estate transactions, a significant amount was also realized from sales of Jewish household furnishings and automobiles. On smaller sales such as these, the assessed fees ranged as high as 50 percent and were paid by the buyers, who, by verbal agreement with Strobl's office, deposited the "donations" directly into one of Streicher's closed bank accounts under the name and number—"Aryanization-14770." In one typical example, a piano retailer named Schroeder paid an average of 369 marks for 17 pianos purchased from Jews. Schroeder deposited 25 percent of the total sum into the above closed account and paid the balance directly to the various Jewish sellers of the pianos.[76]

The purchase of motor vehicles in Franconia also followed this pattern of payment. For example, a Jew, Dr. Lessing, owned an automobile worth at least 2000 marks. Strobl's office "stipulated" the purchase price at 120 marks. The buyer, a party member, paid Lessing 80 marks and deposited 40 marks in Streicher's closed bank account. The procedure for expropriation of motor vehicles typified methods of subterfuge frequently used by Streicher's henchmen to ease the Jews out of their possessions quickly and efficiently. On a certain day, all Franconian Jews who owned motor vehicles received a summons to appear at a certain place, where they were told that specific information about their vehicles was needed. They were ordered to fill out a form containing questions regarding the make of the vehicle, the model year, license number, mileage and general condition. They also had to verify that the vehicle belonged to them and was paid for. After these forms were completed, a Nazi official informed them that unless they signed a bill of sale, agreeing to sell the vehicle for a "stipulated" price, they might find the vehicle destroyed beyond recognition. Except for a few rare cases, the Jewish owners signed away ownership immediately.

Usually the purchaser was a party member who had previously submitted an aryanization requisition with Strobl's office.

As indicated in the above paragraphs, procedures followed in Franconia regarding the payments to the Jews for their aryanized possessions and payments for commissions and "donations" were far from consistent. While Berlin anti-Semitic edicts were often subjected to varied interpretation, it was clear that the late-1938 laws intended that the central government should realize the principal benefits from the appropriation of the Jewish properties. These laws specified that the money due the Jews was not to be paid directly to them, but was to be deposited in closed bank accounts or entered directly into *Reich* account books as payment for some form of debt levied according to *Reich* laws. All securities also were to be deposited with a bank and only with special permission were the Jews allowed to withdraw nominal sums monthly or make some use of their securities. However, the balance in the accounts bearing the Jewish person's name was usually reduced immediately at rates ranging from 25 to 100 percent as special levies for such assessments as *Entjudungsgewinn* (elimination of Jewish influence or profit) or *Suehnabgabe* (atonement fee for a Jewish crime).[77]

In late November, Streicher became very interested in a large block of securities held in a bank for a Nuremberg Jewish businessman named Anton Kohn, who had been sent to the Dachau concentration camp. Kohn was the principal stockholder of a large manufacturing firm registered as Mars-Werke A.G. Streicher evidently realized the possibility of a sizable personal gain at the unfortunate prisoner's expense and decided to acquire Kohn's majority shares of stock in the firm at a fraction of its true value. Details of the Mars-Werke stock acquisition provide a factual illustration of another method used by Streicher as well as other Nazis to enrich themselves through the guise of the government aryanization laws. Specific information about the Mars-Werke stock transfer is especially relevant here because this was a key element in testimony against Streicher in an investigation which eventually led to his political downfall.[78]

To handle the legal details necessary for the acquisition of Kohn's Mars-Werke stock, Streicher engaged the services of a shrewd attorney named Dr. G. Oehl. After some investigation, Oehl went to the Dachau prison, where, by questionable means, he obtained Kohn's signature on a document agreeing to sell these shares of stock to a third party, not named, at a price yet to be determined. With this document, Oehl purchased the shares of stock worth over 350,000 marks for the nominal sum of 35,000 marks. Oehl, in confidence, told Fink that Streicher was the actual purchaser of the shares and that he (Oehl) wanted to become chairman of the board of directors of the Mars-Werke firm. Fink allegedly was ordered by Streicher to arrange for the payment of the shares from *Stuermer* funds.

The large-scale profiteering by illicit aryanization activities of Streicher and his cronies did not go unnoticed by certain authorities. Nuremberg's Police President Martin and his staff accumulated a mass of documentary evidence substantiating these and other activities that violated existing Nazi government laws. As chief law enforcement officer, Martin had tried to curb these violations but found it impossible to overcome Streicher's authority without the aid of superior powers. He duly informed Himmler and Reich Treasurer Schwarz of the evidence he had gathered on cases of profiteering by Streicher and his cronies through illegal appropriations methods. However, no action was taken against the *Gauleiter* by higher Nazi authorities at this time. In spite of this disappointment, Martin continued his attempts to break Streicher's tyrannical actions in Franconia. Some time in early 1938 he was joined by Liebel and others in Nuremberg in this effort.[79]

Martin had been accumulating evidence of Streicher's questionable activities since 1934. At that time he had assigned a special police agent, named Heigl, to compile material for the eventual ouster of the *Gauleiter*. A surveillance program was set up including full-time police guards at Streicher's home and office as well as cameras with telescopic lenses at strategic locations to record all of Streicher's movements and his visitors. A microphone taped to his desk and taps on his telephone line provided police officers with further confidential information for the Streicher police file.

By early 1938, Martin had collected a massive dossier of recorded evidence of illicit acts committed by Streicher, or traceable to him or his close associates. By this time he was not only hated thoroughly by all Jews and their friends, but his name was repulsive to most Franconian citizens as well as to most ranking Nazi officials. Yet, because Martin felt that Streicher was still too solidly protected by Hitler, he made no serious attempt to take his evidence to higher party authorities for action.

Forced to wait until Streicher's transgressions would alienate him from Hitler, his sole protector, Martin embarked on a plan to limit the *Gauleiter's* extortionist activities and to further discredit him in the eyes of his Nazi peers. In mid-summer, 1938, Martin arranged for the distribution of anonymous leaflets about Streicher and his cronies to some 200 small businessmen in Franconia. These tradesmen had been pressured annually by Streicher for "free-will donations" to the local party treasury. In most cases, these persons had responded to the threats of the *Gauleiter's* bullies and had been bled of considerable sums of money in this manner. Martin's anonymous leaflets proved to be very effective. Printed on Berlin stationery the publications criticized the Streicher gang sharply and urged all recipients to refuse further payments to them. It also stated that Hitler and other Nazi officials had received copies of the leaflet. Streicher reportedly became furious and accused both Liebel and Martin as responsible for the publication, but he could not trace the true source of it. As a result of this tactic, most local businessmen managed to evade any payment as a "party donation" that year.[80]

Martin planned a second anonymous publication in early August to be prepared in time for mailing to some one-hundred party officials and foreign visitors who would be attending the 1938 Nuremberg Party-day Rally. This was arranged in the form of a leaflet entitled "The Saint and the Fool" and secretly authored by an SS officer named Schickert, who was secretary of the secret police. The section on Streicher was a satire on the saintly public affections of the *Gauleiter*, oftentimes attempting to emulate a man of God, intoning pledges of righteousness and peace while at the same time privately issuing orders for atrocities to be committed on countless innocent persons. In addition, this section listed many of his immoral personal activities.

The section headed "The Fool" concerned the sordid

affairs of Koenig. Accompanied by a caricature of his face, depicting a buffoon, a detailed article described his shady activities as Streicher's "strongman." However, the focus of the charges against him was on a private scandal dealing with his intimate relations with a young actress named Else Balster. In early 1937, she had become pregnant by Koenig and, not wishing to interrupt her stage career, had engaged the services of a Dr. Simon, who performed an abortion for her.

By early 1938, the scandal had become a sensational topic of local gossip. Nuremberg police had learned of the illegal operation and anonymous letters were sent to Fraeulein Balster, threatening her with prison, and were also sent to some Nuremberg governmental and party officials, informing them of the affair.[81]

Perhaps because of the overshadowing melodrama of the gigantic Party-day Rally, the gossipy revelations in the anonymous leaflets caused nothing more than a wave of whispering among ranking Nazis, who seemed only a little surprised about the alleged transgressions of Streicher and Koenig. According to Martin's later testimony, Streicher appeared more shocked than anyone else, acting like a "foaming lion, " but powerless to retaliate because he could not trace the origin of the leaflets. Martin conjectured that the anonymous attack only served, at the time, to provoke more hatred in Streicher than ever toward his known and unknown enemies.[82]

By the time the Party-day Rally was concluded, Streicher had narrowed the possible sources of the leaflets to either Liebel or Martin. While he lacked positive proof of his suspicions, he nevertheless opened bitter feuds with these two officials, castigating them verbally and in newspaper articles.[83] Almost simultaneously, Liebel dropped his pretense of cooperation with the *Gauleiter* and began acting openly hostile and criticizing him in public.

Martin's determined campaign to gather enough incriminating evidence against Streicher to oust him from public office was made known to him (Streicher) in late November, 1938, by means of a memo from Himmler's office. When Streicher learned of the forces that were beginning to oppose him openly and threaten his position seriously, he reacted with increasing hatred and bitterness in the manner noted by

Martin after the leaflets against him were published in September.

This reaction coincided partially with the pattern of the confirmed, historical anti-Semite who usually responds to open opposition or serious threats to his position by increased aggressiveness and displays of uncontrolled anger. According to some behavioral analysts, racial fanatics also have shown a tendency to react to threatening situations by excessive preoccupation with sex and sexual practices.[84]

It seems feasible that Streicher's reaction to the September leaflets was directly related to the excessive brutality inflicted on Franconian Jews during and after *Kristallnacht*. Although unrecorded, it can only be conjectured that Streicher's hateful attitude triggered or encouraged the extreme cruelty suffered by Nuremberg area Jews at the hands of the *Gauleiter's* bullies. Records indicate that the treatment of the Jewish population in Streicher's *Gau* in late 1938 was more brutal and sadistic than during any other two-months period and worse than in any other district in Germany at this time.[85]

According to later testimony by Fink, Streicher began to act increasingly agitated during November, and by early December he flew into a rage whenever he was presented with a problem concerning the aryanization program, especially the Mars-Werke transaction. It appears almost certain that this state of emotional stress mirrored Streicher's concern over continuing information from Himmler that Martin was requesting official Berlin intervention into the affairs of Franconia. Eventually Streicher was informed that Martin was seeking an audience with Goering and that he (Martin) was armed with a dossier filled with damning evidence of his (Streicher's) illicit activities.[86]

It may have been because of the increasing worry and agitation caused by this news that Streicher suddenly began to seek diversion in concentrating his attention on the sexual practices of other persons. On December 2, he appeared unannounced at the Nuremberg prison accompanied by his twenty-three-year-old son, Lothar, and asked to see eight teen-aged boys who had been jailed on charges of assault and robbery. Although the alleged crimes had been committed against Jewish persons, Streicher did not express interest in these charges. Instead, he tried to make them feel at ease and then began questioning them about their sex practices and how often they masturbated. When one of the young boys said he had never heard of that term and did not know the meaning of it, Streicher explained it to them at great length and in detail. After more than an hour of this sordid discussion, Streicher suddenly flew into a rage and inflicted a beating with his riding whip on the last boy questioned.[87]

About two weeks later, on December 17, Streicher made the long drive to the Dachau concentration camp in order to question some prisoners there. During these sessions, he concentrated on the issue of the prisoners wives' moral conduct at home. Most of the men questioned offered no comment when Streicher asked them if they were certain that their wives were faithful to them while they were gone. His line of question then focused on what the prisoners did to satisfy their sexual desires while they were away from home.

In addition to badgering young boys and Dachau prisoners about their sexual practices Streicher also questioned a young housemaid he had hired recently about her past sexual experiences, especially in connection with the Jewish husband of a woman for whom the girl had formerly worked. Professing that she was still a virgin, the girl could not stop Streicher's badgering until she yielded to his insistence that she consent to an examination by a police doctor and obtain a certificate of her virginity.

Streicher's avid preoccupation with sexual matters in early 1939 was noted by his chauffeur, Fritz Herbert, who related stories about this to Fink. Apparently, Streicher bragged continuously to Fritz about his past sexual exploits and, on one occasion, called the chauffeur to his bedside to show him a large stain on the sheet. Boasting that he wanted to share this evidence of a nocturnal emission, he said: "I just wanted to prove to you that at fifty-four years of age, I'm still a good man!" On yet another occasion later that month, the chauffeur related that he and his boss were at a steam-bath establishment, and while Streicher was receiving a massage with only a sheet over him, he developed an erected penis. Then he called over a young female clerk and pointed to the irregularity in the sheet, exclaiming that he only wanted to show her this because he was certain that she probably never saw something that nice in the middle of the day.[88]

While Streicher's lascivious activities during December and January indicated an almost fanatic interest in sexual matters, he seemed cautious in directing his sordid words only to innocuous and defenseless persons. Eventually, however, he seemed to be so preoccupied in this erotic pastime that he cast all caution aside. Overstepping all bounds of political tact, he carelessly pointed some debauching remarks at Goering, who, next to Hitler, was the most powerful Nazi in Germany. According to a Nuremberg newspaper reporter, Streicher was at a bowling alley and remarked, in the presence of a small crowd, that he had heard a rumor that Goering was impotent and unable to father the recent child of his young wife. Elaborating, Streicher then added words to the effect that he believed that this rumor could be true since Goering was so fat and pompous. During the next few days, Streicher repeated these remarks to a colleague in a telephone conversation, which was intercepted and transcribed by one of Martin's police investigators.[89]

Martin included a copy of this recorded conversation in the large file of evidence against Streicher and went to Berlin in late December to again seek help from higher authorities in bringing Streicher to justice. When Himmler refused to initiate action against Streicher, Martin tendered his resignation, but Himmler flatly refused it with the comment that Martin was needed in Nuremberg to "keep an eye on that fool Streicher." Martin then attempted to see Goering. He failed in this endeavor but managed through an intermediary, General Bodenschatz, to inform Goering of the overwhelming evidence of Streicher's wrongdoings contained in his confidential file. Perhaps realizing that Hitler disliked listening to complaints about Streicher, Goering attempted to settle the matter by calling the *Gauleiter* to Berlin for a meeting to "clean up the mess" in Franconia.

After this meeting with Goering, Streicher returned to Nuremberg visibly shaken. Martin was branded a traitor by the *Gauleiter's* followers, and open threats against his life were made on several occasions. With his life publicly threatened, Martin again appealed to Goering's office in mid-January, and this time was granted a personal interview with the Field Marshal. As Martin presented the contents of his file, he noticed that Goering appeared hesitant and non-committal, evidently uncertain of Hitler's possible hostile reaction to a demand that Streicher undergo official investigation for misconduct of his office. Martin argued that the illegal profiteering in Franconia was detrimental to his (Goering's) well-publicized Four Year Plan for Economic Development. When Goering continued to remain unmoved, Martin presented him a copy of a transcript of Streicher's derogatory remarks about his rumored impotence. At this, Goering was visibly angered and finally agreed with Martin that an official inquiry into the alleged transgressions of Streicher and his cronies should be undertaken. Within two weeks, a special commission, ordered by Goering with Hitler's permission, was formed to launch preliminary investigations in Franconia and to recommend whether or not formal legal proceeding against Streicher should be instituted.[90]

CHAPTER XII

UNFIT FOR LEADERSHIP

In early February, 1939, news about the formation of the Goering commission and the coming investigation reached Nuremberg. Somewhat panicky, Streicher called Koenig immediately expressing his apprehension concerning the Balster woman's abortion. Since Hitler and most ranking Nazis considered abortion a serious crime, Streicher insisted to Koenig that he felt this affair would become the central issue in the impending inquiries. Streicher was also evidently worried that his own reputation would be damaged by the abortion "scandal" because he had known about it before it became public knowledge and he had taken no official action. A little later that day Streicher sent Koenig a loaded pistol and a note telling him that the only way "to keep the party clean" was for him to commit suicide as acknowledgement of the shame he had brought on the local party. Surprisingly, Koenig agreed to this drastic move without argument and later that day, stood in front of a mirror in his bedroom and shot himself fatally.[1]

An intriguing question arises regarding Streicher's honest motives in ordering this suicide. Considering that it was not Koenig but the actress Balster who ordered the abortion, it seems nonsensical to assume that Koenig's gesture of extreme repentance would minimize to any appreciable extent the seriousness of the abortion scandal in the eyes of an investigation commission. On the other hand, Koenig was probably Streicher's closest confidante and perhaps as knowledgeable as anyone else about the *Gauleiter's* personal and business transgressions. Since two of Streicher's inner circle, Fink and Strobl, later became state's witnesses against Streicher, it seems possible that the *Gauleiter* may have questioned the reliability of Koenig under pressure. Capitalizing on the excuse provided by the abortion scandal, he may have magnified the possible implications of it to Koenig in order to rid himself of a potentially damaging witness in the coming inquiries.

In a gesture that may have symbolized partial atonement for the sacrificial death of his erstwhile colleague, Streicher arranged a massive state funeral for Koenig in a ceremony befitting a national hero. The Franconian Nazi bully was awarded special posthumous honors by Streicher, who also delivered a stirring graveside eulogy, praising the martyred Koenig's contributions to the party and to the Franconian people.

A few days after Koenig's funeral the commission organized by Goering began its inquiries. Headed by a high Nazi police official named Meisinger, and including several ranking representatives from the finance and economic ministries, the group soon accumulated a large quantity of incriminating evidence against Streicher from Martin's file. The commission's findings against Streicher were also increased by testimony of a number of witnesses who were afraid to lie under oath or who had personal reasons to turn against the *Gauleiter*.

One of the key witnesses was the embittered former mistress of Streicher, Anni Seitz, who had been recently arrested and jailed on the *Gauleiter's* orders, ostensibly because of his suspicion of her loyalty to him. She testified to her intimate relations with Streicher and stated also that he had used funds from the party newspaper *Fraenkische Tageszeitung* to provide her and her father with steady salaries of 200 to 300 marks monthly. She also stated under oath that according to her best knowledge, the same newspaper also paid for their use of an automobile and expense accounts of approximately 130 marks every month.[2]

Several other witnesses, including Strobl, provided further incriminating evidence against Streicher, such as his role in organizing the illegal aryanization transactions and profiteering from them; his flagrant misuse of party and public funds for his personal construction projects, and for gifts and free services to members of his family as well as to three or four mistresses in addition to Anni Seitz. Two days of the commission's inquiries dealt with Streicher's sadistic beating of Steinrueck in a jail cell in 1934.

After the first round of hearings which lasted about two months, the Meisinger group had recorded an impressive amount of testimony related to the illegal and illicit activities of Streicher and his cronies. Yet, the commission continued the probe throughout the most part of the spring and summer of 1939. Because some commission members were dissatisfied with the answers of Holz, Fink, and others who were possibly intimidated by the *Gauleiter* or fearful of incriminating themselves, Meisinger had persons such as these recalled to answer questions several times. Finally, Fink weakened after a reminder that he could be sent to prison for lying under oath. With his subsequent testimony, Fink proved to be the principal witness in affecting Streicher's eventual fall from political power.[3]

Fink provided the Meisinger commission with the type of confidential information that was perhaps impossible to obtain from any other living individual. Among his many responsibilities in Streicher's affairs, Fink had been business manager for the *Stuermer* and the *Fraenkische Tageszeitung* from 1933 to 1939. While the former newspaper belonged solely to Streicher, the latter was founded by him but was later acquired by the local party. Fink attested to many cases of complying with Streicher's orders to pad the payroll and expense accounts of the *Fraenkische Tageszeitung* in order to make payments to Streicher's family members, his household staff, and some of his mistresses and their parents.[4]

As the chief financial officer of Streicher's publishing companies, Fink admitted that he knew of large sums of money from aryanization profits and commissions that were deposited in bank accounts controlled by Streicher. He cited specific amounts that he (Fink) had withdrawn from these accounts to pay construction costs for buildings on the Pleikershof farm and for a dwelling house for himself with a private suite attached used solely by Streicher for his amorous affairs. In one statement that seems to be somewhat exaggerated, Fink said that the construction costs at Pleikershof totalled two million marks when completed. Fink also provided the commission with specific names of persons, including Koenig's mistress Else Balster, and several intimate female acquaintances, most of them married, who were given sizable monetary gifts from funds belonging to the party and from aryanization proceeds. These gifts totalled between 25 and 30 thousand marks within a period of less than three years.

Perhaps the most crucial revelations by Fink concerned the Mars-Werke transaction, which seemed of utmost importance to Meisinger and his colleagues. This affair was apparently planned by the commission to be highlighted as a prime example of large-scale misappropriation of funds from impounded securities. It became evident later that Goering had instructed Meisinger to look for at least one clear-cut case proving that Streicher instead of the *Reich* had profited from this type of transaction. Unfortunately, the commission did not attempt to seek proof of legal ownership or restitution for the former Jewish owners, but rather centered its questions on the final disposition of the money received for the securities from third parties.

In discussing his involvement of the Mars-Werke stock transfer, Fink told the commission that this recent acquisition appeared to worry Streicher more than any other matter during February and March, 1939. Fink alleged that he had suggested to Streicher in mid-February that he return the shares of stock to Kohn, but that the *Gauleiter* rejected this suggestion. Later, however, Fink said that Streicher deposited the shares with a Nuremberg trust company where he (Streicher) would have the right to dispose of them as he wished. Inasmuch as these shares were presumably still in the vaults of the trust company at the time of the inquiries, Fink could offer no further information regarding their final disposition. Apparently, however, the Mars-Werke shares were never returned to Kohn but were sold to a third party with the proceeds deposited in a *Reich* bank account.[5]

While describing his relationship with Streicher in February, Fink testified that he had repeatedly been called by Streicher to discuss his concern about the pending investigation and especially the Mars-Werke transaction. On one of these occasions, Streicher allegedly insisted to Fink that he must not reveal that he (Streicher) knew that the shares belonged to a Jew and that the stock purchases had been for the party's newspaper. When Fink did not fully agree to tell these lies under oath, Streicher allegedly flew into a rage and thundered: "The best thing is to have you sent where many others already are, or even better for you to shoot yourself!"

As the Meisinger commission continued its inquiries, some of the involved minor party members were arrested and given light prison sentences. A few others, such as Fink, lost their jobs while some were dismissed from the party. Throughout most of the following summer Holz was left untouched and Streicher remained in full power until after the end of the year. On the several occasions of Streicher's appearance before the commission, he generally pleaded innocent of any wrong-doing. Each time documentary proof of illegal activities was presented to him, he placed the blame on others, especially Holz and Fink. When questioned about the possibility of clearance by Hitler for some anti-Semitic measures that had occurred in Franconia, he insisted that he had been extremely limited in his attempts at personal contact with Hitler in recent years. He also added that it had always been difficult for him to be friendly with Hitler, even though he was still one of only three living men who were permitted to address him in the familiar *"du"* form of pronoun.[6]

Streicher's claim that Hitler was virtually inaccessible to him by 1939 was factual. When he tried to complain to his chief in June about the undermining of his authority by Liebel and Martin, he was not permitted to see Hitler personally. Instead he was instructed to send his complaint in an official report through one of Hitler's secretaries, Lammers, who disliked the *Gauleiter* intensely. Although Lammers claimed that he had handed the report to Hitler the same day it was received, Hitler apparently had not bothered to reply in any way. After a few days, Streicher apparently realized the futility of waiting further for Hitler's support in his present dilemma. Observers noted that he appeared haggard and distraught. That same week he left Nuremberg for a convalescent center in the town of Hohenlynchen where he received some needed medical treatment and then spent the next two months vacationing in the company of several local lady friends.[7]

While Streicher was absent from Nuremberg, anti-Semitic activities were noticeably slowed down. Martin reported that the presence of the Meisinger commission may have also contributed to the easing of tensions in Franconia, especially in Jewish neighborhoods. However, it was noted by a newspaper reporter that by this time many Jewish families were living in very crowded conditions, practically destitute. Emigration of jews from Streicher's *Gau* continued as rapidly as the necessary permits could be obtained. In many cases where Jewish families were unable to arrange for travel and accommodations in foreign countries, they moved to other localities in Germany, not knowing of the fate that ultimately awaited them at the hands of the Nazi rulers.

In August, Holz brought on his own demise. He had

embarked on a pleasure trip to Italy with a mistress. While there, he accidentally met an Italian political figure who was somewhat knowledgeable about political affairs in Nuremberg. Holz, a married man, foolishly introduced his mistress as his wife. The next day, Nuremberg newspapers were sent copies of Italian newspaper articles, complete with pictures, of the well-known assistant Franconian *Gauleiter* and his "wife" vacationing in Italy. Liebel and Martin seized on this opportunity to investigate the incident further and to circulate the story to high party officials. When Streicher initially heard about the affair he registered amusement, but later became angry when he heard that it was more than a moral issue and that Martin's police had learned that Holz had given his mistress foreign exchange which was considered a serious violation of *Reich* civil law. The matter was immediately handed over to the highest party court. To avoid prosecution, Holz enlisted in the army at the lowly rank of private.[8]

There is little doubt that Streicher strongly urged Holz to join the army. At that time Hitler's foreign policies had drawn the nation to the brink of war, and recently established military priorities excused volunteers from prosecution for disobedience of most civil laws. Holz's immunity from civil court procedures relieved Streicher of unneeded anxieties as Nuremberg prepared for the annual Party-day Rally, scheduled to begin on September 1. The *Gauleiter* would not be faced with another scandal caused by the almost certain conviction of Holz in the foreign exchange case. He would also be spared the threat that Holz might weaken under further questioning and expose more information about the illicit aryanization transactions in Franconia.

Without informing Streicher, the Meisinger commission had finished its work in early August and had chronicled its findings in two volumes, which were subsequently reproduced and distributed to the offices of Hitler, Goering, Himmler, von Epp, and a few other ranking Nazi officials. Then, to the frustration of a number of persons, especially Martin, Liebel and Meisinger, the case against Streicher seemed to have reached a dead end. Martin learned through Goering's office that no party court or party official was allowed to undertake further legal proceedings against Streicher without Hitler's personal approval, and that Hitler had refused to consider the matter because of his preoccupation with pressing foreign and military affairs.[9]

By September 1, the issue of further legal proceedings against Streicher had seemingly lost political importance in Nuremberg with the busy preparations for the opening of the 1939 Party-day Rally. As in former years, several weeks of concentrated effort by city administrators and police officials had been concentrated on parade plans and accommodations for the hundreds of thousands of visitors and participants expected in Nuremberg by the time opening ceremonies were to take place.

However, this rally, billed as the "Rally for Peace," lasted only a few hours and was to be the last Nazi Party-day Rally ever to be scheduled. After all the preparations, the only event of this rally was a speech by Hitler, which was climaxed with the stunning announcement that since dawn that day, German armed forces had initiated the invasion of Poland. As if by prior instruction, Party Secretary Rudolf Hess and other speakers announced the cancellation of this rally and issued detailed orders for the evacuation of the city by the masses of participants and visitors who had only recently arrived there.

Throughout September, all Nazis and German citizens seemed totally engrossed in the news of the astounding successes of German and Russian forces in Poland and declarations by western European nations indicating the opening of a large-scale international war. Streicher was seen infrequently in Nuremberg, at restaurants or cafes, and spoke two or three times that month at political meetings outside the city. His demeanor and words indicated that he had regained his former arrogance and apparently had ceased concerning himself over the findings of the Meisinger commission. By early October, it seemed to Martin that Streicher had been saved from further proceedings against his past transgressions by the diversion of Hitler's attention to ongoing military developments.

In all likelihood, further legal proceedings against the *Gauleiter* would have been stalled forever if Streicher had not committed two further transgressions which finally eroded the shield of Hitler's long-standing loyalty and protection. On October 8, he received a message ordering him to attend an impromptu meeting of *Gauleiters* at Hitler's headquarters the following day. The single agenda item was an address by the Nazi leader outlining further war plans and needs for the organization of wartime economic measures. Hitler began by describing the need to control the English Channel coastline for the future invasion of Britain. Then, after a few statements emphasizing the confidential nature of what he was discussing, Hitler told of his scheme for a surprise attack westward the following month through neutral Belgium, Holland and Luxembourg. After returning to Nuremberg, Streicher carelessly disclosed the confidential information to a few party comrades, and later to a larger assembly at a political meeting.[10]

Even though it is virtually certain that Hitler learned of Streicher's betrayal of the military secrets almost immediately, he made no apparent gesture to reprimand or punish the *Gauleiter* at this time. Evidently oblivious to the fact that he may have angered Hitler and possibly his generals by leaking important military information, Streicher brought on the wrath of almost the entire army general staff a few weeks later with thoughtless and insulting words at the Nuremberg *Kulturvereinhalle*, while attending an "evening of comradeship" for German war veterans.

After listening to a few speeches which concentrated on the recent brilliant successes in the Polish campaign and the outstanding achievements of some of the military leaders there, Streicher suddenly arose and made his way to the speaker's platform. Although he was not a scheduled speaker, he stood behind the podium and began to address the audience in an excited manner. Taking exception to some of the comments made by the previous speakers, he stated emphatically that sole credit for the military triumphs in Poland was due to Hitler, who had personally directed the invasion and had inspired the troops in heroic fashion. Continuing his verbal torrent, he charged that the previous great war had been lost because of inept military leaders who would not lead their men properly in the front lines. Before he had finished his harangue, many officers in the crowd, who had seen combat service in the last war were on their feet, shaking their fists and shouting angrily at him.[11]

By the next morning, Streicher learned that he had unwittingly incurred the hostility of large numbers of army officers, including general staff members at Hitler's head-

280

quarters. At the insistence of some ranking military leaders he was forced to apologize publicly and publish a retraction of his insulting words. As a result, issues of the *Stuermer* and the *Fraenkische Tageszeitung* the next few days carried front-page articles apologizing to all persons "who might have misunderstood" the *Gauleiter's* words. In a crude attempt to whitewash the meaning of his speech, Streicher managed to create further animosity with a blatant lie, in a *Stuermer* article, that he had actually attempted, in clear words, to compliment the "brave generals" who had won the last war, but were cheated out of their victory by the Jews in the Weimar government who had "handed over the German victory to the enemy nations."[1][2]

Even though subsequent issues carried articles lauding general officers who had died in the service of their country, Streicher's insincere words in his published apology and retraction did nothing to exonerate him in the minds of certain military leaders who evidently voiced continuing complaints to Hitler about Streicher's damaging words to the war effort and to the morale of the army's officers.

By early November, it was apparent that Hitler had lost his patience with the radical antics of his old comrade. Streicher's "fall from grace" was made evident when Hitler purposely denied him the opportunity to participate in the annual commemoration of the 1923 Munich Beer Hall *Putsch.* This formal snub became public knowledge in Nuremberg as a *Fraenkische Tageszeitung* issue carried a front-page article about the meeting in the *Buergerbraeukeller* on the evening of November 8. In a photograph accompanying the article, Streicher was conspicuously absent from the rows of Nazi dignitaries listening to Hitler's traditional speech. However, the *Gauleiter* could be identified in the background, seated among ordinary party members.[1][3]

The highlight of the November 8 Munich meeting was a speech by Hitler, who directed his words at castigating the British and French nations, intimating that their hostile actions would have to be dealt with in the future. His address was unusually brief and he did not stay more than a few minutes, shaking hands and conversing with his followers. Shortly after Hitler left the hall, a bomb exploded in a column next to the speaker's podium, killing seven persons and wounding 63 others. It was learned in the following days that this assassination attempt on Hitler was planned and carried out by a man named Georg Elser, a former Communist who had served a sentence in the Dauchau prison and who was an avowed pacifist. In his confession, Elser stated that he had intended to kill Hitler in order to bring about an end to the war.[14]

Interestingly, it was because Hitler had somehow feared that an attempt would be made on his life in Munich that he had changed his plans and left the beer hall and the city earlier than originally scheduled. He had reportedly heard that rumors of his westward military aggression had been circulated widely and that political liberals and pacifists were determined to take drastic steps to stop him from fulfilling his military ambitions. In view of Hitler's evident knowledge that Streicher had been responsible for at least some of the disclosures of his immediate war plans, it seems reasonable to assume that the assassination attempt may have shocked Hitler into finally yielding to persuasions by Goering and others that Streicher should be brought to trial for the many charges that had been made against him.

While Hitler's reasons for finally agreeing to legal action in Streicher's case remain unclear, it is evident that he intended to remain aloof from the procedural details involved in the matter. He left it up to Goering to organize the formal hearing of the charges against Streicher. Orders emanating from Goering's office in late December stated that legal proceedings against Streicher by a special court would be arranged as soon as possible. The official named to represent Goering in the organization of the court hearings was General Bodenschatz. Rudolph Hess was to supervise the proceedings as Hitler's representative, and Major Walter Buch, chief of the supreme court, was appointed to act as presiding judge. Streicher was informed that evidence against him would be heard by a "jury" composed of six *Gauleiters;* three to be chosen by Rudolf Hess and three chosen by himself. The jurors eventually appointed by Hess were Sauckel of Thuringia, Mutschmann of Saxony, and Koch of East Prussia. Streicher picked three native Bavarians; Wagner of Munich, Schwede of Pomerania, and Forster of Danzig.[15]

The formal hearing took place at the Hotel Regina in Munich and began on February 13, the day after Streicher's fifty-fifth birthday. The proceedings opened with a brief address by Hess, stating that he had been empowered by Hitler to order that the evidence be presented as concisely as possible, and that the "jury" was not authorized to pass judgment or levy a sentence, but only to render an "opinion" about the defendant Streicher. The presentation of evidence lasted a little less than three days and the only witnesses appearing against the defendant were Liebel, Martin and Meisinger. The principal issues and charges against Streicher were the same ones that the Meisinger commission had previously investigated and substantiated. In response to Buch's orders, Streicher attended the hearing but seemed subdued and had little to say except to blame all of the alleged wrong-doings on the actions of others, protesting that he had always wanted fair treatment for the Jews in his *Gau.*[16]

On February 16, the consensus of the *Gauleiter* jurors was read to Streicher by Major Buch. The defendant was found guilty of the principal charge that he had profited from dishonest financial dealings in the confiscation of Jewish property. The official "opinion" referred to Hitler by the jurors was simply that Streicher was found "unfit for leadership." In spite of the terse nature of the report on the findings of this special court, it was stated unofficially that the jurors were also influenced in their decision by evidence that Streicher was also guilty of treason, extreme brutality, and of speaking libelously against army generals and Goering.[17]

Hitler's reaction to the findings and recommendations of the special court was to order that Streicher cease all functions as a *Gauleiter* and make no further public speeches. However, he did not order any prohibition of Streicher's publishing activities and did not strip him of any titles, offices or honorary positions. During the week after this order, Hitler's office named Hans Zimmermann as acting *Gauleiter* of Franconia. Zimmermann had been an unemployed engineer who found work with the party in 1932 and had been promoted to *Kreisleiter* by Streicher because he was an able anti-Semitic speaker and because Streicher allegedly thought Zimmermann was "aryan looking." In 1939, when Streicher seemed to be falling into disgrace, Zimmermann had the foresight to stay away from him.[18]

After Zimmermann was named to take over the duties and

responsibilities of Franconian *Gauleiter*, Streicher quietly moved his place of residence to the Pleikershof farm. During the first few weeks after moving, he traveled the twenty miles to Nuremberg several times to attend to some business matters and to renew acquaintances with some old party comrades. According to Martin, these public appearances in Nuremberg brought reactions of anger among some of the "decent" citizens, who shook their fists at him. Martin said that he informed Hess and Bodenschatz about the disturbances caused by Streicher on these occasions. Evidently in obedience to orders from Berlin, Streicher made no further visits to Nuremberg or any other sizable Franconian town.[19]

Streicher did not seem outwardly resentful about the sentence and subsequent order to banish him from his position of political authority or from his beloved city, Nuremberg. In marked contrast to his usual volatile behavior, he appeared to accept his fate with dignity and stoic silence, making no effort to vindicate himself or question the fairness of the sentence. He probably realized that objections to Hitler's firm order would be futile and might lead to more severe consequences such as the loss of his publishing privileges.

He may have also accepted his banishment because the quietness of farm life came as welcome relief to the mental pressures brought on by his political activities in Nuremberg during recent years. His wife, Kunigunde, also seems to have undergone increasing mental strain after the Meisinger investigations began. She was undoubtedly accustomed to her husband's unpredictable behavior and fits of uncontrolled temper and also must have been aware of his longstanding and habitual infidelity to her. According to insinuations by the chauffeur, Fritz, Streicher had not been interested in sexual relations with Kunigunde during the late 1930 years. However, the added tension brought to the household by Streicher after realizing that he was vulnerable to official censure must have been too much for the woman's emotions, which were notably fragile for many years. She suffered a complete nervous collapse in early 1939 and was committed to a mental sanitorium in Rottermuenster, where she died during the mid-years of the war.[20]

With his wife's deteriorating mental condition and eventual complete emotional breakdown, Streicher employed various women as housekeepers at his home in Nuremberg. At Pleikershof, however, he found the need to expand his domestic staff with the addition of a person to handle the large amount of *Stuermer* correspondence and to perform general stenographic duties. Eventually he voiced this need to his business manager, Hiemer, who recommended his own secretary, Adele Tappe, for the position. After a brief interview and agreement on terms of employment, Adele moved into Streicher's household on June 7, 1940, as his secretary. Lacking authentic description of her physical features, it can only be assumed that at the age of thirty-four she was to Streicher an attractive and personally desirable woman. It is also quite certain that she found him appealing to her feminine instincts and was ideologically compatible to him, especially in racial opinions. Adele had come from Magdeburg to Nuremberg in November, 1938, to work as a staff writer for the *Stuermer* and in recent months had become Hiemer's private secretary.

Adele testified later that soon after she assumed her duties as Streicher's secretary at Pleikershof, he became ill and she helped nurse him back to health. Shortly after this she became his official housekeeper, and to all indications she also became his steady mistress and remained so until late March, 1945.[21]

With the help and companionship of Adele and his chauffeur, Fritz, Streicher seems to have settled into a rather uneventful life-style on the farm. Adele stated later that he had few visitors except Hiemer, who came from Nuremberg about once each week with a briefcase full of material and worked with Streicher on *Stuermer* articles and discussed newspaper editorials, composition, and business problems with him. In the earlier months of his farm life, Streicher was usually at his desk in the early morning hours and expended the rest of his energies helping with the completion of the three large concrete-block and wooden two-story buildings. These were approximately 150 feet long each and arranged squarely, on three sides of a large court-yard. Living quarters for Streicher's household, his chauffeur and several families of farm workers were finished on the upper floor, while the ground floor of the buildings was sectioned off for machinery, grain storage and farm animals. Perhaps in keeping with his questionable personal tastes, Streicher located the indoor pens for his small herd of white pigs directly beneath his own living quarters.[22]

After the building project was completed, Streicher spent his time reading, writing, or working with the farm hands in the fields, breaking stones, cutting hedges or mending fences. He was also keenly interested in the breeding habits of his pigs. During inclement weather he often sat at his easel, painting landscape scenes in watercolor. Several evenings each week he walked the distance of approximately one mile to a small *Bierstube* to drink a few glasses of beer and talk with some village men about farm problems. In a 1971 interview in this establishment with several elderly Pleikershof farmers, it was learned that Streicher seemed to be well-liked there and appeared to other patrons as a somewhat subdued person, causing no excitement or trouble.

While Streicher was undoubtedly genuinely interested in his crops and animals on the Pleikershof farm, his principal concern there until late March, 1945, remained the *Stuermer*. After his dismissal as active *Gauleiter* he had lost his political power which he had formerly used advantageously in promoting and forcing circulation of the newspaper and sales of advertising space. From average sales of 600,000 copies weekly between 1935 and 1939, *Stuermer* circulation dropped to a weekly average of some 425,000 copies between 1940 and early 1945. Streicher may have tried to maintain high circulation figures by appealing to his readers. During the war years every issue included the following message: "*Stuermer*-readers! Don't forget to send the *Stuermer* to your friends and relatives! The men at the front will thank you for this!"[23]

While loyal *Stuermer* readers may or may not have helped maintain fairly high circulation figures, it is certain that the principal source of support for Streicher's newspaper was Hitler, who sanctioned its distribution in greater Germany and in all countries conquered during the war. He also approved its circulation to German soldiers on all fronts. Hitler voiced this support to Propaganda Minister Goebbels in early 1942, in a memo stating that he did not wish the circulation of the *Stuermer* to be reduced or stopped.[24]

Until mid-1942, *Stuermer* editorial contents continued steadily to stress its usual anti-Semitic themes woven about real or imaginary cases that could be interpreted as proof of the "evil nature" of all Jews. Intermittently, Streicher contributed articles suggesting that the time would soon come when the Jewish problem in the *Reich* would have to be solved permanently. On these occasions he wrote that this "final solution" might be the enforced relocation of all European Jews to either the state of Israel or to the French island of Madagascar.[25]

Beginning in early 1940, the scope of *Stuermer* racial themes broadened to include consistent mention of Hitler's military achievements which were always emphasized in editorial articles as proof of Nazi successes in the struggle against the world-wide organization of Jews. At this time a new by-line was added to accompany the standard *Stuermer* proclamation, "The Jews are Our Misfortune," which for seventeen years had appeared across the bottom of the front page in bold type. The new by-line stretched across the bottom of the second page and stated: "The Jews Are To Blame For The War."

Following the lead of this statement, many subsequent *Stuermer* articles asserted that military campaigns on all fronts were initiated by Jewish treachery and greed. In typical fashion, the *Stuermer* reported the invasion of France as an unavoidable consequence of the hostile activities of French army troops responding to orders by their Jewish officers. With his penchant for reinforcing his arguments with historical references, Streicher wrote a series of articles on the 19th-century Dreyfuss affair, distorting the facts of the case to "prove" the long-standing record of Jewish officers undermining discipline or controlling activities of the French army.

In similar fashion, another Streicher series castigated England and dwelled on her imperialistic foreign policy under Prime Minister Benjamin Disraeli as "conclusive evidence" of Britain's selfish interests planned by Jews. One Fips cartoon accompanying these articles showed a British soldier guarding a large warehouse in India, refusing even a small quantity of rice to starving natives. This cartoon's caption indicated that all the rice was consigned to Jewish merchants in London for the war effort.[26]

Hitler's invasion of Russia was hailed in the *Stuermer* as a necessary step to eliminate Germany's eastern menace created by the "Bolshevik-Jew Lenin." In a series of garbled accounts of the Russian Revolution, Streicher attempted to prove that the former Czar was overthrown by the "Jew Kerensky" and that Jews had supported the revolution with money and had been profiting from it since the time of Lenin. In one cartoon, Fips tried to emphasize the presence of Jews in the Kremlin with a drawing of typical "*Stuermer* Jews" compiling long lists of lend-lease commodities from the United States and Great Britain. The caption of this cartoon depicted that the goods received would not be used for the benefit of Soviet troops or citizens, but would be sold to another country and the proceeds divided among the men compiling the list.[27]

Before and after the United States' declaration of war against Germany, *Stuermer* articles lampooned American domination by Jews. Special articles by Streicher focused on certain American families such as Guggenheim and Morgenthau, distorting facts in these cases to "prove" that the theater and the financial affairs in America were controlled by Jews. Throughout the war years, Streicher's favorite American target was President Franklin Roosevelt, who was always dubbed as "the Jew Rosenfeld" in the *Stuermer*. In one misconstrued article dealing with the history of the Roosevelt family, Streicher claimed that the President's ancestor, Theodore "Rosenfeld," was known to be a "greedy Jew imperialist," and since his presidency American politics had been controlled by Jews.

Cartoons by Fips satirized Franklin Roosevelt frequently with the countenance of a "*Stuermer* Jew," always in the presence of other men with similar features, conspiring in various ways to seize all the wealth in the world and to drive all non-Jews into perpetual misery. Featured in several *Stuermer* issues during the war years, Roosevelt's caricature was also included in cartoons illustrating the illusionary threat: "Only the victory of international Jewry will bring the world peace!" On numerous occasions *Stuermer* cartoons lampooning leaders of nations at war with Germany would be arranged with the distorted caricatures in the background and the bold figure of a clean-cut, "aryan" type German soldier in the foreground moving bravely away toward an illuminated horizon.[28]

In the early months of 1942, Streicher authored a series of editorial articles again dealing with possible solutions to the *Reich's* "Jewish question." After thoroughly discussing all the "dangers" existing with the presence of Jews in "aryan" societies, he pointed out that only the total absence of all Semitic persons in greater Germany would assure future generations of prosperity, peace and racial purity. Then one article mentioned that extermination, in addition to expulsion, would be the only method of liberating Europe of Jews. Continuing this theme, Streicher then elaborated on a distorted version of 13th-century history, stating that the Jews were expelled from a number of countries in Europe, but they wandered from place to place and always returned to dominate the societies from which they were expelled. Streicher also cited examples from medieval history where various governments or rulers carried out massacres of Jews to eliminate them from their realms. But, he continued, these attempts at extermination were only partially successful because the massacres usually excluded certain age groups or sexes and eventually future generations of non-Jews were still plagued by the Jews, who had replenished their own numbers.

After completing the details of the above pseudo-historic background, Streicher arrived at the hypothesis of his argument in a profusion of words. Summarized and paraphrased, his hypothesis stated: "Just as we have learned that the expulsion of Jews will lead to temporary and partial success, the extermination of Jews. . .if carried out in small numbers. . .will again be only temporarily and partially successful. . . ."[29]

On later occasions Streicher would be interrogated at length about his recommendations to rid Europe, and also the world, of all Jews by mass murder. While details of some of these interrogations will be discussed in subsequent pages, it is interesting to note here the contradictory reasons cited by Streicher to justify the *Stuermer's* adoption of the hard-line approach to the "final solution" of the "Jewish problem." In a March, 1942 *Stuermer* issue, Streicher stated that he was recommending the removal of the Jews by extermination because Hitler had proclaimed this "solution" on February 24, 1942, in the following public statement:

. . .today. . .my prophecy will find its fulfillment, that in this war not the aryan race will be destroyed, but the Jew will be

exterminated. . .and only then, after the removal of these para-
sites, will there be a long period of understanding among nations,
and hence real peace will come. . . .[30]

A few years later Streicher contradicted himself and
insisted under questioning that he felt compelled to recommend the removal of Jews by extermination only after he
read in the *Voelkischer Beobachter* about a book by an
American Jewish writer named Kaufman. Evidently incensed
by the brutal treatment of fellow Jews at the hands of the
Nazis, Kaufman wrote that the best "solution" to the
European situation would be the eradication of the German
nation by sterilizing all able-bodied German men.

In discussing his reactions to Kaufman's book, Streicher
insisted that until the time he read of the widely published
"threat" to the German nation, he had always recommended
that the Jews should be moved to their own national state.
He alleged further that he knew that Hitler never contem-
plated solving the "Jewish question" in a radical fashion.
Streicher made every attempt to convince his interrogators
that it was only after he learned that the Jews wanted to
exterminate the German nation that he wrote that the Jews
themselves should be exterminated.[31]

Streicher's contradictory reasons for adopting the "hard-
line" in early 1942 were not considered relevant matters to
interrogators who were aware of at least one *Stuermer* article
in 1938 and one in 1939 that alluded to death as the
deserving fate of certain Jews. The crucial issue in judging the
degree of Streicher's criminality would hinge mainly on
certain *Stuermer* articles advocating the mass-murder of Jews
written or approved by Streicher during the war years. In the
early 1942 *Stuermer* article which recommended the extermination of European Jews, Streicher left little to the reader's
imagination as he stated that this means of removal would be
"more complete and successful than expelling the Jews from
Europe."

During his five years at Pleikershof, Streicher wrote or
approved more than twenty-five similar *Stuermer* articles
openly recommending or suggesting death to the Jewish
"race." Excerpts of *Stuermer* articles published during this
period serve as examples of this type of criminous journalism.
In May, 1942, Streicher approved the following statements in

a *Stuermer* article written by Hiemer, which unquestionably urges the removal by death of all Jewish persons in the world:

> . . . .Europe is about to carry out the final solution of the Jewish question. . . .The Jewish question is a world question. Not only is Germany not safe in face of the Jews as long as one Jew lives in Europe, but also the Jewish question is hardly solved in Europe so long as Jews live in the rest of the world. Jewry is organized criminality. The Jewish menace will thus only be eliminated if Jewry in the whole world has ceased to exist. . . .[32]

In a later *Stuermer* article that year, Streicher wrote the following words in foretelling the annihilation of all Jews by the end of the war:

> . . . .My prophecy will find fulfillment that the aryan race is not annihilated by this war. On the contrary, the Jew will be exterminated. Whatever else this struggle leads to or however long it may endure, this will be the final result, and then. . .after the elimination of these parasites, a true peace will arise in a suffering world. . . .[33]

The following phrases from a *Stuermer* article in November, 1943, again reflect Streicher's advocacy of the removal of all Jews by extermination:

> . . . .There it results that the cause for anti-Semitism is in the existence of the Jews itself. One, therefore, only has to exterminate the cause, that is, the Jews, and then the world is free from anti-Semitism. It is clear that the Jews do not wish for such a solution. Moreover, they ask for the extermination of all non-Jews. . . .[34]

The final examples excerpted from articles written by Streicher and published in the *Stuermer* in February, 1944, and December 1944, illustrate that rather than softening, he seemed to have hardened in his criminal genocidal contentions in the last years of the war:

> . . . .Whoever does what a Jew does is a scoundrel and a criminal, and he who repeats and wishes to copy him deserves the same fate. . .annihilation—death!. . .
> . . . .If the danger of the reproduction of that curse of God in

the Jewish blood is finally come to an end, then there is only one way—the extermination of that people whose father is the devil. . . .[35]

It seems unbelievable that a person of full mental facilities could seriously propound total genocide as a course of action at any time or place in the history of mankind. The fact that even during the closing months of World War II, Streicher continued writing *Stuermer* articles of this nature suggests strongly that he may have been mentally unbalanced or at least out of touch with reality by this time. He must have known about the increasing losses by German troops on all fronts by 1942 and 1944 because he admittedly read daily and weekly newspapers from major German cities as well as papers from Switzerland and America. By this time the war was also getting close to Pleikershof as the systematic destruction of Nuremberg by allied bombers had already begun.

On the other hand, it is also possible that Streicher was in possession of full mental capacities at Pleikershof and realized fully that Germany was losing the war. But because of his long-standing conviction that his destiny was irrevocably charted for him in advance, he may have been determined to carry on his "battle" regardless of the consequences. As mentioned earlier in this study, both Streicher and Hitler shared the belief that their personal fate was guided by some mystical force which they frequently called "destiny" or "providence." This possibility seems more likely in view of a strong statement made by Streicher during a surprise visit by Goebbels in May, 1944. Streicher recalled this visit during a later interrogation and stated that Goebbels had conveyed greetings sent by Hitler and that nothing of political importance had been discussed between them. However, as Goebbels was preparing to leave, Streicher said he told him to inform Hitler that he was contented and needed no material help and then said to Goebbels: "Tell the *Fuehrer* that if a national disaster should come down on the German people, I have only one desire, to fall at his side!"[36]

Less than one year later, in early March, 1945, Streicher learned that the disaster of Germany was rapidly approaching its tragic climax. American forces were nearing Franconia from the west and little or no German military strength remained to stop this advance. Streicher must have decided at this time that the fulfillment of his "destiny" was at hand. During the month of March, he enlisted the aid of Adele every evening for about fourteen days to burn and bury valuable and/or incriminating material such as books, correspondence and journals. According to Adele's later testimony, Streicher had made a decision to join in the fighting to defend Nuremberg from falling into enemy hands. Adele also testified that she had insisted on going with him even if it meant dying at his side. In a somewhat melodramatic gesture, Streicher agreed with Adele's wishes, but proposed that she marry him immediately so that they could die as man and wife. She said that they also dug joint graves on the farm for their eventual interment.[37]

They were married on March 30, probably by a local civil service official in a simple ceremony. Adele said that when they began the short journey toward Nuremberg, they were stopped by some German soldiers who advised them to change their plans as American troops were already inside the city limits. Then the newlyweds headed southward, towards Munich, but were stopped on the way and cautioned to avoid that city and to head towards the Tyrolian Alps. Eventually they found refuge as paying guests at a farm near the town of Weidring, some fifteen miles southwest of Berchtesgaden.

Streicher lived out the closing weeks of the war at the modest farmhouse posing as an artist, partially disguised with the growth of a white beard. In all likelihood he had heard radio reports about the marriage of Hitler and his mistress, Eva Braun, on April 29, and their suicides a few hours afterwards. Streicher said later that he had planned a somewhat similar end for himself and his bride when he left Pleikershof, but was "interrupted" by some soldiers and then decided instead to travel southward.[38]

Even before the German surrender on May 6-7, military intelligence units had begun rounding up Nazis who had been considered by a joint board of allied officials as most guilty of aggressive warfare and wartime atrocities and crimes. The names of the Nazis considered to be potential criminals were published in a list circulated to all sectors of Europe. Two weeks after the collapse of Germany, most of the persons of this list had been captured or accounted for except Bormann, Himmler, Ribbentrop and Streicher.

CHAPTER XIII

FINAL JUSTICE AT NUREMBERG

The capture of Streicher by the Jewish-American officer, Major Henry Blitt, on May 23 was probably viewed by some observers as lucky and somewhat comical. However, to those persons who had been victimized by Streicher or were aware of the harm and suffering he had caused countless Jewish people, the event must have been hailed as fatefully ordained and justified.

In his later description of the arrest, Blitt remembered Streicher as appearing to him as disgraceful looking as his evil reputation. Dressed in a collarless, dirty, blue-striped shirt and ragged trousers, Streicher seemed to Blitt as much older than his sixty years, with his shaggy, unkempt white beard.[1]

A few minutes after Streicher was placed under arrest, his wife, Adele, appeared in the doorway of the farmhouse. She seemed stunned as she stared at the American soldiers and her husband, now standing manacled in handcuffs. Answering a few of Blitt's brief questions pertaining to her identity, Adele was also arrested. Shortly afterwards, both Streichers were ordered into the jeep and driven to a U.S. Army compound northeast of Munich. They were then jailed in separate cells at the police station in the town of Freising.[2]

Three days later they were transported to a jail in Wiesbaden and Streicher was taken the next day to the Central Continental Prisoner of War Enclosure near Mondorf, Luxembourg. Adele was kept in custody at various locations until she was taken to Nuremberg in early August, in order to undergo official interrogation.[3]

Streicher had been accompanied from Wiesbaden by Captain John Dolibois of the United States Army Intelligence Service. Dolibois, a native of Luxembourg, had been assigned Streicher, Goering, and a few other major war criminals to act as special liaison officer and preliminary interrogator. Dolibois reportedly treated the Nazi prisoners firmly, but fairly, and gained the confidence of Streicher, who in a friendly manner called Dolibois "Captain Gillen."[4]

Dolibois later related that Streicher complained bitterly of his treatment at the hands of American soldiers before his transfer to Mondorf. Evidently his notoriety as a fanatic racial persecutor was known to the troops at Freising. Streicher claimed that he and his wife were forced by some black American soldiers to walk in public stripped of their clothes. These soldiers allegedly spat on them and extinguished cigarettes on their bare skin. At Mondorf, an unconfirmed report was circulated stating that some soldiers had taken photographs that showed Streicher dressed only in an open coat, with swollen testicles and a crown of thorns on his head with a sign draped over his neck with the words "Julius Streicher, King of the Jews."

However, this unconfirmed report as well as most of Streicher's complaints at Mondorf of barbaric treatment at the hands of American troops are extremely questionable. In a handwritten letter dated in June, 1945, to former *Stuermer* colleagues at Nuremberg, Streicher related some of his experiences after his capture. He complained about the lack of furniture in the jail cell, the uncomfortable handcuffs, and mentioned an incident where he was forced to stamp out cigarettes with his bare feet. This letter contained no other indication of brutality on the part of American soldiers.[5]

While Streicher apparently fabricated some stories to officers at Mondorf about the behavior of some of his captors, his own actions in custody were abnormal and somewhat revolting to those around him. Dolibois related in an interview that Streicher seemed to be obsessed with sexual fantasies and extraordinary sexual desires. Streicher allegedly implored Dolibois on several occasions to bring a woman into his cell for sexual purposes even though this was strictly against the rules of the prison. During most conversations between the two men, Streicher inevitably brought up obscene topics or began relating some of his past sexual conquests.[6]

On one occasion described by Dolibois, Streicher was in his cell when a visitor to Mondorf, Erika Mann, appeared at the prison. Ms. Mann, a masculine-attired authoress, was on a research assignment for the American magazine, *Liberty*. Streicher had previously voiced his resentment at the many visitors who had been permitted to view the Nazi prisoners in their cells. He told Dolibois that he often felt like an animal behind bars at a public zoo. As Streicher heard the visitor approaching his cell he had turned his back to the door, with legs stiff and spread apart. When he heard her voice, he turned, and recognizing her, said sarcastically: "Well, I see you have also come to stare at all the wild animals in the zoo!" After Ms. Mann offered no reply, Streicher continued: "Then you may as well see everything!" With this remark, Streicher unbuckled his trousers and dropped them to the floor, exposing his genital organs to her. According to Dolibois, Ms. Mann stared at him coldly for an instant, then flicked the ash from her small cigar in his direction and turned toward the next cell.

Streicher's obnoxious behavior in his cell may have been partially the result of his frustration with the treatment he received from his fellow Nazi prisoners. Dolibois relates that Streicher was disliked intensely by the other inmates, who seemed embarrassed that he was considered to be one of them. When Streicher entered the dining hall for his first evening meal at Mondorf, all of the Nazis present turned on their heels and left the room. When they complained to the prison commandant, Colonel Burton Andrus, about being forced to eat with Streicher, he patiently asked that at least some of them act cooperatively and eat with Streicher. Only Robert Ley, Hitler's former Labor Minister, responded in a friendly manner toward Streicher and volunteered to share a dining table with him.

Perhaps because of his loneliness and inactive life at Mondorf, Streicher decided to write a political testament in the form of a monograph consolidating the high points of his political career with his principal anti-Semitic ideologies. Dolibois approved of this project and arranged for a minor prisoner, the son of Hitler's Treasury Minister, Franz Schwarz, to transcribe Streicher's dictated words on an old typewriter. When completed in late summer, 1945, the document was entrusted by Streicher to Dolibois, who must have considered it unworthy as archival material or for publication. The manuscript was bulky, containing approximately 15,000 words and was poorly transcribed, containing many typographical errors and misspelled words.

Quite accidentally, Dolibois told of the manuscript's existence thirty years later in the presence of an American university professor, Jay W. Baird, whose academic specialty is 20th-century German history. Baird became interested in the document and subsequently corrected the mechanical errors. After rewriting the political testament, he then wrote a concise introduction, summarizing Dolibois' experiences at Mondorf as well as parts of Streicher's political and journalistic career. The testament and introduction were published in the April, 1978, issue of the *Vierteljahrshefte fuer Zeitgeschichte.*

As presented in its corrected form, the political testament of Streicher appears to be surprisingly well-written as far as grammatical style and word usage. It is difficult to believe that the author of this document was the same person who wrote in the gutter-language and crude style that was typical of Streicher's *Stuermer* articles. In his political testament, Streicher mentions his writing style during his twenty-five years as an anti-Semitic propagandist. He claims that he never intended to address the well-educated classes, and therefore modified his language to be more understandable and impressive to the large masses of workers and farmers, who, he said, were uncomplicated in their thinking processes but capable of strong (anti-Semitic) feelings.

The general literary content of the political testament contains nothing of importance that has not been mentioned previously in this study. However, there are several topics addressed which do not alter the general story of his adult life but which add substance to accounts of his development as a political figure and radical anti-Semite.

The opening section of the document is particularly interesting and deserves mention in some detail here because it provides a clearer insight into reasons why he claimed that his life was guided by fate, which was inevitably linked to the destiny of Germany. The document's first section is fittingly entitled "Call to Destiny." In his opening paragraphs Streicher summarizes his early life until the end of World War I. He mentions that at the age of five he became aware of the word "Jew" from his mother, who had been swindled by a Jewish mail-order firm. He also recalls several other occasions when he heard that Jews were usually involved in shady dealings. However, he affirms that it was only after a spiritual experience in late 1918 that he realized that the salvation of Germany hinged on the successful struggle over Jews and Jewish interests.

In dramatic phrases he describes his despondent feelings after viewing the sorry plight of his fatherland immediately after the end of the war. He recalls that it was in such a

297

moment of melancholy that his "call to destiny" came
through an "inner voice" that cried out, reminding him that
he was a part of the German people and that he would sink
with them into oblivion unless he helped retrieve them all
from this dismal abyss.[7]

After establishing the point that his primary and vital
concern in life after the loss of the war was the salvation of
Germany, Streicher then launches into a lengthy discussion
detailing step by step, but illogically, the development of his
racial beliefs. He attempts to prove by historical references
that all misfortunes of the nordic race stemmed from
interbreeding with inferior races of the southern hemispheres.
His arguments include the hypothesis that Adam and Eve
were misguided by the devil when they committed the
"original sin," which, he states, was sexual intercourse with
other races. In his effort to substantiate the warped concept
of the "original sin," Streicher included references to
questionable sources such as a book published in 1913,
entitled *The Fall of the Major Races*, by an American
writer, Madison Grant.[8]

The political testament then attempts to prove that the
principal villains creating the greatest chaos throughout world
history have been members of the Jewish "race." He begins
this section by referring to the book, *Race and Character*,
by a Jewish author, Otto Weininger. He claims that the
yellowish skin caste, the kinky hair and the thick lips of some
Jewish persons indicates clearly that the Jews were fore-
runners in committing the "original sin."[9] According to
Weininger, the Jewish tribes originated from an early nordic
group that mixed with yellow, brown and black natives while
wandering in search of new lands. Continuing as he often did
in many *Stuermer* articles, but with higher quality word
usage, Streicher embarks on a pseudo-philosophic discussion
using questionable references to validate his argument that
the Jews have behaved like criminals since ancient times
because they have been instructed to commit crimes in their
religious instructions and scriptural lessons.

After arguing his point about the criminous nature of the
Jews, Streicher directs the reader's attention to elements
which "prove" that the Jews were not only the cause of the
outbreak of World War I, but were also responsible for
Germany's defeat as well as for the economic debacle that

befell the Germans in the early 1920's.

The balance of the political testament focuses mainly on Streicher's personal experiences as well as information dealing with the founding and growth of his newspaper, the *Stuermer*. Throughout these sections, Streicher's flair for dramatic journalism is in evidence. In one paragraph he relates details of his first major anti-Semitic address in Nuremberg in 1919 before an audience of 10,000 persons. He recalls that after he had finished his three-hour speech he felt certain that his words had touched the hearts of most of his listeners, and then he offered a "silent prayer of heavenly thanks" because he knew at that moment that he had found his proper role in fulfilling his purpose in life.

Near the end of the document, Streicher describes his rise to power. These paragraphs are highlighted with praises about Hitler, whom he obviously has never ceased to venerate. He describes in reverent terms his experience the first time he heard Hitler speak in 1922, when be became aware that he was witnessing a spiritual event so moving that he imagined he saw a halo over Hitler's head. He relates his role with Hitler in the abortive Munich Beer Hall *Putsch* and his imprisonment later at Landsberg with Hitler. He also includes a brief section to Hitler's benevolence in choosing Nuremberg as the "capital city" of the National Socialist movement.

The document's closing pages include brief sections on the recent war, the question of war-guilt, and Hitler's spiritual legacy. Streicher blames the war on the selfish manipulations of the world-wide association of Jews and follows with his conclusion that the Jews should be tried and convicted as the parties guilty for all war crimes committed. In defending Hitler to the end, Streicher implores that the enemies of Hitler will eventually sink into their graves and be forgotten, but the spirit of Hitler will continue to live and will eventually bring freedom to those who deserve it.

Streicher ends his monograph with a statement that is a reversion from his many assertions in later *Stuermer* articles that the "final solution" of the "Jewish question" should be extermination or mass-murder. He may have been attempting to vindicate himself somewhat in the eyes of his captors when he dictated the following closing lines to his political testament:

As long as the Jews are forced to co-exist with other peoples, anti-Semitism will continue to exist. World peace, long sought by other peoples, can only become a reality if a national state for all the world's Jews is established.[10]

Within a few weeks after completing his political testament, Streicher was moved to a prison cell in the compound of Nuremberg's Palace of Justice, the place chosen for the formal trial of major Nazi war criminals. A commission of legal representatives of the United States, Great Britain, France, and the Soviet Union had finalized almost all details of this unprecedented judicial proceeding by August, 1945. While numerous issues dealing with such matters as the trial's procedures and the wording of the indictments were hotly debated by members of the commission, there had been little or no disagreement over the selection of Nuremberg as the site of the trial. The principal factor in this unanimous decision was Nuremberg's infamous reputation as the focal point of Nazi anti-Semitism.

When Streicher disembarked at the large building housing the cell blocks in the Nuremberg prison compound, he remarked to persons around him that he was glad to be back in familiar surroundings. Somewhat braggingly, he told of his incarceration in this prison several times before, during the 1920's.[11] A few days after his return to Nuremberg, preliminary legal proceedings against him were initiated. Beginning on September 1, this phase of inquiries began with a series of interrogations under oath conducted principally by Colonel Howard Brundage of the United States Army's judicial section. On at least one occasion, Brundage also questioned Streicher's wife, Adele.

Transcripts of these interrogation sessions with Streicher are extremely bulky, containing numerous innocuous informational questions and answers. However, the major reason for the unusual verbosity of these inquiries was the overly wordy responses by Streicher to straightforward questions. In all sessions Brundage was obliged at times to cut off Streicher's answers which often degenerated into long diatribes, completely irrelevant to the subject under discussion. However, the transcripts also contain information which is crucial to Streicher's case. When compared to the complete record of Streicher's testimony during the later, formal proceedings which was published by the International Military Tribunal, the transcripts of these preliminary interrogations include all but a few critical questions upon which Streicher's case was judged.

Close study of the line of inquiry by Brundage reveals that he was primarily interested in obtaining Streicher's pre-trial testimony regarding several major points dealing with the principal charges contained in the indictments under consideration by prosecutors for most of the Nazi defendants. While official reading of the general indictments did not occur until late in November, a brief listing of them here may aid in understanding Brundage's main points of concern as he questioned Streicher. The four counts of the indictments were stated in rather lengthy terms, but their major points may be summarized as follows:

Count One—The common plan or conspiracy to wage aggressive war....The acquiring of totalitarian control in Germany....
Utilization of Nazi control for foreign aggression....
Count Two—Crimes against peace....Violation of international treaties, agreements, and assurances....
Count Three—War crimes...Murder of civilian populations....and prisoners of war....Deportation for slave labor....Killing of hostages....
Count Four—Crimes against humanity....Murder, extermination, enslavement....Persecution on political and racial grounds....[12]

The manner in which Brundage examined Streicher was skillful. He mixed his questions dealing with serious issues with others that could be answered easily in order to relax the tension in the room. He also allowed Streicher to brag about his imagined accomplishments. However, most of the time Streicher appeared wary. He seemed to know intuitively when to evade answering certain issues in definite terms. Even though he did not have knowledge of the formal charges under which his guilt or innocence would be judged, his evasiveness at times indicates that he must have known that he belonged to a party that committed illegal and immoral acts. His responses also indicate that he must have known that a number of his own activities, especially verbal expressions, would be considered criminous according to international law. In addition, some of his answers to Brundage's queries reveal opinions and attitudes never previously stated by Streicher and thus provide further insight into his anti-Semitic mind.

In the early sessions, Brundage directed his questions toward Streicher's implication in acts included under Counts One and Four. His initial focus was on the issue of the Nazis acquiring totalitarian control in Germany. After obtaining Streicher's admission that he was instrumental in helping to organize the Nazi party as well as its very rigid internal control of the nation after 1933, Brundage asked about the various means used by the Nazis to secure and maintain this control. Streicher described the highly organized National Socialist political system beginning at the lowest levels with cells in factories and party wards in all urban neighborhoods and villages. He said that by 1935, every house in Germany had a Nazi member or was under the jurisdiction of a political ward. He also agreed that the SS and the *Gestapo* were the principal agents used to root out persons considered politically or racially undesirable by the party.[13]

This line of questioning led to the matter of procedures used in Hitler's regime to punish these "undesirable" citizens. Streicher volunteered that after attaining political power, "the Nazi party created a law in which the party heads were protected, then whoever insulted them would be punished the legal way." At the mention of the term "legal way," Brundage pursued the question of punishment meted out by the Nazis to dissident or undesirable individuals. Streicher finally admitted that if an individual was considered undesirable or dissident according to party standards, then it was "legal" if they were put into a concentration camp without first going through any court process. However, Streicher consistently denied that he ever issued a direct order that an individual be sent to a concentration camp. Interestingly, Streicher patently denied knowledge of the treatment of prisoners inside the concentration camps, yet he bragged that he managed to persuade Himmler not to erect one in his *Gau*. He said he did this because a concentration camp was "not a nice thing to have in my *Gau*."

Returning to issues directly concerned with Count One, Brundage inquired into the extent of Streicher's political jurisdiction outside Franconia. He claimed that long before 1933 he was left outside Hitler's inner circle and was never consulted or informed about national policy decisions. He added that he was the only *Gauleiter* in Germany who served without pay, and that his principal concern in this position was the matter of race and questions of race "purity." He answered negatively to questions about his active role in the authoritative governance of his *Gau*. He added that his assistant *Gauleiter* took care of these political matters.

Brundage then asked Streicher his opinion of Hitler's well-publicized concept that more *Lebensraum* (living space) was part of the National Socialist program for future Germany. Streicher then answered that as far as he was concerned, this concept did not necessarily mean acquiring land from other nations forcefully. He said that he always interpreted Hitler's references to *Lebensraum* to mean that German citizens would be re-settled in areas within the boundaries of the country formerly uninhabitable, but reclaimed, such as swamplands.

Streicher was then queried about his knowledge of Hitler's armament buildup and subsequent invasion of Poland and other countries. His answers were innocuous, admitting that he knew that Germany was re-arming, but adding that most people in the nation also knew this. He also stated that most people felt that re-armament was a necessary move for defensive purposes. Regarding the issue of the Polish war, Streicher affirmed that he felt Hitler justified in attacking that country because he believed newspaper accounts which told of 60,000 Germans being killed in Poland before the German armies swept into that country in September, 1939.

After listening to answers such as these, Brundage must have realized that it was useless to inquire further into Streicher's possible implication in matters dealing with war plans or military campaigns. Streicher seemed as poorly informed about the aggressive nature of the Polish invasion as any ordinary German citizen. In addition, there was no existing documentary proof that could have linked him to Hitler's military plans at any time. His activities between 1934 and 1940 were fairly easy to trace through the volumes of evidence compiled by Police President Martin and the Meisinger commission. Records of police surveillance on Streicher could substantiate his consistent denial of having any liaison with Hitler or his staff of military planners immediately prior to the opening of the Polish war. And with the repeated phrase "I was on vacation after 1940," Streicher was able to clear himself of implications in the actual planning of aggressive wars after that time. His "retirement" in early 1940 also served to exonerate him from charges of crimes against peace and war crimes under Counts Two and Three of the general indictments. Throughout the series of interrogations, Brundage asked only a few questions that could have been related to issues under these two counts.

The principal thrust of questions during all interrogation sessions was aimed at Streicher's involvement in points listed under Count Four, crimes against humanity. In obvious pursuit of information useful to the prosecution of Streicher under this count, Brundage returned many times to the matter of the concentration camps. He seemed especially tenacious in his queries about the extent of Streicher's knowledge of the torture and mass killing that occurred inside the enclosures of these huge prison compounds. Remarking that he realized that the question of the concentration camps was a decisive factor in the coming judicial proceedings, Streicher responded initially: "...I hereby declare honorably that I never knew what was going on in concentration camps until now." A few minutes later, he attempted to clarify his answer and explained that it was only when he was shown some pictures at Mondorf that he learned of the atrocities committed in those places.[14]

Evidently disbelieving Streicher's claims that he only recently learned about happenings inside the concentration camps, Brundage persisted in questions dealing with the "strange circumstance" that no one in Germany seemed to know about the fate of millions of Jewish persons after they were sent to the concentration camps. Streicher answered these questions evasively. He attempted to establish the fact of his unawareness of the bestialities perpetrated on Jewish victims by digressing into lengthy accounts of his charitable acts toward some Communist prisoners at Dachau. He especially dwelled upon the story of his bringing busloads of Dachau prisoners to their homes in Nuremberg to a Christmas celebration with their families.

While Brundage continued asking why no German citizen seemed to know anything about the horrors that occurred inside the concentration camps, Streicher insisted repeatedly that these matters were always kept highly secret. Then he added the following somewhat preposterous reply:

Inside the party, Mr. Himmler was a dictator by himself, and I believe. . .that if the *Fuehrer* would have known what was going on, he would have dropped dead with fright. . . .Himmler had his ideas and his affairs shut in as behind a big iron door. . . .[15]

Streicher also repeated during this line of questioning that he never had anything to do with sending Jews away from his *Gau* and further, that he never worried about them after they did not return because he probably assumed that they had eventually emigrated to other countries.

Brundage then turned the direction of his inquiry toward Streicher's long-lasting, fanatic anti-Semitic propaganda. One key question dealt with the possibility that the concentration camp atrocities may have been partially the result of this brain-washing technique. Streicher's response to this question was interesting. He implied that he was no more guilty of inciting mass murder than certain well-known citizens of other countries who also preached anti-Semitism in public:

Anti-Semitism is all over the world. There are about 12 anti-Semitic newspapers in the United States. Mr. (Henry) Ford published an article in one of his papers. Radio Priest (Father) Coughlin can speak (about anti-Semitism) openly in the States. (Sir Oswald) Mosely in England pronounced anti-Semitism in the open, and if the declaration about race-hatred which I preached would lead to mass murder, we would have had a mass murder right in this town of Nuremberg, which is the most anti-Semitic city in Germany. . . .[16]

After another of Streicher's lengthy answers regarding his anti-Semitic propaganda, Brundage asked somewhat mildly if he (Streicher) was ashamed of anything he ever said about the Jews. When Streicher emphatically answered in the negative, Brundage then queried that if this was the case, then why did he bother to bury and burn large volumes of books and papers at Pleikershof before he left. Streicher's denials to these deeds were thwarted when Brundage calmly stated that American forces had located evidence of burned papers and had uncovered caches of at least 200 books and a somewhat lesser number of household articles buried in various places on the farm. After hearing this, Streicher admitted to the burning of some documents and letters, but refused to answer further questions regarding the contents of the burned papers or other buried material.[17]

Returning to lines of inquiry concerning Streicher's possible guilt under Count Four, Brundage asked a number of questions about his role in the formulation of the Nuremberg Laws and his involvement in the 1938 *Kristallnacht* pogrom in Franconia. Streicher answered questions about the Nuremberg Laws quite truthfully, stating that he was not consulted when the racial edicts were written. But he also said that he agreed totally with the legal prohibition of sexual intercourse between Jews and non-Jews. However, he was evasive and untruthful in his responses to queries dealing with the *Kristallnacht* issue. He claimed that he had given strict orders prohibiting any acts of violence against Jewish persons before the demonstrations began. Then he contradicted himself and said that he had no knowledge of the "unusual acts" until the morning after they occurred. According to Streicher's answers, damage in Nuremberg had been minimal, with one synagogue burned and a few windows broken.[18]

He also refused to admit having stated the following day that the Jews were deserving of the treatment they had received. He also claimed that he knew nothing about orders that resulted in the arrest of several thousands of Jews in Franconia in the days immediately following November 8, 1938. Brundage presented a document sent from Nazi police headquarters in Munich immediately after the *Kristallnacht* violence had occurred. One section was read to Streicher which issued the order for the arrest of the wealthiest Jewish persons in all areas. An addendum to this document stated that all *Gauleiters* should be informed of this order. Yet Streicher pretended that he was oblivious to this order and insisted that he knew practically nothing of the arrest of between 3,000 and 4,000 Jews in his *Gau* until some days after it happened. He agreed, however, that most of these arrested persons were eventually shipped to the Dachau concentration camp.

Perhaps the most crucial questions posed by Brundage during all the interrogation sessions pertained to *Stuermer* articles recommending extermination as the "final solution" to the "Jewish question" in Nazi Germany. After a number of attempts at evading a definite answer, Streicher admitted that he used words such as "exterminate," "annihilate" and "liquidate" while discussing racial topics in the *Stuermer*.

However, he refused to agree that these harsh words meant mass-murder as the intended fate for the Jews. He insisted that the word "exterminate" meant "getting rid of" the Jews by exporting them to other countries. In similar fashion, he tried to explain that in his usage of the words "annihilate" and "liquidate" he did not intend killing, but that these terms meant that Jews should not be allowed to mix sexually with non-Jews or to acquire political power in any country.[19]

After it became evident to Brundage that Streicher would not admit to the fact that he meant mass-murder when he used these destructive terms, he switched the focus of his queries back to the topic of the concentration camps. The aim of this line of inquiry was to establish an approximate date that Streicher became knowledgeable about the mass killings of Jews in the Nazi death camps. Under intensive questioning, Streicher finally admitted that he had learned about these executions while at Pleikershof sometime in 1944, while reading Jewish newspapers from Switzerland and America.

When Brundage asked Streicher how he felt after he learned about the gas chamber operations, Streicher answered unconvincingly: "I would not be able to kill anybody or have anybody killed."

The next question was evidently intended to bait Streicher into telling the truth. Brundage asked somewhat cynically: "You were one of the principal leaders in fomenting measures against the Jews. You must have been proud when they found a man (Himmler) strong enough and bloody enough to go in and wipe them off the earth."

Streicher responded promptly to this question revealing perhaps truthfully that his only disagreement with mass killing as the "final solution" to the "Jewish question" was that it was timed poorly. He must have used bragging tones when he stated: "If I had been the leader of the State, I would surely not have thought of doing such a thing in the moment when it was certain that we could not win the war."

In all the interrogation sessions with Brundage, Streicher went no further than the above statements in admitting that he recommended or agreed to the mass execution of the Jews in the concentration camps.

On October 19, Brundage opened his questions with

references to the copy of the formal indictment that Streicher and the other defendants had received that morning. This document named Streicher as defendant in the commission of various crimes. When Streicher appeared somewhat bewildered at the number of detailed charges levied against him, Brundage volunteered to clarify the document during future sessions. He added that the trial was scheduled to open in approximately thirty days and that all defendants would be provided legal counsel to be chosen from an approved list. Brundage closed this brief meeting with a remark that further interrogation sessions between them would take place only upon Streicher's request.[20]

The final meeting between Streicher and a pre-trial interrogator occurred on November 6. This session was conducted by Colonel S. W. Brookhart, a colleague of Colonel Brundage. The questions and answers during this session revealed no important information that has not been previously discussed here and serve no useful purpose in repeating. However, one interesting comment by Streicher seems worthy of mention because it implies that he might have been influenced less by "mystical forces" and more by a desire for public popularity when he chose anti-Semitism as a career. Replying to a question regarding his life-long campaign against the Jews, Streicher stated:

> ...Anyone who wants to become well-known in the world need only touch on the Jewish question. Anyone who wants to write about the Chinese or Japanese, or whatever it is, Indians, that would not interest anybody in the world. That is a proof that there is a Jewish problem, because there is an immediate reaction if anybody says a word about the Jews.[21]

On November 20, 1945, the Nuremberg Trials of Major War Criminals formally opened. The panel of four judges presiding over the trial's procedures and ultimately rendering verdicts and sentences on the Nazi defendants was called the International Military Tribunal (IMT). Prosecuting attorneys as well as the judges had been selected equally from the four victorious allied nations. Attorneys for each defendant had been selected individually from a list approved by the IMT. The large courtroom was equipped with special four-language microphones, lights, and cameras in order to transcribe properly all the historic proceedings about to take place.

Eventually all details of the trials would be published by the IMT in forty-two large volumes in all modern languages.

Events of the first day were limited to readings of the indictments and an opening address for the prosecution by an American jurist, Robert Jackson. While many of the 21 Nazi defendants were charged with all four counts of the indictment, Streicher was charged under Counts One and Four. Every defendant rendered the same "not guilty" plea after listening to the charges read against him.

The group of men labelled Major Nazi War Criminals was viewed with mixed feelings by many observers who saw them as only a token assortment of personalities who may or may not have been the key figures in planning and implementing the crimes listed in the indictments. Three persons, Hitler, Himmler, and Goebbels, who were unquestionably rated as "major" Nazi criminals, had evaded the trial by suicide. Others in this class, such as Martin Bormann, had been identified but were yet to be found. Still others, later to be recognized as directly responsible for some of the most heinous crimes committed, were yet to be brought to justice. The 21 Nazis who heard the charges read against them at Nuremberg are listed below in alphabetical order:

Doenitz, Karl—Grand Admiral of the German Navy and named in Hitler's last testament as Head of State

Frank, Hans—Hitler's lawyer and later Governor-General of occupied Poland

Frick, Wilhelm—Nazi Minister of the Interior since early 1933

Fritzsche, Hans—Radio Propaganda Chief in Goebbels' Propaganda Ministry

Funk, Walter—Nazi Minister of Economics after 1938

Goering, Hermann—Chief of the German Air Force, *Reichstag* President, Head of the Four-Year Economic Plan. Hitler's nominal successor until the last stages of World War II

Hess, Rudolf—Hitler's Chief Secretary and Number Three Nazi until his flight to England on a questionable mission in 1941

Jodl, Alfred—General of the German Army High Command, Chief of Military Operations, one of Hitler's top military advisors

Kaltenbrunner, Ernst—Chief of Himmler's Security Headquarters

Keitel, Wilhelm—Field Marshall and Chief of Staff of the Army High Command, known as Hitler's "yes man" in military affairs

Neurath, Konstantin—A German Baron, Foreign Minister and later Protector of Bohemia and Moravia von Papen, Franz—*Reich* Chancellor before Hitler, Ambassador to Austria and Turkey

Raeder, Erich—Grand Admiral of the German Navy, Chief of Submarine Operations

von Ribbentrop, Joachim—Hitler's Foreign Minister

Rosenberg, Alfred—Former editor of the *Voelkischer Beobachter*, Chief Nazi Racial Philosopher, *Reichsminister* for the Eastern Occupied Territories

Sauckel, Fritz—Hitler's Chief of slave labor recruitment

Schacht, Hjalmar—President of *Reichsbank* and Minister of Economics until early 1939, later arrested and imprisoned as a Nazi enemy at Dachau

von Schirach, Baldur—Hitler Youth Leader and later *Gauleiter* of Vienna

Seyss-Inquart, Arthur—Chancellor of Austria and later *Reichs*-Commissioner for the Netherlands

Speer, Albert—*Reichsminister* of German Armaments and Munitions

Streicher, Julius—*Gauleiter* of Franconia, newspaper publisher, known as the Number One Nazi Jew-Baiter

Penetrating insights into the thoughts and behavior of most of the Nazi defendants during the long period of their imprisonment and trials at Nuremberg were made public by an American psychologist, Dr. G. M. Gilbert. As a German-speaking intelligence officer, Gilbert had visited some of the concentration camps immediately after they were liberated and had seen the stark evidence of the Nazi atrocities at these places. Partially because of these experiences, he became keenly interested in the human qualities of persons capable of such atrocious deeds. Gilbert welcomed the assignment as a liaison officer between the prisoners and the prison commandant, Colonel B. C. Andrus, former head of the Mondorf compound. Gilbert maintained close daily contact with the defendants and was allowed free access to their cells from the time of the indictments to the executions. The results of his discussions and observations during his approximate one year in the Nuremberg prison were carefully noted and later compiled into a popular paperback volume entitled *Nuremberg Diary*.

Gilbert had arrived at Nuremberg on October 20, and during his first round of making acquaintances with the prisoners, visited the cell of Robert Ley, who appeared to be in a very agitated state over the accusations against him in his copy of the indictment. The next day Ley was found dead, having hung himself with a piece of towel from a toilet pipe. While most other prisoners took the news of the suicide quite casually, Streicher was the only one who seemed to mourn Ley's passing. As leader of Hitler's labor front he had aided Streicher's publishing business by forcing German workers to subscribe to the *Stuermer*. In addition, Ley had been the only Nazi prisoner at Mondorf to voluntarily share a dining table with Streicher.[22]

According to Gilbert, other prisoners felt that they considered Streicher unfit to associate with. Later evidence indicates that his social standing among the defendants at Nuremberg was as lowly as it had been at Mondorf. Whenever the Nazis were able to associate with one another, Streicher's attempts at greetings or small talk were met with contemptuous stares or icy silence. Some of the more arrogant defendants, such as Goering and Schacht, spoke out in Streicher's presence about their feeling of degradation at being tried in the same courtroom with him. After Ley's death none of the other prisoners were willing to eat in the same room with Streicher. When von Ribbentrop and Raeder were finally ordered to share the same dining room with Streicher, they literally howled their complaints of humiliation to prison officials. While Streicher made no complaints to Gilbert about this treatment, his demeanor after several months at the Nuremberg prison indicated that he felt isolated and downcast. He became subdued and withdrawn in the company of his fellow prisoners and made little attempt to even acknowledge their presence when he was among them.[23]

The reasons for the intense dislike of Streicher by all other Nuremberg defendants were numerous and justified. As described in previous chapters, he had incurred the animosity of almost every Nazi official he encountered during his political career. Except for Hitler's intercession he would have been banned from the party before 1933. His newspaper, the *Stuermer*, was an embarrassment to many ranking party officials. In addition to all this, his behavior at Mondorf and Nuremberg in the presence of his peers was considered inexcusable and most obnoxious.

All of the captured Nazis at Mondorf and at Nuremberg

were forced to view photographs and films of the horrid scenes discovered at some of the Nazi concentration camps. The tangle of arms, legs and bodies of murdered Jewish victims in piles or in mass graves in these pictures brought tears and expressions of shame to many of the defendants. Yet, even after witnessing this "harvest" of Hitler's racial policies, Streicher continued to sing praises of Hitler's greatness and preach the righteousness of his anti-Semitic doctrines to anyone who would listen. Goering may have been expressing the feelings of all the prisoners who had listened to Streicher on the witness stand making ludicrous statements about his "racial theories." During a brief intermission after Streicher had left the stand, Goering and Hess were discussing Streicher's testimony. Goering said: "Well at least we did one good thing—getting that prick kicked out of office." Hess agreed whole-heartedly.[24]

Streicher's reputation became as lowly among the doctors, lawyers and other prison personnel as it was with his fellow prisoners. His insistence on preaching his radical anti-Semitic ideas to everyone he encountered raised questions by his own counsel and other court representatives about the possibility of mental derangement. In an intelligence test administered by Gilbert, Streicher rated the only below-average-intelligence score, 106, which was the lowest among all other prisoners.

Because of his abnormal behavior and low test score, the IMT ordered an examination of him by a psychiatric commission consisting of a team of three physicians representing the Soviet Union, France, and the United States. Streicher tried to turn the examination into an anti-Semitic lecture, telling the doctors that after 25 years of studying the racial subject he knew more about the Jewish problem than anyone else. When the doctors asked Streicher to undress for a physical examination, he noticed the female Russian interpreter step aside and turn her back. At this, Streicher allegedly leered and said: "What's the matter? Are you afraid of seeing something nice?"[25]

After the examination, Streicher was diagnosed as not insane but suffering from a neurotic obsession, and fit to stand trial. Gilbert states that this neurotic condition was illustrated frequently when he visited Streicher's cell. In the following example of one of Streicher's typical tirades in the

Nuremberg prison, he still maintained that he was (somehow) "called " to the anti-Semitic cause and that by this time he believed himself to be the world's leading historical anti-Semite:

> I am the only one in the world who clearly saw the Jewish menace as an historical problem. I didn't become anti-Semitic because of any personal mistreatment or grudge—not at all—I was *called* to it! My realization of the Jewish menace came from the *Talmud* itself—the so-called Jewish Holy Book. . .which shows that the Jews are governed by racial law. . . .And that is how they maintained their racial purity and survived for centuries. . . .

In a manner suggesting a seer revealing an important, secret truth, Streicher squinted his eyes and wagged a finger at Gilbert and added:

> . . .one can learn much from the *Talmud.* The Jews knew about such things. But we must be masters, not they.[26]

Throughout the period of approximately one year that Streicher spent at the Nuremberg prison, he never ceased attempting to impress everyone he talked with of his superior knowledge about anti-Semitism. He claimed to Gilbert that he could identify "races" such as Jews and Negroes by means of visual identification. In this manner, he said, he was certain that three of the four principal judges at the trials were Jews. He also claimed that in this manner he knew that Himmler was not a pure aryan because his features betrayed that he had some Negro blood in him.[27]

The defense counsel selected for Streicher was a reputable German attorney named Dr. Marx. From the time of the first meeting between the two, it became evident to Gilbert that neither could have the respect or confidence of the other. Marx seemed to be a busy man and had little patience for Streicher's digressions. Streicher continually tried to impress Marx with his knowledge of racial issues and thought that his (imagined) standing as an authority on anti-Semitism should comprise the principal strategy of his defense. After each session between counsel and client, Marx left in exasperation after futile attempts to organize some form of logical defense strategy.

According to the trial's procedural rules, each defendant

was to have the benefit of hearing the specific charges and issues of the prosecution's case against him before being subjected to any cross-examination. On January 10, 1946, a British lawyer, Mr. Griffith-Jones, summarized the charges and cited the sources of proof to be used in the prosecution's case against Streicher. Most of the issues included in the charges had been raised by Brundage in the pre-trial sessions. In presenting the sources of proof that Streicher was guilty of inciting the vicious persecution of Jews over a long period of time, Griffith-Jones referred to political speeches and *Stuermer* articles, quoting excerpts as substantiation. For example, he cited the following brief passage from a 1926 political speech to illustrate that he could prove Streicher's vicious anti-Semitic propaganda began in the early years of the Nazi movement: "For thousands of years the Jew has been destroying nations. Let us make a new beginning today so that we can annihilate the Jew."[28]

Armed with a large bundle of *Stuermer* back issues, the British attorney quoted a number of articles which typified Streicher's major racial theories and arguments with which he attempted to poison the minds of his readers. As an example, Griffith-Jones read an excerpt of a 1938 *Stuermer* copy to illustrate one of Streicher's favorite pseudo-scientific anti-Semitic claims:

> The male sperm in cohabitation is partially or completely absorbed by the female, and thus enters her bloodstream. . .and is sufficient to poison her blood forever. . . .Never will she be able to bear purely aryan children. . . .Now we know why the Jew uses every artifice of seduction in order to ravish German girls at as early an age as possible; why the Jewish doctor rapes his patients while they are under anesthetic. . . .[29]

In a similar manner, Griffith-Jones illustrated that the *Stuermer* frequently recommended the extermination and annihilation of the Jews even after Streicher had learned of the gas chamber operations in the eastern concentration camps. The case for the prosecution also included accounts of Streicher's profiteering from the Nazi aryanization programs and a summary of the reasons why he was judged "unfit to rule" in 1940.

In the week following the presentation of the prosecution's case against Streicher, an articulate French jurist delivered a bitter denunciation against Nazi anti-Semitism. A few days later, Gilbert paid a visit to Streicher's cell to see if there might be some change in his attitude. However, Streicher seemed unchanged and as obsessed as ever with his racist ideas. Almost immediately after Gilbert entered the cell, Streicher began to preach that the Jews were still a world power. Then he tried to explain how Christianity was being duped by the Jews, and that Christ wasn't a Jew. Becoming excited, he made some further statements that revealed how his own sordid thoughts were projected onto the Jews:

> Do you know what the *Talmud* says about Christ? It says he was born on a dungheap—yes—and it says he was the son of a whore. . . .She was not married, and that story about getting the child from God. Now you know. . . .it is true that according to that story she must have been a whore. . . .

Continuing to discuss the vulgar thoughts in his mind, Streicher then began to harp on the subject of circumcision:

> Circumcision was the most amazing stroke of genius in history! Just think of it. It wasn't for sanitary reasons or anything like that. . . .It was to preserve racial consciousness. 'Thou shalt always remember that thou art a Jew and shall have Jewish children with Jewish women![30]

Gilbert stated that he left Streicher's cell after remaining only 15 minutes because that length of time was about all he could stand listening to the ramblings of Streicher's perverted mind.

Dr. Marx must have been subjected to similar racial harangues as he attempted for more than three months to prepare for Streicher's defense. It became evident that no mutual agreement had been reached between Marx and his client by the time Streicher's formal defense opened on April 26. Streicher took the witness stand for the initial phase of the case for his defense. According to trial procedures, the defendants themselves were allowed to make opening statements before undergoing cross-examination by opposing counsels. In his opening sentences, Streicher denounced Dr. Marx for not cooperating with him in preparing the case as he wished. Marx then interrupted proceedings and offered to resign his position as Streicher's defense counsel. He explained to the court that he did not wish to defend Streicher's anti-Semitism and could only continue in the case if the court understood his position. After a brief conference, the judges agreed that Marx should continue as Streicher's defense counsel under these circumstances.[31]

Streicher then launched into an emotional tirade, describing himself as a fate-ordained apostle of the struggle against the Jews. He told of the super-natural "inner voice" which told him of his destiny and how he met and was inspired by Hitler when he first saw him. He mentioned also that he was certain that a halo appeared over Hitler's head as he spoke fervently about the goals of the National Socialist party in 1922. Continuing, Streicher described the findings of his "research" into the Jewish question and cited *Old Testament* passages to "prove" his theories regarding the evil goals of Jews throughout history.

Streicher focused his entire address on his radical racist beliefs. Gilbert noted that his words were evidently embarrassing to other Nazi defendants in the courtroom. Goering buried his head in his hands as though he was becoming sick. Doenitz shook his head sadly and closed his eyes. Some of the others grimaced as if in pain. Before Streicher finished his anti-Semitic polemic, he was interrupted by one of the judges because he had called a previous witness, named Gisevius, a traitor to the memory of Hitler. In his closing statement Streicher praised Hitler as a man of genius whose only mistake was listening to sadists and fools, such as Himmler and Bormann.

After Streicher had finished his long oration the court was recessed. Gilbert noted later that most of the other defendants voiced bitterness and disgust over Streicher's insistence on harping on the dangers of the Jews especially after spending long periods of time in the courtroom viewing scenes of Nazi atrocities against them. In their defense presentations, the other prisoners tried to avoid discussing the Nazi party's anti-Semitic policies. Von Schirach remarked: "He (Streicher) certainly showed what a fanatic fool he is in court."

Schacht appeared very agitated at Gilbert's mention of Streicher's name. He said: "You just have to look at that worm (Streicher) and see the kind of man Hitler protected. . . ."

Doenitz told Gilbert that none of his naval officers would ever have touched Streicher's "filthy Sheet" *(Stuermer)* even with a pair of tongs.

Jodl stated that Streicher's performance was almost laughable and that he was obviously only trying to put on a show to attract attention to himself. Intimating that he wouldn't be surprised to learn that Streicher had adopted anti-Semitism as a career only to gain political influence, he added: "These school-teachers were always looking for a chance to get some power and respectability." When Gilbert seemed puzzled by this remark, Jodl explained that the position of grammar school teacher, especially in Bavaria, was the most looked-down-upon profession in the country; that they were merely looked upon as a lackey of the local priest who dictated what they could or could not teach.

When the court re-convened, Streicher was called to the stand again and asked if he had anything further to state before cross-examination began. This time he spoke more rationally than he did previously. He pleaded that he was not guilty of the charges against him in the indictments. He said that the mass killings were carried out in complete secrecy by Himmler's SS troops upon orders by higher government authorities and that the German people had no knowledge that Jews were being killed systematically in the concentration camps.

Streicher appeared somewhat confident as he pointed out to the tribunal that he was certain that the prosecution could not prove that neither he nor his *Stuermer* had any connection with the planning and implementation of the mass-murders of the Jews. In attempting to strengthen this point, he said that it was clearly established that when he was ordered to lead the anti-Jewish boycott on April 1, 1933, he, as *Gauleiter*, neither ordered, demanded, nor participated in any acts of violence against the Jews.

Continuing in his denial of guilt, Streicher stated that it had been established that in many articles in the *Stuermer* he had advocated the Zionist demand for the creation of a Jewish state as the natural solution of the Jewish problem. In concluding this point, he added: "These facts prove that I did not want the Jewish problem to be solved by violence."

Then, as as if anticipating one of the major weaknesses in his case, Streicher attempted to explain away the intent of the *Stuermer* articles in which mass-murder was recommended as a deserving fate of all Jews. He said that if he or others in the *Stuermer* mentioned destruction or extermination of Jewry, then these articles were not to be taken seriously as they were merely replies to Jewish writers who advocated and demanded extermination of the German people. Streicher said further that the mass-murders may not have been ordered by Hitler, but they were most likely a result of his attitude against the Jews; and that the *Fuehrer* may have stated that he wanted them punished for unleashing the war and bombing the German civilian population.

Nearing the end of his plea, Streicher repeated that he regretted the mass killings which could only be traced to the acts of higher government authorities. Streicher closed his defense address with the following righteous words directed toward the panel of judges:

> I repudiate the mass killings which were carried out, in the same way that they are repudiated by every decent German. . . .Neither in my capacity as *Gauleiter* nor as a political author have I committed a crime and I therefore look forward to your judgment with a good conscience.[32]

After Streicher had finished his defense plea, Griffith-Jones proceeded with his cross-examination. He re-phrased many of the same questions asked during Streicher's earlier interrogation sessions, which focused on issues dealing with crimes listed under Count One of the indictment. As in the pre-trial inquiries, Streicher was able to establish quite conclusively that he had not been a member of Hitler's inner circle since the mid-1920's and that he had not been in a position to take part in any plans dealing with foreign policy or war. After a number of questions it must have become evident to Griffith-Jones that it was useless to try establishing that Streicher had anything important to do in forming specific policies of war or in general conspiracy to wage aggressive acts of war.

The prosecutor then turned to the subject of Streicher's anti-Semitic propaganda. After a few questions, Griffith-Jones obtained Streicher's admission that he was chiefly responsible for all articles and editorials published in the *Stuermer*. Then he read a number of excerpts from back issues of the newspaper which he presented as exhibits in his case. These included accounts of the alleged Hebrew ritual murders and stories directed to children advocating hatred of all things Jewish. However, Griffith-Jones concentrated these readings on articles in which the extermination, annihilation, or destruction of all Jews was recommended.

During the citations from the *Stuermer* articles, most of which were published during the later war years, the prosecutor hammered questions at Streicher in the effort to bring out plainly that when they were written, he must have known that Jews, in large numbers, were already being killed in the East. Ostensibly to emphasize the point of his allegation, Griffith-Jones cited a sentence written by Streicher in a November, 1943 *Stuermer* issue: "It is possibly true that the Jews are, so to say, disappearing from Europe."

Streicher acknowledged writing the sentence but denied that it indicated that he knew anything about the mass-murder programs. The prosecutor countered with a document to prove that a *Stuermer* press photographer had visited ghettoes in the East, in Spring, 1943, when the Warsaw ghettoes were destroyed. The same photographer was also reported to have visited at least one of the death camps during this trip.[33]

Continuing his questions, Griffith-Jones obtained the admission from Streicher that he received the Jewish newspaper, *Israelitisches Wochenblatt*, and that at Pleikershof he read it quite regularly. After this admission by Streicher, the prosecutor virtually clinched his case. By reading excerpts from this newspaper, he illustrated to the court that it carried continuous accounts of Nazi atrocities against the Jews. These articles included numbers and names of Jews deported from different places and listed those that were known to have met death in the concentration camps. Then Griffith-Jones referred to the sentence quoted above from the November, 1943, *Stuermer* issue. In this particular article, Streicher had taken the sentence stating that the Jews were virtually disappearing from Europe as a verbatim quotation from the *Israelitisches Wochenblatt*. In discussing this sentence from the *Stuermer* article, Streicher had commented: "This is *not* a Jewish lie!"[34]

Squirming under Griffith-Jones' cross-examination, Streicher responded weakly that he did not remember writing those things, and that even if he had read about the atrocities against Jews carried on in the East in those newspapers he would not have believed it. He kept repeating that when he had used terms such as "exterminating the Jews" he had not meant them literally. He also tried to excuse himself of the guilt to incite mass murder on the grounds of literary license, practiced in some foreign countries under the constitutional right of freedom of the press. In addition, he tried to defend himself by repeating that he had often recommended in the *Stuermer* that the Jews should be resettled in Madagascar or some other place.

After Griffith-Jones finished his cross-examination, Dr. Marx began to ask Streicher questions aimed at emphasizing his deeds of charity as *Gauleiter* and his many published *Stuermer* articles which ordered that Jews were not to be physically harmed in Franconia. Evidently becoming impatient with Marx's deliberate court-room manner, Streicher refused to answer one of the questions and insulted Marx with crude words. The court then warned him that further insolence of this nature would cause the termination of the examination.

Streicher's hostile attitude did not help Marx in his difficult task. Yet, he proceeded painstakingly to strengthen Streicher's previous claims of innocence of charges under Count One of the indictment. He also established quite clearly that Streicher had nothing to do with ordering or implementing the large-scale execution of the Jews. However, Marx could do little in his cross-examination to offset the prosecution's strong case relative to Streicher's intent to incite the mass killings even after he had knowledge that the death camps were already in operation. After Marx dismissed Streicher from the stand, he called on Adele Streicher for cross-examination. Her testimony was innocuous, with only an affirmation of belief that her husband was a "good man." The prosecution did not bother to cross-examine her.[35]

After his April appearance on the witness stand, Streicher spent the next three months waiting for the completion of the defense pleas and cross-examinations of the balance of the prisoners. Then, before the tribunal retired to deliberate on the verdicts and sentences of the defendants, the defense attorneys and the defendants were allowed a brief final plea. Also, a representative jurist of each of the four allied nations involved in the trials presented a blanket summation for the prosecution.

On July 12, Dr. Marx made his final pleas in Streicher's defense. Marx depicted him as being obsessed with his life-long crusade against the Jews. To Streicher's outward annoyance, Marx emphasized that the *Stuermer* was so radical that none of the German people took it or its owner seriously. While Marx admitted that Hitler supported the *Stuermer* to the end, he argued that even Hitler did not consider it worthy of reading. Marx tried to reason that Streicher did not have anything to do with the extermination of the Jews and most likely did not even know that the death camps were operating; however, it may have appeared that he did.[36]

The day after Marx's defense summation, Gilbert visited Streicher's cell for a short talk. Somewhat surprisingly, Streicher made no mention of Marx's defense strategy. Instead he seemed anxious to continue proving his superior knowledge about the subject of anti-Semitism. He stated that Hitler had made a mistake in allowing so many Jews to be killed because they were now a martyred race. After Streicher mentioned the term "racial blood," Gilbert interrupted, remarking that it was not easy to identify racial characteristics. Streicher then said that he could always identify a Jew by his eyes because they were different. Gilbert asked how a Jewish person's eyes were different. Streicher could only say that they were "just different."

Wagging his head in pretended wisdom, Streicher continued that he could also identify a Jew by his behind and "by the way they talked with their hands." When Gilbert looked at him questioningly, Streicher said: "Oh, the Jewish behind is not like a Gentile behind...(it) is so feminine—so soft and feminine...and you can tell from the way it wobbles when they walk." Then he added: "I have made quite a study of this for 25 years, and nobody understands this problem as well as I do. ....I can recognize a Jew in a few minutes while the others have to study a man for days before they realize I am right." Streicher then claimed that he had identified almost all jurists on the prosecution team as Jews. Gilbert asked if he thought Prosecutor Jackson was a Jew. Streicher answered quickly, saying that of course he thought Jackson was a Jew and his real name was probably Jacobson.[37]

About two weeks after this conversation with Gilbert,

Streicher sat in the courtroom with the other prisoners and heard Justice Robert Jackson's summation speech for the American delegation. Jackson did not spare Streicher in his condemnations of those he felt most guilty for all the Nazi crimes committed during the recent years:

> Streicher, the venomous vulgarian, manufactured and distributed obscene racial libels which incited the populace to accept and assist the progressively savage operation of 'race purification.'[38]

After Jackson's address, which denounced all of the defendants in harsh terms, many of the prisoners appeared shocked to realize that they were still considered criminals. Some registered dismay with remarks that their defense testimony had seemingly been ignored by the allied jurists. Streicher, however, appeared unperturbed by Jackson's denunciation of him. Without commenting on the prosecution's summation, he addressed Gilbert with a series of enthusiastic but confusing statements which apparently were intended to stress that he had always disapproved of the mass killing of Jews and had sincerely wanted them to emigrate from Europe to a national state of their own. However, neither Gilbert nor any of the other prisoners who heard Streicher's remarks on this occasion seemed to consider them seriously or worthy of meaningful comment.

Following Jackson's prosecution summation, representative jurists from Great Britain, France, and the Soviet Union presented their final statements in condemnation of the defendants. These addresses were generally bitter and vindictive as well as somewhat repetitious. Perhaps the most vitriolic presentation was by the Chief British Prosecutor, Sir Hartley Shawcross. He began by a review of the Nazi military action which resulted in billions of dollars worth of property damage and the loss of some ten million human lives. When he came to the subject of the extermination of the Jews, Shawcross quoted passages written and spoken by Streicher and other Nazis who, he felt, were most guilty for inciting such horrible deeds. Then he read a vivid, but terrible eyewitness account of a mass execution by gunfire written by an SS "Action Commando:"

> ...these people undressed, stood around in family groups...and

waited for a sign from another SS man, who stood by the pit with a whip in his hand. . . .People were closely wedged together and lying on top of each other. . . .Nearly all had blood running over their shoulders from their heads. . . .The pit was already two-thirds full. . .it already contained 1000 people. . . .Then I heard a series of shots. I looked into the pit and saw that the bodies were twitching. . . .[39]

While some of the defendants paled and expressed shame at this horrid account, others, including Streicher, remained expressionless, or sat reading their transcripts. Shawcross may have directed his next words at Streicher when he quoted the German writer, Goethe, as saying that some day fate would strike the German people because "they ingenuously submit to any mad scoundrel who appeals to their lowest instincts, who confirms them in their vices and teaches them to conceive nationalism as isolation and brutality."

Then in a dramatic gesture of emphasis, Shawcross peered at the judges while he pointed at the prisoners sitting in the dock: "With what a voice of prophecy he spoke, for these are the mad scoundrels who did these very things!"

After all the prosecution summations were completed, the trial continued for about another month with arguments concerning the responsibilities of the Nazi organizations such as the SS and the General Military Staff. Then, on August 31, 1946, the last day of the trial, the 21 defendants made their final defense speeches.

Most of the prisoners acknowledged that there had been horrible crimes committed, but claimed that they had only followed orders of superior officers or had followed the laws of the land. Most also claimed that they had not intended such terrible things to happen. Streicher again attempted to expound on his knowledge of anti-Semitism and the dangers of the world association of the Jews. However, he was interrupted quickly by one of the judges and instructed to keep his statements brief and restricted to questions pertaining to his defense. After this, Streicher could only state weakly that he disapproved of the mass killing of the Jews. He also reiterated that he had proven by citing passages from his speeches and *Stuermer* writings that he had always aimed only at a peaceful solution to the problem of race purification of the German people.

On September 30, the tribunal rendered its verdict and

read its judgment of the 21 defendants. Three of them, Fritzsche, von Papen, and Schacht, were found not guilty. Doenitz and von Neurath were sentenced respectively to 10 and 15 years imprisonment, while von Schirach and Speer received 20-year prison sentences. Funk, Hess, and Raeder were sentenced to life imprisonment. The remaining 11, Frank, Frick, Goering, Jodl, Kaltenbrunner, Keitel, Ribbentrop, Rosenberg, Sauckel, Seyss-Inquart, and Streicher, were sentenced to death by hanging.

In relating its judgment on Streicher, the tribunal began by stating that they found that the prosecution had failed to provide evidence establishing Streicher's participation in conspiracy or common plan to wage aggressive war. Therefore, he was found not guilty under Count One of the indictment. However, the tribunal continued, it had determined Streicher guilty under Count Four, crimes against humanity.[40]

As substantiation, the panel of judges cited that Streicher had preached hatred of Jews for 25 years especially through his newspaper, *Der Stuermer*. By this means, the panel decreed, he had unquestionably infected the minds of countless Germans against Jewish people and had incited vicious persecution of Jews. The tribunal also mentioned that the *Stuermer* must have been widely read with its circulation averaging 600,000 copies weekly after 1935. Reference was also made to Streicher's involvement in the Jewish boycott of April 1, 1933, his advocacy of the Nuremberg Laws, and his responsibility for the demolition of the Nuremberg synagogue in November, 1938. In addition, the tribunal cited excerpts of many of the 26 *Stuermer* articles, written after August, 1941, which demanded extermination and annihilation of Jews.

Referring to these writings as positive proof that Streicher deserved the odious sub-title, "Number One Nazi Jew-Baiter," in exhorting the mass killing of Jews, the tribunal concluded its judgment of Streicher:

> . . .Streicher's incitement of murder and extermination at the time when Jews in the East were being killed under the most horrible conditions clearly constitutes persecution on political and racial grounds in connection with war crimes, as defined by the Charter, and constitutes a crime against humanity.

Verdict: GUILTY on Count Four
Sentence: Death by hanging[41]

After the defendants heard the final judgment and sentence pronounced, they were returned to their cells where Gilbert managed to talk to most of them in turn. Some prisoners, such as Goering, Kaltenbrunner, and Raeder were evidently too emotionally upset to offer comment. The military men, Jodl and Keitel, did not seem overly disappointed at receiving the death sentence. However, they both appeared highly agitated at the idea of dying a cowardly death at the end of a rope. To them, the most important issue seemed that they would not be executed by a firing squad as they had requested. Aside from the three acquitted men, five others, Frank, Frick, Hess, Seyss-Inquart and Streicher did not complain about their sentences, or said that they had not expected what they received.

Streicher met Gilbert with a crooked smile on his face. Almost light-heartedly he said without being questioned: "Death, of course—just what I expected. You must have known about it all along."[42]

Julius Streicher's last full day alive was spent alone in his prison cell, patiently writing a half-dozen letters and reading intermittently from a book by A. Jelusik, entitled *The Soldier*. Military police guards at the prison noted no outward show of emotion from him. That evening, at 9 PM on October 15, 1946, one of the white-helmeted guards brought Streicher his last supper consisting of potato salad, cold cuts, black bread and tea. At the same time, the prison lights dimmed and attitudes of the guards and other prison personnel seemed to reflect the ominous anticipation of death.[43]

At 10:45, Colonel Andrus, Prison Commandant, left his office to see if the machinery for the scheduled executions of the 11 condemned Nazi criminals was in readiness. Just about then, Hermann Goering, still considered the most important Nazi alive, bit into a vial of potassium cyanide. Somehow, unexplainably, Goering had managed to have possession of the vial at the right time. Defiant to the end, he had denied the large group of international witnesses already gathered in the temporary execution chamber the spectacle that many had come expressly to see.

Goering's suicide did not delay the final preparations inside the small prison gymnasium for carrying out the death sentence of the remaining Nazi criminals. Three black gallows, standing eight feet apart, had been erected on one side of the gymnasium floor under the supervision of the chief executioner, United States Master Sergeant John C. Woods, who was well experienced for this assignment. Woods, of San Antonio, Texas, had been active as an army executioner for 15 years. Throughout his career, he had hanged 347 people.[44]

The gallows each stood eight feet high and measured eight feet square. From each platform rose two heavy beams supporting a heavy cross-piece with a hook for the rope fastened in the center. On the floor of the platform was a trap-door, controlled by a lever to be operated by an assistant executioner. The space beneath the platform was hidden by black curtains.

The first of the condemned men to be hanged that night was Joachim von Ribbentrop. He was led across a small courtyard from the cell block into the makeshift gallows chamber and entered the dimly lit gymnasium at 1:11 AM on October 16. All witnesses rose from their seats and stood at attention. At the foot of the steps leading up to the gallows' platform, Ribbentrop's wrist manacles were removed. After he mounted the 13 steps he was placed on the trap-door and Woods slipped the noose around his neck. Told that he could make a last statement, Ribbentrop, with enforced bravery, said: "My last wish. . .is an understanding between East and West."[45]

As Woods tightened the noose and placed a black hood over the prisoner's head, a chaplain on the platform began to pray. All witnesses removed their hats just before the lever releasing the trap was pulled. The condemned man's body disappeared below the platform and the rope was suddenly taut, swinging back and forth with a creaking sound. After Ribbentrop was pronounced dead by an international team of physicians, the rope holding him in the air was cut and his body laid behind a curtain.

Similar procedures were followed in approximate ten-minute intervals with the prisoners that followed: Wilhelm Keitel, Ernst Kaltenbrunner, Hans Frank and Wilhelm Frick. With little protest, these men bore themselves erectly and spoke their last words in dignity.

When the white-helmeted guards came for the next prisoner, Streicher, they found him in his pajamas, lying on his cot, reading. Streicher ignored the guards' orders to get up and dress. He said defiantly that if they wanted him to go someplace, then they could dress and carry him. The burly guards manacled Streicher's wrists and lifted him bodily and dragged him by the armpits in his pajamas across the courtyard to the foot of the gallows' steps. Adding to the ignobility of the scene, Streicher intermittently cried out profanities, objecting to his rough treatment. Protesting his innocence, he shouted almost incoherently that this act was final proof of the treachery of the Jews.[46]

Pushed and pulled up the steps to the platform, Streicher appeared wild-eyed. When the noose was slipped over his head, he screamed *"Heil* Hitler! *Heil* Hitler!" When he was asked his name, he snarled "You know it well!" Then he shouted at the witnesses: "Purim Festival 1946!"[47] and "The Bolsheviks will hang you all one day."

The chaplain followed the hangman's signal and began to pray. When the black hood was placed over Streicher's head, he uttered his last words: "Adele—my dear wife."

At 2:14 AM October 16, 1946, Julius Streicher disappeared behind the black curtain.[48]

NOTES

PROLOGUE

1. Joe J. Heydecker and Johannes Leeb, *The Nuremberg Trial* (New York: 1962), pp. 42-43.

2. *Ibid.*, which is also the source for the following.

3. *Time*, June 4, 1945, p. 39.

4. *Ibid.*

5. Edward Peterson, *Limits of Hitler's Power* (Princeton, N.J.: 1969), p. 228.

6. National Archives, Washington, (cited hereafter as NAW), *Interrogation of Adele and Julius Streicher by U. S. Army Officers in Nuremberg*, (cited hereafter as IAJS), October 10, 1945.

CHAPTER I.

1. Stadtbibliothek, Nuremberg, (cited hereafter as SBN), Manfred Ruehl, *Der Stuermer und sein Herausgeber*, 1960, p. 39.

2. *Ibid.*

3. *Ibid.*, p. 37.

4. Jay W. Baird, "Streicher, Julius, Das Politische Testament," in *Vierteljahrshefte fuer Zeitgeschichte* (Stuttgart, April, 1978), p. 670.

5. SBN, Ruehl, *Der Stuermer*, p. 38.

6. Bayerisches Staatsarchiv, *Personalakten Julius Streicher*, (cited hereafter as BSA, PAJS), vol. I, documents number 16 and 18. August 4, 1904 and November 19, 1906. Protocol of Inspector's Visitation of the Boys' School at Lauingen, January 31, 1907. Streicher's salary for the substitute assignments was 820 marks annually. His salary for the Lauingen position was the same plus 100 marks annually for living expenses.

7. SBN, Ruehl, *Der Stuermer*, p. 38.

8. BSA, PAJS, vol. I, folder 1730. Police report of a political meeting, April 4, 1922.

9. Peterson, *Limits of Hitler's Power*, p. 228.

10. BSA, PAJS, vol. I, doc. nr. 25. Notice from Royal Bavarian Government to Streicher, September 11, 1908. Streicher's starting salary was to be 1,000 marks annually, with additional allowances of 120 marks for living expenses and 72 marks for old-age pension.

11. *Ibid.*, Streicher was notified on September 11, 1908, to begin his new assignment at Mindelheim as soon as possible after his release from military duty on October 20, 1908.

12. SBN, Ruehl, *Der Stuermer*, p. 38.

13. International Military Tribunal, *Trial of Major War Criminals* (hereafter cited as IMT), vol. 12, pp. 307-308.

14. *Ibid.*

15. NAW, IAJS, Testimony of Julius Streicher, September 1, 1945.

16. BSA, PAJS, vol. 1, folder 1730. Report from the file of the Police Office at Ansbach, June 3, 1914.

17. *Ibid.*

18. SBN, Ruehl, *Der Stuermer*, p. 40. It is uncertain whether Streicher joined the army voluntarily or responded to orders as a reservist.

19. *Ibid.*, which is also the source for the following.

20. NAW, IAJS, Testimony of Julius Streicher, September 1, 1945.

CHAPTER II.

1. IMT, vol. 12, p. 308.

2. *Ibid.*

3. Allan Mitchell, *Revolution in Bavaria: 1918-1919* (Princeton, New Jersey: 1965), p. 192.

4. SBN, Arnd Mueller, *Geschichte der Juden in Nuernberg: 1146-1945*, 1968, p. 191.

5. NAW, IAJS, Testimony of Streicher, September 1, 1945.

6. Franz Neumann, *Behemoth, the Structure and Practice of National Socialism—1933-44* (New York: 1942), pp. 102-103.

7. SBN, Ruehl, *Der Stuermer*, p. 43.

8. Baird, *Das Politische Testament*, p. 670. See also NAW, IAJS, Testimony of Julius Streicher, September 1, 1945.

9. SBN, Ruehl, *Der Stuermer*, p. 41

10. IMT, vol. 12, p. 308.

11. Peterson, *Limits of Hitler's Power*, p. 226.

12. *Ibid.*, p. 225.

13. Hannah Arendt, *Antisemitism* (New York: 1951), p. x.

14. Jean-Paul Sartre, *Anti-Semite and Jew* (New York: 1948), p. 17.

15. *Ibid.*, p. 25-27, which is also the source for the following.

16. Robert Waite, "Hitler's Anti-Semitism," in Benjamin Wolman's *The Psychoanalytic Interpretation of History* (New York: 1971), p. 199. Waite comments that it is the opinion of a number of psychologists and psychiatrists that the study of many cases of anti-Semitics reveals a variety of recognizable clinical syndromes.

17. Frederick Schuman, *The Nazi Dictatorship* (New York: 1939), p. 13. See also Mitchell, *Revolution in Bavaria*, p. 208.

18. Schuman, *Nazi Dictatorship*, p. 13.

19. Ludwig Wagner, *Hitler, Man of Strife* (New York: 1942), p. 95.

20. *Ibid.*

21. SBN, Mueller, *Geschichte der Juden*, pp. 188-189.

22. Dietrich Orlow, *The History of the Nazi Party: 1919-1933* (Pittsburgh: 1969), p. 18.

23. SBN, Mueller, *Geschichte der Juden*, p. 190.

24. SBN, Ruehl, *Der Stuermer*, p. 43.

25. *Ibid.*, The Deutsch-Sozialistische Partei is not to be confused with the Deutsch-Sozialen Partei which was under the leadership of one Richard Kunze.

26. *Ibid.*, p. 87.

27. BSA, PAJS, vol. 1, folder 1730. Report to the Middle Franconian Police Commissioner, August 2, 1920. Streicher eventually became the publisher and the business office was located in Nuremberg.

28. *Deutscher Sozialist*, nr. 1, June, 1920.

29. *Ibid.*, nrs. 3 and 4, June, 1920. See also SBN, Ruehl, *Der Stuermer*, pp. 43-44. Out of 1,657,000 total votes, the *DSP* candidate polled only 2, 351 in the election.

30. BSA, PAJS, vol. I, folder nr. 1739. Report to Middle Franconian Police Commissioner, July 21, 1921, which is also the source for the following.

31. *Ibid.*

32. SBN, Ruehl. *Der Stuermer*, p. 103.

33. *Ibid.*, p. 47.

34. *Ibid.*, p. 103.

35. *Ibid.*.

36. *Ibid.*, Ruehl states that the membership of the DW was recognized as "much more sizable" after Streicher joined it.

37. *Ibid.*

38. The Ohio State University, Captured German Documents (on microfilm), (hereafter cited as OSU, CGD), series T-580, roll 306.

39. *Deutscher Volkswille*, November 11, 1921.

40. *Ibid.*, April 4, 1922 and May 10, 1922.

41. BSA, PAJS, doc. nr. 2217/22. Copy of legal brief from trial at Schweinfurt, September 5, 1922. Recordings of speeches by Nazi leaders are available at most university libraries.

42. BSA, PAJS, vol. I, folder 1730. Report on Nuremberg meeting from files of Nuremberg police office, February 27, 1922. See also Wagner, *Hitler, Man of Strife*, p. 113. At the time of this speech, Hitler was serving a jail sentence for causing a riot in Munich. Although Rathenau was not murdered until June 24, 1922, rumors in the Munich streets prophesied his assassination some months earlier in threatening limericks sung aloud by *voelkisch* hoodlums.

43. *Deutscher Volkswille*, March 3, 1922.

44. BSA, PAJS, vol. I, folder 1730. Extract from day-book of the office of the Middle Franconian police office, March 14, 1922.

45. *Ibid.*, Report on the meeting at Schonungen in the files of the Nuremberg police office, March 16, 1922.

46. *Ibid.*, doc. nr. 2217/22. Copy of legal brief from the trial at Schweinfurt, September 5, 1922.

47. *Ibid.* doc. nr. 2207/22. Copy of legal brief accompanying

verdict of appeals court at Schweinfurt, November 10, 1922.

48. *Ibid.*

49. *Ibid.*, doc. nrs. 2217/22 and 2207/22.

50. *Ibid.*, vol. I, folder 1730. Report to Bavarian Police Office from Neustadt City Government, March 28, 1922.

51. *Ibid.*, vol. I, doc. nr. 2978. Reports to Bavarian Government Police Office, April 4 and April 11, 1922. Both meetings were held at the Herkules Velodrom, Nuremberg.

52. *Ibid.*

53. SBN, Ruehl, *Der Stuermer*, p. 104.

54. *Ibid.* Since the DW had approximately one-half their members in the Augsburg district, Streicher lost many subscribers by this edict.

55. BSA, PAJS, vol. I, folder 1730. Extract from day book of the office of the Middle Franconian police department, March 14, 1922.

56. SBN, Ruehl, *Der Stuermer*, p. 104.

CHAPTER III.

1. SBN, Ruehl, *Der Stuermer*, p. 51.

2. IMT, vol. 12, p. 309.

3. Kurt Ludecke, *I Knew Hitler* (New York: 1937), p. 16. Ludecke became disenchanted with Hitler's cruelties and escaped from Germany in 1934.

4. Orlow, *History of the Nazi Party*, p. 29.

5. William Shirer, *The Rise and Fall of the Third Reich* (New York: 1959), p. 46, which is the source for the following.

6. Ibid., pp. 46-48. See also Orlow, *History of the Nazi Party*, p. 27.

7. SBN, Ruehl, *Der Stuermer*, p. 104.

8. *Ibid.*, pp. 50-51, which is also the source for the following.

9. Ludwig Wagner, *Hitler, Man of Strife* (New York: 1942), p. 110.

10. Ludecke, *I Knew Hitler*, p. 99.

11. Adolf Hitler, *Mein Kampf* (Munich: 1925), p. 575.

12. William E. Dodd, *Ambassador Dodd's Diary* (New York: 1941), p. 106. Dodd warned the Nazi government that Streicher's violent anti-Semitic attacks were hurting business between the U.S. and Germany. Hitler not only refused to interfere, he complimented Streicher on his "effective writing."

13. SBN, Ruehl, *Der Stuermer*, p. 70. The other three men who shared this privilege were Drexler, Roehm, and Esser.

14. Peterson, *Limits of Hitler's Power*, p. 226. See also Bullock, *Hitler*, p. 24.

15. NAW, IAJS, Testimony of Julius Streicher, September 1, 1945. See also Bullock, *Hitler*, p. 53.

16. Waite, "Hitler's Anti-Semitism," p. 199 ff. Hitler's racist

symptoms are paralleled here with recognized symptoms of clinically observed anti-Semites. Streicher exhibited most of these same characteristics.

17. SBN, Mueller, *Geschichte der Juden*, p. 191.

18. *Ibid.*

19. OSU, CGD, series T-580, roll 307.

20. SBN, Ruehl, *Der Stuermer*, p. 53.

21. OSU, CGD, series T-580, roll 307.

22. SBN, Ruehl, *Der Stuermer*, p. 53.

23. Schuman, *Nazi Dictatorship*, p. 33.

24. U.S. Office of the Chief Counsel for Prosecution of Criminality, *Nazi Conspiracy and Aggression* (Washington: 1946), vol. VIII, p. 10.

25. BSA, PAJS, vol. I, folder 1730. Report from Nuremberg police to the Bavarian Government Office, December 15, 1922.

26. *Ibid.*

27. SBN, Mueller, *Geschichte der Juden*, p. 191.

28. BSA, PAJS, vol. I, folder 1730. Police report to Bavarian Government, Ansbach, November 9, 1922.

29. OSU, CGD, series T-580, roll 307.

30. SBN, Ruehl, *Der Stuermer*, p. 54.

31. *Ibid.*, pp. 53-54.

32. BSA, PAJS, vol. I, folder 1730. Police report to Bavarian Government, Ansbach, December 10, 1922.

33. *Ibid.*

34. SBN, Ruehl, *Der Stuermer*, p. 54.

CHAPTER IV.

1. F. L. Carsten, *The Rise of Fascism* (Los Angeles:1967), p. 108. In 1914 the German mark was valued at approximately four to one U.S. dollar. At the end of the inflationary spiral in late 1923, the ratio was 4,200,000,000 marks to one U.S. dollar.

2. SBN, Ruehl, *Der Stuermer*, p. 55.

3. Schuman, *Nazi Dictatorship*, p. 482.

4. Peterson, *Limits of Hitler's Power*, p. 226.

5. *Ibid.*

6. SBN, Ruehl, *Der Stuermer*, p. 53.

7. BSA, PAJS, vol. I, doc. nr. 59. Report to the Bavarian Government Office, Ansbach, dated February 20, 1923. His class at this time consisted of 40 girls of the eighth grade.

8. *Ibid.*, doc. nr. 60. Report from District Inspector to Bavarian Government Office, Ansbach, January 27, 1923.

9. *Ibid.*

10. *Ibid.*

11. *Ibid.*, doc. nr. 62. Report from Grim to Bavarian Government Office, Nuremberg, February 2, 1923.

12. *Ibid.*

13. *Fraenkische Tagespost*, February 10, 1923.

14. *Nuernberger Anzeiger*, March 10, 1923.

15. BSA, PAJS, vol, vol. I; doc. nr. 72. Report from Ministry of Culture at Ansbach to Nuremberg School Board, March 12, 1923. Article 118 RV of the Bavarian Constitution is cited here.

16. *Ibid.*

17. *Ibid.*, Even if the appropriate official had received Streicher's written request on Saturday he could not have reached him to affirm or deny it.

18. *Ibid.*

19. *Ibid.*, doc. nr. 80. Letter and enclosure from Luppe to the President of the Middle Franconian Government, April 17, 1923. Hans Sachs was born in Nuremberg and was revered as the most prolific German poet and dramatist of the 16th Century. Streicher's accusation regarding Luppe's plans to demolish this statue was perhaps intended to arouse "tradition minded" Nuremberg citizens to oppose the mayor.

20. *Ibid.*

21. *Ibid.*, doc. nr. 87. Letter from Government Office in Ansbach to the City Council of Nuremberg, May 1, 1923.

22. *Ibid.*, doc. nr. 90. Letter from Dr. Huber to Luppe, June 5, 1923.

23. *Ibid.*, folder nr. 1730. Police report of a NSDAP meeting in Nuremberg, May 11, 1923.

24. *Ibid.*, doc. nr. 96. Letter from Luppe to Huber, June 12, 1923.

25. *Ibid.*, doc. nr. 102. Report to the Government Office in Ansbach from the Uffenheim police office, June 20, 1923.

26. *Ibid.*, doc. nr. 132. Report for the file by Dr. Huber, December 7, 1923.

27. *Ibid.*, Because of the rampant inflation the actual value of the cash donated to the refugees by the children did not amount to more than a few pennies of U.S. money.

28. Orlow, *History of the Nazi Party*, pp. 42-43. See also Wagner, *Hitler*, p. 119.

29. SBN, Ruehl, *Der Stuermer*, p. 55.

30. Orlow, *History of the Nazi Party*, pp. 42-43. See also Wagner, *Hitler*, p. 119.

31. Schuman, *Nazi Dictatorship*, p. 81. The event was so venerated that Hitler often used one of the blood-stained flags of the *Putsch* to consecrate new Nazi flags in ceremonies and rallies.

32. BSA, PAJS, vol. I, doc. nr. 132. Report from the files of Dr. Huber, December 7, 1923.

33. *Ibid.*

34. Bullock, *Hitler*, p. 108.

35. SBN, Ruehl, *Der Stuermer*, p. 53. See also *Fraenkische Tageszeitung*, nr. 262, November 8, 1938.

36. SBN, Ruehl, *Der Stuermer*, p. 59. See also Harold J. Gordon, Jr., *Hitler and the Beer Hall Putsch* (Princeton, New Jersey: 1972) pp. 334-335. In addition to description, Gordon includes a photograph of Streicher speaking from a truck in the Marienplatz, a very large square in Munich which was jammed to capacity with people listening to Streicher.

37. Hanns Hoffmann, *Der Hitlerputsch* (Munich: 1961), pp. 100-102. See also SBN, Ruehl, *Der Stuermer*, p. 59.

38. SBN, Ruehl, *Der Stuermer*, pp. 59-60.

39. Berndorff, *General Zwischen Ost und West*, p. 112. See also Heiden, *Der Fuehrer*, p. 198.

40. SBN, Ruehl, *Der Stuermer*, p. 61.

41. BSA, PAJS, vol. I, folder 1730. Police report to Bavarian Government Office at Ansbach, February 2, 1924.

42. *Ibid.* See also OSU, CGD, series T-580, roll 310.

43. BSA, PAJS, vol. I, folder 1730. Police report to Bavarian Government Office at Ansbach, February 2, 1924.

44. *Ibid.*, doc. nr. 202/1, folder 1730. Protocol signed by Streicher in defense of his innocence regarding events in Munich, November 8 and 9, 1923.

45. *Ibid.*, doc. nr. 201, folder 1730. Letter from Attorneys Kelber and Titus to the Nuremberg Police Department, November 14, 1923.

46. *Ibid.*, doc. nr. 132. Directive signed by Huber, December 10, 1923.

47. *Ibid.*, doc. nr. 1652. Notice to the Nuremberg School Board from Huber, December 11, 1923.

48. *Ibid.*, doc. nr. 143, folder 1730. Letter from Streicher to Office of School District IV, Ansbach, December 11, 1923.

49. *Ibid.*

50. *Ibid.*

51. *Ibid.*, doc. nr. 205/9. Report from Police Inspector to Nuremberg Police Office, January 3, 1924.

52. *Ibid.*, doc. nr. 126, folder 1730. Report by Nuremberg Police Inspector to Bavarian Government Office at Ansbach, December 7, 1923.

53. SBN, Ruehl, *Der Stuermer*, p. 63.

54. Personal interview with Dr. Benno Martin, dated August 4, 1970.

55. Wagner, *Hitler*, pp. 128-129.

56. Bundesarchiv Koblenz, (cited hereafter as BAK), *Streicher Nachlasse*, diary of Streicher from January 18 to February 24, 1924.

57. Wagner, *Hitler*, p. 132. Guertner was quoted as saying: "After all, the National Socialists are flesh of our flesh."

58. Shirer, *Rise and Fall*, p. 75.

59. BSA, PAJS, vol. I, doc. nr. 166. Bavarian Government report signed by Kahr, January 22, 1924.

60. *Ibid.*

61. *Ibid.*, No specific term of confinement was mentioned in this order.

62. BAK, *Streicher Nachlasse*, Streicher's diary. It is not likely that Kunigunde smiled because she was happy about the arrest. Throughout her married life she remained loyal and dutiful to her husband.

63. *Ibid.*

64. Interview with Dr. Benno Martin in Munich, August 4, 1970.

65. BAK, *Streicher Nachlasse*, Streicher's diary.

66. *Ibid.*, Streicher noted that he accepted the disciplinary punishment and declared with a laugh that if he had another chance he would commit the same "crime" again.

67. *Ibid.*

68. Alan Bullock, *Hitler, A Study in Tyranny* (New York: 1962), p. 115. See also most other biographical works on Hitler's life.

69. SBN, Ruehl, *Der Stuermer*, p. 96.

70. *Der Stuermer*, nr. I, April 20, 1923. This phrase, with slight alteration, remained the byline of the newspaper for 22 years.

71. *Ibid.*, April to November, 1923.

72. *Ibid.*, nr. 6, July, 1923.

73. English synonyms for the German word *Stuermer* include "stormer," "assailant," and "forward."

74. SBN, Ruehl, *Der Stuermer*, p. 98.

75. *Ibid.*, p. 99. Ruehl stated that he took this excerpt from Goebbels' newspaper, *Der Angriff.*

76. *Der Stuermer*, nr. 11, August, 1923.

77. *Ibid.*

78. SBN, Ruehl, *Der Stuermer*, p. 99.

CHAPTER V.

1. Ernest Hanfstaengl, *Hitler—The Missing Years* (London:1957), p. 108. See also Payne, *The Life and Death*, p. 181.

2. Wagner, *Hitler*, pp. 130-131.

3. Gordon, *Beer Hall Putsch*, p. 572.

4. SBN, Ruehl, *Der Stuermer*, p. 64.

5. *Ibid.* See also Gordon, *Beer Hall Putsch*, p. 572.

6. *Fraenkischer Kurier*, nr. 64, March 4, 1924.

7. *Ibid.*, nr. 65, March 5, 1924.

8. *Ibid.*

9. For details of the "coat affair" see the previous chapter.

10. *Fraenkischer Kurier*, nr. 65, March 5, 1924.

11. BSA, PAJS, vol. I, doc. nr. 206. Report from the Nuremberg Provincial Court, June 13, 1924.

12. *Fraenkischer Kurier*, nr. 72, March 12, 1924.

13. *Ibid.*

14. *Ibid.*, nrs. 72 and 74, March 12 and March 15, 1924.

15. BSA, PAJS, vol. I, doc. nr. 206. Report from the Nuremberg police files, June 13, 1924.

16. *Fraenkischer Kurier*, nr. 74, March 15, 1924.

17. BSA, PAJS, vol. II, folder nr. 1731. Police report on political meeting at the Geissmannssaal in Fuerth, March 15, 1924.

18. George L. Mosse, *Nazi Culture* (New York: 1966), p. 41.

19. BSA, PAJS, vol. II, folder nr. 1731. Police report on political meeting at the Geissmannssaal in Fuerth, March 15, 1924, which is also the source for the following.

20. *Ibid.* Report to the Police Office at Nuremberg, April 3, 1924, which is also the source for the following.

21. *Der Stuermer*, nr. 15, May, 1924.

22. BSA, PAJS, vol. II, folder nr. 1731. Report from Nuremberg police files, May 20, 1924.

23. Heiden, *Der Fuehrer*, p. 250.

24. *Ibid.*, p. 251.

25. BSA, PAJS, vol. II, folder nr. 1731. Report from Nuremberg police files, May 20, 1924.

26. Heiden, *Der Fuehrer*, p. 254.

27. *Der Stuermer*, nr. 15. May, 1924.

28. Douglas Reed, *Nemesis* (Boston: 1940), p. 78.

29. Heiden, *Der Fuehrer*, p. 254.

30. BSA, PAJS, vol. II, folder nr. 1731. Report from Nuremberg police files, May 20, 1924.

31. Wagner, *Hitler*, p. 139, which is also the source for the following.

32. SBN, Ruehl, *Der Stuermer*, pp. 65-66.

33. BSA, PAJS, vol. II, folder nr. 1731. Report from Nuremberg police files, July 17, 1924.

34. *Ibid.* Report from Nuremberg police files, July 30, 1924, which is also the source for the following.

35. *Ibid.*

36. *Fraenkischer Kurier*, July 29, 1924.

37. *Ibid.*

38. *Der Stuermer*, special issue, July 22, 1924. See also BSA, PAJS, vol. II, folder 1731. Report from Nuremberg police files, July 30, 1924.

39. *Voelkisches Echo*, nr. 56, July 22, 1924.

40. *Ibid.*

41. *Deutsche Presse*, August 4, 1924.

42. BSA, PAJS, vol. II, folder 1731. Report from Nuremberg police files, August 16, 1924, which is also the source for the following.

43. *Deutsche Presse,* August 4, 1924. When offered a committee position in the *Landtag,* he had always refused in arrogant terms.

44. *Oberfraenkische Volkszeitung,* nr. 231, August, 1924.

45. *Deutsche Presse,* August 4, 1924.

46. BSA, PAJS, vol. II, folder 1731. Report from Nuremberg police files, August 3, 1924.

47. *Ibid.*

48. *Ibid.* Report from Nuremberg police files, September 23, 1924.

49. *Ibid.*

50. *Ibid.* Report from Nuremberg police files, September 30, 1924.

51. *Ibid.* Report from Nuremberg police files, October 1, 1924, which is also the source for the following.

52. IMT, vol. 12, pp. 334-335. Also substantiated by author's personal interview in Munich, July 1970, with Dr. Benno Martin, former Police President in Nuremberg in the 1930's. Martin stated that between 1933 and 1938 Streicher transported busloads of Communist prisoners from Dachau to Nuremberg where they were served dinner with their families and allowed a few days home during the Christmas holidays.

53. Personal interview in Nuremberg, March, 1971, with Fritz Nadler, author and former Nuremberg newspaper reporter. Nadler verified Streicher's acts of kindness toward Communist prisoners during holiday seasons. Nadler also related a story of his friend, Herr Umlauf, a former Communist, whose marriage at Dachau was arranged by Streicher.

54. BSA, PAJS, vol. II, folder 1731. Report from Nuremberg police files, May 23, 1925.

55. *Nordbayerische Zeitung,* nr. 253, October 27, 1924.

56. BSA, PAJS, vol. II, folder 1731. Report from Nuremberg police files, November 28, 1924.

57. *Ibid.* Letter from Luppe to Huber, December 5, 1924.

58. *Ibid.* Report from Nuremberg police files, November 28, 1924.

59. *Ibid.*

60. *Bayerischer Kurier.* January 1, 1925, which is also the source for the following.

61. BSA, PAJS, vol. II, folder 1731. Letter from Huber to Nuremberg School Board, May 12, 1925. In addition to these incomes, Streicher received 288 marks monthly as a suspended teacher. There is no record of his income from political activities or from his publications. At this time the German mark was valued at approximately 25 cents, U. S. currency.

62. SBN, Ruehl, *Der Stuermer,* p. 106. This slogan was printed in the same place in all subsequent issues.

63. SBN, Ruehl, *Der Stuermer,* p. 106.

64. *Ibid.*

65. *Der Stuermer,* nr. 25, December, 1925.

66. *Ibid.*, nr. 18, October, 1941.

67. SBN, Ruehl, *Der Stuermer*, p. 120.

68. *Ibid.*, p. 114.

69. *Ibid.*, p. 111.

70. *Der Stuermer*, nr. 25, December, 1925.

71. *Ibid.*, nr. 10, March, 1924.

72. *Ibid.*, nr. 21, October, 1925.

73. *Ibid.*, nr. 20, May, 1927.

74. *Ibid.*, nr. 24, June, 1927.

75. SBN, Ruehl, *Der Stuermer*, p. 125.

76. *Ibid.*, p. 107.

77. OSU, CGD, series T-580, reel nr. 268. Excerpt from *Der Stuermer*, October 4, 1924.

78. SBN, Ruehl, *Der Stuermer*, p. 116. This library survived the destruction of Nuremberg in World War II. It contained over 8000 volumes. Streicher collected these volumes by confiscations from Jewish homes and by donations from readers who responded to *Stuermer* articles requesting books thought, or known to be Jewish literature.

79. Schlomo Gliksman, *My Lawsuit Against Julius Streicher and Co., and the Forgeries and Falsifications in Anti-Semitic Literature* (Cleveland, Ohio: 1941), p. 25.

80. *Ibid.*, p. 27.

81. *Ibid.*, p. 26.

82. *Der Stuermer*, nr. 6, July, 1923.

83. *Ibid.*

84. *Ibid.*, nr. 17, September, 1924.

85. *Ibid.*, nr. 13, August, 1925.

86. *Ibid.*, nr. 20, October, 1925.

87. SBN, Ruehl, *Der Stuermer*, p. 161. Streicher charged about three-fourths of one mark per column inch for these ads.

88. *Ibid.*, p. 155.

89. *Ibid.* Ruehl adds that this information could not be substantiated by valid documentation.

90. *Ibid.*, p. 156.

91. BSA, PAJS, vol. II, folder nr. 1731. Report from Nuremberg police office, June 12, 1924.

92. SBN, Ruehl, *Der Stuermer*, p. 156.

CHAPTER VI.

1. Wagner, *Hitler*, p. 141.

2. Ludecke, *I Knew Hitler*, p. 261. See also Shirer, *Rise and Fall*, p. 123.

3. Ludecke, *I Knew Hitler*, p. 261.

4. Orlow, *History of the Nazi Party*, p. 51.

5. Wagner, *Hitler*, p. 142.

6. *Ibid.*, pp. 142-143.

7. *Ibid.*, p. 143, which is also the source for the following.

8. Peterson, *Limits of Hitler's Power*, p. 226.

9. BSA, PAJS, vol. II, folder 1731. Police report of GVG meeting in Nuremberg, January 21, 1925, which is also the source for the following.

10. Wagner, *Hitler*, p. 142.

11. Bullock, *Hitler*, pp. 128-129.

12. Orlow, *History of the Nazi Party*, pp. 52-53.

13. *Voelkischer Beobachter*, February 25, 1925. See also Bullock, *Hitler*, p. 129.

14. Wagner, *Hitler*, p. 143.

15. Orlow, *History of the Nazi Party*, pp. 53-54.

16. Wagner, *Hitler*, p. 144, which is also the source for the following.

17. Bullock, *Hitler*, pp. 130-131.

18. Wagner, *Hitler*, p. 144.

19. *Ibid.*, p. 145.

20. BSA, PAJS, vol. II, folder 1731. Police report on Nuremberg meetings, March 2, 1925, which is also the source for the following.

21. Since the 1924 currency stabilization in Germany, the highest admission fee to any Nuremberg GVG meeting had been 80 pfennig. At most meetings there was no admission fee charged. The audience was requested to contribute what they could as they left the hall.

22. *Ibid.*

23. *Ibid.*

24. *Ibid.* See also SBN, Ruehl, *Der Stuermer*, Stuermer, p. 67. The term Franconia, as used in connection with Streicher's area of political influence, is actually the Bavarian province of Mittelfranken.

25. Wagner, *Hitler*, p. 148. In early 1925, the Nazis were one of the smallest political parties in Germany, with a membership of approximately 17,000.

26. Orlow, *History of the Nazi Party*, p. 61.

27. Bullock, *Hitler*, p. 132.

28. *Der Stuermer*, nr. 10, April, 1925.

29. *Ibid.*, nr. 11, April, 1925.

30. Wagner, *Hitler*, p. 149, which is also the source for the following.

31. BSA, PAJS, vol. II, folder 1731. Police report on NSDAP meeting in Nuremberg, April 21, 1925, which is also the source for the following.

32. *Ibid.* Report on court hearing in Nuremberg, April 30, 1925. Streicher was fined ten marks for this violation.

33. *Ibid.* Letter from Huber to Luppe, January 9, 1925. Parliamen-

tary immunity is provided in Article 39 of the Bavarian Constitution.

34. BSA, PAJS, vol. II, folder 1731. Letter from the Franconian Government Disciplinary Office to Luppe, July 15, 1925.

35. U. S. Office for Prosecution of Axis Criminality, *Nazi Conspiracy*, vol. VIII, doc. nr. M-30, pp. 16-17. Speech by Julius Streicher at *Landtag* session, June 25, 1925, which is also the source for the following.

36. Orlow, *History of the Nazi Party*, p. 66.

37. *Ibid.* See also Bullock, *Hitler*, p. 136.

38. Orlow, *History of the Nazi Party*, p. 66.

39. BSA, PAJS, vol. II, folder 1731. Police report on NSDAP meeting at Fuerth, September 28, 1925, which is also the source for the following.

40. Orlow, *History of the Nazi Party*, p. 68.

41. Joseph Goebbels, *The Early Goebbels Diaries* (New York: 1963), p. 45, which is also the source for the following.

42. Heiden, *Der Fuehrer*, p. 287. See also Payne, *Life and Death*, p. 215.

43. Bullock, *Hitler*, p. 127.

44. *Fraenkischer Kurier*, nr. 319, November 17, 1925.

45. *Ibid.*, nr. 321, November 19, 1925. See also SBN, Mueller, *Geschichte der Juden*, p. 143. Karl Holz, Streicher's principal associate, was expelled from the city council in May, 1925, for publishing secret council information. Before this, both he and Streicher did all they could to disrupt council sessions.

46. *Fraenkischer Kurier*, nr. 329, November 27, 1925.

47. *Ibid.*, nr. 333, December 1, 1925.

48. *Ibid.*, nr. 336, December 4, 1925.

49. *Ibid.*, nr. 344, December 12, 1925.

50. *Ibid.*, nr. 349, December 17, 1925.

51. BSA, PAJS, vol. II, folder 1731. Copy of court proceedings of Nuremberg Juror's Court, December 30, 1925, which is also the source for the following.

52. *Ibid.* Notice from the Interior Office of the Franconian Government to the President of the Nuremberg Juror's Court, August 10, 1926.

53. *Fraenkischer Kurier*, nr. 485, September 15, 1926.

54. *Der Stuermer*, nrs. 35-39, *November 20 to December 20, 1925.*

55. BSA, PAJS, vol. II, folder 1731. Police report on *voelkisch* political meeting, Nuremberg, January 18, 1926, which is also the source for the following.

56. *Fraenkischer Kurier*, nr. 2, January 12, 1926.

57. BSA, PAJS, vol. II, folder 1731. Police report on *voelkisch* political meeting, Nuremberg, January 18, 1926. Closing sentences of the report noted that many people left the hall grumbling, and that Ludendorff left the premises practically unnoticed. See also *Fraen-*

kischer Kurier nr. 2, January 12, 1926.

58. Orlow, *History of the Nazi Party*, p. 69. See also Payne, *Life and Death*, p. 216.

59. Orlow, *History of the Nazi Party*, p. 70.

60. Shirer, *Rise and Fall*, pp. 128-129. See also Payne, *Life and Death*, p. 217.

61. Orlow, *History of the Nazi Party*, p. 70.

62. *Ibid.*, p. 71.

63. BSA, PAJS, vol. II, folder 1731. Police report on open meeting of the NSDAP, Nuremberg, March 20, 1926, which is also the source for the following.

64. Goebbels, *Diaries*, p. 45, p. 71.

65. Shirer, *Rise and Fall*, p. 128. See also Heiden, *Der Fuehrer*, p. 290.

66. BSA, PAJS, vol. II, folder 1731. Police report on open meeting of the NSDAP, Nuremberg, March 20, 1926.

67. Heiden, *Der Fuehrer*, p. 292.

68. *Der Stuermer*, nrs. 10 and 11, April, 1926.

69. *Ibid.*, nr. 11, April, 1926.

70. *Ibid.*, nr. 12, May, 1926.

71. SBN, Ruehl, *Der Stuermer*, p. 155.

72. Orlow, *History of the Nazi Party*, p. 72.

73. *Ibid.* See also BSA, PAJS, vol. II, folder 1731. Report from police files, Nuremberg, May 15, 1926.

74. BSA, PAJS, vol. II, folder 1731. Report from police files, Nuremberg, May 15, 1926.

75. Heiden, *Der Fuehrer*, p. 292.

76. *Ibid.*, p. 293.

77. Payne, *Life and Death*, p. 217. See also Bullock, *Hitler*, p. 139.

78. Hamilton T. Burden, *The Nuremberg Party Rallies: 1923-39* (New York: 1967), p. 33.

79. *Voelkischer Beobachter*, July 3, 1926.

80. *Ibid.*

81 Payne, *Life and Death*, p. 217. See also Burden, *Nuremberg Rallies*, p. 33.

82. *Der Stuermer*, nr. 14, July, 1926. See also Payne, *Life and Death*, p. 217.

83. *Voelkischer Beobachter*, July 5, 1926. See also Orlow, *History of the Nazi Party*, p. 74.

84. Payne, *Life and Death*, p. 217. See also Burden, *Nuremberg Rallies*, p. 35.

CHAPTER VII.

1. Orlow, *History of the Nazi Party*, p. 76.

2. *Ibid.*, p. 78. These questions were more in the form of arguments for and against a definitive commitment to support only left-wing causes.

3. BSA, PAJS, vol. I, folder 1732. Police reports of NSDAP meetings in Nuremberg, August 10, 1926, January 21, 1927.

4. *Ibid.*

5. *Ibid.* Police report of NSDAP meeting in Nuremberg, August 10, 1926, which is also the source for the following.

6. OSU, CGD, series T-580, reel nr. 267. Court order to Streicher from the President of the Nuremberg Common Pleas Court, August 8, 1926.

7. BSA, PAJS, vol. I, folder 1732. Letter from Luppe to Dr. Huber, August 12, 1926.

8. *Ibid.* Report from Nuremberg police files, August 16, 1926.

9. *Ibid.*

10. *Voelkischer Beobachter*, August 18, 1926.

11. BSA, PAJS, vol. I, folder 1732. Report from Nuremberg police files, August 16, 1926.

12. *Der Stuermer*, August 18 and August 26, 1926, which is also the source for the following.

13. *Ibid.* See also BSA, PAJS, vol. I, folder 1732. Police report on NSDAP meeting, August 20, 1926, which is also the source for the following.

14. *Die Bombe*, September 5, 1926.

15. *Der Stuermer*, August 26, to December 1, 1926.

16. BSA, PAJS, vol. I, folder 1732. Letter from Franconian Office of the Bavarian Interior Ministry to the Provincial Court, Nuremberg, August 30, 1926.

17. *Ibid.* This figure is an estimate taken from the undocumented statement that 17,000 to 20,000 copies per month were sold at 90 pfennig per month.

18. BSA, PAJS, vol. I, folder 1732. Letter from Nuremberg Common Pleas Court to Streicher, September 5, 1926. See also *Der Stuermer*, September, 17, 1926.

19. *Die Bombe*, September 9. 1926.

20. BSA, PAJS, vol. I, folder 1732. Letter from Dr. Huber to Nuremberg Police Office, September 12, 1926.

21. *Der Stuermer*, September 17, 1926.

22. *Voelkischer Beobachter*, August 23 to December 7, 1926.

23. BSA, PAJS, vol. I, folder 1732. Report from Nuremberg police files, December 10, 1926, which is also the source for the following. See also *Der Stuermer*, December 9, 1926, (special edition) which is also the source for the following.

24. Mosse, *Nazi Culture*, p. 47.

25. *Fraenkischer Kurier*, nr. 1, Jan. 2, 1940.

26. Oswald Dutch, *Hitler's Twelve Apostles* (London: 1939), p. 175.

27. *Der Stuermer*, January 21, 1927; June 7, 1927; July 10, 1929.

28. *Die Bombe*, December 20, 1926. See also *Nuernberg-Fuerth Morgenpresse*, December 23, 1926.

29. BSA, PAJS, vol. II, folder 1733. Police report on Nuremberg NSDAP meeting, January 21, 1927. Streicher disclosed this information in a speech.

30. *Nuernberg-Fuerth Morgenpresse*, June 14, 1928.

31. BSA, PAJS, vol. II, folder 1733. Report from Nuremberg police files on criminal hearing in Nuremberg common pleas court, July 17, 1928.

32. *Nuernberg-Fuerth Morgenpresse*, July 18, 1928; August 30, 1928.

33. *Der Stuermer*, July 17, 1928.

34. BSA, PAJS, vol. I, folder 1732. Report from Nuremberg police files on *Landsturm* meeting, February 22, 1926.

35. *Der Stuermer*, August 18, 1926.

36. BSA, PAJS, vol. I, folder 1732. Letter from Rettig to NSDAP headquarters, Munich, September 3, 1926.

37. *Der Stuermer*, October 5, 1927.

38. Orlow, *History of the Nazi Party*, p. 113, which is also the source for the following.

39. *Der Stuermer*, May 13, 1927.

40. Alan Wykes, *The Nuremberg Rallies* (New York: 1970), p. 10.

41. *Ibid.*, pp. 98-99. See also Burden, *Nuremberg Party Rallies*, pp. 38-39. The figure of 160,000 visitors is questionable. Some opposition newspapers estimated total attendance at less than 10,000. It is likely that the correct number is somewhat less than that cited by the Nazis. There was no official estimate made by attending police.

42. Burden, *Nuremberg Party Rallies*, p. 39.

43. *Der Stuermer*, special issue, August 21, 1927, which is also the source for the following.

44. Wykes, *The Nuremberg Rallies*, pp. 98-99. See also Burden, *Nuremberg Party Rallies*, p. 39.

45. BSA, PAJS, vol. I, folder 1732. Letters from Luppe to the Nuremberg disciplinary court for non-judicial officials, March 10, 1925 and June 13, 1926.

46. *Ibid.* Letter from Nuremberg disciplinary court for non-judicial officials, June 25, 1926.

47. *Nuernberger-Buerger-Zeitung*, January 13, 1928, which is also the source for the following.

48. BSA, PAJS, vol. II, folder 1733. Police report on NSDAP meeting in Nuremberg, January 23, 1928. Streicher discussed this hearing and his feelings about the "unfair Jewish judges" who ruled against him before a large audience.

49. *Nuernberger-Buerger-Zeitung*, January 20, 1928. See also *Der Stuermer*, nr. 3, 1928.

50. *Voelkischer Beobachter*, May 25, 1928. See also *Der Stuermer*, nr. 22, May, 1928, which is also the source for the following.

51. BSA, PAJS, vol. II, folder 1733. Notice from the office of the Franconian Minister of the Interior, to the District Revenue Office in Nuremberg, May 25, 1928.

52. *Ibid*. Report from Nuremberg police files on meeting at Breidenbach's Department Store, Nuremberg, February 5, 1928, which is also the source for the following.

53. *Deutsche Volkszeitung*, February 24; March 4, 1928, which is also the source for the following.

54. *Ibid*., March 11, 1928.

55. BSA, PAJS, vol. IV, folder 1733. Political circular from Nuremberg police files, March 12, 1928.

56. Orlow, *History of the Nazi Party*, p. 135.

57. BSA, PAJS, vol. IV. folder 1733. Police report on NSDAP meeting in Nuremberg, March 14, 1928, which is also the source for the following.

58. *Der Stuermer*, nrs. 14, 15, 16, 17, and 18, April and May, 1928, which are also the sources for the following.

59. BSA, PAJS, vol. IV, folder 1733. Police reports on campaign meetings for NSDAP candidates at Schwabach and Rothenberg, April 28 and May 3, 1928, which are also the sources for the following.

60. BSA, PAJS, vol. IV. folder 1733. Police report on campaign meeting for NSDAP candidates at Fuerth, May 12, 1928.

61. *Der Stuermer*, nr. 18, May. 1928.

62. Max H. Kele, *Nazis and Workers* (Chapel Hill, North Carolina: 1927), p. 125.

63. Orlow, *History of the Nazi Party*, pp. 129-130. Franconia led all other electoral districts in percentage of votes cast for Nazi candidates at 8.1%.

64. Wykes, *The Nuremberg Rallies*, pp. 93-96.

65. Orlow, *History of the Nazi Party*, p. 131.

66. *Voelkischer Beobachter*, June 3, 1928. See also *Der Stuermer*, nr. 21, 1928.

67. Orlow, *History of the Nazi Party*, pp. 129-130.

68. *Ibid.*, The urban plan was an organizational scheme followed after August, 1928, in an attempt to win the urban masses to the Nazi cause.

69. *Ibid.*, p. 135. See also *Der Stuermer*, nr. 21, June, 1928.

70. *Der Stuermer*, nr. 32, August, 1928. See also *Voelkischer Beobachter*, August 3, 1928.

71. *Voelkischer Beobachter*, August 5, 1928.

72. *Der Stuermer*, nrs. 36, 37, 38, August and September, 1928.

73. *Ibid.*, See also BSA, PAJS, vol. IV, folder 1733. Police reports on NSDAP meetings at Marktbreit and Neustadt, September 30 and October 5, 1928.

74. BSA, PAJS, vol. IV, folder 1733. Police report on NSDAP meeting at Iphofen, October 10, 1928.

75. *Ibid.* Police report on NSDAP meeting at Schwabach, December 15, 1928.

76. *Der Stuermer*, nrs. 6 and 7, February, 1929.

77. *Ibid.*, nr. 14, April, 1929.

78. *Ibid.*, nr. 23, June, 1929. See also *Voelkischer Beobachter*, June, 10, 1929.

79. *Der Stuermer*, nr. 25, June, 1929. See also *Voelkischer Beobachter*, June 30, 1929, and *Fraenkischer Kurier*, June 28, 1929.

80. BSA, PAJS, vol. IV, folder 1733. Report from Nuremberg police files. Criminal proceedings in the provincial court, Nuremberg, September 26, 1931. Streicher was sentenced to a fine of 500 marks and ordered to pay for the publication of an apology in three local newspapers.

81. Manvell and Fraenkel, *Inside Adolph Hitler*, p. 76. While party membership figures for Franconia are unavailable, the following statistics for overall membership year by year show that increases for that year doubled the increases of the previous year: 1927-72,000 members; 1928-108,000 members; 1929-178,000 members.

82. William S. Allen, *The Nazi Seizure of Power* (Chicago: 1965); p. 24.

83. Orlow, *History of the Nazi Party*, p. 166.

84. Wykes, *The Nuremberg Rallies*, pp. 103-104.

85. *Der Stuermer*, nr. 25. June, 1929.

86. Burden, *The Nuremberg Party Rallies*, p.49.

87. Named after an American banker, Owen Young, who headed a committee of international banking experts to determine Germany's future reparations payments. The committee signed a report on June 7, 1929, setting Germany's payments at a lower amount and extending them over a longer period of years than originally specified in the Versailles Treaty.

88. *Der Stuermer*, nr. 31, August, 1929.

89. Burden, *The Nuremberg Party Rallies*, pp. 50-51.

90. *Ibid.*, p. 55. See also Orlow, *History of the Nazi Party*, p. 166.

CHAPTER VIII.

1. *Voelkischer Beobachter*, September 7, 1929.

2. Orlow, *History of the Nazi Party*, p. 173. See also Ludecke, *I Knew Hitler*, p. 340.

3. *Voelkischer Beobachter*, September 7, 1929.

4. Orlow, *History of the Nazi Party*, p. 173.

5. BSA, PAJS, vol. IV, folder 1733. Police report on NSDAP meeting in Nuremberg, September 10, 1929.

6. Konrad Heiden, *A History of National Socialism.* (London: 1934), p. 112. See also *Der Stuermer*, nr. 34, September, 1929, and also Ludecke, *I Knew Hitler*, p. 340. Hitler explained that Hugenberg had agreed to pay large sums of money and also place his film studios and news services at the party's disposal.

7. Orlow, *History of the Nazi Party*, p. 174. See also Bullock, *Hitler*, p. 149, and Ludecke, *I Knew Hitler*, p. 341.

8. *Der Stuermer*, nr. 36, September, 1929.

9. BSA, PAJS, vol. IV, folder 1733. Police reports on NSDAP meetings in Nuremberg and Rothenberg, September 30 and October 5, 1929. See also *Der Stuermer*, nr. 36, September 1929 and nr. 37, October, 1929.

10. Bullock, *Hitler*, p. 148. See also Ludecke, *I Knew Hitler*, p. 341.

11. *Voelkischer Beobachter*, October 20, 1929.

12. SBA, Ruehl, *Der Stuermer*, pp. 187-188. See also BSA, PAJS, vol. IV, folder 1733. Report from Nuremberg police files. Criminal proceedings in Nuremberg Common Pleas Court, November 13, 1929, which is also the source for the following.

13. *Der Stuermer*, nr. 42, November 29, 1929.

14. *Ibid.*, nr. 45, December, 1929.

15. BSA, PAJS, vol. IV, folder 1733. Police report on NSDAP meeting in Nuremberg, December 10, 1929.

16. *Der Stuermer*, nr. 46. December, 1929.

17. Orlow, *History of the Nazi Party*, p. 176.

18. *Ibid.*, p. 177.

19. *Der Stuermer*, nr. 47, December, 1929. See also BSA, PAJS, vol. II, folder 1735. Police report on NSDAP meeting in Nuremberg, December 23, 1929.

20. *Der Stuermer*, special issue, December 17, 1929.

21. Orlow, *History of the Nazi Party*, pp. 192 and 237.

22. BSA, PAJS, vol. II, folder 1734. Report from Nuremberg police files on *SA* action in Nuremberg, January 2, 1930.

23. Wagner, *Hitler*, p.101.

24. *Der Stuermer*, nr. 2, January, 1930.

25. SBN, Ruehl, *Der Stuermer*, p. 190. See also BSA, PAJS, vol. I, folder 1734. Report from Nuremberg police files on *SA* action in Nuremberg, January 22, 1930.

26. *Der Stuermer*, nr. 10, March, 1930.

27. BSA, PAJS, vol. I, folder 1734. Police report on NSDAP meeting in Nuremberg, March 7, 1930, which is also the source for the following.

28. *Der Stuermer*, nr. 19, March, 1930.

29. *Ibid.*, nrs. 20 and 21, March and April, 1930.

30. *Ibid.*, nr. 22, April, 1930.

31. BSA, PAJS, vol. I, folder 1734. Police report on NSDAP meeting at Nuremberg, May 11, 1930, which is also the source for the following.

32. The building project was started later in the year, but for unexplained reasons (probably shortage of funds) it was not completed until late 1933. The theater project was dropped after two months for lack of attendance.

33. *Stuermer* issues in May and June advertised and promoted all these schemes but did not mention the degree of success of any of them. Hitler's speech was cancelled later, but ticket holders were not refunded their money. Instead, they were told that the tickets would be honored the next time Hitler spoke in Nuremberg, which was in April, 1932.

34. BSA, PAJS, vol. I, folder 1734. From Nuremberg police files. Report to Dr. Huber from superior court in Munich, June 12, 1930, which is also the source for the following.

35. Orlow, *History of the Nazi Party*, p. 182. See also Bullock, *Hitler*, p. 159.

36. *Der Stuermer*, nr. 29, July, 1930. See also Orlow, *History of the Nazi Party*, p. 183.

37. *Der Stuermer*, nr. 32, 1930, See also BSA, PAJS, vol. I, folder 1734. Police report on NSDAP meeting in Gunzenhausen, August 10, 1930.

38. *Der Stuermer*, nr. 31, 1930.

39. *Ibid.*, See also BSA, PAJS, vol. I, folder 1734. Police report on joint political meeting in Nuremberg, August 13, 1930, which is also the source for the following.

40. Bullock, *Hitler*, p. 160. See also Peterson, *Limits of Hitler's Power*, p. 227.

41. *Voelkischer Beobachter*, August 27, 1930, which is also the source for the following.

42. Orlow, *History of the Nazi Party*, p. 185. See also Bullock, *Hitler*, p. 161.

43. In the 1928 *Reichstag* election, the Franconian percentage of 8.1 was followed by upper Bavaria-Schwaben with 6.2. All other electoral districts recorded lesser percentage figures than these.

44. Orlow, *History of the Nazi Party*, p. 130.

45. James K. Pollock, "An Areal Study of the German Electorate, 1930-1933," *American Political Science Review*, XXXVII (February: 1944), pp. 90-91, which is also the source for the following.

46. Pollock, "An Areal Study of the German Electorate," pp. 90-91. See also Orlow, *History of the Nazi Party*, p. 130.

47. *Voelkischer Beobachter*, October 20, 1930. See also *Der Stuermer*, nr. 43, October, 1930.

48. *Voelkischer Beobachter*, October 28, 1930.

49. *Ibid.*, See also BSA, PAJS, vol. I, folder 1734. Police report on NSDAP meeting at Nuremberg, October 30, 1930.

50. BSA, PAJS, vol. I, folder 1734. Police report on NSDAP meeting at Nuremberg, October 30, 1930. See also *Der Stuermer*, nr. 44, October, 1930, which are also the sources for the following.

51. Orlow, *History of the Nazi Party*, pp. 188-189.

52. Orlow, *History of the Nazi Party*, p. 193. *Gleichschaltung*, briefly described, is a process to coordinate non-Nazi organizations and institutions with the Nazi regime by replacing the leaders with loyal Nazis and running the organizations according to Nazi principles.

53. *Ibid.*, p. 207.

54. Peterson, *Limits of Hitler's Power*, p. 253.

55. BSA, PAJS, vol. I, folder 1734. Police report on meeting of Erlangen National Socialist Student Association, Erlangen, February 15, 1930, which is also the source for the following.

56. *Ibid.*, Police report on union meeting at Essen, April 14, 1931, which is also the source for the following.

57. *Ibid.*, Official memo from the Prussian Prosecution Counsellor to the Nuremberg Police Office, September 21, 1931.

58. *Ibid.* Official Nazi party notice from Strasser to Streicher, May 6, 1931.

59. *Ibid.* Letter from Streicher to Strasser, May 27, 1931.

60. *Ibid.* Letter from Streicher to Strasser, June 9, 1931.

61. *Ibid.* Letter from Streicher to Strasser, May 27, 1931, which is also the source for the following.

62. Kelley, *22 Cells in Nuremberg*, p. 87.

63. SBN, Mueller, *Geschichte der Juden*, p. 130.

64. *Der Stuermer*, nr. 28, 1931, which is also the source for the following.

65. Articles of this nature appeared irregularly in the *Stuermer* until the mid-1930's.

66. *Der Stuermer*, nr. 28, 1931, which is also the source for the following.

67. SBN, Ruehl, *Der Stuermer*, p. 113.

68. *Der Stuermer*, nr. 28, July, 1931.

69. *Ibid.* Police report on NSDAP meeting in Nuremberg, July 24, 1931, which is also the source for the following.

70. Heiden, *Der Fuehrer*, pp. 4-6. The *Protocols* was propagandized by the Nazis as an authentic tract, discovered in Moscow in 1917, but supposedly written by a group of Jews in Switzerland, in 1897. It was actually written by a French lawyer, Maurice Joly, as a satire against Emperor Napoleon III, and published in 1863.

71. BSA, PAJS, vol. I, folder 1734. Police report on NSDAP meeting in Nuremberg, July 24, 1931.

72. *Der Stuermer*, nr. 36, September, 1931. See also Orlow, *History of the Nazi Party*, p. 233.

73. Bullock, *Hitler*, p. 184.

74. *Der Stuermer*, nr. 36, September, 1931.

75. Peterson, *Limits of Hitler's Power*, pp. 228-229.

76. *Der Stuermer*, nr. 38, September, 1931.

77. *Ibid.*, nr. 40, October, 1931.

78. Orlow, *History of the Nazi Party*, p. 236. See also Bullock, *Hitler*, p. 189.

79. Orlow, *History of the Nazi Party*, p. 239. The party membership figure is noted by Orlow to be an educated, but reasonable guess. Lacking official documentation, this figure was used because there were 129,563 members registered on September 14, 1930, and 719,446 at the end of January, 1933. See also Bullock, *Hitler*, p. 190. Bullock's estimate of Nazi membership at the end of 1931 was 800,000. However, this figure is probably an exaggerated guess and less reliable than the Orlow estimate.

CHAPTER IX.

1. The illusion of "endless columns" of parading Nazis was probably due to the fact that the troopers literally marched in a circle, around a large city block and past the reviewing stand two or three times.

2. Bullock, *Hitler*, p. 190.

3. *Der Stuermer*, special issue, January 1, 1932, which is also the source for the following.

4. BSA, PAJS, vol. II, folder 1735, Police report on NSDAP-sponsored meeting at Fuerth, January 7, 1932.

5. *Ibid*. Police report on NSDAP-sponsored meeting at Rothenburg, January 8, 1932.

6. *Ibid*. Police report on NSDAP-sponsored meeting at Schwabach, January 17, 1932.

7. BSA, PAJS, vol II, folder 1735. Official notice from Dr. Huber to Streicher, January 19, 1932.

8. *Der Stuermer*, nr. 4, January, 1932.

9. BSA, PAJS, vol. II, folder 1735. Report from Nuremberg police files regarding Streicher's speech prohibition, which is also the source for the following.

10. Heiden, *Der Fuehrer*, p. 433.

11. Heiden, *Der Fuehrer*, pp. 434-435. See also Bullock, *Hitler*, pp. 192-193.

12. Heiden, *Der Fuehrer*, p. 436. See also Bullock, *Hitler*, p. 194.

13. Orlow, *History of the Nazi Party*, p. 250.

14. BSA, PAJS, vol. II, folder 1735. Report from Nuremberg police files, February 28, 1932, which is also the source for the following.

15. *Der Stuermer*, nr. 10, March, 1932.

16. *Ibid.*, nr. 12, March, 1932.

17. BSA, PAJS, vol. II, folder 1735. Police reports on NSDAP meetings at Nuremberg and Fuerth, March 3 and March 5, 1932, which is also the source for the following.

18. *Der Stuermer*, nrs. 10 and 12, March 1932.

19. Orlow, *History of the Nazi Party*, p. 249.

20. Bullock, *Hitler*, p. 201.

21. Pollock, "An Areal Study of the German Electorate," p. 93.

22. Orlow, *History of the Nazi Party*, p. 250, which is also the source for the following.

23. *Der Stuermer*, nr. 12, March, 1932.

24. *Ibid.*, nrs. 13, 14, 15 and 16, March and April, 1932.

25. Pollock, "An Areal Study of the German Electorate," p. 93.

26. Bullock, *Hitler*, p. 203.

27. Orlow, *History of the Nazi Party*, p. 251.

28. *Der Stuermer*, nrs. 15 and 16, March and April, 1932.

29. Orlow, *History of the Nazi Party*, p. 253.

30. *Der Stuermer*, nr. 18, April, 1932.

31. *Ibid.*, nr. 19, April, 1932.

32. *Der Stuermer*, nrs. 19 and 20, April, 1932.

33. Bullock, *Hitler*, p. 205.

34. *Der Stuermer*, nr. 21, April, 1932.

35. BAK, *Streicher Nachlasse*, folder 342, which is also the source for the following.

36. Orlow, *History of the Nazi Party*, p. 250.

37. BSA, PAJS, vol. II, folder 1735. Police report on NSDAP meeting in Nuremberg, May 14, 1932.

38. *Der Stuermer*, nr. 26, June, 1932.

39. Orlow, *History of the Nazi Party*, p. 260, which is also the source for the following.

40. *Ibid.*, p. 226. See also *Der Stuermer*, nr. 27, June, 1932.

41. Bullock, *Hitler*, p. 213.

42. *Ibid.*, pp. 216-217.

43. *Ibid.*, p. 217

44. *Der Stuermer*, nr. 34, July, 1932. See also Pollock, "An Areal Study of the German Electorate," p. 93.

45. Bullock, *Hitler*, p. 222. See also *Der Stuermer*, nr. 40, September, 1932.

46. Orlow, *History of the Nazi Party*, pp. 281-282.

47. *Institut fuer Zeitgeschichte*, Munich, (cited hereafter as IFZ), Anton Wegner, *Kurs Martin-Polizei, Einmal Anderes*, 1947, p. 117, which is also the source for the following.

48. *Der Stuermer*, nr. 36, August, 1932.

49. BSA, PAJS, vol. II, folder 1735. Police report on Nuremberg SA activities, September 18, 1932.

50. *Ibid.* Police report on NSDAP meeting in Nuremberg, September 24, 1932.

51. *Ibid.* Police report on Nuremberg SA activities, September 28, 1932.

52. *Der Stuermer*, nr. 45, October, 1932.

53. IFZ, Wegner, *Kurs Martin*, p. 117.

54. BSA, PAJS, vol. II, folder 1735. Report from Bavarian Police to Huber, October 20, 1932.

55. *Der Stuermer*, nr. 46, October, 1932.

56. Bullock, *Hitler*, p. 230.

57. Pollock, "An Areal Study of the German Electorate," p. 93.

58. Peterson, *Limits of Hitler's Power*, p. 229.

59. *Ibid.* See also Wegner, *Kurs Martin*, p. 118.

CHAPTER X.

1. John Toland, *Adolf Hitler* (New York: 1976), pp. 396-397.

2. Eliott Wheaton, *The Nazi Revolution, 1933-1935* (New York: 1969) p. 226.

3. Toland, *Adolf Hitler*, p. 401.

4. *Fraenkischer Kurier*, nr. 33, February 2, 1933, which is also the source for the following.

5. *Der Stuermer*, special issue, March 6, 1933. See also Wheaton, *The Nazi Revolution*, pp. 269-271. The national average of the Communist vote in this election was 12.3 percent, with the district of Berlin polling the highest number of Communist votes at 30.1 percent.

6. Peterson, *Limits of Hitler's Power*, p. 229.

7. Hermann Hanschel, *Oberbuergermeister Hermann Luppe* (Nuremberg: 1977) pp. 380-382, which is also the source for the following.

8. Hermann Luppe and Mella Heinsen-Luppe, *Mein Leben* (Nuremberg: 1977) p. 288 ff. Luppe survived the Nazi years and the war in Kiel and later Berlin but was killed there in 1945, during an air raid.

9. SBN, Ruehl, *Der Stuermer*, p. 20.

10. Lucy Dawidowicz, *The War Against the Jews, 1933-1945* (New York: 1975) p. 69. See also IFZ, folder 1241, doc. nr. 2157-PS.

11. IFZ, folder 1241, doc. 2155-PS. Copy of Streicher's Boycott Decree, March 30, 1933.

12. SBN, Mueller, *Geschichte der Juden* pp. 220-221. See also *Voelkischer Beobachter*, March 29, 1933.

13. *Ibid.*

14. Peterson, *Limits of Hitler's Power*, p. 231.

15. Dawidowicz, *The War Against the Jews*, p. 77.

16. Peterson, *Limits of Hitler's Power*, p. 232.

17. *Ibid.*

18. *Ibid.*, p. 235. See also *Muenchener Neueste Nachrichten*, February 13, 1937.

19. NAW, Berlin Document Center, File of Malsen-Ponickau.

20. *Ibid.* See also IFZ, Wegner, *Kurs-Martin*, pp. 179-181, which is also the source for the following.

21. Peterson, *Limits of Hitler's Power*, p. 246.

22. *Ibid.*, p. 249.

23. *Times,* October 15, 1934. See also Karlsbad *Neuer Vorwaerts,* November 4, 1934.

24. IFZ, Wegner, *Kurs Martin,* pp. 185-187.

25. Discussions by the author with older Franconian farmers between 1970-1975, revealed a general non-interest in national political happenings of past decades.

26. BSA, PAJS, vol. III, doc. nr. 1725, which is also the source for the following.

27. *Der Stuermer,* November 20, 1934.

28. SBN, Mueller, *Geschichte der Juden,* pp. 280-285, which is also the source for the following.

29. Wheaton, *The Nazi Revolution, 1933-1935,* p. 438.

30., SBN, Mueller, *Geschichte der Juden,* pp. 280-285, which is also the source for the following.

31. *Ibid.*, p. 219, which is also the source for the following.

32. Peterson, *Limits of Hitler's Power,* p. 256.

33. BSA, PAJS, Bavarian Interior Ministry, doc. nr. 73708, which is also the source for the following.

34. *Pariser Tageblatt,* March 15, 1934.

35. *Der Stuermer,* March and April, 1934.

36. BSA, PAJS, vol. IV, nr. 73708.

37. *Fraenkfurter Zeitung,* nr. 416, August 16, 1935.

38. Hitler, *Secret Conversations,* pp. 168; 393.

39. Even though Streicher was shorn of his political authority by Hitler in 1940, he was permitted to continue publication and nationwide circulation of the *Stuermer* and other racist material until early 1945, solely on Hitler's orders.

40. SBN, Ruehl, *Der Stuermer,* pp. 69-70.

41. *Fraenkischer Kurier,* February 12, 1945, which is also the source for the following.

42. BSA, PAJS, vol. II, official notice from the Bavarian State Ministry for Education and Culture to the Franconian Office of the Interior. At this time the German mark was valued at almost one quarter of a U.S. dollar, or 25 cents.

43. *Ibid.*, vol. I, speech by Hitler in Nuremberg, December 5, 1929.

44. SAN, *Schicksal juedischer Mitbuerger in Nuernberg 1850-1945,* p. 202.

45. Wykes, *The Nuremberg Rallies,* p. 129 ff., which is also the source for the following.

CHAPTER XI.

1. *Pariser Tageblatt,* September 20 and 22, 1935.

2. SBN, Mueller, *Geschichte der Juden,* p. 230 ff.

3. *Ibid.* See also Wheaton, *The Nazi Revolution*, pp. 519-521.

4. Toland, *Adolf Hitler*, p. 687.

5. SBN, Mueller, *Geschichte der Juden*, p. 230 ff., which is also the source for the following.

6. Toland, *Adolf Hitler*, p. 687.

7. SBN, Mueller, *Geschichte der Juden*, p. 230 ff.

8. Wheaton, *The Nazi Revolution*, pp. 518-519.

9. Dawidowicz, *The War Against the Jews*, pp. 261-262.

10. SBN, Mueller, *Geschichte der Juden*, p. 230 ff., which is also the source for the following.

11. IFZ, Streicher file, doc. nr. 3351-PS.

12. *Pariser Tageblatt*, May 13, 1935.

13. *Ibid.*

14. *Der Stuermer*, October 2, 1935.

15. *Ibid.*, January 10, 1936.

16. SBN, Ruehl, *Der Stuermer*, pp. 147-148.

17. *Ibid.*, p. 152. See also IMT, *Trial of Major War Criminals*, vol. XVII, p. 204. After early 1940, these circulation figures dwindled rapidly. The average price for a regular *Stuermer* subscription was 84 pfennig monthly. This was approximately 20 cents in American money. Even at this low price, Streicher's monthly gross income from the *Stuermer* averaged about $100,000 between late 1935 and early 1940. This does not include income from *Stuermer* advertisers.

18. Hannah Vogt, *The Burden of Guilt* (New York: 1964), p. 222. This author repeats the theme of acceptance, or indoctrination, of many German citizens during this period because of the Nazi party's continued repetition of its anti-Semitic doctrines.

19. SBN, Ruehl, *Der Stuermer*, p. 156.

20. *Ibid.*, pp. 180-181.

21. *Ibid.*, p. 179. Also interview with Fritz Nadler, Nuremberg journalist and author, March, 1971.

22. Louis Bondy, *Racketeers of Hatred* (London: 1946), p. 42.

23. *Fraenkischer Kurier*, nr. 285, October 14, 1935, which is also the source for the following.

24. Nadler, *Eine Stadt im Schatten Streichers*, pp. 35-37.

25. *Ibid.* See also *Neue Freie Presse, Wien*, March 16, 1937.

26. BSA, PAJS, vol. II, folder 1731. Letter from the Archbishop of Bamberg to Ritter von Epp, November 11, 1936, which is also the source for the following.

27. *Fraenkischer Kurier*, October 10, 1936.

28. BSA, PAJS, vol. II, folder 1731. Letter from the Archbishop of Bamburg to Ritter von Epp, November 11, 1936.

29. *Ibid.*, folder 1733. Letter to Ernest Hiemer from the Director of the Secret State Police, Karlsruhe, October 27, 1936.

30. *Der Stuermer*, November 3, 1936.

31. BSA, PAJS, vol. II, folder 1733. Letter to Ernest Hiemer from

the Director of the Secret State Police, Karlsruhe, November 24, 1936.

32. *Der Stuermer*, December 5, 1936.
33. Peterson, *Limits of Hitler's Power*, pp. 259-260.
34. *Der Stuermer*, June 10, 1935.
35. *Ibid.*, July 5, 1935.
36. SAN, *Stuermer Archiv*, folder nr. XVII. Copy of court proceedings against Streicher, case nr. 2U2923-37, which is also the source for the following.
37. *Der Stuermer*, nr. 10, March, 1936.
38. *Ibid.*
39. SBN, Ruehl, *Der Stuermer*, p. 177.
40. *Ibid.*, p. 145-147, which is also the source for the following.
41. *Ibid.*, pp. 163-164.
42. *Ibid.*, pp. 170-171. See also SBN, Mueller, *Geschichte der Juden*, pp. 257-259.
43. SBN, Ruehl, *Der Stuermer*, pp. 141-142.
44. SBN, Mueller, *Geschichte der Juden*, pp. 256-261, which is also the source for the following.
45. *Fraenkische Tageszeitung*, May 25, 1938, which is also the source for the following.
46. Sartre, *Anti-Semite and Jew*, p. 32.
47. BSA, PAJS, vol. III, folder 2132. Nuremberg police files, anonymous letter to Streicher, dated June 15, 1938.
48. *Der Stuermer*, January 20, 1938, which is also the source for the following.
49. *Prager Tageblatt*, January 22, 1938. See also *Wiener Neueste Nachrichten*, January 22, 1938.
50. NAW, Interrogation of Max Fink by U.S. Office of Chief of Counsel (cited hereafter as NAW-IMF); doc. Nr. 3346-PS.
51. *Ibid.*
52. Nadler, *Eine Stadt im Schatten Streichers*, pp. 27-32, which is also the source for the following.
53. Dawidowicz, *The War Against the Jews*, p. 127.
54. *Fraenkische Tageszeitung*, December 16, 1937.
55. SBN, Mueller, *Geschichte der Juden*, pp. 231-233.
56. Franz Neumann, *Behemoth: The Structure and Practice of National Socialism, 1933-1944* (New York: 1942), p. 118.
57. SBN, Mueller, *Geschichte der Juden*, p. 235 ff., which is also the source for the following.
58. *Ibid.*, pp. 245-251, which is also the source for the following.
59. *Ibid.*
60. *Ibid.*
61. *Fraenkische Tageszeitung*, August 11, 1938.
62. *Ibid.*
63. SBN, Mueller, *Geschichte der Juden*, p. 237.
64. Wykes, *The Nuremberg Rallies*, pp. 10-23, which is also the

source for the following.

65. Peterson, *Limits of Hitler's Power*, p. 270.
66. Dawidowicz, *The War Against the Jews*, pp. 133-134.
67. *Ibid.*, pp. 135-137.
68. IFZ, Martin file, doc. nr. 3253-PS. See also NAW, IMF, doc. nr. 3346-PS., which are also the sources for the following.
69. BAK, Wegner, *Kurs Martin*, pp. 13-14.
70. Dawidowicz, *The War Against The Jews*, pp. 137-138. See also Neumann, *Behemoth*, pp. 119-120.
71. NAW, IMF, doc. nr. 3347-PS., which is also the source for the following.
72. IFZ, Goering file, doc. nr. 1757-PS.
73. SBN, Mueller, *Geschichte der Juden*, pp. 247-249, which is also the source for the following.
74. *Ibid.*, p. 249. See also Peterson, *Limits of Hitler's Power*, p. 271.
75. NAW, IMF, doc. nr. 3346-PS.
76. SBN, Mueller, *Geschichte der Juden*, pp. 244-248, which is also the source for the following.
77. *Ibid.*, pp. 249-251.
78. NAW, IMF, doc. nr. 3346-PS, which is also the source for the following.
79. BAK, Wegner, *Kurs Martin*, pp. 11-12, which is also the source for the following.
80. *Ibid.*
81. NAW, IMF, doc. nr. 3346-PS.
82. BAK, Wegner, *Kurs Martin*, p. 12.
83. *Der Stuermer*, October 2, 1938.
84. Sartre, *Anti-Semite and Jew*, pp. 46-48.
85. SBN, Mueller, *Geschichte der Juden*, p. 247.
86. BAK, Wegner, *Kurs Martin*, p. 8, See also NAW, IMF, doc. nr. 3346-PS.
87. IFZ, *Goering Commission Report*, doc. nr. 1757-PS., which is also the source for the following.
88. NAW, IMF, doc. nr. 3346-PS.
89. BAK, Wegner, *Kurs Martin*, pp. 9-11, which is also the source for the following.
90. *Ibid.* See also IFZ, *Goering Commission Report*, doc. nr. 1757-PS.

CHAPTER XII.

1. NAW, IMF, doc. nr. 3346-PS. See also IFZ, *Goering Commission Report*, doc. nr. 1757-PS., which are also the sources for the following.
2. IFZ, *Goering Commission Report*, doc. nr. 1759-PS.
3. *Ibid.*, doc. nr. 1760-PS.

4. *Ibid.*, doc. nr. 1757-PS, which is also the source for the following.

5. NAW, IMF, doc. nr. 3346-PS., which is also the source for the following.

6. IFZ, *Goering Commission Report*, doc. nr. 1757-PS.

7. BAK, Wegner, *Kurs Martin*, p. 9. and p. 140. See also Peterson, *Limits of Hitler's Power*, p. 283.

8. Peterson, *Limits of Hitler's Power*, p. 283.

9. BAK, Wegner, *Kurs Martin*, p. 9.

10. David Irving, *Hitler's Wars* (London: 1976), p. 40.

11. Nadler, *Eine Stadt im Schatten Streichers*, pp. 30-32.

12. *Der Stuermer*, November 2, 1939. See also *Fraenkische Tageszeitung*, November 3, 1939.

13. *Fraenkische Tageszeitung*, November 10, 1939.

14. Toland, *Adolf Hitler*, p. 808.

15. Nadler, *Eine Stadt im Schatten Streichers*, p. 30.

16. BAK, Wegner, *Kurs Martin*, p. 10.

17. Irving, *Hitler's Wars*, pp. 74-75.

18. Peterson, *Limits of Hitler's Power*, p. 232.

19. BAK, Wegner, *Kurs Martin*, p. 10.

20. BAK, *Streicher Nachlasse*, doc. nr. 1715.

21. NAW, IAJS, Testimony of Julius Streicher, October 10, 1945.

22. The Pleikershof farm and buildings were sold in 1946 to displaced persons from East Germany who are the present occupants. In the mid-1970's a large herd of white pigs was observed on the farm by the writer.

23. *Der Stuermer*, November 25, 1943.

24. Joseph Goebbels, *The Goebbels Diaries* (New York: 1948), p. 47.

25. *Der Stuermer*, March 10, 1941.

26. *Ibid.*, November 18, 1943.

27. *Ibid.*, February 27, 1942.

28. *Ibid.*, as well as many other issues published during the years of World War II.

29. *Der Stuermer*, March 26, 1942.

30. *Ibid.*

31. NAW, IAJS, Testimony of Julius Streicher, October 7, 1945.

32. *Der Stuermer*, May 7, 1942.

33. *Ibid.*, August 21, 1942.

34. *Ibid.*, November 18, 1943.

35. *Ibid.*, February 12, 1944; December 5, 1944.

36. NAW, IAJS, Testimony of Julius Streicher, November 6, 1945.

37. NAW, IAJS, Testimony of Julius Streicher, October 10, 1945.

38. Baird, *Das Politische Testament*, p. 662.

CHAPTER XIII.

1. Heydecker and Leeb, *The Nuremberg Trials*, pp. 42-43.

2. Fred Hahn, *Lieber Stuermer* (Stuttgart: 1978), Letter by Streicher to Hiemer, June, 1945.

3. *Ibid.*

4. Baird, *Das Politische Testament*, pp. 660-661, which is also the source for the following.

5. Hahn, *Lieber Stuermer*, Letter by Streicher, June, 1945.

6. Baird, *Das Politische Testament*, pp. 662-664, which is also the source for the following.

7. *Ibid.*, pp. 670-671.

8. *Ibid.*, p. 674. Grant stated in his book that the most active race is the nordic race and through the mixing of the races the nordic race will go down in "a race of swamps."

9. *Ibid.*, pp. 674-683, which is also the source for the following.

10. *Ibid.*, pp. 684-693.

11. IMT, vol. 22, p. 547.

12. Gilbert, *Nuremberg Diary* (New York: 1947), pp. 37-38.

13. NAW, IAJS, Testimony of Julius Streicher, September 1, 1945, which is also the source for the following.

14. *Ibid.*, September 8, 1945, which is also the source for the following.

15. *Ibid.*, September 1, 1945.

16. *Ibid.*

17. *Ibid.*, October 11, 1945.

18. *Ibid.*, September 8, 1945, which is also the source for the following.

19. *Ibid.*, October 17, 1945.

20. *Ibid.*, October 19, 1945.

21. *Ibid.*, November 6, 1945.

22. Gilbert, *Nuremberg Diary*, p. 13. See also Baird, *Das Politische Testament*, p. 663.

23. Gilbert, *Nuremberg Diary*, p. 261.

24. *Ibid.*, p. 113.

25. *Ibid.*, p. 14.

26. *Ibid.*, p. 15.

27. *Ibid.*, p. 43.

28. IMT, vol. 22, p. 451.

29. *Ibid.* See also *Der Stuermer*, September 15, 1938.

30. Gilbert, *Nuremberg Diary*, p. 119.

31. *Ibid.*, p. 276 ff. See also IMT, vol. 22, p. 385 ff., which are also the sources for the following.

32. IMT, vol. 22, pp. 387-390, which is also the source for the following.

33. IMT, vol. 22, pp. 391-395, which is also the source for the following.

34. *Ibid.* See also *Der Stuermer*, November 18, 1943.

35. IMT vol. 22, pp. 395-397.

36. *Ibid.*, vol. 22, pp. 450-451.

37. Gilbert, *Nuremberg Diary*, p. 376.

38. *Ibid.*, p. 381. See also IMT, vol. 22, pp. 469-470.

39. IMT, vol. 22, pp. 475-476.

40. *Ibid.*, vol. 22, p. 547 ff.

41. *Ibid.*

42. Gilbert, *Nuremberg Diary*, p. 394.

43. Heydecker and Leeb, *The Nuremberg Trials*, p. 381.

44. *Time*, October 28, 1946.

45. Heydecker and Leeb, *The Nuremberg Trials*, p. 384.

46. *Ibid.*, p. 386.

47. "Purim Festival 1946." This utterance by Streicher was an effort at irony in reference to a traditional Jewish Spring festival commemorating the hanging of a fifth-century B. C. Jew-baiter named Haman, by Persia's King Xerxes.

48. *Time*, October 28, 1946.

BIBLIOGRAPHY

Unpublished Sources

Bayerisches Staatsarchiv, Munich and Nuremberg (cited as BSA)

Personalakten Julius Streicher der Bayerischen Regierung von Mittelfranken—Kammer des Innern. Volumes I through V (cited as PAJS and referred to by volume and document, or folder number)

Bundesarchiv Koblenz (cited as BAK)

Miscellaneous documents (cited by folder number)

Stuermer Archiv (cited by folder number)

Streicher Nachlass (cited by folder and document numbers)

Institut fuer Zeitgeschichte, Munich (cited as IFZ)

Goering Commission Reports (cited by document number)

Kurs Martin—Polizei Einmal Anderes. Manuscript by Anton Wegner.

National Archives, Washington, D. C. (cited as NAW)

Files of captured German documents microfilmed at the Berlin Document Center (cited by series and roll numbers)

Interrogation of Adele and Julius Streicher by U.S. Army officers, Nuremberg, Germany, September 1, to November 6, 1945 (cited as NAW-IAJS)

Interrogation of Max Fink by U.S. Office of Chief of Counsel (cited as NAW-IMF)

The Ohio State University Library (cited as OSU)

Files of captured German documents microfilmed at the Hoover Institute on War, Revolution, and Peace. Stanford University (cited by series and roll numbers)

Stadtarchiv Nuremberg (cited as SAN)

Schicksal Juedischer Mitbuerger in Nuernberg, 1850-1945.

Stuermer Archiv (cited by folder number)

Stadtbibliothek Nuremberg (cited as SBN)

Blut und Boden, Manuscript written by Julius Streicher, 1938.

Der Aufstieg der NSDAP in Mittel und Oberfranken, 1925-1933. Manuscript written by Rainer Hambrecht, 1976.

Der Stuermer und sein Herausgeber. Dissertation written by Manfred Ruehl, 1960.

Die Anfaenge der Voelkischen Bewegung in Franken. Dissertation written by Heinz Preiss, 1937.

Die Judengesetze Grossdeutschlands. Manuscript written by Peter Deeg, 1939.

Geschichte der Juden in Nuernberg, 1145-1945. Manuscript written by Arnd Mueller, 1968.

Newspapers

Der Angriff
Bayerischer Kurier
Die Bombe
Deutsche Presse
Deutsche Volkszeitung
Deutscher Sozialist
Deutscher Volkswille
Frankfurter Zeitung
Fraenkische Tagespost
Fraenkische Tageszeitung
Fraenkischer Kurier
Muenchener Neueste Nachrichten
Neue Freie Presse, Wien
Neuer Vorwaerts
Nordbayerische Zeitung
Nuernberg-Fuerther Morgenpresse
Nuernberger Anzeiger
Nuernberger Buerger-Zeitung

Oberfraenkische Volkszeitung
Pariser Tageblatt
Prager Tageblatt
Der Stuermer
Times
Voelkischer Beobachter
Voelkisches Echo
Wiener Neueste Nachrichten

Published Sources

Dodd, William E., *Ambassador Dodd's Diary*. New York: Harcourt, Brace and Co., 1941.

Freud, Sigmund, *The Basic Writings of Sigmund Freud*. Translated and edited by A.A. Brill. New York: Random House, Inc., 1938.

Fromm, Bella, *Blood and Banquets: A Berlin Social Diary*. New York: Harper and Bros., 1942.

Gilbert, G. M., *Nuremberg Diary*. New York: Farrer, Straus and Co., 1947.

Goebbels, Joseph, *The Early Goebbels Diaries*, 1925-1926. Edited by Helmut Heiber. Translated by Oliver Watson. New York: Frederick A. Praeger, 1963.

——————————, *The Goebbels Diaries, 1942-1943*. Edited and translated by Lois Lochner. New York: Doubleday and Co., Inc., 1948.

Hitler, Adolf, *Mein Kampf*. Munich: Zentralverlag der NSDAP, 1925.

——————————, *The Speeches of Adolf Hitler*. Translated and edited by Norman H. Baynes. London: Oxford University Press, 1942.

——————————, *Hitler's Secret Conversations*, 1941-1944. New York: Farrar, Straus and Young, 1953.

International Military Tribunal, *Trial of the Major War Criminals*. Volumes 12 and 24. Nuremberg: Secretariat of the Tribunal, 1948.

Luppe, Hermann, and Luppe-Heinsen, Mella, *Mein Leben*. Selbstverlag des Stadtrats zu Nuernberg, 1977.

Speer, Albert, *Inside the Third Reich*. Translated by Richard and Clara Winston. New York: The Macmillan Co., 1970.

Streicher, Julius, "Das Politische Testament." Edited and foreword by Jay W. Baird. *Vierteljahrshefte fur Zeitgeschichte*. Stuttgart: Deutsche Verlags-Anstalt, April, 1978.

United States Office of the Chief of Counsel for Prosecution of Axis Criminality, *Nazi Conspiracy and Aggression*. Volumes I through VIII. Washington: U.S. Printing Office, 1946.

Books and Articles

Allen, William., *The Nazi Seizure of Power*. Chicago: Quadrangle

Books, Inc., 1965.

Arendt, Hannah, *Totalitarianism*. New York: Harcourt, Brace and World, Inc., 1951.

—————, *Antisemitism*. New York: Harcourt, Brace and World, Inc., 1951.

Armstrong, Hamilton F., *Thus Speaks Germany*. Edited by W. W. Cole and M.F. Potter. New York: Harper and Bros., 1941.

Berndorff, H. R., *General Zwischen Ost und West*. Hamburg: Hoffman und Campe, 1951.

Bondy, Louis W., *Racketeers of Hatred*. London: Newman Wolsey Ltd., 1946.

Bossenbrook, William J., *The German Mind*. Detroit: Wayne State University Press, 1961.

Bullock, Alan, *Hitler: A Study in Tyranny*. New York: Harper and Row, 1964.

Burden, Hamilton T., *The Nuremberg Party Rallies—1923-1939*. New York: Praeger Press, 1967.

Carsten, F. L., *The Rise of Fascism*. Los Angeles: University of California Press, 1967.

Creel, George, *War Criminals and Punishment*. New York: MacBride and Co., 1944.

Dawidowicz, Lucy S., *The War Against the Jews, 1933-1945*. New York: Holt, Rinehart and Winston, 1975.

Deuel, Wallace R., *People Under Hitler*. New York: Harcourt, Brace and Co., 1942.

Dutch, Oswald, (pseud) *Hitler's 12 Apostles*. New York: MacBride and Co., 1940.

Fest, Joachim C., *The Face of the Third Reich*. Translated by Michael Bullock. New York: Random House, 1970.

Gliksman, Schlomo, *My Lawsuit Against Julius Streicher and Co., and the Forgeries and Falsifications in Anti-Semitic Literature*. Cleveland, Ohio: Schlomo Gliksman, 1941.

Gordon, Harold J., Jr., *Hitler and the Beer Hall Putsch*. Princeton, New Jersey: Princeton University Press, 1972.

Hahn, Fred, *Lieber Stuermer*. Stuttgart: Sewald Verlag, 1978.

Hanfstaengel, Ernst, *Hitler: The Missing Years*. London: Eyre and Spottiswoode, 1957.

Hanschel, Hermann, *Oberbuergermeister Hermann Luppe*. Nuremberg: Selbstverlag des Vereins fuer Geschichte der Stadt Nuernberg, 1977.

Heiden, Konrad, *Der Fuehrer*. Translated by Ralph Manheim. New York: Howard Fertig, 1966.

—————, *A History of National Socialism*. Translated by Anonymous. London: Methuen and Co., 1934.

Heydecker, Joe J., and Leeb, Johannes, *The Nuremberg Trial*. Translated and edited by R. A. Downie. New York: The World

Publishing Co., 1962.

Hoehne, Heinz, *The Order of the Death's Head.* Translated by Richard Barry. New York: Coward-Mac Cann, Inc., 1970.

Hoffmann, Hanns, H., *Der Hitlerputsch.* Munich: Nymphenburger Verlagshandlung, 1961.

Irving, David, *Hitler's Wars.* New York: The Viking Press, 1977.

Kele, Max H., *Nazis and Workers.* Chapel Hill, North Carolina: University of North Carolina Press, 1972.

Kelley, Douglas M., *22 Cells in Nuremberg.* New York: Greenberg, 1947.

Lesser, Jonas, *Germany: The Symbol and the Deed.* London: Thomas Yoseloff, Ltd., 1965.

Loewenberg, Peter, "The Unsuccessful Adolescence of Heinrich Himmler." *The American Historical Review,* vol. 72, (June 1971), 612-641.

Ludecke, Kurt G., *I Knew Hitler,* New York: Charles Scribner's Sons, 1937.

MacGovern, James, *Martin Bormann.* New York: William Morrow and Co., 1968.

Manchester, William, *The Arms of Krupp—1587-1968.* Boston: Little, Brown, and Co., 1964.

Manvell, Roger, and Fraenkel, Heinrich, *Inside Adolph Hitler.* New York: Pinnacle Books, Inc., 1973.

Mitchell, Allan, *Revolution in Bavaria, 1918-1919.* Princeton, New Jersey: Princeton University Press, 1965.

Mosse, George L., *Nazi Culture.* New York: Grosset and Dunlap, 1966.

Nadler, Fritz, *Eine Stadt im Schatten Streichers.* Nuremberg: Fraenkische Verlagsanstalt und Buchdruckerei GMBH, 1969.

Neumann, Franz, *Behemoth, The Structure and Practice of National Socialism: 1933-44.* New York: Harper and Row, 1942.

Nyomarkay, Joseph, *Charisma and Factionalism in the Nazi Party.* Minneapolis: University of Minnesota Press, 1967.

Orlow, Dietrich, *The History of the Nazi Party.* Pittsburg: University of Pittsburg Press, 1969.

Payne, Robert, *The Life and Death of Adolf Hitler.* New York: Praeger, 1973.

Peterson, Edward N., *The Limits of Hitler's Power.* Princeton, New Jersey: Princeton University Press, 1969.

Pollock, James K., "An Areal Study of the German Electorate, 1930-1933." *American Political Science Review,* XXXVII (Feb. 1944).

Pope, Ernest R., *Munich Playground.* New York: G. B. Putnam's Sons, 1941.

Rauschnigg, Hermann, *Men of Chaos.* New York: G. B. Putnam's Sons, 1942.

Reed, Douglas, *Nemesis.* Boston: Houghton, Mifflin Co., 1940.

Roberts, Stephen H., *The House That Hitler Built*. New York: Harper and Brothers, 1938.

Sartre, Jean-Paul, *Anti-Semite and Jew*, Translated by George Becker. New York: Schocken Books, Inc., 1973.

Schoenbaum, David, *Hitler's Social Revolution: Class and Status in Nazi Germany, 1933-39*. Garden City, New York: Doubleday and Co., Inc., 1966.

Schuman, Frederick L., *The Nazi Dictatorship*. New York: Alfred A. Knopf, 1939.

Shirer, William L., *The Rise and Fall of the Third Reich*. New York: Simon and Schuster, 1959.

Toland, John, *Adolf Hitler*. New York: Ballantine Books, 1976.

Vogt, Hannah, *The Burden of Guilt*. New York: Oxford University Press, Inc., 1964.

Wagner, Ludwig, *Hitler, Man of Strife*. New York: W. W. Norton and Co., Inc., 1942.

Wheaton, Eliot B., *The Nazi Revolution—1933-35, Prelude to Calamity*. Garden City, New York: Doubleday and Co., Inc., 1969.

Wolman, Benjamin B., Ed., *The Psychoanalytic Interpretation of History*, New York: Harper and Row, 1971.

Wykes, Alan, *The Nuremberg Rallies*, New York: Ballantine Books, 1970.

Zimmermann, Werner G., *Bayern und das Reich—1918-1923*. Munich: Richard Pflaum Verlag, 1953.

INDEX

Schacht, Dr. Hjalmar, 181, 214, 216, 223, 252, 310-311, 316, 324
Schirach, Baldur von, 162, 310, 316, 324
Schutzstaffel (SS), 165, 171, 174-176, 183, 205, 210-211, 255-256, 262, 302, 317, 323
Seitz, Anni, 251, 274
Seyss-Inquart, Arthur, 310, 324-325
Speer, Albert, 310, 324
Steel Helmet Party (*Stahlhelm*), 180, 182-183
Stegmann, Wilhelm, 165, 171-172, 176-179, 196
Strasser, Gregor, 74, 79-81, 87, 105-106, 110-112, 115, 130, 150, 160-161, 172, 174
Streicher, Adele Tappe (second wife), 14, 17-19, 285, 293-295, 300, 320, 327
Streicher, Anna Weiss (mother) 23-24, 297
Streicher, Elmar, (younger son), 29, 68-69, 129
Streicher, Friedrich (father), 23-24, 35
Streicher, Julius: reputation and biographical summary, 12-13; joins forces with Hitler, 12, chapt. III *passim;* loyalty to Hitler, 12, 46, 79-80, 292, 312, 327; clinical anti-Semitic tendencies and behavior, 13, 20, 33-34, 48, 232, 248, 269, 295-296; Jewish economic boycott, 13, 199-202, 214-215, 223, 252, 317; marries mistress, 13, 293; post-war arrest and early imprisonment, 13, 17-19, 294-299; polical testament, 13, 296-300; as an arrogant Nazi bully, 17, 117, 213, 250-251; as a broken, disreputable old man, 17, 294; some abnormal behavioral traits, 20, 25, 28, 31-32, 77; personality swings to normal,

gentle or benevolent behavior, 20, 64-66, 83, 89, 160-162, 167-168, 235-236, 284; family background and early life, 23-26; teaching experiences, 24-26, 55-56; World War I activities and citations, 27-28, 48, 74; motivation by "fate" or "destiny", 28, 292, 297-298, 316; anti-Semitic speeches and polemics, 19, 29, 38, 49-51, 78, 80, 103, 108-109, 167, 183, 313, 315, 321; sudden dedication to anti-Semitism, 31-33; possibility of Jewish ancestry, 32; attacks against Catholic church and clergy, 35, 237-239; at odds with Hitler, 38, 44; propounds Jewish "blood-ritual" theory, 39-40, 51, 119, 154, 167; court trials for slander or libel, 39-40, 74-76, 112-115, 148, 154-155, 240-241; partiality shown by biased jurists, 39-40, 57, 76, 107, 125, 136, 240-241; allusions to Hitler as a supernatural being, 42-43, 299, 316; as a political asset to Hitler, 46-47, 102-105; parallelisms to Hitler, 47-48, 292; Nazi party organizational activities, 42-43, 49-51, 54, 82, 102-104, 175; accusations or evidence of immoral behavior, 52-53, 59, 86, 128, 131-132, 250, 269-271, 295-296; in Munich *putsch,* 1923, 60-63; suspended as a teacher, 63-65; imprisonment in Landsberg prison, 67-69; appeal to female audiences, 77-78, 88; questionable involvement with Communists, 88-89; named Franconian *Gauleiter,* 104, racial indoctrination of school children, 109, 244-248; as Hitler's special political